T0335484

Optimizing Information Security and Advancing Privacy Assurance:

New Technologies

Hamid R. Nemati
University of North Carolina at Greensboro, USA

Managing Director:	Lindsay Johnston
Senior Editorial Director:	Heather Probst
Book Production Manager:	Sean Woznicki
Development Manager:	Joel Gamon
Development Editor:	Myla Harty
Acquisitions Editor:	Erika Gallagher
Typesetters:	Milan Vracarich, Jr.
Cover Design:	Nick Newcomer, Greg Snader

Published in the United States of America by
Information Science Reference (an imprint of IGI Global)
701 E. Chocolate Avenue
Hershey PA 17033
Tel: 717-533-8845
Fax: 717-533-8661
E-mail: cust@igi-global.com
Web site: http://www.igi-global.com

Library of Congress Cataloging-in-Publication Data

Optimizing information security and advancing privacy assurance: new technologies / Hamid R. Nemati, editor.
    p. cm.
 Includes bibliographical references and index.
  ISBN 978-1-4666-0026-3 (hbk.) -- ISBN 978-1-4666-0027-0 (ebook) -- ISBN 978-1-4666-0028-7 (print & perpetual access) 1. Computer security. 2. Information technology--Security measures. 3. Computer networks--Security measures. 4. Data protection. I. Nemati, Hamid R., 1958-
  QA76.9.A25O685 2012
  005.8--dc23
                        2011049414

British Cataloguing in Publication Data
A Cataloguing in Publication record for this book is available from the British Library.

All work contributed to this book is new, previously-unpublished material. The views expressed in this book are those of the authors, but not necessarily of the publisher.

Table of Contents

Preface xi

Chapter 1
Provable Security for Outsourcing Database Operations 1
    Sergei Evdokimov, Humboldt-Universität zu Berlin, Germany
    Matthias Fischmann, Humboldt-Universität zu Berlin, Germany
    Oliver Günther, Humboldt-Universität zu Berlin, Germany

Chapter 2
A Host-Based Intrusion Detection System Using Architectural Features to Improve
Sophisticated Denial-of-Service Attack Detections 18
    Ran Tao, Louisiana State University, USA
    Li Yang, University of Tennessee at Chattanooga, USA
    Lu Peng, Louisiana State University, USA
    Bin Li, Louisiana State University, USA

Chapter 3
A Keystroke Biometric System for Long-Text Input 32
    Charles C. Tappert, Pace University, USA
    Sung-Hyuk Cha, Pace University, USA
    Mary Villani, Pace University, USA
    Robert S. Zack, Pace University, USA

Chapter 4
A Six-View Perspective Framework for System Security: Issues, Risks, and Requirements 58
    Surya B. Yadav, Texas Tech University, USA

Chapter 5
Are Online Privacy Policies Readable? 91
    M. Sumeeth, University of Alberta, Canada
    R.I. Singh, University of Alberta, Canada
    J. Miller, University of Alberta, Canada

Chapter 6
Protecting User Privacy Better with Query l-Diversity 115
    Fuyu Liu, University of Central Florida, USA
    Kien A. Hua, University of Central Florida, USA

Chapter 7
Globalization and Data Privacy: An Exploratory Study 132
    Robert L. Totterdale, Robert Morris University, USA

Chapter 8
Security Issues for Cloud Computing 150
    Kevin Hamlen, The University of Texas at Dallas, USA
    Murat Kantarcioglu, The University of Texas at Dallas, USA
    Latifur Khan, The University of Texas at Dallas, USA
    Bhavani Thuraisingham, The University of Texas at Dallas, USA

Chapter 9
Global Information Security Factors 163
    Garry White, Texas State University - San Marcos, USA
    Ju Long, Texas State University - San Marcos, USA

Chapter 10
The Integrated Privacy Model: Building a Privacy Model in the Business Processes
of the Enterprise 175
    Munir Majdalawieh, American University of Sharjah, UAE

Chapter 11
Policy Enforcement System for Inter-Organizational Data Sharing 197
    Mamoun Awad, UAE University, UAE
    Latifur Khan, The University of Texas at Dallas, USA
    Bhavani Thuraisingham, The University of Texas at Dallas, USA

Chapter 12
Goals and Practices in Maintaining Information Systems Security 214
    Zippy Erlich, The Open University of Israel, Israel
    Moshe Zviran, Tel-Aviv University, Israel

Chapter 13
Factors Influencing College Students' Use of Computer Security 225
    Norman Pendegraft, University of Idaho, USA
    Mark Rounds, University of Idaho, USA
    Robert W. Stone, University of Idaho, USA

Chapter 14

A Game Theoretic Approach to Optimize Identity Exposure in Pervasive Computing
Environments 235

    Feng Zhu, The University of Alabama in Huntsville, USA
    Sandra Carpenter, The University of Alabama in Huntsville, USA
    Wei Zhu, Intergraph Co., USA
    Matt W. Mutka, Michigan State University, USA

Chapter 15

Hiding Message in Map along Pre-Hamiltonian Path 255

    Sunil Kumar Muttoo, University of Delhi, India
    Vinay Kumar, National Informatics Centre, India

Chapter 16

Probabilistic Inference Channel Detection and Restriction Applied to Patients'
Privacy Assurance 270

    Bandar Alhaqbani, Queensland University of Technology, Australia
    Colin Fidge, Queensland University of Technology, Australia

Compilation of References 295

About the Contributors 316

Index 321

Detailed Table of Contents

Preface xi

Chapter 1
Provable Security for Outsourcing Database Operations 1
    Sergei Evdokimov, Humboldt-Universität zu Berlin, Germany
    Matthias Fischmann, Humboldt-Universität zu Berlin, Germany
    Oliver Günther, Humboldt-Universität zu Berlin, Germany

In this chapter, the authors present a new definition of security for homomorphic database encryption schemes that avoids these flaws and show that it is difficult to build a privacy homomorphism that complies with this definition. As a practical compromise, the authors present a relaxed variant of the security definition and discuss arising security implications. They present a new method to construct encryption schemes for exact selects and prove that the resulting schemes satisfy this notion.

Chapter 2
A Host-Based Intrusion Detection System Using Architectural Features to Improve
Sophisticated Denial-of-Service Attack Detections 18
    Ran Tao, Louisiana State University, USA
    Li Yang, University of Tennessee at Chattanooga, USA
    Lu Peng, Louisiana State University, USA
    Bin Li, Louisiana State University, USA

In this chapter, the authors identify the following hardware architecture features: Instruction Count, Cache Miss, Bus Traffic and integrate them into a HIDS framework based on a modern statistical Gradient Boosting Trees model. Through the integration of application, operating system and architecture level features, the proposed HIDS demonstrates a significant improvement of the detection rate in terms of sophisticated DoS intrusions.

Chapter 3
A Keystroke Biometric System for Long-Text Input 32
    Charles C. Tappert, Pace University, USA
    Sung-Hyuk Cha, Pace University, USA
    Mary Villani, Pace University, USA
    Robert S. Zack, Pace University, USA

A novel keystroke biometric system for long-text input was developed and evaluated for user identification and authentication applications. The system consists of a Java applet to collect raw keystroke data over the Internet, a feature extractor, and pattern classifiers to make identification or authentication decisions. This chapter describes the development and evaluation of a keystroke biometric system for long-text input.

Chapter 4

A Six-View Perspective Framework for System Security: Issues, Risks, and Requirements 58
    Surya B. Yadav, Texas Tech University, USA

The proposed framework presents a synergistic view of the system security in which the author presents an extensive list of heuristics/guidelines under each view, discussing security issues, risks, and requirements. Through a case study, the authors shows that a multiple view perspective of system security is effective in determining a more complete set of security requirements than the traditional approach of focusing on threats alone.

Chapter 5

Are Online Privacy Policies Readable? 91
    M. Sumeeth, University of Alberta, Canada
    R.I. Singh, University of Alberta, Canada
    J. Miller, University of Alberta, Canada

This chapter examines the question of are on-line privacy policies understandable to the users of the Internet? This examination is undertaken by collecting privacy policies from the most popular sites on the Internet, and analyzing their readability using a number of readability measures. The study finds that the results are consistent regardless of the readability measure utilized.

Chapter 6

Protecting User Privacy Better with Query l-Diversity 115
    Fuyu Liu, University of Central Florida, USA
    Kien A. Hua, University of Central Florida, USA

This paper examines major privacy concerns in location-based services. Most user privacy techniques are based on cloaking, which achieves location k-anonymity. The key is to reduce location resolution by ensuring that each cloaking area reported to a service provider contains at least k mobile users.

Chapter 7

Globalization and Data Privacy: An Exploratory Study 132
    Robert L. Totterdale, Robert Morris University, USA

Using an established privacy management framework, this study provides a summary of major data privacy laws in the U.S., Europe, and India, and their implication for businesses. Additionally, in this paper, relationships between age, residence (country), attitudes and awareness of business rules and data privacy laws are explored for 331 business professionals located in the U.S and India.

Chapter 8

Security Issues for Cloud Computing 150

    Kevin Hamlen, The University of Texas at Dallas, USA
    Murat Kantarcioglu, The University of Texas at Dallas, USA
    Latifur Khan, The University of Texas at Dallas, USA
    Bhavani Thuraisingham, The University of Texas at Dallas, USA

In this chapter, the authors discuss security issues for cloud computing and present a layered framework for secure clouds and then focus on two of the layers, i.e., the storage layer and the data layer. In particular, the authors discuss a scheme for secure third party publications of documents in a cloud.

Chapter 9

Global Information Security Factors 163

    Garry White, Texas State University - San Marcos, USA
    Ju Long, Texas State University - San Marcos, USA

In this chapter, the authors explore the global nature of information security from the perspectives of corporate professionals. Through an empirical study with corporate professionals, who have first-hand information security knowledge, the authors confirm that the proposed knowledge topics are relevant toward a comprehensive understanding of information security issues. Analyzing the empirical data, the authors found two global security factors: business protection of data and government/social issues.

Chapter 10

The Integrated Privacy Model: Building a Privacy Model in the Business Processes
of the Enterprise 175

    Munir Majdalawieh, American University of Sharjah, UAE

This chapter discusses the challenges that faced in the "DigNet" age in terms of privacy and proposes a framework for privacy protection. This framework is integral in ensuring that personal data protection is impeded part of business processes of any systems that are involved in collecting, disseminating, and accessing an individual's data.

Chapter 11

Policy Enforcement System for Inter-Organizational Data Sharing 197

    Mamoun Awad, UAE University, UAE
    Latifur Khan, The University of Texas at Dallas, USA
    Bhavani Thuraisingham, The University of Texas at Dallas, USA

In this chapter, the authors describe a Data Sharing Miner and Analyzer (DASMA) system that simulates data sharing among N organizations. Each organization has its own enforced policy. The N organizations share their data based on trusted third party. The system collects the released data from each organization, processes it, mines it, and analyzes the results.

Chapter 12

Goals and Practices in Maintaining Information Systems Security 214

    Zippy Erlich, The Open University of Israel, Israel
    Moshe Zviran, Tel-Aviv University, Israel

In this chapter, the authors discuss the goals of information systems security and the techniques to achieve them. Specifically, the paper focuses on access control and the various authentication approaches, as well as intrusion detection and prevention systems.

Chapter 13
Factors Influencing College Students' Use of Computer Security 225
    Norman Pendegraft, University of Idaho, USA
    Mark Rounds, University of Idaho, USA
    Robert W. Stone, University of Idaho, USA

A theoretically sound model linking student and system security characteristics to students' security behaviors is developed and presented in this paper. The model is operationalized using student responses to a web-based questionnaire. The empirical results show that training to use security measures has no impact on students' security behaviors while experience with security does.

Chapter 14
A Game Theoretic Approach to Optimize Identity Exposure in Pervasive Computing
Environments 235
    Feng Zhu, The University of Alabama in Huntsville, USA
    Sandra Carpenter, The University of Alabama in Huntsville, USA
    Wei Zhu, Intergraph Co., USA
    Matt W. Mutka, Michigan State University, USA

In this paper, the authors propose the Hierarchical Identity model, which enables the expression of one's identity information ranging from precise detail to vague identity information. The authors model privacy exposure as an extensive game. By finding subgame perfect equilibria in the game, the approach achieves optimal exposure. It finds the most general identity information that a user should expose and which the service provider would accept. The authors' experiments show that their models can reduce unnecessary identity exposure effectively.

Chapter 15
Hiding Message in Map along Pre-Hamiltonian Path 255
    Sunil Kumar Muttoo, University of Delhi, India
    Vinay Kumar, National Informatics Centre, India

In this paper, an algorithm to embed information in a map along Hamiltonian path is presented. A file based data structure in which a graph is treated as a composition of three components, node, segment and intermediate points that constitute a segment, is used to store a graph.

Chapter 16
Probabilistic Inference Channel Detection and Restriction Applied to Patients'
Privacy Assurance 270
    Bandar Alhaqbani, Queensland University of Technology, Australia
    Colin Fidge, Queensland University of Technology, Australia

In this paper, the authors present definitions and algorithms for detecting inference channels in a probabilistic knowledge base and maximising an attacker's uncertainty by restricting selected inference channels to comply with data confidentiality and privacy requirements. As an illustration, a healthcare scenario is used to show how inference control can be performed on probabilistic relations to address patients' privacy concerns over Electronic Medical Records.

Compilation of References 295

About the Contributors 316

Index 321

Preface

It is obvious that Information Technologies (IT) have had a major impact on all aspects of our lives. Information Technologies have made us more productive in our workplaces, brought us closer together, transformed our lives and ultimately, defined who we are as humans. We live in an age where information defines us. We are able to communicate more freely and effortlessly with one another, make more informed decisions, and have a higher standard of living, all, resulting from advances in Information Technologies (IT). The growth in Internet usage and e-commerce has offered businesses and governmental agencies the opportunity to collect and analyze information in ways never previously imagined. One result of the fast expansion of Information Technology in our daily lives is that it generates a large amount of data. The number of Americans who utilize the Internet for their daily business such as online purchasing, conducting online banking, and for entertainment value has increased in the past few years. Technological advances and the World-Wide-Web revolution have allowed for vast amounts of data, both internal and external sources, to be generated, collected, stored, processed, analyzed, distributed, and used at an ever-increasing rate by organizations and governmental agencies. According a survey by US Department of Commerce there is an astonishingly large growth in data, and this can be traced to the ever increasing number of Americans who are online on daily basis and are engaged in several activities, including engaging in online purchases and e-commerce, conducting banking online, learning, entertaining each other and being entertained by others, and above all, interacting socially. As a result, the size of a typical business database has grown a hundred-fold during the past five years. Data experts estimate that in 2008 the world generated 75 exabytes of data. While this amount of data is more than all the words ever spoken by human beings, it is far less than what was produced just a year later, in 2009. The rate of growth is just as staggering – the amount of data produced in 2008 was up 35% from previous years. The rate of growth in data has not slowed. International Data Corporation (IDC) estimates that the amount of data generated in 2009 was 1.2 million Petabytes. (A Petabyte is a million gigabytes.). Although this seems to be an astonishingly large amount of data, it is paled in compression to what IDC estimates to be the amount of data that will be generated in 2020. IDC estimates that the amount of data generated in 2020 will be 44 times as much as this year's and will reach an incomprehensible amount of 35 Zettabytes (A Zettabyte is 1 trillion gigabytes).

Assuring the trustworthiness of this massive amount of data and the integrity of the technologies supporting it are formidable challenges facing organizations. Without security that guarantees the trustworthiness of the data and the integrity of the supporting technologies, the data cannot be used appropriately. This is chiefly due to realization that concerns over security of what is collected and the potential harm from personal privacy violations resulting from their unethical uses have also skyrocketed. This implies that securing data and related technologies and ensuring the privacy of that information contained with it will be major areas of concern for researchers and practitioners alike.

With the emergence of the new paradigm in Information Technology, the role of information security and privacy will evolve. As a result, information security and privacy will be everyone's business, not just IT's. This change in the way companies view and approach information security and privacy will be driven primarily due to consumer demand. Consumers will demand more security for information about them and will insist on better ethical uses of that information. This demand will drive business profitability measures and will ultimately manifest itself as pressure on the government and other regulatory agencies to pass tougher and more intrusive legislation and regulations, resulting in greater pressure on the business organizations to comply and to demonstrate a commitment to information security and privacy. Therefore to be successful, organizations need to focus on information security not just as an IT issue, but rather as a business imperative. It is obvious that information security is a priority for the management, as it should be. Regardless of the source, the impact on organization can be severe ranging, from interruption in delivery of services and goods, loss of physical and other assets, loss of customer good will and confidence in the organization, to disclosure of sensitive data. Such sensitive data breaches can be very costly to the organization.

As we move forward, new security and privacy challenges will likely to emerge. It is essential that we are prepared for these challenges in order to take full advantage of the opportunities. This book is an attempt to help researchers and practitioners seeking answers to these complex problems. *Optimizing Information Security and Advancing Privacy Assurance: New Technologies* is a comprehensive collection of 16 chapters that explain the changing roles of Information Technology and its impact on security and privacy.

In chapter 1, "Provable Security for Outsourcing Database Operations," written by Evdokimov, Fischmann, and Gunther, the authors present a new method to construct encryption schemes for exact selects and prove that the resolution schemes satisfy this notion.

In chapter 2, "A Host-Based Intrusion Detection System Using Architectural Features to Improve Sophisticated Denial-of-Service Attack Detections," Tao, Yang, Peng, and Li identify hardware architecture features and integrate them into HIDS framework bases on a modern statistical Gradient Boosting Trees model.

In chapter 3, "A Keystroke Biometric System for Long-Text Input," written by Tappert, Cha, Villiani, and Zack, describes the development and evaluation of a keystroke biometric system for long-text input.

Chapter 4, "A Six-View Perspective Framework for System Security: Issues, Risks, and Requirements," by Yadav, proposes framework that presents a synergistic view of the system security in which the author presents an extensive list of heuristics/guidelines under each review, discussion security issues, risks and requirements.

In chapter 5, Sumeeth, Singh, and Miller examine the question of online privacy policies in their chapter "Are Online Privacy Policies Readable?" This examination is undertaken by collecting privacy policies from the most popular sites on the Internet and analyzing their readability.

In chapter 6, "Protecting User Privacy Better with Query l-Diversity," Liu and Hua examine major privacy concerns in location-based services. Most user privacy techniques are based on cloaking, which achieves location k-anonymity. The key is to reduce location resolution by ensuring that each cloaking area reported to a service provider contains at least k mobile users.

Chapter 7, "Globalization and Data Privacy: An Exploratory Study," by Totterdale, provides a summary of major data privacy laws in the U.S., Europe, and India, and their implication for businesses.

Additionally, in this chapter, relationships between age, residence (country), attitudes, and awareness of business rules and data privacy laws are explored for 331 business professionals located in the U.S and India.

Next, "Security Issues for Cloud Computing" by Hamlen, Kantarcioglu, Khan, and Thuraisingham, discusses security issues for cloud computing, presents a layered framework for secure clouds, and then focuses on two of the layers, i.e., the storage layer and the data layer. In particular, the authors discuss a scheme for secure third party publications of documents in a cloud.

Chapter 9, "Global Information Security Factors," by White and Long, explores the global nature of information security from the perspectives of corporate professionals. Through an empirical study with corporate professionals, who have first-hand information security knowledge, the authors confirm that the proposed knowledge topics are relevant toward a comprehensive understanding of information security issues. Analyzing the empirical data, the authors found two global security factors: business protection of data and government/social issues.

In chapter 10, "The Integrated Privacy Model: Building a Privacy Model in the Business Processes of the Enterprise," Majdalawieh discusses the challenges that faced in the "DigNet" age in terms of privacy and proposes a framework for privacy protection. This framework is integral in ensuring that personal data protection is part of business processes of any systems that are involved in collecting, disseminating, and accessing an individual's data.

In chapter 11, "Policy Enforcement System for Inter-Organizational Data Sharing," Awad, Khan, and Thuraisingham describe a Data Sharing Miner and Analyzer (DASMA) system that simulates data sharing among N organizations. Each organization has its own enforced policy. The N organizations share their data based on trusted third party. The system collects the released data from each organization, processes it, mines it, and analyzes the results.

In chapter 12, "Goals and Practices in Maintaining Information Systems Security," by Erlich and Zviran, the authors discuss the goals of information systems security and the techniques to achieve them. Specifically, the chapter focuses on access control and the various authentication approaches, as well as intrusion detection and prevention systems.

In chapter 13, "Factors Influencing College Students' Use of Computer Security," by Pendegraft, Rounds, and Stone, the authors present and develop theoretically sound model linking student and system security characteristics to students' security behaviors.

In chapter 14, "A Game Theoretic Approach to Optimize Identity Exposure in Pervasive Computing Environments," by Zhu, Carpenter, Zhu, and Mutka, the authors propose the Hierarchical Identity model, which enables the expression of one's identity information ranging from precise detail to vague identity information. The authors model privacy exposure as an extensive game. By finding subgame perfect equilibria in the game, the approach achieves optimal exposure. It finds the most general identity information that a user should expose and which the service provider would accept. The authors' experiments show that their models can reduce unnecessary identity exposure effectively.

In chapter 15, "Hiding Message in Map along Pre-Hamiltonian Path," by Muttoo and Kumar, the authors present an algorithm to embed information in a map along Hamiltonian path. A file based data structure in which a graph is treated as a composition of three components, node, segment, and intermediate points that constitute a segment, is used to store a graph.

In chapter 16, "Probabilistic Inference Channel Detection and Restriction Applied to Patients' Privacy Assurance," by Alhaqbani and Fidge, the authors present definitions and algorithms for detecting inference channels in a probabilistic knowledge base and maximising an attacker's uncertainty by restricting selected inference channels to comply with data confidentiality and privacy requirements. As an illustration, a healthcare scenario is used to show how inference control can be performed on probabilistic relations to address patients' privacy concerns over Electronic Medical Records.

Hamid R. Nemati
The University of North Carolina at Greensboro, USA

Chapter 1
Provable Security for Outsourcing Database Operations

Sergei Evdokimov
Humboldt-Universität zu Berlin, Germany

Matthias Fischmann
Humboldt-Universität zu Berlin, Germany

Oliver Günther
Humboldt-Universität zu Berlin, Germany

ABSTRACT

Database outsourcing has become popular in recent years, although it introduces substantial security and privacy risks. In many applications, users may not want to reveal their data even to a generally trusted database service provider. Several researchers have proposed encryption schemes, such as privacy homomorphisms, that allow service providers to process confidential data sets without learning too much about them. In this paper, the authors discuss serious flaws of these solutions. The authors then present a new definition of security for homomorphic database encryption schemes that avoids these flaws and show that it is difficult to build a privacy homomorphism that complies with this definition. As a practical compromise, the authors present a relaxed variant of the security definition and discuss arising security implications. They present a new method to construct encryption schemes for exact selects and prove that the resulting schemes satisfy this notion.

DOI: 10.4018/978-1-4666-0026-3.ch001

INTRODUCTION

The alternative [to rigorous proofs of security] is to design systems in an ad hoc manner, and to simply hope for the best. As we have seen, this approach often ends in disaster, or at least, an embarrassing mess.-- Victor Shoup, IBM, 1998

In this paper, we assess cryptographic solutions to the problem that some client party (Alex) wants to outsource database operations on sensitive data sets to a service provider (Eve) without having to trust her. Forming contracts and relying on law enforcement are options, but for various reasons their effectiveness is limited and the costs for negotiations, auditing and prosecution are considerable (Boyens & Günther, 2002). Alex would prefer to encrypt his data in a way that enables Eve to perform operations on the ciphertext yielding encrypted results, which Alex could in turn decrypt. All this should ideally take place without revealing anything to Eve about the plaintext data or the operations.

Consider two examples:

1. If the service provider (say, Peoplesoft) changes owners, it is unclear whether the new owner (say, Oracle) is still legally bound by the same contract, regardless of pre-existing privacy policies.[1] As Amazon has phrased it in a similar context:[2]

In the unlikely event that Amazon.com Inc., or substantially all of its assets are acquired, customer information will of course be one of the transferred assets.

Alex has good reasons to be worried about this situation if he has to give away sensitive data in the clear. However, if the data were never exposed to any service provider, no contract would be required in the first place.

2. Celebrity Paris Hilton's personal phone book was stolen and leaked to the public in 2005.[3]

The data had been stored in a T-Mobile server farm and used from a mobile device. One theory of what happened is that hackers got access to the central server, where the data was stored in plaintext. If a secure privacy homomorphism had been used, the hackers would have obtained only useless ciphertext.

The security requirements of Alex heavily depend on the application. The strongest notion of confidentiality keeps every single bit of information on queries as well as data secret from Eve, no matter how many queries she can observe, or how clearly she breaks the contract. This notion would allow for doing business with arbitrarily malicious service providers, but we will see shortly that it is impossible to achieve.

Confidentiality against an adversary that can do computations on the ciphertext (even with encrypted output) is difficult. Traditionally, confidentiality is defined precisely in terms of the adversary's incapability of doing any such computations. Even if the adversary cannot necessarily understand the outcome of the computation, confidentiality and processability are strong antagonists.

Worse, the application to databases is extreme in this respect: Relational algebra is a rich formalism that imposes a complex structure on the data being processed. If Eve were supposed to process arbitrary terms of relational algebra, she would need to have a lot of structural information on the ciphertext, which, together with a plausible amount of context knowledge, would most likely allow her to deduce at least fractions of the secret data.

The idea that encryption schemes for situations like these could exist has been brought up almost 30 years ago (Rivest, Adlerman & Dertouzos, 1978) under the name *privacy homomorphism*. Our aim is to find privacy homomoprhisms for database outsourcing that transform relational data sets and queries into ciphertext such that (*i*) the data is *securely hidden* from Eve, although she has unlimited access to the ciphertext; and (*ii*) Eve can compute ciphertext results from ciphertext queries that Alex can *efficiently* decrypt to obtain plaintext results. We will also perform a rigorous analysis of security definitions that are both possible to meet and satisfactory to a large potential user base.

As we explore these issues, we will find that privacy homomorphisms are rare indeed, and that many reasonable and highly desirable security notions are extremely hard to meet by any possible encryption scheme. Fortunately, there are more relaxed scenarios that still have important practical applications. For example, Alex may be comfortable to merely make sure that if Eve turns adversarial *after* (not *while*) processing his data, she has no way of decrypting the ciphertext. If she does (and if he is aware of the change in her attitude), he can simply stop sending queries. Then Eve has no encrypted queries or encrypted query results to use in her assumed attack, and finding encryption algorithms for keeping the data safe becomes feasible. This security notion fits our Example 1 (PeopleSoft vs. Oracle) nicely --- change of ownership is a public process that can be witnessed by Alex easily. We will present a class of privacy homomorphisms suitable for this scenario and rigorously prove its security.

The remainder of this paper is structured as follows: In Section 2, we review some of the literature relevant to homomorphic encryption, give formal definitions of encryption schemes and privacy homomorphisms, and describe a widely known notion of security used in (non-homomorphic) cryptography called *indistinguishability*. In Section 3, we outline the limitations of indistinguishability, analysing the security of existing homomorphic encryption schemes in more detail. We then introduce new and more suitable definitions and assess their utility. In Section 4, we introduce a solution for some subsets of relational algebra (in particular, exact selects and, with some limitations, range selects) using privacy homomorphisms for searching on unstructured documents as building blocks. We prove that the resulting scheme is secure if the

original scheme is. By using a scheme from (Song, Wagner & Perrig, 2000) as a building block that comes with its own proof of security, we obtain a privacy homomorphism for databases that is provably secure and imposes very little cryptographic performance overhead. In Section 5, we discuss extensions and apply our results to the domain of secure remote file systems and related areas. Section 6 concludes with a summary and an outlook.

RELATED WORK AND RELEVANT NOTIONS OF SECURITY

In (Hacıgümüs, Iyer, Li & Mehrotra, 2002) a database encryption scheme for full SQL is proposed. The idea is that every tuple is encrypted with a secure cipher first, then weakly encrypted attributes are attached to the ciphertext. These weak encryptions are obtained by taking a plaintext attribute value, mapping it to a containing interval, and encrypting that interval using a secret permutation. Two plaintexts produce the same containing-interval ciphertext not only if they are equal, but even if they are similar. While the information left undistorted by weak encryption is enough to query the encrypted database, one hopes that Eve still does not obtain *too much* information on the data if the partitionings into intervals and the other security parameters have been chosen properly. It is clear Eve will learn *something* about the data (like the number of tuples in the table, or which tuples have similar values in which secret attributes). But there are less obvious problems that have led to modifications of the original scheme by, among others, (Damiani, De Capitani Vimercati, Jajodia, Paraboschi & Samarati, 2003) and (Fischmann & Günther, 2003). Boyens and Fischmann (2003) suggested a more general framework for encrypting data in outsourced applications and showed how aggregate operations on encrypted databases can be performed. Still, there is no clear notion of what amount of information leakage is *too much* for

Alex, and whether the scheme or its variants can fulfill Alex' requirements.

All these solutions have a common structure that can be described using the notion of privacy homomorphisms (Rivest et al., 1978), although this has been done in the database area only relatively recently (Boyens et al., 2002).

Intuitively, a privacy homomorphism maps plaintext data into ciphertext that looks meaningless to the naive adversary, but still has a similar structure to that of the plaintext. In particular, the adversary can apply certain operations to the ciphertext, producing encrypted results, without learning anything about the data. In more rigorous terms, these concepts can be defined as follows:

Definition 2.1 (Encryption Scheme)

An encryption scheme is a tuple (K,E,D), where $E : K \times X \mapsto C, D : K \times C \mapsto X$ are encryption and decryption functions that convert a plaintext $x \in X$ into the corresponding ciphertext $y \in C$ and back using a secret key $k \in K$. For all $x \in X$, we have $D_k(E_k(x)) = x$. Keys are chosen uniformly at random from the key space K. The bit length $n = \log(|K|)$ of all keys is called the *security parameter* of the scheme.

Where it is obvious from the context, we omit the keys to simplify notation and write $D(x), E(x)$. Note that nothing has been said about the security of a given encryption scheme yet. Whether an adversary can compute (part of) the matching plaintext from some ciphertext, and under what conditions, is subject of a separate class of definitions, cf. Definition 2.4.

Definition 2.2 (Privacy Homomorphism)

An encryption scheme (K,E,D) is a privacy homomorphism (*PH* for short), mapping a system of plaintexts $(X, \{\phi_i\})$, where $\{\phi_i\}$ is a set of operations $\phi_i : \underbrace{X \times \ldots \times X}_{l_i} \mapsto X$, to a system of

ciphertexts $(C, \{\psi_i\})$, where $\{\psi_i\}$ is a set of operations $\psi_i : \underbrace{C \times \ldots \times C}_{l_i} \mapsto C$, if for any

$x \in X$, the equation

$$E_k(\phi_i(x_1, \ldots, x_{l_i})) = \psi_i(E_k(x_1), \ldots, E_k(x_{l_i}))$$

holds.

Privacy homomorphisms have been proposed for a number of operations, such as modulo arithmetics (Rivest et al., 1978), (Domingo-Ferrer, 2002) or full-text search on document sets (Song & Wagner, 2000). In this paper, we are mainly concerned with relational databases. In that case, X is a set of plaintext tables and $\{\phi_i\}$ is a set of relational operations defined on these tables. Note that the set of operations can be confidential in its own right, i.e., Alex may want to hide what he is asking even if that does not tell Eve anything about the results of the query. But more importantly, in Section 3 we will show that if Eve knows a few plaintext queries and some encrypted data, she can decrypt a significant fraction of the database. Therefore, the transformation of $\{\phi_i\}$ into $\{\psi_i\}$ is itself secret, i.e., an encryption operation. We call this transformation E^*.

Let $R = (a_1 : D_1, a_2 : D_2, \ldots, a_l : D_l)$ be a database schema, where a_i denotes an attribute name and D_i the domain of attribute a_i (all domains are finite). Then,

$$\text{Tup}(R) =$$
$$\{\langle a_1 : d_{k1}, \ldots, a_l : d_{kl} \rangle | d_{ki} \in D_i, a_i \neq a_j, i \neq j\},$$

is the set of all possible data tuples allowed by R, where k is the tuple index and i,j are column numbers. Every subset $T(R) \subseteq \text{Tup}(R)$ is called an *instance* of R (or a *table* fitting schema R). When it is clear from a context which schema is implied we just write T. $\mathsf{R} = (\text{Tup}(R))^s$ is the set of all possible instances of R, i.e., the power set of $\text{Tup}(R)$. Let $\{q_i\}$ be a set of relational operations. Then a database PH can be defined as follows:

Definition 2.3 (Database Privacy Homomorphism)

A database privacy homomorphism is a PH $(K,(E,E^*),D)$ where $E : K \times \mathsf{R} \mapsto \mathsf{C}$ encrypts tables, $E^* : K \times \{q_i\} \mapsto \{\psi_i\}$ encrypts queries, and $D : K \times \mathsf{C} \mapsto \mathsf{R}$ decrypts tables.

We usually write (K,E,E^*,D) for simplicity. The transformations E and E^* draw a single key from the set K. If the two algorithms require independent keys, we simply define them to use different parts of the bit representation of a given shared k. If they require keys that functionally depend on each other, then we can encode this function dependence in the algorithms as well.

The most common notions of security are based on games between an honest user (such as Alex) and an adversary (such as Eve) modeled by a probabilistic polynomial-time (PPT) algorithm (cf. Goldreich, 2001; Goldreich, 2004) for an exhaustive introduction to cryptographic theory). A scheme is secure if Eve can only win the game with *negligible* probability. A probability value x is called *negligible* if $x < 1 / 2 + 1 / p(n)$ for *every* polynomial p and all sufficiently large n.

Let us recall the basic concept of indistinguishability as defined in text books on cryptography. (Unless stated otherwise, encryption keys are always chosen uniformly at random at the beginning of the game.)

Definition 2.4 (Indistinguishability)

An encryption scheme (K,E,D) is indistinguishable if Eve cannot win the following game:

Eve chooses two plaintexts x_1,x_2 of the same length and presents them to Alex.

Alex chooses $i \in \{1,2\}$ uniformly at random and presents $E_k(x_i)$ to Eve.

Eve must guess i with non-negligible probability. She wins if her guess is correct.

It may seem surprising that Eve only needs to recover one bit of entropy from the ciphertext of which she already knows everything else. Weaker definitions could reduce the amount of plaintext knowledge or increase the amount of information that Eve must guess correctly in order to succeed. This would make attacks more difficult, and more schemes would be secure in this weaker sense. However, such weaker levels of security introduce considerable risks. For example, it often happens in communication that only one bit of information is of interest to Eve (e.g., in the acknowledgement resp. canceling of a stock order). It is also hard to find plausible bounds for what Eve already knows about the plaintext from context (such as communicating parties and time of communication). If we think of schemes as building blocks for securing complex applications, Eve must be assumed to know everything about the application down to the source code. Using weaker adversary models (or no model at all) has been tried and given way to a rich history of failures.[4]

A SECURITY ANALYSIS OF DATABASE PRIVACY HOMOMORPHISMS

Known Database PHs

For most existing database PHs, it is straightforward to find adversaries that win the game described in Definition 2.4. Consider the scheme proposed in (Hacıgümüş et al., 2002) and the following game. Eve produces two pairs of table and query. The tables are different, but the query is the same in both cases (for 4900 and 5400, choose any two values that do not end up in the same bucket) (Figures 1 and 2):

SELECT * FROM t WHERE salary=4900

Both tables and queries are presented to Alex for encryption. Eve obtains a ciphertext from Alex. Since the encryption is homomorphic, she can run the query on the table and examine the result. As each tuple is encrypted separately and, with high probability, only matching tuples are included in the result, Eve can look at the size of the encrypted result: If the encrypted result is half the size of the encrypted table, then Eve outputs 1; otherwise, she outputs 2. A similar attack works on the scheme in (Damiani et al., 2003).

To take another example, consider the scheme in (Boyens et al., 2003). Again, Eve maintains a table of encrypted salaries for Alex but this time the arithmetic mean of these salaries is of interest, not the unaggregated data itself. To this end, a privacy homomorphism for addition is used and Eve computes the encrypted sum of all ciphertexts plus the number of ciphertexts, leaving the division to Alex. In order to launch an attack, Eve can produce the same two tables as above, but this time, the plaintexts are obtained by computing *two* queries on each table:

SELECT SUM(salary) FROM t

SELECT SUM(salary) FROM t WHERE salary=4900

If the ciphertext results obtained by running these two queries are identical, then Eve outputs 2; otherwise, she outputs 1. She wins with probability 1.

Security Levels and Limitations

Privacy homomorphisms are a subset of the set of all encryption schemes, therefore insights into the latter are also applicable to the former. However, the ability to transform plaintext operations into corresponding ciphertext operations yields new possibilities for an adversary to get insights into encrypted data. In this section, we will show that traditional definitions of security do not guarantee the secrecy of the data encrypted by a database PH, provide new definitions and explore how much security can and can not be achieved.

Consider a database PH (K,E,E^*,D) such that the encryption scheme (K,E,D) is indistinguishably secure and such that for all q, $E^*(q)=q$, which means that the issued queries are not being encrypted. Assume an adversary Eve runs the query $q_j = E^*(\sigma_{a_i:d_i})$ on the encrypted table, where $\sigma_{a_i:d_i}$ is a query returning all tuples where a value of attribute a_i is equal to d_i (in the following we will refer to such queries as "exact selects"). As result of her computation, Eve obtains a set of encrypted tuples. Although she cannot decrypt them, she can infer that the value of the attribute a_i of these tuples is d_i merely from the fact that they are in the query result. So even though we used a rigorous security definition, our scheme is far less secure than the two we attacked in the last section.

How is it possible that a database PH based on a perfectly secure table encryption scheme can still leak so much information? What tricked us here is an ill-applied adversary model. The classical model does not consider that the adversary might

Figure 1. Example pair of table and query

ID	salary
171	4900
481	5400

Figure 2. Example pair of table and query

ID	salary
171	4900
481	4900

be provided additional information when receiving and processing the queries. Our example showed that these computations can cause unsuspected leaks. In order to capture this new situation, we need to craft new security definitions that are aware of the adversary's new capabilities. In other words, we need to take E^* into account. Kantarcioglu and Cliffton (2004) propose a definition that addresses this problem and requires that, in addition to encrypting tables, the queries should be securely encrypted as well:

Definition 3.1 (Kantarcioglu-Clifton Security for Databases)

A database PH is secure according to the Kantarcioglu-Clifton model (or *KC-secure*) if

1. Any two tables of the same size are indistinguishable (i.e., secure in the sense of Definition 2.4).
2. Two queries that run on the same set of tables and return results with the same number of tuples are indistinguishable.

Kantarcioglu and Clifton suspected that their definition may already be too strong for any scheme to exist that satisfies it. While we show that this is not true by presenting a scheme satisfying it in Section 4, the definition has another serious problem: It does not match our intuition of what security means. A scheme that is KC-secure may still reveal information about encrypted tables.

As an example consider a database PH $(K \times K, E, E^*, D)$ that allows exact select queries. Let $T = \{\langle x_1 \rangle, ..., \langle x_m \rangle\}$ be a table consisting of one attribute and filled with m tuples, (K, E, D) be an indistinguishably secure stream cipher and (k_1, k_2) be a pair of keys randomly and uniformly chosen from the key space $K \times K$. To encrypt table T each of its attribute values is encrypted with (K, E, D) encryption scheme and key k_1 and the set of resulting ciphertexts is again encrypted with the same encryption scheme and key k_2:

$E_k(T) = E_{k_1}(\{\langle E_{k_2}(x_1) \rangle, ..., \langle E_{k_2}(x_m) \rangle\})$. To run an exact select query $q = \sigma_x$ on outsourced and encrypted table T the query is encrypted as $\psi = \sigma_{E_{k_2}(x)}$, appended key k_1 and pair (ψ, k_1) is sent to Eve. By using obtained key k_2, Eve removes the first "encryption layer" from the table: $D_{k_1}(E_k(T)) = \{\langle E_{k_2}(x_1) \rangle, ..., \langle E_{k_2}(x_m) \rangle\}$, and then identifies tuples that contain x as the attribute value by consequently comparing $E_{k_2}(x)$ with attribute values $E_{k_2}(x_i), i = 1, ..., m$.

Due to the indistinguishable security of encryption scheme (K, E, D) any two tables of the same size as well as any two exact select queries returning the same amounts of tuples are indistinguishable. Thus, the proposed database PH satisfies the definition of KC-security. However, it is also obvious that this database PH provides very limited security, since as soon as the first query is processed the complete table becomes susceptible to a statistical attack.

This yields the following

Theorem 3.1

KC-security is weak in the sense that even though encrypted databases and encrypted queries, are secure in the sense of Definition 2.4, the combination of encrypted databases and matching encrypted queries is insecure in the sense of Definition 2.4.

Based on this insight, we propose the following improved definition. (We write $\overline{q} = (q_1, ..., q_l)$ for a sequence of queries, and $\overline{E}^*(\overline{q}) = (E^*(q_1), ..., E^*(q_l))$ for the sequence of encryptions.)

Definition 3.2 (Database PH Indistinguishability)

A database PH (K, E, E^*, D) is indistinguishably secure if Eve cannot win the following game:

1. Eve chooses two tables T_1, T_2 with the same attributes and the same number of tuples, two sequences of queries $\overline{q}_1 = (q_1^1, \ldots, q_l^1)$, $\overline{q}_2 = (q_1^2, \ldots, q_l^2)$ and presents pairs $(T_1, \overline{q}^1)$, $(T_2, \overline{q}^2)$ to Alex.

2. Alex chooses $i \in \{1,2\}$ uniformly at random and presents $(E_k(T_i), \overline{E}_k^*(\overline{q}_i))$ to Eve.

3. Eve must guess i. She wins if her guess is correct with non-negligible probability.

Unlike KC-security, this definition confronts Eve with a challenge that includes tuples of encrypted table and associated encrypted queries. Such a tuple is in fact what a service provider will gather from her client over time. Besides repairing the flaw we have just exposed in KC-security, it is also a more accurate representation of reality.

But how, looking at a database PH, can we tell whether it is secure or not? If a database PH does not hide the size of the query results, this definition allows Eve to compose pairs (T_1, q_1), (T_1, q_2) such that $q_1(T_1) = \varnothing$ and $|q_2(T_2)| > 1$. Eve can use this to distinguish between $(E(T_1), E^*(q_1))$ and $(E(T_2), E^*(q_2))$ with non-negligible probability. An attempt to hide the size by adding random tuples to the result that Alex discards during decryption is either ineffective or overwhelmingly inefficient. In order to prevent Eve from distinguishing a query returning the whole table from one that returns nothing, each query must return the whole table.

In order to find necessary conditions for a database PH to be secure, the related concept of *computational Private Information Retrieval* (cPIR) (Chor & Gilboa, 1997) proves helpful. A cPIR scheme allows a client to query a computationally bounded database server without revealing any information about the *query* (not about the *data*).

Definition 3.3 (Computational Private Information Retrieval)

Let (D, E) be a family of query mappings $D \times E : \{q_i\} \to \{\psi_i\}$. A querying protocol provides *computational Private Information Retrieval* for table T if Eve cannot win the following game:

1. Eve knows T.
2. Eve chooses two sequences of queries for table T $\overline{q}_1 = (q_1^1, \ldots, q_l^1)$, $\overline{q}_2 = (q_1^2, \ldots, q_l^2)$ and presents $\overline{q}_1, \overline{q}_2$ to Alex.
3. Alex chooses $i \in \{1,2\}$ uniformly at random and presents $\overline{E}_k^*(q_i)$ to Eve.
4. Eve must guess i. She wins if her guess is correct with non-negligible probability.

CPIR is a variant of Private Information Retrieval problem (PIR) (Chor, Goldreich, Kushilevitz & Sudan, 1995). In PIR, the adversarial server has unlimited computing powers, and the only solution that is secure in PIR and does not rely on multiple replicated database servers is the trivial one to download the entire database for each query. The restriction on the adversary in cPIR that makes the model weaker than the PIR model is that she can only do computations of polynomial complexity. All of public-key cryptography makes the same assumption, so cPIR is still a good foundation for strong security.

With cPIR, the necessary conditions for indistinguishable security of a database PH follow. We start with a condition that is necessary, but not sufficient.

Theorem 3.2

A database PH (K, E, E^*, D) is indistinguishably secure in the sense of Definition 3.2 only if

1. Encryption scheme (K, E, D) is indistinguishably secure.

2. The database PH provides cPIR.

Proof. For each condition, we construct a direct contradiction to Definition 3.2 from assuming its violation. *(1)* Assume (K,E,D) is distinguishable, or that there exist such T_1,T_2 that Eve can distinguish between $E_k(T_1)$ and $E_k(T_2)$ with non-negligible probability. Then Eve can distinguish between $(E_k(T_1),\bar{E}_k(\bar{q}_1))$ and $(E_k(T_2),\bar{E}_k(\bar{q}_2))$, even if she simply ignores any $\bar{q}_1$ and $\bar{q}_2$. *(2)* If the database PH is insecure in cPIR, then Eve can use the query sequences $\bar{q}_1,\bar{q}_2$ from any cPIR attack to distinguish between $(E_k(T),\bar{E}_k^*(\bar{q}_1))$ and $(E_k(T),\bar{E}_k^*(\bar{q}_2))$ with non-negligible probability.

These conditions are significantly stronger than KC-security. Also, there is a gap between Definition 3.2 and Theorem 3.2: The latter gives a set of *necessary*, not *sufficient* conditions for the former to hold. Even if we find a database PH that satisfies the latter, we have no guarantee that it is secure. The existing cPIR algorithms impose a significant computational and communication overhead on the client and service provider. The only algorithm known to the authors that provides both cPIR and hides the queried data is described in (Boneh, Kushilevitz, Ostrovsky, & Skeith, 2007). However, though being of sub-linear communication complexity, the communication overhead is large enough to make the algorithm unpractical. A client wishing to privately outsource his database could consider a trade-off between privacy and functionality. For instance, if Alex issues only exact selects to the outsourced database, a possible trade-off may be to allow each query to reveal the number tuples in the result while keeping all other information hidden. This is formalized in the following relaxation of Definition 3.2:

Definition 3.4 (Database PH Indistinguishability up to Frequency)

A database PH (K,E,E^*,D) is indistinguishably secure up to frequency (of queried elements) if

1. The encryption scheme (K,E,D) is indistinguishably secure.

For every probabilistic polynomial-time algorithm A there exists a probabilistic polynomial-time algorithm A' such that for every table T, every sequence of different exact select queries $\bar{q} = (q_1,...,q_l)$, every polynomially bounded function f, every polynomial p and all sufficiently large n:

$$\Pr[A(E_k(T),\bar{E}^*(\bar{q})) =$$
$$f(T)] < \Pr[A'(E_k(T),\bar{N}(\bar{q}(T))) = f(T)] + \frac{1}{p(n)},$$

where $\bar{N}(\bar{q}(T)) = (N(q_1(T)),...,N(q_l(T)))$ are the numbers of tuples in the resulting sets of each query.

In the remainder of this paper, in order to make reasoning about this definition more straightforward, we restrict ourselves to database PHs that encrypt tables tuple by tuple. We will discuss in Section 5.2 that this technical move does not sacrifice the generality of our results.

Definition 3.4 suggests a statistical attack exploiting possible dependencies between the information that is legitimately leaked and the information that is supposed to stay secret. By monitoring the encrypted flow of queries and their results, Eve may be able to gather enough information about the distribution of values of the queried attributes to launch such an attack.

As an example of such an attack, suppose an indistinguishably secure up to frequency database PH that allows for exact selects only, and a patient database with statistics for three hospitals. For each patient, we store HIV status and the hospital they are assigned to:

id hospital hivNow suppose that Eve knows the database schema, the number of hospitals, has good estimates of the distribution of patients among hospitals (0.2,0.3,0.5, respectively) and the percentage of HIV-positive patients (say, 8%).

Alex issues the following queries:

SELECT * FROM table WHERE hospital = 1;
SELECT * FROM table WHERE hospital = 2;
SELECT * FROM table WHERE hospital = 3;
SELECT * FROM table WHERE hiv = "positive";

Since the sizes of the results are sufficiently different, Eve can guess the queries with high confidence. This in itself is not a problem: our concern is privacy of the database, not privacy of the queries. But by intersecting the answers to the first and the fourth query, Eve can now infer the ratio of HIV-positive patients in hospital 1.

In order to find a way to rule out this threat, we can impose validity restrictions on what Alex can do with the database. So we can easily limit the queries to those that do not reveal anything if the frequencies are revealed. We call those queries *safe* .

Definition 3.5 (Safe and Unsafe Queries)

A safe query with respect to some subset $T^* \subseteq R$ of all possible instances of R is a query that yields always exactly one output tuple if run on any instance $T \in T^*$. Unsafe queries are queries that are not safe.

As an example, consider a radio frequency ID reader that reads a unique identification code from a tag attached to some item and extracts information associated with this code (name, price, etc.) from an encrypted outsourced database. Since for every item the code is unique and the reader sends requests only for existing codes, the reader issues only safe queries.

Are there queries that are intuitively safe but are not covered by this definition? If the number of resulting tuples varies freely, the hospital example on page 10 demonstrates how Eve can run a successful attack on the encrypted database and infer some sensitive information. Note that if all the queries return exactly k tuples for $k>1$, assuming tuple-wise encryption of the tables

it is possible to craft tables with two attributes a_1, a_2 and queries q_1, q_2 such that for one table the queries produce intersecting result sets, and for another they produce non-intersecting result sets. This allows Eve to infer dependencies between values of different attributes and use them for an attack. For example, if the adversary suspects that attribute a_1 contains names of hospitals and a_2 contains last names of patients, by observing such intersections she can try to estimate the number of family members that were treated in the same hospital. Hence, Definition 3.5 is optimal in the sense that any relaxation would include queries that are breaking Definition 3.4.

PRIVACY HOMOMORPHIC EXACT SELECT

In this section, we describe an approach for building database PHs that preserve exact selects. The resulting homomorphisms satisfy Definition 3.4 and can be used for scenarios in which the adversary never gets access to unsafe encrypted queries. This is sufficient in all scenarios described above where Alex trusts Eve not to abuse her access to unsafe queries. It is also applicable if Alex accesses his data only via exact selects on existing values of the primary key: Any such query is safe by definition.

Our approach is based on the intuitive analogy between running exact selects on a database table and searching a set of documents by keyword. A table can be seen as a set of documents: Each tuple is one document, and the attribute--value pairs of the tuples are the words of the document. We formally establish a structure-preserving mapping from a database table to such document sets. An algorithm for secure full-text keyword search on encrypted data (referred to as *searchable encryption scheme* in the following) can then be used to implement exact selects (and some more). Searchable encryption schemes allow to encrypt a set of plaintext documents and then perform word search on encrypted documents without decrypting them (or the search word). Boneh, Crescenzo, Ostrovsky, & Persiano (2004), Chang, & Mitzenmacher (2005), Goh (2003), and Song et al. (2000), among others, have proposed such schemes. We use (Song et al., 2000) to demonstrate our results but any other scheme can be used as well.

Mapping

In this section we define a mapping from tables to sets of documents. Given some relational schema R, let $D = \{a_i : d_{ki}\}, d_{ki} \in D_i$ be the set of all attribute-value pairs in R, and let $W = \{w_i\}$ be a set of words (i.e., finite bit strings) such that the total number of words:

$$|W| = |D| = \sum_{i=1...l} |D_i|.$$

There is always a bijective mapping from attribute-value pairs to words:

$$\Phi : D \mapsto W,$$

$$\Phi(a_i : d_{ki}) = w_m$$

For any tuple $\langle a_1 : d_{k1}, ..., a_l : d_{kl} \rangle$ there is a corresponding set

$$V_k = \{\Phi(a_1 : d_{k1}), \Phi(a_2 : d_{k2}), ..., \Phi(a_l : d_{kl})\}$$

of corresponding words. V_k is called the *document* corresponding to tuple k.[5] For every table T (which is a tuple set), there is a corresponding document set $U = \{V_1, ..., V_m\}$. Analogous to R, we write $U = \{V_k\}^s$ for the set of all document sets. Using the bijection Φ, we obtain a mapping $\Lambda : R \mapsto U$ of tables to document sets:

$$\Lambda(\{\langle a_1 : d_{m1}, ..., a_l : d_{ml}\rangle\}_m) = \{\{\Phi(a_1 : d_{m1}), ..., \Phi(a_l : d_{ml})\}\}_m \qquad (1)$$

Note that the mapping $\Lambda : R \mapsto U$ is bijective.

Homomorphism

We now show that Λ maps the set U with keyword search to an equivalent schema R with exact selects. In other words, we define a homomorphism which projects keyword searches into exact selects. This is not a database PH yet, because there are no confidentiality considerations involved; In this section, we only construct a correspondence between the two, in the next section, we will build encryption around this correspondence. We define keyword search on document sets as follows:

Definition 4.1 (Keyword Search)

Let $w \in W$. Then $\phi_w : U \mapsto U$ is a *keyword search operation* if

$$\phi_w(U) = \{V_k | V_k \in U, w \in V_k\}$$

ϕ_w maps a set of documents to the subset of these documents all of which contain w. For example:

$$\text{if} \quad U = \begin{Bmatrix} \{``ab", ``ac", ``bc"\} \\ \{``a", ``cba", ``c"\} \\ \{``ac", ``ca", ``aa"\} \end{Bmatrix},$$

$$\text{then} \quad \phi_{``ac"}(U) = \begin{Bmatrix} \{``ab", ``ac", ``bc"\} \\ \{``ac", ``ca", ``aa"\} \end{Bmatrix}$$

Now consider the systems $(R, \{\sigma_{a_i:d_j}\})$ on the one hand and $(U, \{\phi_{w_{ij}}\})$ on the other. Using the bijection Φ between attribute-value pairs and words, we can define a mapping between the two search operations:

$$\Psi : \{\sigma_{a_i:d_j}\} \mapsto \{\phi_{w_{ij}}\}, \Psi(\sigma_{a_i:d_j}) = \phi_{\Phi(a_i:d_j)} \qquad (2)$$

that defines the pairs of operations preserved by the homomorphism.

The mapping Λ is a homomorphism with respect to $(\mathsf{R}, \sigma_{a_i:d_j})$ and $(\mathsf{U}, \phi_{\Phi(a_i:d_j)})$: If $T \in \mathsf{R}$, then

$$\Lambda(\sigma_{a_i:d_j}(T)) = \Psi(\sigma_{a_i:d_j})(\Lambda(T))$$

Defining the Database PH

The elements of set U are sets of documents. So,

if $U = \{V_1, \dots, V_m\} \in \mathsf{U}$,

then $V_k = \{w_{k1}, \dots, w_{kl}\} \in U$

represents a document, consisting of the words w_i. Now, search on encrypted data is another instance of the privacy homomorphism idea: A searchable encryption scheme is a tuple $\Gamma = (K, E, E^*, D)$, where $E : K \times U \mapsto C$ maps a key $k \in K$ and a set of documents U into a ciphertext C, $E^* : K \times \{\phi_i\} \mapsto \{E^*(\phi_i)\}$ maps a key $k \in K$ and a search query ϕ to an encrypted query $E^*(\phi)$ and $D : K \times \mathsf{C} \mapsto \mathsf{U}$ maps a key k and a ciphertext C back to a plaintext U (As in the case of database PHs, there is no need for decryption of the queries.)

For any such searchable encryption scheme and the mappings Λ and Ψ introduced above, there is a database PH that preserves exact selects:

Theorem 4.1

If (K,E,E^*,D) is a searchable encryption scheme with plaintext $(\mathsf{U}, \{\phi_i\})$ to ciphertexts $(\mathsf{C}, \{E^*(\phi_i)\})$, then $(K, E \circ \Lambda, E^* \circ \Psi, \Lambda^{-1} \circ D)$ is a privacy homomorphism mapping the plain-

text system $(\mathsf{R}, \{\sigma_{a_i:d_j}\})$ to the ciphertexts system $(\mathsf{C}, \{(E^* \circ \Psi)(\sigma_{a_i:d_j})\})$.

Proof. Directly follows from the fact that Λ is bijective and homomorphic, and from Definition 2.3.

Theorem 4.1 constitutes a method to build secure database PHs preserving exact selects: If we are given relational schema R and searchable encryption scheme $\Gamma = (K, E, E^*, D)$, then a database PH for R is built as follows:

1. Choose a set W such that $|W| = |\mathsf{D}|$.
2. Choose a bijective mapping $\Phi : \mathsf{R} \mapsto W$ suitable to Γ.
3. Using W and Φ, generate Λ and Ψ.
4. Output $\Delta = (K, E \circ \Lambda, E^* \circ \Psi, \Lambda^{-1} \circ D)$.

By Theorem 4.1, Δ is a privacy homomorphism on R that maps tables T and exact select operations $\sigma_{a_i:d_j}$ to ciphertexts C, $(E^* \circ \Psi)(\sigma_{a_i:d_j})$, respectively.

Security Proof

It remains to be shown that the database PH Δ inherits the security characteristics of the searchable encryption scheme Γ, i.e., that it is secure if Alex is not submitting any unsafe queries to Eve.

First, we introduce a definition of security for a searchable encryption scheme that is an analogue of Definition 3.4:

Definition 4.2 (Indistinguishability up to Frequency for Text Search)

A searchable encryption scheme $\Gamma = (K, E, E^*, D)$ reveals nothing but the frequencies of searched words if

1. Encryption scheme (K,E,D) is indistinguishably secure.

    For every probabilistic polynomial-time algorithm A there exists a probabilistic polynomial-time algorithm A' such that for every sequence of search queries $\bar{\phi}$, every set of documents U, every polynomially bounded function f, every polynomial p and all sufficiently large n:

$$Pr[A(E_k(U), E_k^*(\bar{\phi})) = f(U)]$$
$$< \quad Pr[A'(E_k(U), \bar{N}(\bar{\phi}(U))) = f(U)]$$
$$+ \frac{1}{p(n)}$$

Then we prove that the proposed database PH Δ is secure in the sense of the introduced security definition:

Theorem 4.2

Let (K,E,E^*,D) be a a secure (in the sense of Definition 4.2) searchable encryption scheme. Then the database PH $\Delta = (K, E^* \circ \Psi, E \circ \Lambda, \Lambda^{-1} \circ D)$ as constructed in Theorem 4.1 is secure (in the sense of Definition 3.4).

Proof. We show that any violation of Definition 3.4 for Δ yields a violation of Definition 4.2 for Γ.

1. Say $(K, E \circ \Lambda, \Lambda^{-1} \circ D)$ is not indistinguishably secure, i.e., there exist tables T_1 and T_2 such that Eve can distinguish between $E_k \circ \Lambda(T_1)$ and $E_k \circ \Lambda(T_2)$ (with non-negligible probability). Then given two encrypted sets of documents $\Lambda(T_1), \Lambda(T_2)$ Eve can distinguish between $E_k(\Lambda(T_1))$ and $E_k(\Lambda(T_2))$, since $E_k(\Lambda(T_i)) = (E_k \circ \Lambda)(T_i)$. This violates condition 1 of Definition 4.2.

2. Since (K,E,E^*,D) reveals nothing but the frequencies of searched words, for every probabilistic polynomial-time algorithm A there always exists a probabilistic polynomial-time algorithm A' such that for any set of documents $\Lambda(T)$, any sequence of search queries $\bar{\Psi}(\bar{q})$, and any polynomially bounded function $f \circ \Lambda^{-1}$, every polynomial p and all sufficiently large n:

$$Pr[A(E_k(\Lambda(T)), \bar{E}_k^*(\bar{\Psi}(q))) = (f \circ \Lambda^{-1})(\Lambda(T))]$$
$$< Pr[A'(E_k(\Lambda(T)), \bar{N}(\bar{\Psi}(\bar{q})(\Lambda(T)))) = (f \circ \Lambda^{-1})(\Lambda(T))]$$
$$+ \frac{1}{p(n)}$$

Observe that

$$(E_k \circ \Lambda)(T) = E_k(\Lambda(T))$$

$$\overline{(E_k^* \circ \Psi)}(\bar{q}) = \bar{E}_k^*(\bar{\Psi}(\bar{q}))$$

$$\bar{N}(\bar{q}(T)) = \bar{N}(\bar{\Psi}(\bar{q})(\Lambda(T)))$$

$$f(T) = (f \circ \Lambda^{-1})(\Lambda(T))$$

Therefore the upper inequality can be rewritten as

$$Pr[A((E_k \circ \Lambda)(T), \overline{(E_k^* \circ \Psi)}(\bar{q})) = f(T)]$$
$$< Pr[A'((E_k \circ \Lambda)(T), \bar{N}(\bar{q}(T))) = f(T)]$$
$$+ \frac{1}{p(n)}$$

and condition 2 of Definition 3.4 for Δ is satisfied.

Example

We now deploy the method described in the last section to construct a database PH based on the searchable encryption scheme proposed in (Song et al., 2000). Word length and document length are global constants. (There are simple extensions that allow for variable-length words and documents, but for our simple database schema this does not help much, and we skip it here for the sake of clarity.) We write $a\mathbf{P}b$ for concatenation of strings a and b. '#' is the padding symbol.

We use the database schema

$Emp(name : string[9], dept : string[5], salary : int)$

The privacy homomorphism is defined as follows:

$W =$
$\{d_1\mathbf{P}"NM", d_2\mathbf{P}"DP", d_3\mathbf{P}"SL" | d_1, d_2, d_3 \in string[9]\}$

$\Phi(name:d) =$
$pad(d)\mathbf{P}"NM", where\, pad(d) \in string[9]$

$\Phi(dept:d) =$
$pad(d)\mathbf{P}\#\#\#\#\mathbf{P}"DP", where\, pad(d) \in string[5]$

$\Phi(salary:d) =$
$pad(toString(d))\mathbf{P}\#\#\#\#\#\mathbf{P}"SL", where\, d \in int$

Then, Λ maps tuples as follows (see ((1))):

$V_k = \Lambda(\langle name:"Montgomery", dept:"HR", salary:7500\rangle)$
$= \{\Phi(name:"Montgomery"), \Phi(dept:"HR"), \Phi(salary:7500)\}$
$= \{"MontgomeryNM", "HR\#\#\#\#\#\#\#DP", "7500\#\#\#\#\#\#SL"\}$

Analogously, other tuples are mapped to sets, which are stored as strings, consisting of 3 words of 12 bytes each. But we need to be careful with the linear representation of sets we chose. In relational algebra, tuple attributes are not ordered. The set $V_k = \{w_{k1}, ..., w_{kl}\}$ is not ordered either. However, the resulting document strings fix the order of elements w_{ki} and, hence, the order of the attributes in the tuples. In order to be consistent with the framework described above, words of each string must be permuted randomly and independently of all other document strings, such that the position of a word in a document is uniformly random. Any correlation between word

order and attributes would allow Eve to distinguish queries with different attributes in the equality conditions, and that would break the security of the database PH. $\overset{R}{\rightarrow}$ is a probabilistic mapping from words sets into the set of permutation strings:

$\{"MontgomeryNM", "HR\#\#\#\#\#\#\#DP", "7500\#\#\#\#\#\#SL"\}$

$\overset{R}{\rightarrow} "HR\#\#\#\#\#\#\#DPMontgomeryNM7500\#\#\#\#\#\#SL"$

At this point, the resulting strings are encrypted using the searchable encryption scheme and stored on Eve's server.

Ψ, as introduced in ((2)), establishes the link between exact select and keyword search. For example, the exact select query $\sigma_{name:"Montgomery"}$ will be mapped to the search operation $\phi_{"MontgomeryNM"}$, and processed as a search operation, returning a set of encrypted strings. This set is then decrypted and by applying Λ^{-1} mapped to corresponding tuples producing the result of the issued query.

Following *Fehler!*, the searchable encryption scheme indistinguishably encrypts sets of documents and reveals nothing but the number of documents sharing the queried word. Thus, according to Theorem 4.2, the resulting database PH is secure in the sense of Definition 3.4.

Complexity

The performance of the obtained database PHs is affected by the time required for processing exact select queries and the time required for encryption and decryption. The plaintext tuples are encrypted once when inserted into the encrypted table. Decryption is performed on the results, which are usually significantly smaller than the queried tables. Therefore, the most time consuming operation is the processing of the exact select queries. The time required for processing one such query on a table consisting of l columns and m tuples is the same as the time required to perform search on m encrypted documents consisting of l words. Searchable encryption schemes available at present perform such a search in time varying from $O(m)$ to $O(m \cdot l)$, depending on the scheme being used. Therefore, processing an exact select query will also require $O(m)$ or $O(m \cdot l)$ time. Currently there is no support for indexing encrypted tables.

Some searchable encryption schemes (and in particular the one we used as an example) may erroneously return documents not containing the keyword. That means that the database PH built on the basis of that scheme may also return erroneous tuples. However, the probability of such an error is sufficiently small; so the erroneous tuples do not create a significant traffic overhead and can easily be filtered out by Alex.

DISCUSSION AND REMARKS

We conclude our paper by tying a few loose ends.

Boolean Expressions

It is possible to increase the subset of SQL that can be handled by boolean operations and process exact selects with conjunctions, disjunctions, and negations of multiple equality conditions. This is because boolean operations in select conditions are really set operations:

$$\sigma_{(a_1:d_1 \vee (a_2:d_2 \wedge a_3:d_3))} = \sigma_{a_1:d_1} \cup (\sigma_{a_2:d_2} \cap \sigma_{a_2:d_2})$$

For every OR operation, the query is split in two (one for each operand), and the result is the union of the results of the two queries. AND can be implemented similarly with an intersect operation, and NOT by subtracting the un-negated result from the entire table. All set operations can be carried out by the server with constant cryptographic overhead.

Tuple-Wise Encryption

We have only considered tuple-wise encryption of the tables, which allows to naturally perform insert,

Conceivably, there may be a database PH that does not operate tuple-wise and thus is not restricted by the upper bounds we establish in this paper. However, we are not aware of any publication investigating this option. In fact, we can not hope to gain much from spreading one plaintext tuple over a larger part of the ciphertext than the corresponding number of bits. As long as Alex doesn't provide Eve with any queries, even tuple-wise encryption is safe. But in order to process queries in any assumed encryption scheme that is not tuple-wise, either Eve has to apply some transformation on the ciphertext to shrink it into the size of the plaintext, or communication complexity, which is the bottleneck of most distributed algorithms, is increased. Either way, the complexity of the attack can only be grown linearly in the overhead imposed on Alex for additional security. In other words, the computational complexity the attacker can handle must be smaller than the computational complexity Alex is willing to handle for normal operation of the database service. Given the unknown resources of an unknown adversary in practical scenarios, this is unacceptable.

Linear increase in complexity on both user and adversary level is considered a fatal flaw for any cryptographic primitives. To pick an arbitrary example, consider one-way functions, which are used in the theoretical foundations of cryptography to define concepts like encryption and authentication. A (trap-door) one-way function is a function that can be computed in polynomial time, whereas its inverse can not (unless one has the key to the trap-door). If encryption is a function that can be proven to be (trap-door) one-way, then the adversary can not compute the plaintext from the ciphertext in polynomial time (unless she has the key). However, if the lower bound on the attack complexity against an encryption scheme is only doubled by doubling the effort of Alex to perform a round of encryption and decryption, the underlying function is not one-way any more.

CONCLUSION AND FUTURE WORK

If a database production system is deployed, nobody questions the virtue of a sound theory of databases that the system is based on. If an insecure network connection is used between client and server for sensitive applications, reliable encryption and authentication mechanisms are used to protect the user against attacks. However, solutions for the problem that the database server itself goes adversarial have so far often been based on much lower standards: Rather than focusing on acceptable worst-case bounds of security, researchers have been more concerned with minimizing their performance overhead.

In this paper, we have given several new security definitions for database privacy homomorphisms, a cryptographic technique that allows for secure processing of encrypted data in the presence of an untrusted database service provider. We have showed that no database PH can securely protect the client a truly malicious service provider.

We could also show, however, that a combination of trust and appropriate technical means can protect a client from undesired security breaches if the range of operations outsourced to the service provider is limited.

In particular we presented a database PH that is secure in a relaxed, but still rigorous and plausible sense under widely accepted cryptographic assumptions, together with a proof of security.

Security engineering requires extreme care in order for the outcome to work. We must always expect a system to degenerate into the worst state possible, no matter how unlikely, because an adversary drives it there. We hope that our approach of establishing suitable security definitions first and then finding encryption schemes that satisfy them will prove valuable for future work in this area, in particular in light of our constructive results.

Many interesting questions remain. There may be extensions to our query language of exact selects. Projection, joins, secure aggregations and arithmetics, or more complex selection conditions need to be investigated. Some solutions for these have been proposed but should be analyzed in the light of our understanding of what constitutes a secure privacy homomorphism. Also there is a chance that we can find weaker but yet useful security definitions for other application scenarios. Finally, we are currently trying to understand how our new class of database PHs works with indexing data structures, and whether it is suitable for high-performance applications.

REFERENCES

Boneh, D., Crescenzo, G., Ostrovsky, G., & Persiano, G. (2004). Public-key Encryption with Keyword Search. In *Proceedings of the European Conference on Cryptology (EUROCRYPT)*.

Boneh, D., Kushilevitz, E., Ostrovsky, R., & Skeith, W. (2007). *Public Key Encryption that Allows PIR Queries* (Cryptology ePrint Archive, Rep. No. 2007/073). Retrieved from http://eprint.iacr.org/

Boyens, C., & Fischmann, M. (2003). Profiting from Untrusted Parties in Web-Based Applications. In *Proceedings of the 4th International Conference on Electronic Commerce and Web Technologies (EC-Web)*.

Boyens, C., & Günther, O. (2002). Trust Is not Enough: Privacy and Security in ASP and Web Service Environments. In *Proceedings of the Sixth East-European Conference on Advances in Databases and Information Systems*.

Chang, Y., & Mitzenmacher, M. (2005). Privacy Preserving Keyword Searches on Remote Encrypted Data. In *Proceedings of the Applied Cryptography and Network Security, Third International Conference,* New York (pp. 442-455).

Chor, B., & Gilboa, N. (1997). Computationally private information retrieval (extended abstract). In *STOC '97: Proceedings of the Twenty-Ninth Annual ACM Symposium on Theory of Computing* (pp. 304-313). New York: ACM Press.

Chor, B., Goldreich, O., Kushilevitz, E., & Sudan, M. (1995). Private Information Retrieval. In *Proceedings of the IEEE Symposium on Foundations of Computer Science*.

Damiani, E., De Capitani Vimercati, S., Jajodia, S., Paraboschi, S., & Samarati, P. (2003). Balancing Confidentiality and Efficiency in Untrusted Relational DBMSs. In *CCS '03: Proceedings of the 10th ACM Conference on Computer and Communications Security.* New York: ACM Press.

Domingo-Ferrer, J. (2002). A Provably Secure Additive and Multiplicative Privacy Homomorphism. In *Proceedings of the Information Security, 5th International Conference*.

Fischmann, M., & Günther, O. (2003). Privacy Tradeoffs in Database Service Architectures. In *Proceedings of the First ACM Workshop on Business Driven Security Engineering (BIZSEC)*.

Goh, E.-J. (2003). *Secure Indexes* (Cryptology ePrint Archive: Rep. No. 2003/216). Retrieved from http://eprint.iacr.org/2003/216/

Goldreich, O. (2001). Foundations of Cryptography: *Vol. I. Basic Tools*. Cambridge, UK: Cambridge University Press.

Goldreich, O. (2004). Foundations of Cryptography: *Vol. II. Basic Applications*. Cambridge, UK: Cambridge University Press.

Hacıgümüs, H., Iyer, B., Li, C., & Mehrotra, S. (2002). Executing SQL over Encrypted Data in the Database-Service-Provider Model. In *Proceedings of the 28th SIGMOD Conference on the Management of Data*. New York: ACM.

Kantarcioglu, M., & Clifton, C. (2004). *Security Issues in Querying Encrypted Data* (Tech. Rep. TR-04-013). West Lafayette, IN: Purdue University.

Rivest, R., Adleman, L., & Dertouzos, M. (1978). On Data Banks and Privacy Homomorphisms. In DeMillo, R., Dobkin, D., Jones, A., & Lipton, R. (Eds.), *Foundations of Secure Computation*. New York: Academic Press.

Song, D., Wagner, D., & Perrig, A. (2000). Practical Techniques for Searches on Encrypted Data. In *Proceedings of the IEEE Symposium on Security and Privacy*.

ENDNOTES

[1] Oracle press release on the take-over of PeopleSoft [http://www.oracle.com/corporate/press/2004_dec/acquisition.html].

[2] Wired article "Amazon's Privacy Policy Altered" [http://www.wired.com/news/politics/0,1283,38572,00.html].

[3] CNN article "Paris Hilton Hacking Victim?" [http://money.cnn.com/2005/02/21/technology/personaltech/hilton_cellphone/]

[4] The Risks Digest [http://catless.ncl.ac.uk/Risks] represents an extensive collection of such failures.

[5] One could model documents as sequences and not sets, but sets are strictly more general, and for us the word order is irrelevant.

This work was previously published in International Journal of Information Security and Privacy, Volume 4, Issue 1, edited by Hamid Nemati, pp. 1-17, copyright 2010 by IGI Publishing (an imprint of IGI Global).

Chapter 2

A Host-Based Intrusion Detection System Using Architectural Features to Improve Sophisticated Denial-of-Service Attack Detections

Ran Tao
Louisiana State University, USA

Li Yang
University of Tennessee at Chattanooga, USA

Lu Peng
Louisiana State University, USA

Bin Li
Louisiana State University, USA

ABSTRACT

Application features like port numbers are used by Network-based Intrusion Detection Systems (NIDSs) to detect attacks coming from networks. System calls and the operating system related information are used by Host-based Intrusion Detection Systems (HIDSs) to detect intrusions toward a host. However, the relationship between hardware architecture events and Denial-of-Service (DoS) attacks has not been well revealed. When increasingly sophisticated intrusions emerge, some attacks are able to bypass both the application and the operating system level feature monitors. Therefore, a more effective solution is required to enhance existing HIDSs. In this article, the authors identify the following hardware architecture features: Instruction Count, Cache Miss, Bus Traffic and integrate them into a HIDS framework based on a modern statistical Gradient Boosting Trees model. Through the integration of application, operating system and architecture level features, the proposed HIDS demonstrates a significant improvement of the detection rate in terms of sophisticated DoS intrusions.

DOI: 10.4018/978-1-4666-0026-3.ch002

INTRODUCTION

Denials of Service (DoS) attacks impose serious threat on the availability and quality of Internet services (Moore, Voelker, & Savage, 2001). They exhaust limited resources such as network bandwidth, DRAM space, CPU cycles, or specific protocol data structures, inducing service degradation or outage in computing infrastructures for the clients. System downtime resulting from DoS attacks could lead to million dollars' loss.

Generally, DoS attacks can be either flooding-based or software exploit-based. In a flooding-based DoS attack, a malicious user sends out a tremendously large number of packets aiming at overwhelming a victim host. For example, in a SYN-flooding attack, a significant number of TCP SYN packets are sent towards a victim machine, saturating resources in the victim machine. We can observe a surge of TCP connections in a short time, which are modeled by a tuple of application features <*source IP, destination IP, source port, destination port*>. In exploit-based DoS attacks, specially crafted packets are sent to the victim system targeting at specific software vulnerabilities in the operating system, service or application. The success of exploitation will either overwhelm or crash the target system. An existing solution to the exploit-based attacks is to patch and update software frequently.

Currently, research work on DoS intrusion detections mainly rely on Network-based Intrusion Detection Systems (NIDSs) (Chen et al., 2005; Handley et al., 2001; Hussain et al., 2003; Jin et al., 2003; Chari et al., 2003; Kuzmanovic et al., 2003; Wang et al. 2003). The NIDSs monitor features extracted from network packet headers at the application layer such as packet rate and traffic volume. Ramp-up behaviors and frequency domain characteristics are also studied to aid in improving the accuracy and performance of IDS (Chen et al., 2005; Hussain et al., 2003). On the other hand, Host-based Intrusion Detection Systems (HIDSs) which widely employ audit trails

and system call tracking can effectively identify buffer overflow (BoF) attacks (Chari et al., 2003; Chaturvedi et al., 2006; Wagner et al., 2002). However, the DoS attacks are not easily observed by such an HIDS and not widely researched in the HIDS literature. Some researchers have proposed to limit the bound of certain system calls (Chari et al., 2003) such as fork(). However, with the advent of large-scale application software, such bounds may seriously impair the performance of normal applications. Moreover, DoS attacks may not involve huge number of system calls at all. Therefore, a more generic solution is needed to detect DoS attacks.

When increasingly sophisticated techniques are adopted by attackers, multi-tier attacks and IP spoofing are emerging to amplify destructive effects and evade detections. The attack patterns or behaviors will be difficult to identify by using only header-based network traffic analysis. For example, in a complicated scenario that an attacker gets around the network monitoring sensors and launches DoS attacks locally, a NIDS may not able to detect this intrusion. In such a scenario, non-privileged access is well enough to successfully initiate a DoS attack against the host machine: once the attacker obtains the access to the victim machine, even if it is not root-privileged and difficult to further elevate to carry out other destructive or stealthy behaviors, he/she can still easily upload a DoS daemon to massively consume the machine's limited resources. Instead of network information only, information originated and resided on the victim machine should be used to track and monitor such undergoing attacks in this case.

In this paper, we propose an HIDS with multi-level integrated information from application, operating system (OS), and architecture levels to improve the detection rate of sophisticated DoS attacks. According to our experiments, even if DoS attacks could successfully evade captures of NIDS monitors, architectural behaviors will still be triggered: a tremendous jump of *Instruction Count*,

Cache Miss, *Bus Traffic* can be found. Based on this observation, a novel HIDS employing a modern statistical *Gradient Boosting Trees (GBT)* model is proposed to detect sophisticated DoS intrusions through the integration of application, OS, and architecture features. Our experiments test three different types of exploits: self-developed local DoS exploits, real-world remote DoS exploits and real-world local DoS attacks. The results show that the inclusion of architecture features can significantly improve the detection rate of evasive DoS intrusions.

The rest of this paper is organized as follows: related work is discussed in section 2; our proposed IDS methodology and framework is elaborated in section 3. The experiment results are shown and discussed in section 4. We conclude the paper in Section 5.

RELATED WORK

Modern DoS attacks employ many advanced and sophisticated techniques to amplify the damage and elude detections or mitigations of counter-measures. IP spoofing is widely adopted by hackers to mask the real source of attacks, or launch reflective DoS attacks; Distributed DoS is used to initiate attacks from multi-source; low-rate pulsing method is utilized to reduce average packet rate and evade network monitors. Based on a header analysis, frequency domain characteristics are studied to improve the IDS performance (Chen et al., 2005; Hussain et al., 2003), a ramp-up behavior is also considered as a way to distinguish between single- or multi-source attacks. In (Chari et al. 2003, Kuzmanovic et al., 2003), authors propose to take a spectral analysis to detect shrew attacks which consist of short time bursts repeating at a maliciously chosen low frequency. This kind of low-rate attack sends out packets at certain fixed intervals, to intentionally reduce the average packet rate, rendering the IDS unable to discover undergoing attacks. To defend against IP spoof-ings, various off-line IP trace-back techniques are proposed to pinpoint the real origin of DoS attack (Savage et al. 2000; Snoren et al., 2001), some on-line countermeasures are also developed to filter out those spoofed packets, help sustain service availability during attacks: (Jin et al. 2003) presents a Hop-Count Filtering scheme to utilize the Time-to-Live(TTL) value in the IP header to filter out spoofed IP packets.

Recent work on intrusion countermeasures include machine learning IDS techniques, alert correlation, alert fusion and feature analysis. *Machine learning techniques*, such as decision tree, neural network, Bayesian network, are applied to detect network intrusions. *Alert correlation* attempts to correlate IDS alerts based on the similarity between alert attributes, previously known attack scenarios, or prerequisites and consequences of known attacks (Ning & Xu, 2004). *Alert fusion* combines detection outputs of the same attack from different independent detectors. *Feature Analysis* tries to optimize the information gained from multiple dimensional features through feature bagging, relevance and redundancy analysis, and feature weight classification (Lazarevic et al., 2005; Li & Guo, 2008; Liu & Yu, 2005; Yu & Liu 2004).

In the HIDS literature, various techniques utilizing system call tracking and auditing trails are proposed. System call arguments are integrated to capture data-flow behaviors of programs, and improve attack detections in HIDS (Chaturvedi et al., 2006). A policy-driven solution is presented in (Chari et al., 2003) to define and enforce process behavior rules controlling processes' access to system resources. All system behaviors are monitored in real-time by a modified kernel.

Basically, research works investigating DoS attack utilize sniffer-based methodologies. They only rely on analyzing network traffic information at the application level. These network-based schemes suffer from fast traffic, switched network, information encryption, and most importantly, they have little knowledge of what is really going on in the victim machine. Significant useful information on the victim host is neglected. HIDS against DoS attacks are not widely researched since it is difficult to find a generic and low-cost way to defend against such attacks. We propose to utilize the strong correlation of architectural behaviors with DoS attacks, and employ multi-layer features to construct an IDS model. Close to our work, Woo & Lee (2007) have observed performance degradation of multi-threaded workload under architectural DoS attacks. However, they do not further study the correlation of architectural behavior and DoS attacks and apply into an IDS in identifying and preventing such attacks. In our work, we are exploring architecture features to enrich the existing feature set used for intrusion detection research and demonstrate its effectiveness in a systematic approach.

In our recent paper (Tao et al., 2009), we demonstrated the effectiveness of integrating architectural level events into the HIDS. This paper further extends (Tao et al., 2009) by including experiments on real-world local exploits which can be easily detected by our HIDS.

THE IDS FRAMEWORK

A. Methodology

Our proposed scheme is one of the anomaly-based intrusion detection systems. We employ a modern statistical model, Gradient Boosting Trees, to build up a knowledge base from an offline training dataset. This knowledge base contains patterns of benign and malicious behaviors which are learned from observed traffic, and has the ability to predict whether a network connection is an attack.

In our proposed IDS system, multi-layer information will be integrated to detect sophisticated DoS. The correlation of system architectural behaviors and DoS attacks is analyzed by the statistical model employing Gradient Boosting Trees techniques. Architectural features are explored to improve the IDS performance.

The training set and the real-time traffic include the following application and architectural level features.

1. Application (APP) Features: *proto-col_type, service, duration, size_from_client, size_from_server, packet_rate and wrong_checksum_rate.*
2. Operating System (OS) Features: *forked_socket_session, forked_shell, forked_from_shell, coincided_pid.*
3. Architectural (ARCH) Features: *instruction_retired, L1_cache_miss, L2_cache_miss, and bus_access.* We select them because a typical network DoS attack can be monitored by observing these events (Woo & Lee, 2007).

As shown in Figure 1, our proposed scheme involves multiple steps listed as follows.

Step 1: Data Collection

At different levels, we use different schemes and tools to collect data. *Tcpdump* utility is used to record header information of network packets transmitting towards/from the host computer. A system call tracking function embedded in the Linux kernel is employed to log all system call events. Architectural behaviors are recorded using a kernel module which periodically samples CPU performance counters and dumps out the performance variation trace.

Step 2: Feature Extraction and Correlation

Our desired application level features are extracted using a custom network traffic parser which models records by network sessions identified by a format of "src_ip:src_port <-> dst_ip:dst_port". We modified the system tracking function to export detailed information of all network socket sessions, in order to be able to map OS events

Figure 1. The framework of our Intrusion Detection System

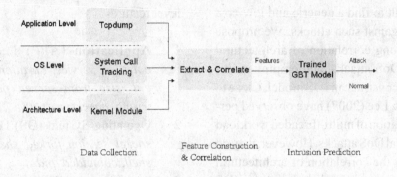

with other level events. Architectural records are processed as a ratio of event numbers during the current session to a pre-measured normal session without attacks. Since features of different levels are obtained by different collecting processes, we append a timestamp to each record for the correlation between architectural events and application events during the same session.

Step 3: Intrusion Prediction

As a standard workflow, in this step, each correlated record is fed to the statistical model which has learned the patterns of normal and attack behaviors from the training dataset. It will raise an alert if the given record deviates from normal behaviors.

B. The Gradient Boosting Trees (GBT) Model

The statistical model that we employed for intrusion detection is based on Gradient Boosting Trees (GBT), originally proposed in (Friedman, 2001). GBT is one of several techniques that aim to improve the performance of a single model by fitting many models and combining them for prediction. GBT uses two algorithms: "trees" from the Classification and Regression Tree and

"boosting" which builds and combines a collection of models, i.e. trees.

From a user's point of view, GBT has the following advantages. First, GBT is inherently non-parametric and can handle mixed-type of input variables. Both discrete and continuous data are supported. There is no need of data discretization. GBT doesn't need to make any assumptions regarding the underlying distribution of the values for the input variables. For example, GBT can relieve researchers from determining whether variables are normally distributed, and making transformations if they are not. Second, the tree is adept at capturing complex-structured behavior, i.e. complex interactions among predictors are routinely and automatically handled with relatively few inputs required from the analyst. This is in marked contrast to some other multivariate nonlinear modeling methods, in which extensive input from the analyst, analysis of interim results, and subsequent modification of the method are required. Third, the tree is insensitive to outliers, and unaffected by monotone transformations and differing scales of measurement among inputs. Despite clear evidence of strong predictive performance, boosting-based learning methods have been rarely used in computer intrusion detection (Yu & Tsai, 2007).

Consider the binary classification problem with n observations of the form $\{y_i, \boldsymbol{x}_i\}$, i=1,...,n, where x_i is a multi-dimensional input vector and y_i is the binary response $y_i \in \{-1, +1\}$. In this paper, x_i is the feature in multiple levels and y_i is the prediction result, i.e., attack or not. The negative log-likelihood for the binomial model or *deviance* (also known as cross-entropy) is used as the loss function:

$$L\left(y, \hat{f}\right) = \log\left(1 + \exp\left(-2y\hat{f}\right)\right).$$

The population minimizer of the loss function is at the true probabilities:

$$\arg\min_{f(\mathbf{x})} E_{Y|\mathbf{x}}\left[L\left(y, f\left(\mathbf{x}\right)\right)\right] =$$

$$f^*\left(\mathbf{x}\right) = \frac{1}{2}\log\left[\frac{\Pr\left(y = 1 \mid \mathbf{x}\right)}{\Pr\left(y = -1 \mid \mathbf{x}\right)}\right]$$

or equivalently,

$$\Pr\left(y = 1 \mid \mathbf{x}\right) = \frac{1}{1 + e^{-2f^*(\mathbf{x})}},$$

where $E_{Y|\mathbf{x}}\left[L\left(y, f\left(\mathbf{x}\right)\right)\right]$ is the expectation value of the loss function over Y given the input X.

The detailed algorithm for GBT in binary classification is the following.

1. Initialize $\hat{f}_0\left(\mathbf{x}_i\right) = \frac{1}{2}\log\left(\frac{1 + \bar{y}}{1 - \bar{y}}\right)$, where $\bar{y}$ is the average for $\{y_i\}$.

2. Repeat for m = 1, 2, ..., M:
    a. Set the negative gradient

    $$\tilde{y}_{im} = -\left[\frac{\partial L\left(y_i, \hat{f}_{m-1}\left(\mathbf{x}_i\right)\right)}{\partial \hat{f}_{m-1}\left(\mathbf{x}_i\right)}\right], \quad i = 1, ..., n.$$

    b.

    $$\left\{R_{hm}\right\}_{h=1}^{H} =$$

    $H -$ terminal node tree based on $\{\tilde{y}$.

    c.

    $$\gamma_{hm} = \arg\min_{\gamma} \sum_{\mathbf{x}_i \in R_{hm}} L\left(y_i, \hat{f}\left(\mathbf{x}_i\right) + \gamma\right)$$

    d.

    $$\hat{f}_m\left(\mathbf{x}\right) = \hat{f}_{m-1}\left(\mathbf{x}\right) + \nu \times \gamma_{hm} I\left(\mathbf{x} \in R_{hm}\right)$$

3. End algorithm.

Note that ν is the "shrinkage" parameter between 0 and 1 and controls the learning rate of the procedure. Empirical results have shown that small values of ν always lead to better generalization error rates (Friedman, 2001). In this study, we fix ν at 0.01. At each iteration, an H-terminal node tree, which partitions the x space into H-disjoint regions $\left\{R_{hm}\right\}_{h=1}^{H}$, is fitted based on the current negative gradient for the loss function.

EXPERIMENTAL RESULTS

We use an Intel Pentium-D PC installed with Redhat Linux 9.0, and connect it to a department LAN. Network traffic information is captured with the *tcpdump* tool. Our modified parser based on an open source utility *Chaosreader* extracts desired information in the application level out from the recorded tcpdump files, and groups packets into sessions by src_ip:src_port <-> dst_ip:dst_port, thus we will obtain a set of preprocessed data in the format that each entry represents a network connection, together with application features flagged accordingly.

The Intel Pentium-D processor provides us with adequate performance counters to illustrate the CPU's dynamic performance profile. A kernel module is implemented to sample the performance counters in regular intervals. We set the sampling interval to 0.5s, balancing the tradeoff between system performance overhead and accuracy of monitored performance variation. Thus, at regular interval, the values of these four architectural counters which have most representative architectural variation under a DoS attack

Table 1. The self-developed DoS exploits

Attack Type	Description
L2 Cache DoS	Target L2 cache, sweep through L2 cache space
BSB DoS	Target backside bus bandwidth, sweep through twice the L1 D$ size, saturate backside bus
FSB DoS	Target front-side bus bandwidth, sweep through twice L2 cache size, saturate front-side bus.
Memory DoS	Target memory space; keep allocating memory space, max out memory usage.
Loop DoS	Target CPU usage, infinite dummy instruction.

are recorded and dumped to a trace file. The time-stamp recorded together with other performance counters is used to correlate architectural events with network connections parsed from tcpdump files. The exploits are triggered manually against the target machine. For each exploit, it will take about an hour to collect the traffic. In addition, several hours' normal traffic is also collected to add to the dataset.

Experiments with Developed Exploits

More sophisticated techniques are emerging to bypass IDS detections; in this work, we assume crackers have gained unauthorized access to the victim machine (they may not have a root-privilege), and then intend to launch local DoS daemons. To emulate this scenario, we design five local DoS exploits which are used to model local DoS exploits exhausting different system resources. Each type of exploit targets a type of system resources, intentionally exhausting a particular resource, and rendering the system unavailable to legitimate users. Detailed descriptions are shown in Table 1. First three attacks are traversing a certain memory space with the stride of the cache line size (64 bytes in our system).

We launch these exploits multiple times over a LAN to obtain five different training datasets, each containing only four exploit types. Details of the training and testing sets are listed in Table 2.

Table 2. Dataset construction

Dataset	Combination
Training 1	l2 + bsb + fsb + mem
Training 2	l2 + bsb + fsb + loop
Training 3	l2 + bsb + mem + loop
Training 4	l2 + fsb + mem + loop
Training 5	bsb + fsb + mem + loop
Testing	l2 + bsb + fsb + mem + loop + noise

The testing dataset includes a full set of the above five exploit types, 25 attack instances in total, and is injected with noise traffic data of CPU or memory intensive operations such as tar, compile, scp, etc. Those noises are included in order to evaluate the ability of the IDS to differentiate normal operation from attack traffic. In addition, we also include 3630 normal connections.

Firstly, we train an IDS using the GBT model solely with the application level features listed in Section 3. The testing results demonstrate that the APP features are not sufficient to detect the testing DoS intrusions accurately. Results shown in Figure 2 reveal that IDS built on the application features alone can only recognized around 30% of such DoS attacks (refer to the light bar group in Figure 2).

This result is expectable since we assume that our multi-step attacks can bypass the application level feature monitors and launch DoS exploits locally. The network connection behaves exactly the same as other normal connections. No DoS attack followed by unauthorized access can be detected by application features only. Therefore, the IDS can not differentiate them from other normal operations.

We first conduct the experiment with assistance of architectural features to evaluate effectiveness of architectural features in detecting multi-step DoS attacks. From the Figure 2, we can see that the capability to detect novel multi-step DoS attacks is greatly improved to an average of 91.2% by integrating ARCH features. For training set 3, 4 and 5, we achieve a detection rate almost to 100%.

A few example records are shown in Table 3 to illustrate the different behaviors of malicious and benign operations monitored from multi-layer features. For the ARCH events including ic, l1_m, l2_m, and bus_acc, we list the ratio of the numbers of the event during a session to a pre-measured normal session. The first entry is a normal *ssh* connection that is commonly seen in a local network. The next three entries are BSB, loop, memory DoS attacks. Each of them has manifest architectural variations (see the bolded italic numbers), which mean they are predicted as an attack as shown in pred_2 column. However, the application (APP) layer features manifest the same pattern as a normal connection as shown in pred_1 column. The IDS built with only APP features can not distinguish such attacks from other normal sessions. Therefore, it lacks sufficient information to make a correct judgment.

However, ARCH features also bring in false positives compared to pure APP feature framework as shown in Table. 4. Even though the false positive rate is as low as an average of 0.17%,

considering the amount of normal connections is large, over 3000 records, the actual number of false alerts is not negligible. The most challenging issue to integrate ARCH features into IDS is how to reduce false positives, since at ARCH level, memory or CPU intensive workloads, and malicious DoS attacks have similar characteristics which is difficult to differentiate at the this level.

To solve this problem, we first analyze the way by which crackers may log in to the victim system. In practice, remote Buffer-over-flow (BoF) and guessing password are mainly used to gain unauthorized access to the target machine. After crackers gain illegal access to the victim system, a DoS attack may be launched. In this paper, we assume that an illegal user will conduct a BoF attack first to obtain access to the target system then start a DoS attack since guessing password can be easily locked down by restricting number

Figure 2. Detection rate of IDS with different feature sets

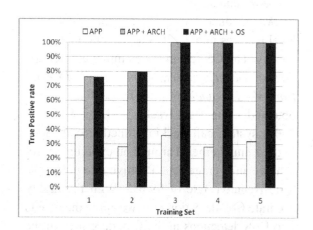

Table 3. Sample records. The label is the actual attribute of the connection, pred_1 is prediction from APP framework, pred_2 is prediction result from APP + ARCH framework.

Num	service type duration size_server size_client pkt_r wrong_cks_r ic l1_m l2_m bus_acc label pred_1 pred_2
1	ssh tcp 77.26 3993 2004 2.01 0.05 1.14 1.48 2.67 1.73 normal_ normal normal
2	ssh tcp 355.16 10407 2148 0.77 0.05 *55.75 3602.53* 1.18 0.96 attack_ normal attack
3	ssh tcp 219.15 11393 3540 1.62 0.03 *264.11* 0.81 0.84 0.87 attack_ normal attack
4	ssh tcp 228.68 17121 3300 1.97 0.03 *11.73* 2.56 3.27 *25.56* attack_ normal attack
...	...

Table 4. False alarm rate of IDS for different feature sets

Training Set	False Positive Rate (%)		
	APP	APP + ARCH	APP + ARCH + OS
1	0	0.19	0.00051
2	0	0.08	0.00022
3	0	0.19	0.00051
4	0	0.19	0.00051
5	0	0.19	0.00051

of continuous failed logins. In this scenario, we enforce the IDS with BoF detection capability with OS level monitors then record prediction results into the system event log. We can distinguish between a normal heavy duty program and an illegal DoS attack in this way: we search the event log and check if a BoF exploit was found in this connection before. If it was found and architectural events also show an abnormal pattern, we think that the system is under DoS attack; otherwise, we believe that there is a legal heavy duty program running on the target machine, i. e., the system is in a normal state.

We conducted experiments integrating OS level features into the IDS to detect remote BoF attacks. The OS features we employed include: *forked_socket_session, forked_shell, forked_ from_shell, coincided_pid*. Those features are obtained using BackTracker's (King & Chen, 2003) system call tracking function embedded in the Linux kernel. Through an experiment, we achieve an average True Positive rate of 90.3%, True Negative rate of 99.6%. With the highly accurate BoF detection rate, we apply the results into DoS detections in the way described in the last paragraph to reduce false alarm rate induced by ARCH monitors. As shown in the last column of Table 4, the false positive rate is almost reduced to zero in all of the cases. The true positive rate is slightly affected as shown by the dark bar in Figure 2. But its average, 90.96%, is still considered as good performance in detecting sophisticated DoS attacks.

Note that we only take BoF for example here, just to demonstrate that additional information could be utilized to reduce the false positives. Guessing password can also be accurately identified by extracting other information from the application payload data.

Interestingly, the system behavior under DoS attacks is barely revealed at the OS level. Although the APP + OS framework works well for BoF attacks, it can not tell DoS attacks in an easy way. If hackers launch remote DoS attacks, the APP + OS IDS will not be able to identify any of these intrusions. Its detection rate is as low as the light bars in Figure 2. Therefore, we don't show the data in this figure.

Experiments with Mixed Exploits

Besides our crafted exploits, we also evaluate our proposed scheme using mixed data with crafted exploits and real-world remote exploits. Remote DoS exploits involve a simpler attack scenario. Attackers only need to initiate a one-step procedure: launch the attack against a target system remotely. Using this set of datasets, we intend to simulate a realistic situation that both remote DoS and sophisticated DoS exploits are mixed together. Real network traffic tend to be sophisticated, it will rarely contain only one type of attacks. The description of real-world exploits in the experiment is listed in Table 5.

We also divide the data into five training datasets and one testing dataset. There is no training

Table 5. Real-world remote DoS exploits

Attack	Description
CVE-2003-0132	Apache memory leak, drains memory via large chunks of linefeed characters.
CVE-2003-0543	OpenSSL integer overflow, causes Apache server to enter CPU intensive loop.
CVE-2004-0493	Apache memory exhaustion.
CVE-2004-0942	Apache multiple space header DoS, drains CPU resource.

Table 6. Our IDS performance for mixed datasets

Training Set	# of False Alarms		# of Missed Attacks	
	APP	APP + ARCH + OS	APP	APP + ARCH + OS
1	28	12	2	0
2	33	11	2	0
3	50	11	3	0
4	36	17	2	0
5	47	9	2	0

dataset containing all types of exploits, while the testing dataset includes all types of exploits. A huge number of noise traffic is injected into the testing data. The training and testing division are designed to evaluate the capability of our IDS in detecting never-seen-before attacks. Results using mixed dataset (shown in Table 6) also prove the effectiveness of integrating architectural level features. In this experiment, the total number of normal connections is 9412 and the total number of attack instances of 472.

Experiments with Real-World Local Exploits

Having shown how ARCH features benefit the IDS using our developed exploits, we test the system with two real-world local DoS exploits (Table 7) separately to further demonstrate the soundness of our work. These two exploits have been used by real hackers in the world, to impair production servers. We tweak the mem-leak-dos-2 exploit to extend the attack timeframe by adding a loop. Mem-dos-exploit-1 is launched 6 times; exploit-2 is launched 5 times. Both are fed with varied parameters in each run.

We use two sets of training data: one constructed with only the hand-crafted exploits, the other one mixed with real-world remote DoS exploits. Note that for both sets, first five training data only contains a subset of all exploit types, and the training 6 contains a full set of all exploit types.

Table 7. Real-world local DoS exploits

Attack	Description
Memory leak local DoS - 1	Kernel vulnerability causing exhaustion of system memory resource, inducing system crash.
Memory leak local DoS - 2	Kernel vulnerability allows non-privileged users to read kernel memory and system performance degradation.

Figure 3. IDS performance comparison (group a's training data consists of self-developed exploits, group b's training data consists of mixed-data)

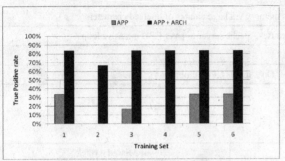

a(1) Detection rate of IDS with different feature
      sets tested using the Mem-leak-dos-1 exploit

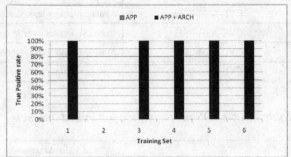

a(2) Detection rate of IDS with different feature
      sets tested using the Mem-leak-dos-2 exploit

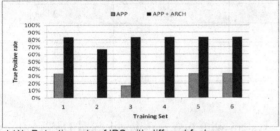

b(1) Detection rate of IDS with different feature
      sets tested using the Mem-leak-dos-1 exploit

b(2) Detection rate of IDS with different feature
      sets tested using the Mem-leak-dos-2 exploit

Figure 3 shows the comparison of True Positive rates using different training and testing datasets. Table 8 outlines the number of false alarms of different experimental sets. In Figure 3, group a's results are based on training sets which are combinations of self-developed exploits. The APP + ARCH IDS achieves an average detection rate of 80.6% for Mem-leak-dos-1 attack, and 80.3% for Mem-leak-dos-2 attack (five out of six datasets have 100% detection rate). Meanwhile, the APP IDS's average detection rates in these two cases are 19.4% and 0 separately. The reason why the APP + ARCH IDS detects none of the mem-leak-dos-2 exploit when trained using training set 2 is that the exploit type missing from the training set, which is memory-dos, has the exact same architectural features as the attack. Therefore, even though the IDS is well trained with other exploit types, it fails to detect this particular exploit efficiently. The result of training set 6 tells that when trained

with full set of all exploit types, the IDS can accurately identify all intrusion instances.

For group b, which is trained with mixed datasets of developed and real-world remote exploits, the average TP rates for APP + ARCH IDS are 88.9% and 100% for Mem-leak-dos-1 and Mem-leak-dos-2 separately; APP IDS can only detect 30.6% or none of those two types of attack instances. The injected real-world remote exploits in the training data improve the detection rate of APP + ARCH IDS as compared to group a. They remedy the degradation induced by absence of the memory-dos from the training data 2, since they bring in similar exploit types that have the same architectural behavior as the testing exploit. The 100% accuracy is obtained in attack detection using this set of training data. This indicates that with more comprehensive training data, our proposed IDS can achieve more accurate detection results.

Table 8. IDS performance comparison (in each table, left group of columns indicates the IDS is trained with self-developed exploits, right group's training data is based on mixed datasets)

| Training Set | # of False Alarms | | | |
| | Crafted Exploits | | Crafted + Real-world Exploits | |
	APP	APP + ARCH	APP	APP + ARCH
1	2	0	1	2
2	1	0	1	0
3	1	0	1	0
4	1	0	1	0
5	1	0	1	0
6	1	0	1	0

a. Number of false alarms for Mem-leak-dos-1

| Training Set | # of False Alarms | | | |
| | Crafted Exploits | | Crafted + Real-world Exploits | |
	APP	APP + ARCH	APP	APP + ARCH
1	1	0	1	2
2	1	0	4	0
3	2	0	2	0
4	1	0	0	0
5	1	0	0	0
6	1	0	0	0

b. Number of false alarms for Mem-leak-dos-2

Number of false alarms is shown in Table 8 by grouping the results by the testing data. Table 8(a) lists the results for two sets of training data detecting mem-leak-dos-1 attack. The APP IDS raises an average of 1.17 or 1 false alarm for two training sets, and the APP + ARCH IDS raises 0.33 or no false alarm for those two training sets. When the volume of network traffic grows, the difference of number of false alarms raised by the two IDSs will increase significantly. Table 8(b) shows the average number of false positives for APP IDS is 1.17 and 1 tested using mem-leak-dos-2 exploit, while the average number is 0 and 0.33 for APP + ARCH IDS.

In conclusion, the testing results demonstrate that ARCH features are of significant use in identifying sophisticated DoS attacks. APP features alone can not reveal the intrusive behaviors by monitoring at the application level. By using our crafted exploits or real-world exploits, attackers can manage avoid detection by APP monitors, and directly induce drastic system performance degradation, with the APP monitors still showing everything is normal. With addition of ARCH features, alarms will be triggered in this case because DoS attack can not be achieved without inducing numerous ARCH level activities. Even though attackers could escape from being caught at other levels, ARCH features will show all suspicious activities.

CONCLUSION

We have conducted experiments to demonstrate that an IDS using only application features failed to detect sophisticated DoS attacks because these attacks appear normal if their behaviors are only monitored by the application feature set. In order to detect the missed DoS attacks, we use a combination of application, OS and architecture feature set. Our experimental results showed improved IDS performance. In summary, we propose the idea that if crackers use sophisticated schemes to evade defense, the architectural level behavior provides us valuable information to improve the IDS against such DoS attacks.

REFERENCES

Chari, S. N., & Cheng, P. C. (2003). BlueBoX: A Policy-Driven, Host-Based Intrusion Detection System. *ACM Transactions on Information and System Security*, *6*(2), 173–200. doi:10.1145/762476.762477

Chaturvedi, A., Bhatkar, E., & Sekar, R. (2006). Improving Attack Detection in Host-Based IDS by Learning Properties of System Call Arguments. In *Proceedings of the IEEE Symposium on Security and Privacy.*

Chen, Y., Hwang, K., & Kwok, Y.-K. (2005). *Collaborative Defense against Periodic. Shrew DDoS Attacks in Frequency Domain.* ACM Transactions on Information and System Security.

Friedman, J. H. (2001). Greedy function approximation: a gradient boosting machine. *Annals of Statistics*, *29*(5), 1189–1232. doi:10.1214/aos/1013203451

Handley, M., Kreibich, C., & Paxson, V. (2001). Network Intrusion Detection: Evasion, Traffic Normalization, and End-to-End Protocol Semantics. In *Proceedings of the USENIX Security Symposium* (pp. 115-131).

Hussain, A., Heidemann, J., & Papadopoulos, C. (2003). A Framework for Classifying Denial of Service Attack. In *Proceedings of ACM SIGCOMM* (pp. 99-110).

Jin, C., Wang, H., & Shin, K. G. (2003). Hop-Count Filtering: An Effective Defense against Spoofed Traffic. In *Proceedings of the 10th ACM conference on Computer and Communications Security* (pp. 30-41).

King, S. T., & Chen, P. M. (2003). Backtracking intrusions. *SIGOPS Oper. Syst. Rev.*, *37*(5), 223–236. doi:10.1145/1165389.945467

Kuzmanovic, A., & Knightly, E. W. (2003). Low-Rate TCP-Targeted Denial of Service Attacks. In *Proceedings of ACM SIGCOMM* (pp. 75-86).

Lazarevic, A., & Kumar, V. (2005). Feature bagging for outlier detection. In *Proceedings of the Eleventh ACM SIGKDD international Conference on Knowledge Discovery in Data Mining* (pp. 157-166).

Lee, W., & Stolfo, S. (1998). Data mining approaches for intrusion detection. In *Proceedings of the 7th USENIX Security Symposium*, San Antonio, TX (pp. 79-94).

Li, Y., & Guo, L. (2008). TCM-KNN scheme for network anomaly detection using feature-based optimizations. In *Proceedings of the ACM Symposium on Applied Computing* (pp. 2103-2109).

Liu, H., & Yu, L. (2005). Towards integrating feature selection algorithms for classification and clustering. *IEEE Transactions on Knowledge and Data Engineering*, *17*(3), 1–12.

Luo, X., & Chang, R. K. C. (2005). On a New Class of Pulsing Denial-of-Service Attacks and the Defense. In *Proceedings of Network and Distributed System Security Symposium*.

Moore, D., Voelker, G. M., & Savage, S. (2001). Inferring Internet Denial-of-Service Activity. In *Proceedings of the 10th USENIX Security Symposium*.

Ning, P., & Xu, D. (2004). Hypothesizing and reasoning about attacks missed by intrusion detection systems. *ACM Transactions on Information and System Security*, 7(4), 591–627. doi:10.1145/1042031.1042036

Savage, S., Wetherall, D., Karlin, A., & Anderson, T. (2000). Practical network support for IP traceback. In *Proceedings of ACM SIGCOMM*, Stockholm, Sweden (pp. 295-306).

Snoren, A. C., Partridge, C., Sanchez, L. A., Jones, C. E., Tchakountio, F., Kent, S. T., et al. (2001). Hash-based IP Traceback. In *Proceedings of ACM SIGCOMM '2001*, San Diego, CA (pp. 3-14).

Tao, R., Yang, L., Peng, L., Li, B., & Cemerlic, A. (2009). A Case Study: Using Architectural Features to Improve Sophisticated Denial-of-Service Attack Detections. In *Proceedings of 2009 IEEE Symposium on Computational Intelligence in Cyber Security*, Nashville, TN (pp. 13-18).

Wagner, D., & Soto, P. (2002). Mimicry Attacks on Host-Based Inrusion Detection Systems, *Proceedings of the 9th ACM conference on Computer and communications security*, November 18–22, pp. 255 - 264

Wang, H., Zhang, D., & Shin, K. (2004). Change-Point Monitoring for Detection for DoS Attacks. *IEEE Transactions on Dependable and Secure Computing*, 193–208. doi:10.1109/TDSC.2004.34

Woo, D. H., & Lee, H.-H. S. (2007). Analyzing Performance Vulnerability due to Resource Denial-of-Service Attack on Chip Multiprocessors. In *Proceedings of the 1ˢᵗ workshop on Chip-Multiprocessor Memory Systems and Interconnects* (pp. 33-40).

Yu, L., & Liu, H. (2004). Efficient Feature Selection via Analysis of Relevance and Redundancy. *Journal of Machine Learning Research*, 5, 1205–1224.

Yu, Z., & Tsai, J. (2007). An efficient intrusion detection system using a boosting-based learning algorithm. *International Journal of Computer Applications in Technology*, 27(4), 223–231. doi:10.1504/IJCAT.2006.011994

This work was previously published in International Journal of Information Security and Privacy, Volume 4, Issue 1, edited by Hamid Nemati, pp. 18-31, copyright 2010 by IGI Publishing (an imprint of IGI Global).

Chapter 3
A Keystroke Biometric System for Long-Text Input

Charles C. Tappert
Pace University, USA

Sung-Hyuk Cha
Pace University, USA

Mary Villani
Pace University, USA

Robert S. Zack
Pace University, USA

ABSTRACT

A novel keystroke biometric system for long-text input was developed and evaluated for user identification and authentication applications. The system consists of a Java applet to collect raw keystroke data over the Internet, a feature extractor, and pattern classifiers to make identification or authentication decisions. Experiments on more than 100 participants investigated two input modes—copy and free-text—and two keyboard types—desktop and laptop. The system can accurately identify or authenticate individuals if the same type of keyboard is used to produce the enrollment and questioned input samples. Longitudinal experiments quantified performance degradation over intervals of several weeks and two years. Additional experiments investigated the system's hierarchical model, parameter settings, assumptions, and sufficiency of enrollment samples and input-text length. Although evaluated on input texts up to 650 keystrokes, the authors found that input of 300 keystrokes, roughly four lines of text, is sufficient for the important applications described.

DOI: 10.4018/978-1-4666-0026-3.ch003

INTRODUCTION

This paper describes the development and evaluation of a keystroke biometric system for long-text input. The system has user-identification and user-authentication Internet applications that are of increasing importance as the population of application participants continues to grow. An example user-authentication application is verifying the identity of students taking online quizzes or tests, an application becoming more important with the student enrollment in online classes increasing and instructors becoming concerned about evaluation security and academic integrity. Similarly, in a business setting employees can be required to take online examinations in their training/orientation programs where the companies would like the exam-takers authenticated. An example user-identification application in a small company environment is a closed system of known employees where there has been a problem with the circulation of inappropriate (unprofessional, offensive, or obscene) e-mail, and it is desirable to identify the perpetrator. Because the inappropriate email is being sent from computers provided by the company for employees to send email and surf the Internet during lunch and coffee breaks, there are no ethical issues in capturing users' keystrokes. In addition, as more businesses moving to e-commerce, the keystroke biometric in Internet applications can provide an effective balance between high security and customer ease-of-use (Yu & Cho, 2004).

Keystroke biometric systems measure typing characteristics believed to be unique to an individual and difficult to duplicate (Bolle, Connell, Pankanti, Ratha, & Senior, 2004; Jin, Ke, Manuel, & Wilkerson, 2004). The keystroke biometric is one of the less-studied behavioral biometrics. Most of the systems developed previously have been experimental in nature. However, several companies such as AdmitOne (2008) and Bio-Chec (2008) have recently developed commercial products for hardening passwords (short input) in computer security schemes.

The keystroke biometric is appealing for several reasons. First, it is not intrusive and computer users type frequently for both work and pleasure. Second, it is inexpensive since the only hardware required is a computer with keyboard. Third, keystrokes continue to be entered for potential repeated checking after an authentication phase has verified a user's identity (or possibly been fooled) since keystrokes exist as a mere consequence of users using computers (Gunetti & Picardi, 2005). This continuing verification throughout a computer session is sometimes referred to as dynamic verification (Leggett & Williams, 2005; Leggett, Williams, Usnick, & Longnecker, 1991).

Most of the previous work on the keystroke biometric has dealt with user authentication, and while some studies used long-text input (Bergadano, Gunetti, & Picardi, 2002; Gunetti & Picardi, 2005; Leggett & Williams, 2005), most used passwords or short name strings (Bender & Postley, 2007; Bolle et al., 2004; Brown & Rogers, 1993; Giot, El-Abed, & Rosenberger, 2009a; Monrose, Reiter, & Wetzel, 2002; Monrose & Rubin, 2000; Obaidat & Sadoun, 1999; Revett, 2008; Rodrigues et al., 2006). Fewer studies have dealt with user identification (Gunetti & Picardi, 2005; Peacock, Ke, & Wilkerson, 2004; Song, Venable, & Perrig, 1997). Gunetti and Picardi (2005) focused on long free-text passages, similar to this research, and also attempted the detection of uncharacteristic patterns due to fatigue, distraction, stress, or other factors. Song et al. (1997) touched on the idea of detecting a change in identity through continuous monitoring.

Researchers tend to collect their own data and no known studies have compared techniques on a common database, although a recent study made a password database available to the scientific community (Giot, El-Abed, & Rosenberger, 2009b). Nevertheless, the published literature is optimistic about the potential of keystroke dynamics to benefit computer system security and usability

(Woodward, Orlans, & Higgins, 2002). Gunetti and Picardi (2005) suggest that if short inputs do not provide sufficient timing information, and if long predefined texts entered repeatedly are unacceptable, we are left with only one possible solution, using users' normal keyed text-input interactions with computers, *free text*, as we do in this research.

Generally, a number of measurements or features are used to characterize a user's typing pattern. These measurements are typically derived from the raw data of key press times, key release times, and the identity of the keys pressed. From key-press and key-release times a feature vector, often consisting of keystroke duration times and keystroke transition times, can be created (Woodward et al., 2002). Such measurements can be collected from all users of a system, such as a computer network or web-based system, where keystroke entry is available, and a model that attempts to distinguish an individual user from others can be established. For short input such as passwords, however, the lack of sufficient measurements presents a problem because keystrokes, unlike other biometric features, convey only a small amount of information. Moreover, this information tends to vary for different keyboards, different environmental conditions, and different entered texts (Gunetti & Picardi, 2005).

The keystroke biometric system reported here is unique in several respects. First, it collects raw keystroke data over the Internet, which is desirable for Internet security applications such as those described above. Second, it focuses on long-text input where sufficient keystroke data are available to permit the use of powerful statistical feature measurements – and the number, variety, and strength of the measurements used in the system are much greater than those used by earlier systems reported in the literature. Third, it focuses on applications using arbitrary text input because copy texts are unacceptable for most applications of interest. However, because of the statistical nature of the features and the use

of arbitrary text input, special statistical fallback procedures were incorporated into the system to handle the paucity of data from infrequently used keyboard keys.

This paper extends two previous studies on the *identification* application and a third that included *authentication* results. The first previous study showed the feasibility of an early version of the identification system on a text copy task (Curtin et al., 2006). The second showed the effectiveness of an improved system under ideal conditions of a fixed text and keyboard, and under less favorable conditions of arbitrary texts and different keyboard types for enrollment and testing (Villani et al., 2006). The third extended the earlier studies by presenting the identification results in a clearer manner; by developing an authentication classifier and presenting associated results; by collecting new data and performing several-week and two-year longitudinal studies; and by conducting experiments to investigate the system models, the parameter settings, the normal distribution assumption for feature measurements, and the sufficiency of the number of enrollment samples and input text length (Tappert, Villani, & Cha, 2009). This paper further clarifies the presentation of results, and presents new authentication results and a novel method of obtaining Receiver Operating Characteristic (ROC) curves from the nearest-neighbor non-parametric classifier.

The organization of the remainder of the paper is straightforward: methodology, results, and conclusions. The next section describes the long-text keystroke biometric system, which has components for data capture, feature extraction, classification for identification and authentication, and ROC curve derivation. The following section describes the experimental design and data collection. The next section describes the experimental results on identification, on authentication, on the longitudinal studies, and on the system model and parameters. The final section presents the conclusions and suggestions for future work.

Figure 1. Java applet for data collection, reprinted with permission from Villani et al. (2006)

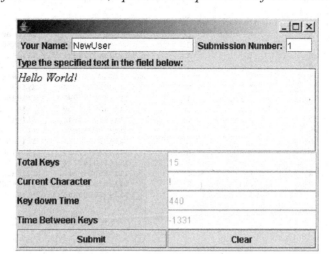

KEYSTROKE BIOMETRIC SYSTEM

The keystroke biometric system consists of four components: raw keystroke data capture, feature extraction, classification for identification, and classification for authentication.

Raw Keystroke Data Capture

A Java applet collects keystroke data over the Internet (Figure 1). The user is required to type in his/her name, but no data is captured on this entry. The submission number is automatically incremented after each sample submission, so the participant can immediately start typing the next sample. If the user is interrupted during data entry, the "Clear" button blanks all fields, except name and submission number, allowing the user to redo the current entry.

Upon pressing submit, a raw-data text file is generated, which is delimited by the '~' character. Figure 2 shows the aligned version of the "Hello World!" raw data file. The raw data file contains the following information for each entry: 1) entry sequence number, 2) key's character, 3) key's code text equivalent, 4) key's location (1 = standard, only one key location; 2 = left side of keyboard; 3 = right side of keyboard), 5) time the key

was pressed (milliseconds), 6) time the key was released (milliseconds). The number of left-mouse-click, right-mouse-click, and double left-mouse-click events during the session (these are events in contrast to key presses) are listed at the end of the file.

Feature Extraction

The system extracts a feature vector from the information in a raw data file. The features are statistical in nature and designed to characterize an individual's keystroke dynamics over writing samples of 200 or more characters. Most of the features are averages and standard deviations of key press duration times and of transition times between keystroke pairs, such as digraphs (Obaidat & Sadoun, 1999; Peacock et al., 2004). Figure 3 shows the transition between keystrokes measured in two ways: from the release of the first key to the press of the second, t_1, and from the press of the first to the press of the second, t_2. While the second measure, t_2, is always positive because this sequence determines the keyboard output, the first measure, t_1, can be negative. We refer to these two measures of transition time as type-1 and type-2 transition features.

Figure 2. Aligned raw data file for "Hello World!," reprinted with permission from Villani et al. (2006)

```
NewUser      Submission 1
  Entry #    Key         Keycode    Location    Press             Release
  Num 1      ?           Shift      2           1114450735680     1114450736962
  Num 2      H           H          1           1114450735991     1114450736311
  Num 3      e           E          1           1114450737653     1114450738144
  Num 4      l           L          1           1114450738735     1114450739256
  Num 5      l           L          1           1114450739786     1114450740277
  Num 6      o           O          1           1114450740998     1114450741399
  Num 7                  Space      1           1114450742090     1114450742420
  Num 8      ?           Shift      2           1114450743542     1114450745004
  Num 9      W           W          1           1114450743872     1114450744263
  Num 10     o           O          1           1114450745755     1114450746216
  Num 11     r           R          1           1114450747017     1114450747437
  Num 12     l           L          1           1114450748138     1114450748549
  Num 13     d           D          1           1114450749310     1114450749771
  Num 14     ?           Shift      2           1114450751373     1114450753776
  Num 15     !           1          1           1114450752445     1114450752885
  Left Clicks     0
  Right Clicks    0
  Double Clicks   0
```

While key press duration and transition times are typically used as features in keystroke biometric studies, our use of the statistical measures of means and standard deviations of the key presses and transitions is uncommon and only practical for long text input. Because we use long text input of several hundred keystrokes we are usually able to estimate the averages and standard deviations of the common letter durations and diagram transitions, like the key press time of the letter "e" and the transition time of the "th" sequence, and the fallback procedure described below handles the few-sample cases of particular keys or key transitions. The use of such statistical measures at the granular level is clearly not possible for short inputs like passwords. As additional features, we use percentages of key presses of many of the special keys. Some of these percentage features are designed to capture the user's preferences for using certain keys or key groups – for example, some users do not capitalize or use much punctuation. Other percentage features are designed to capture the user's pattern of editing text since there are many ways to locate (using keys – Home, End, Arrow keys – or mouse clicks), delete (Backspace or Delete keys, or Edit-Delete), insert (Insert, shortcut keys, or Edit-Paste), and move (shortcut keys or Edit-Cut/Edit-Paste) words and characters.

Figure 3. A two-key sequence (th) shows the two transition measures: t_1 = press time of second key – release time of first, and t_2 = press time of second key – press time of first. A keystroke is depicted as a bucket with the down arrow marking the press and the up arrow the release time. Part a) non-overlapping keystroke events (t_1 positive), and b) overlapping keystroke events where the first key is released after the second is pressed (t_1 negative). Reprinted with permission from Villani et al. (2006).

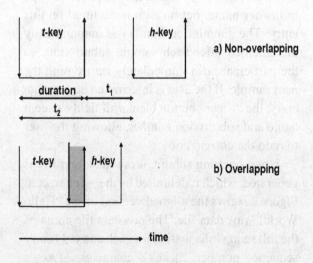

Figure 4. Hierarchy tree for the 39 duration categories (each oval), reprinted with permission from Villani et al. (2006)

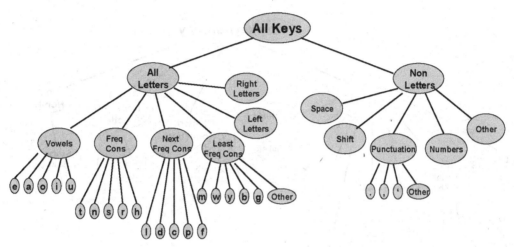

This study used 239 feature measurements (a complete list is presented in the Appendix). These features make use of the letter and digraph frequencies in English text (Gaines, 1956), and the definitions of left-hand-letter keys as those normally struck by fingers of a typist's left hand (q, w, e, r, t, a, s, d, f, g, z, x, c, v, b) and right-hand-letter keys as those struck by fingers of the right hand (y, u, i, o, p, h, j, k, l, n, m). The features characterize a typist's key-press duration times, transition times in going from one key to the next, the percentages of usage of the non-letter keys and mouse clicks, and the typing speed. The granularity of the duration and transition features is shown in the hierarchy trees of Figures 4 and 5. For each of these trees, the granularity increases from gross features at the top of the tree to fine features at the bottom. The least frequent letter in the duration tree is "g" with a frequency of 1.6%, and the least frequent letter pair in the transition tree is "or" with a frequency of 1.1% (Gains, 1956). The six least frequent letters are grouped under "other" and the infrequent digraphs are also grouped. The 239 features are grouped as follows:

- 78 duration features (39 means and 39 standard deviations) of individual letter and non-letter keys, and of groups of letter and non-letter keys (Figure 4)

- 70 type-1 transition features (35 means and 35 standard deviations) of the transitions between letters or groups of letters, between letters and non-letters or groups thereof, between non-letters and letters or groups thereof, and between non-letters and non-letters or groups thereof (Figure 5)

- 70 type-2 transition features (35 means and 35 standard deviations) identical to the type-1 transition features except for the method of measurement (Figure 5)

- 19 percentage features that measure the percentage of use of the non-letter keys and mouse clicks

- 2 keystroke input rates: the unadjusted input rate (total time to enter the text / total number of keystrokes and mouse events) and the adjusted input rate (total time to enter the text minus pauses greater than ½ second / total number of keystrokes and mouse events)

The computation of a keystroke-duration mean (μ) or standard deviation (σ) requires special handling when there are few samples. For

Figure 5. Hierarchy tree for the 35 transition categories (each oval) for type 1 and type 2 transitions, reprinted with permission from Villani et al. (2006)

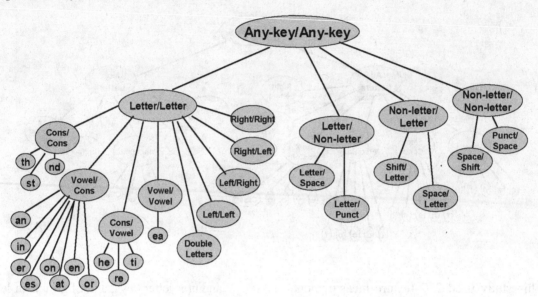

this we use a fallback procedure which is similar to the "*backoff*" procedures used in natural language processing (Jurafsky & Martin, 2000). To compute μ for few samples – that is, when the number of samples is less than $k_{fallback-threshold}$ (an experimentally-optimized constant) – we take the weighted average of μ of the key in question and μ of the appropriate fallback as follows:

$$\mu'(i) = \frac{n(i) \cdot \mu(i) + k_{fallback-weight} \cdot \mu(fallback)}{n(i) + k_{fallback-weight}}$$

(1)

where $\mu'(i)$ is the revised mean, $n(i)$ is the number of occurrences of key i, $\mu(i)$ is the mean of the $n(i)$ samples of key i, $\mu(fallback)$ is the mean of the fallback, and $k_{fallback-weight}$ is the weight (an experimentally-optimized constant) applied to the fallback statistic. The appropriate fallback is determined by the next highest node in the hierarchy tree. For example, the "m" falls back to "least frequent consonants", which falls back to "all letters", which falls back to "all keys". Because we are dealing with long-text input,

fallback is necessary for only infrequently used keys; thus, it is based primarily on frequency of use, and fallback of more than one level is rare. The $\sigma(i)$ are similarly computed, as are the means and standard deviations of the transitions. Thus, we ensure computability (no zero divides) and obtain reasonable values for all feature measurements.

Two preprocessing steps are performed on the feature measurements, outlier removal and feature standardization. Outlier removal is particularly important for these features because a keyboard user could pause for a phone call, for a sip of coffee, or for numerous other reasons, and the resulting outliers – overly long transition times – would skew the feature measurements. Overly long key presses can also occur but are rare. Outlier removal consists of removing any duration or transition time that is far (more than $k_{outlier-\sigma}$ standard deviations) from the participant's $\mu(i)$ or $\mu(i, j)$, respectively. After outlier removal, averages and standard deviations are recalculated. An experimentally optimized parameter, $k_{outlier-pass}$, determines how many passes of outlier removal are performed (a large number causes removal recursively until no further outliers can be removed)

The four parameters mentioned above were optimized using a hill-climbing method on different data from an earlier study (Curtin et al., 2006): the two for fallback – $k_{fallback-threshold}$ and $k_{fallback-weight}$ – and the two for outlier removal – $k_{outlier-\sigma}$, and $k_{outlier-pass}$.

After performing outlier removal and recalculation, we standardize the measurements by converting raw measurement x to x' by the formula,

$$x' = \frac{x - x_{min}}{x_{max} - x_{min}} \qquad (2)$$

where min and max are the minimum and maximum of the measurement over all samples from all participants (Dunn & Everitt, 2004). This provides measurement values in the range 0-1 to give each measurement roughly equal weight.

Classification for Identification

For both identification and authentication the k-nearest-neighbor (kNN) classifier, using Euclidean distance, was employed. This method classifies patterns based on the nearest training examples in feature space. It is a highly accurate non-parametric method with strong consistency results, used when the form of the underlying distributions is not known. It is also one of the simplest machine learning classification algorithms which can be slow because it is computationally intensive for large training sets. The special case of k = 1 is called the nearest neighbor algorithm.

We used the nearest neighbor algorithm (k = 1) for identification and the kNN algorithm (with k > 1) for authentication. For identification, the feature vector of the test sample in question is compared against those of the training set and the author of the training sample having the smallest Euclidean distance to the test sample is identified as the author of the test sample.

Classification for Authentication

For authentication, a vector-difference model transforms a multi-class (polychotomy) problem into a two-class (dichotomy) problem (Figure 6). For this application the resulting two classes are "within-class, you are authenticated" and "between-class, you are not authenticated." This is a strong inferential statistics method found to be particularly effective for multidimensional feature-space problems (Cha & Srihari, 2000; Choi, Yoon, Cha, & Tappert, 2004; Srihari, Cha, Arora, & Lee, 2002; Yoon, Choi, Cha, Lee, & Tappert, 2005).

To explain the dichotomy transformation process, take an example of three people $\{P_1, P_2, P_3\}$ where each person supplies three biometric samples. Figure 6 (a) plots the biometric sample data for these three people in the feature space, exemplifying the polychotomy model. This feature space is transformed into a distance vector space by calculating vector distances between pairs of samples of the *same* person (*intra-person distances*, denoted by $x_\oplus$) and distances between pairs of samples of *different* people (*inter-person distances*, denoted by $x_\varnothing$). Let d_{ij} represent the feature vector of the ith person's j^{th} biometric sample, then $x_\oplus$ and $x_\varnothing$ are calculated as follows:

$$x_\oplus = |d_{ij} - d_{ik}| \; where \; i=1 \; to \; n, \; and \; j,k=1 \; to \; m, \; j \neq k \qquad (3)$$

$$x_\varnothing = |d_{ij} - d_{kl}| \; where \; i,k=1 \; to \; n, \; i \neq k \; and \; j,l=1 \; to \; m$$

where n is the number of people and m is the number of samples per person. Figure 6 (b) shows the transformed feature distance space for the example problem.

Yoon et al. (2005) derive the numbers of the inter- and intra-person distances. If n people provide m biometric samples each, the numbers of intra-person and inter-person distance samples, respectively, are:

Figure 6. Authentication transformation from (a) Feature space to (b) Feature distance space, reprinted with permission from Yoon et al. (2005)

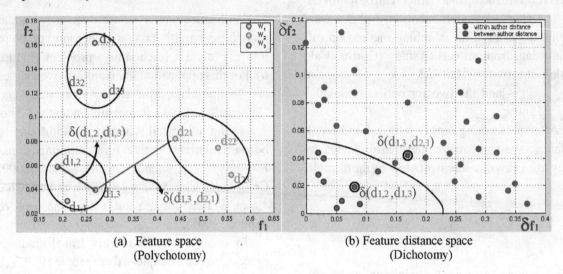

(a) Feature space
(Polychotomy)

(b) Feature distance space
(Dichotomy)

$$n_\oplus = \frac{m \times (m-1) \times n}{2} \text{ and}$$

$$n_\varnothing = m \times m \times \frac{n \times (n-1)}{2} \qquad (4)$$

In the authentication process, a user's keystroke sample requiring authentication is first converted into a feature vector. The difference between this feature vector and an earlier-obtained enrollment feature vector from this user is computed, and the resulting difference vector is classified as within-class (intra-person) or between-class (inter-person). The classification is performed by the k-nearest-neighbor method, using Euclidean distance, to compare this feature difference vector against those in the training set.

To obtain system performance we simulate the authentication process of many true users trying to get authenticated and of many imposters trying to get authenticated as other users. This is done by using the numbers of the inter- and intra-person distances explained above. For example, if we have five keystroke samples from each of 18 users, then (from equation 4) there are 180 intra-person distances to simulate true users and 3825 inter-person distances to simulate imposters.

The feature distance space is populated similarly during training. These numbers of five samples from each of 18 users were the numbers used to measure authentication system performance in the experimental section below.

RECEIVER OPERATING CHARACTERISTIC (ROC) CURVE DERIVATION

In biometric authentication systems the ROC curve is a graphical representation of the trade-off between the False Accept Rate (FAR) and the False Reject Rate (FRR), and the ROC curve is important in describing the performance of the system and in determining where to set the operating point. ROC curves were obtained for authentication by considering the *k* nearest neighbors. Two procedures for obtaining ROC curves were created – an unweighted *m*-match, *k*-nearest-neighbor (*m-kNN*) procedure and a weighted *m*-match, *k*-nearest-neighbor (*wm-kNN*) procedure.

Unweighted *m*-Match, *k*-Nearest-Neighbor (*m-kNN*) Procedure

For each Q (questioned) test sample, the *m-kNN* procedure examines the *k*-nearest-neighbor outputs and counts the number of within-class matches (Figure 7).

If the number of within-class matches is greater or equal to a threshold *m*, the user is authenticated (5), i.e. accepted as being *w* (within-class), and otherwise rejected as *b* (between-class). In Figure 7 the user represented by the questioned sample would be authenticated for *m = 0* through *m = 4*.

$$c(Q) = \begin{cases} w & \text{if } fw(Q) \geq m \\ b & otherwise \end{cases} \quad (5)$$

The ROC curve is obtained from (5) by letting *m* vary from 0 to *k* and calculating the FAR and FRR in each case. For *m = 0*, we authenticate a user (decide within-class) if 0 or more of the *k* choices are *w* (within-class), and clearly all users are accepted in this case, yielding FRR = 0.0 (0%) and FAR = 1.0 (100%). For *m = 1*, we authenticate a user if 1 or more of the *k* choices is *w* and obtain the FAR and FRR. We do the same for *2* or more and continue in this manner until all *k* of the *k* choices must be *w*, obtaining FAR and FRR in each case. Now, plotting the *k+1* (FRR, FAR) pairs yields an ROC curve (FRR on the x-axis and FAR on the y-axis). For the last point, when we require all *k* outputs to be *w* for authentication, FRR is usually large and FAR small.

Weighted *m*-Match, *k*-Nearest-Neighbor (*Wm-kNN*) Procedure

It seems reasonable to weight higher choices more heavily than lower ones because the first choice should clearly be more valuable than the second, the second more valuable than the third, etc. We use a linear rank weighting, assigning the first

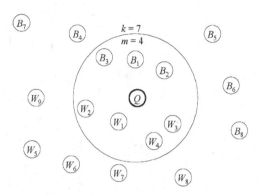

Figure 7. The m-match, k-nearest-neighbor (m-kNN) procedure with k = 7 and m = 4

choice a weight of *k*, second a weight of *k*-1, ..., and the *k*th choice a weight of 1. The maximum score when all choices are within-class is *k+(k-1)+...+1 = k(k+1)/2*, and the minimum score is *0*. Now, consider that we authenticate a user if the weighted-within-class choices are greater or equal to *m*, where *m* varies from *0* to *k(k+1)/2*, and compute the (FRR, FAR) pairs for each *m* to obtain an ROC curve.

EXPERIMENTAL DESIGN AND DATA COLLECTION

In this study, we vary two independent variables – keyboard type and input mode – to determine their effect on both identification and authentication performance. The keyboard types were desktop and laptop PC keyboards. The input modes were a copy task and free (arbitrary) text input. By varying these independent variables, we determined the distinctiveness of keystroke patterns when training and testing on long-text input under ideal conditions (same input mode and keyboard type for enrollment and testing) and under non-ideal conditions (different input mode, different type of keyboard, or both, for enrollment and testing).

All the desktop keyboards were manufactured by Dell and the data obtained primarily in classroom environments; over 90% of the smaller

Figure 8. Experimental design showing the participant pool, adapted with permission from Villani (2006)

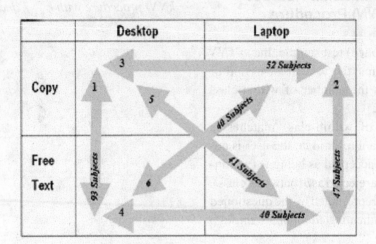

laptop keyboards (mostly individually owned) were also by Dell, and the others were a mix of IBM, Compaq, Apple, HP, and Toshiba keyboards.

We used two input modes: a copy-task in which participants copied a predefined text of 652 keystrokes (515 characters with no spaces, 643 with spaces, and a total of 652 keystrokes when including 9 shift-key presses for uppercase), and free-text input in which participants typed arbitrary emails of at least 650 keystrokes. The participants were instructed to correct errors, further increasing the number of keystrokes.

Figure 8 summarizes the experimental design and shows the participant pool. The two independent variables – the two keyboard types and the two input modes – yield four data quadrants. Data were collected in each quadrant: desktop copy, laptop copy, desktop free text, and laptop free text. There are four ideal (optimal) conditions – enrollment and testing on data within each of the four quadrants.

There are six non-ideal experimental groups corresponding to the six arrows in Figure 8 – training on data at one end of the arrow and testing on data at the other end (and since either end of an arrow can be the starting point, there are a total of 12 non-ideal experimental conditions). Groups 1 and 2 compare the two input modes on the desktop and laptop keyboards, respectively. Groups 3 and 4 compare the two keyboard types on the copy-task and free-text inputs, respectively. Finally, groups 5 and 6 compare the two possible ways of having different keyboard types and different input modes for enrollment and testing. Note that although there are six experimental groups (arrows), there are three major experimental groupings – training and testing on different input modes (the two vertical arrows), different keyboard types (the two horizontal arrows), and both different input modes and different keyboard types (the two diagonal arrows).

For data collection, the participants were asked to complete a minimum of two of the four quadrants as indicated by the two horizontal and two vertical arrows in Figure 8. A participant completes a quadrant by typing a minimum of 5 samples of that category. Data samples were obtained from students in introductory computer classes (accounting for the majority of the data samples); from students in classes at the masters and doctoral levels; and from friends, family, work colleagues, and fellow academics. Although all participants were invited to participate in all four quadrants of the experiment, due to time or equipment limitations some opted for two (minimum)

Table 1. Summary of participant demographics, adapted with permission from Villani (2006)

Age	Female	Male	Total
Under 20	15	19	34
20-29	12	23	35
30-39	5	10	15
40-49	7	11	18
50+	11	5	16
All	50	68	118

while others participated in three or four quadrants of the experiment.

A total of 118 participants supplied keystroke data in 2006, each supplying five samples in at least two quadrants of the experiment (incomplete sample sets were discarded), and 36 completed all four quadrants of the experiment (Figure 8, Table 1). To collect reasonable amounts of data quickly the timing of the input samples was not controlled, and about half input all their keystroke data samples in one sitting, while the others input their samples over several days or weeks. Similar data were collected in 2008 for the longitudinal studies, but the recording times of these data were accurately controlled.

For the copy and free-text tasks on a desktop keyboard (group 1), the participants typed a copy of the predefined passage five times and then typed five arbitrary emails on a desktop keyboard. For the copy and free-text tasks on a laptop keyboard (group 2), the typing was similar but on a laptop keyboard. These two experimental groupings were most suited for participants having access to only one keyboard. Groups 3 and 4 required the participants to type in the same mode but on different keyboards. Finally, groups 5 and 6 required the participants to type in different input modes and on different keyboard types.

EXPERIMENTAL RESULTS

Experimental results are presented here for biometric identification, for biometric authentication, for longitudinal studies on both identification and authentication, and for an investigation of the system hierarchical model and parameter settings.

Identification Experimental Results

The identification results of the study are summarized in Tables 2 and 3, and corresponding Figures 9 and 10, respectively. Table 2 and Figure 9 present the results under the *ideal conditions* of training (enrollment) and testing on data obtained using the same keyboard type and the same input mode. Since training and testing were under the same conditions, the leave-one-out procedure was used in order to test on data different from that used for training. As anticipated, performance (accuracy) is high under these ideal conditions – greater than 98% when the population of users is relatively small (36-participant experiment), and decreasing for larger numbers of participants. This performance decrease as the number of participants increases is highlighted in the average of the four cases at the bottom of Table 2, which indicates that doubling the number of participants increases the error rate by about a factor of four (from 0.7% to 2.6%). The graphs of the four ideal-condition cases in Figure 9 also show the large effect of population increase on performance.

Under ideal conditions in the 36-participant experiment, accuracy varied somewhat from quadrant to quadrant. For example, accuracy was a little higher on the copy task compared to free-text input – 99.4% compared to 98.3% on desktop keyboards, and 100.0% compared to 99.5% on laptop keyboards. These differences, however, were not statistically significant – for example, the first difference yielded a null hypothesis $p = 0.3$ (Chi-square was used for all tests of statistical significance). Higher copy task accuracy is understandable since the copy samples were of the

Table 2. Identification performance under ideal conditions, adapted with permission from Tappert, Villani, & Cha, 2009

Conditions	36-Participant		Full-Participant	
Train and Test	Participants	Accuracy	Participants	Accuracy
DeskCopy	36	99.4%	93	99.1%
LapCopy	36	100.0%	47	99.2%
DeskFree	36	98.3%	93	93.3%
LapFree	36	99.5%	47	97.9%
Average	**36**	**99.3%**	**70**	**97.4%**

Table 3. Identification performance under non-ideal conditions, adapted with permission from Tappert, Villani, & Cha, 2009

	36-Participant		Full-Participant	
Group	Participants	Accuracy	Participants	Accuracy
1	36	90.5%	93	77.4%
2	36	88.6%	47	83.9%
3	36	60.7%	52	53.2%
4	36	60.0%	40	60.7%
5	36	54.8%	41	51.4%
6	36	51.2%	40	47.8%

Figure 9. Identification performance under ideal conditions, graphs of results from Table 2, adapted with permission from Tappert, Villani, & Cha, 2009

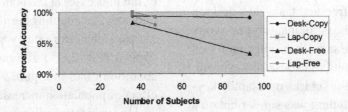

same text whereas the free-text samples were of different texts. Also, other variables being equal, accuracy was a little higher on the laptop keyboards compared to the desktop keyboards – 100.0% compared to 99.4% for the copy task, and 99.5% compared to 98.3% for free-text input. These differences were also not statistically significant. The reason for higher laptop accuracy is likely the greater variety of laptop keyboards used in

the experiments and the participant's greater familiarity with the laptops since they were usually owned by the participants.

Table 3 and Figure 10 present the results under the *non-ideal conditions* of training and testing under different conditions – different input modes, different keyboard types, or both different input modes and different keyboard types. These results clearly show the degradation in performance as

Figure 10. Identification performance under non-ideal conditions, graphs of results from Table 3, adapted with permission from Tappert, Villani, & Cha, 2009

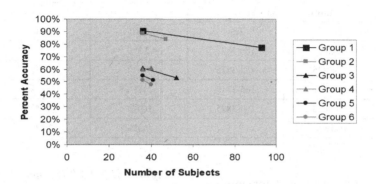

the conditions for training and testing go from different input modes (groups 1 and 2), to different keyboard types (groups 3 and 4), and finally to both different input modes and different keyboard types (groups 5 and 6). They also show the decrease in performance as the population increases.

Under non-ideal conditions in the 36-participant experiment, accuracy decreased from about 99% under ideal conditions to about 90% when the participants used the same keyboard type but different input modes (the four cases in groups 1 and 2). This decrease was statistically significant ($p < 0.0001$). Accuracy dropped even more significantly (from about 99% to about 60%) when the participants used the same copy or free-text input mode but different keyboard types for enrollment and testing (groups 3 and 4). Finally, accuracy decreased most significantly, from about 99% to about 53%, when the participants used different input modes and different keyboard types (groups 5 and 6). These results suggest that an individual's keystroke patterns differ for the different input modes and the different keyboard types, and differ more for different keyboard types than for different input modes. Figure 10 graphically shows the performance on the major conditions of training and testing on different input modes (groups 1 and 2), different keyboard types (groups 3 and 4), and both different input modes and different keyboard

types (groups 5 and 6), as well as the performance decrease as the number of participants increases.

Authentication Experimental Results

Table 4 presents the results under *ideal conditions* (same conditions for training and testing) on the 36-participant data, using 18 participants for training and the remaining 18 for testing; the results shown here are somewhat better than those reported earlier (Tappert, Villani, & Cha, 2009) which were discovered to have come from the touch-type model described below. For the first test in Table 4, for example, the training and testing sets each consisted of 90 samples (18 participants contributing 5 samples each), with all samples obtained under the DeskCopy conditions. The intra- and inter-class sizes were 180 and 3825, respectively (in the third test the smaller intra- and inter-class sizes are due to a few missing samples).

The results presented above used the nearest-neighbor (i.e., 1-nearest-neighbor) procedure for classification. Using a greater number of neighbors was explored, and Figure 11 graphs the average performance of the 1, 3, 5, 7, and 9-nearest-neighbor procedures. Here, we see a significant improvement in going from 1 to 3 neighbors and slight improvements in going from 3 to 5 and to higher nearest neighbors.

Table 4. Authentication performance under ideal conditions, train 18 and test 18 different participants using all inter-class samples

| Conditions | Intra-Inter Class Sizes | | FRR | FAR | Performance |
	Train	Test			
DeskCopy	180-3825	180-3825	2.8%	2.1%	97.9%
LapCopy	180-3825	180-3825	3.3%	4.0%	96.0%
DeskFree	176-3576	165-3740	21.0%	1.1%	98.0%
LapFree	180-3825	180-3825	10.0%	3.3%	96.4%
Average			9.3%	2.6%	97.1%

We now present ROC curves and, for simplicity, only for the DeskCopy ideal condition. Figure 12 presents the ROC curves for the unweighted *m-kNN* and the weighted *wm-kNN* procedures for $k = 10$, 15, and 20. As k increases, more data points are generated and the curves tend to improve slightly (FAR decreases). The Equal Error Rate (EER) can be approximated as 2.7% from these curves.

Plots of FAR and FRR versus the threshold m can also be obtained. Figure 13 shows the plots of FAR and FRR versus the threshold m for the unweighted *m-kNN* procedure for $k = 10$. Similar plots with more points have been obtained for $k = 15$ and 20. Having 20-times more between-class samples than within-class samples likely accounts for the FAR curve being smoother than the FRR curve.

Figure 14 compares the unweighted and weighted ROC curves for $k = 10$, 15, and 20. Compared to the unweighted, the weighted method provides more coordinate data points. The weighted method also appears to be superior to the unweighted one for this DeskCopy condition.

Longitudinal Study Results

In order to study the accuracy of identification and authentication over time, we performed studies at two-week intervals and at a two-year interval. The two-week interval study used 13 participants who had not participated in the earlier experi-

Figure 11. Performance for 1, 3, 5, 7, and 9-nearest-neighbors

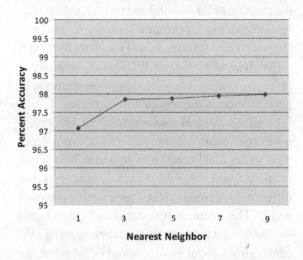

ments, and the two-year interval study brought back 8 of the participants of the earlier 36-participant study for additional data samples. All the longitudinal experimental results were obtained under *non-ideal conditions* – different keyboard type, different input mode, or both, for training (enrollment) and testing – because insufficient data were available for the ideal condition (same quadrant) experiments.

The identification and authentication results of the two-week-interval study are presented in the Tables 5 and 6, respectively. Baseline results were obtained by training and testing on data from the same week – week 0 (W0-W0), week 2 (W2-

Figure 12. DeskCopy ROC curves for the m-kNN procedure (left) and wm-kNN procedure (right) for k = 10, 15, and 20

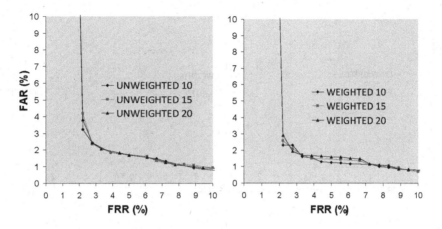

Figure 13. FAR and FRR versus the threshold m for the unweighted m-kNN procedure for k = 10

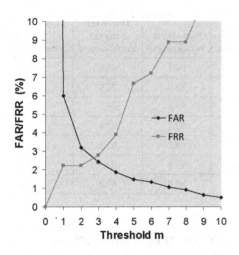

each quadrant, for a total of 65 samples per file (with the exception of the week-4 laptop copy file, which was missing one sample for a total of 64 samples). Percentages shown are the percent of the samples correctly identified. The identification results (Table 5) shows the degree of performance degradation over time, summarized by the average performance (bottom line of table).

The authentication results (Table 6) showed less performance degradation than the identification results over the two- and four-week intervals.

For the two-year interval study, we contacted each of the participants who participated in the earlier 36-participant study in 2006 (Y0), and asked them to enter new complete data sets (5 samples in each of the four quadrants). New data sets were obtained from 8 of these individuals in 2008 (Y2), approximately two years after obtaining their earlier data. Since each of the 8 participants submitted five samples in each of four quadrants, there were a total of 40 samples in each quadrant.

Both the Y0 and Y2 data from these 8 participants were run through the system. The results of training and testing on data recorded in the same year, Y0-Y0 and Y2-Y2, were averaged. Table 7 shows the percent of the samples (80 samples in the "Same Year", half in Y0 and half in Y2;

W2), and week 4 (W4-W4), and these three sets of results were combined to obtain overall "Same-Week" performance. For the two-week interval, results were obtained by training on week 0 and testing on week 2 (W0-W2) and by training on week 2 and testing on week 4 (W2-W4), and these two sets of results were combined for the overall "Two-Week Interval" performance. For the "Four-Week Interval", results were obtained by training on week 0 and testing on week 4 (W0-W4). Five samples were collected from each participant in

Figure 14. ROC curves for the unweighted and weighted methods for k = 10, 15, 20

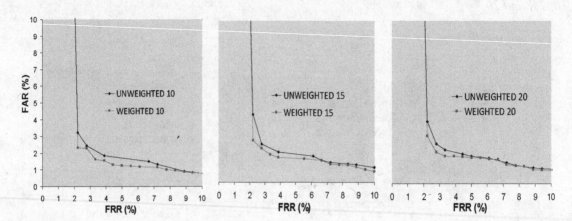

Table 5. Identification performance on 13 participants over two-week intervals, adapted with permission from Tappert, Villani, & Cha, 2009

	Same Week	Two Week Interval	Four Week Interval
1	95.9	82.7	84.6
2	93.0	91.1	89.9
3	93.5	93.4	87.6
4	91.0	85.4	82.3
5	85.7	77.1	76.9
6	79.9	81.8	78.2
Avg	**89.9**	**85.3**	**83.3**

Table 6. Authentication performance on 13 participants over two-week intervals, adapted with permission from Tappert, Villani, & Cha, 2009

Group	Same Week Performance	Two-Week Interval Performance	Four-Week Interval Performance
1	96.1	95.9	95.7
2	83.0	77.9	68.5
3	96.8	96.1	97.6
4	93.2	92.9	90.4
5	93.7	92.5	93.5
6	91.4	93.5	96.5
Avg	**89.8**	**87.4**	**85.3**

and 40 in the "Two-Year Interval") accurately identified. The resulting substantial degradation in performance indicates that one's keystroke patterns change significantly over a two-year interval.

Authentication performance (Table 8) is better, with an average accuracy of 92% with a two-year interval between the training and test sets. Although this performance is better than that obtained over two- and four-week intervals, this is likely due to the smaller number of participants in the two-year study.

System Hierarchical Model and Parameter Experiments

The hierarchical model was investigated and alternative models were evaluated. The system parameters were analyzed by measuring accuracy as a function of the outlier removal parameters (the number of outlier passes and the outlier distance), accuracy as a function of the number of enrollment samples, and accuracy as a function of input text length. The parameter experiments were performed on the identification system using the full-participant ideal DeskFree condition, or both the DeskFree and DeskCopy conditions

Table 7. *Identification performance on 8 participants over a two-year interval, adapted with permission from Tappert, Villani, & Cha, 2009*

Group	Same Year Performance	Two-Year Interval Performance
1	95.0	66.2
2	99.4	58.7
3	81.9	66.3
4	78.1	80.0
5	76.2	58.7
6	75.7	70.0
Avg	84.4	66.7

Table 8. *Authentication performance on 8 participants over a two-year interval, adapted with permission from Tappert, Villani, & Cha, 2009*

Group	Same Year Performance	Two-Year Performance
1	91.1	89.7
2	97.1	95.2
3	94.1	91.6
4	95.0	95.5
5	90.9	89.7
6	92.8	90.8
Avg	93.5	92.1

– the conditions having the largest number of 93 participants. Finally, the normal distribution assumption of the statistical features was verified.

Hierarchical Fallback Model

We investigated the fallback aspect of the hierarchical model by comparing the hierarchical fallback as described above to simply falling back to the top nodes of the hierarchy trees as was done in an earlier study (Curtin et al., 2006). For the desktop-free condition, the hierarchical fallback procedure increased identification accuracy from 91.0% to 93.3% (a 26% decrease in error rate). For the desktop-copy condition, identification accuracy increased from 98.1% to 99.1% (a 53% decrease in error rate). Using the hierarchical model for fallback is therefore highly beneficial.

An analysis of the fallback model showed that fallback never occurred more than one level up from the leaf nodes and that most of the one-level-up nodes were essentially never used for fallback (vowel, frequent consonant, all letters, non-letters) because their leaf nodes were sufficiently frequent to not require fallback. Thus, the original fallback model was essentially a frequency of use model with the infrequent letters falling back to a group average of the infrequent letters.

Two new fallback models were investigated (Ritzmann, 2009). The first, a touch-type model, was based on the fingers used to strike keys by touch typists (Figures 15 and 16), thinking that this model should be superior to the one described above that is frequency oriented but not particularly relevant to typing. The second was a statistical model that groups keys displaying similar key-strike statistics. The results of the touch-type model were similar to those obtained above but not significantly different. The statistical model was significantly poorer than the other two.

Outlier Parameters

We verified the method of performing outlier removal recursively – that is, continuing to remove outliers until a complete pass through the data resulted in no further outliers being removed (Figure 17). We then measured accuracy as a function of the outlier removal distance (in terms of the number of σ from the μ), finding that the 2σ distance used in the experiments was close to the optimal value of 1.75σ (Figure 18). Note that the parameter settings used in this study were established on different data from an earlier study (Curtin et al., 2006).

Figure 15. Touch-type hierarchy tree for durations, adopted with permission from Ritzmann (2009)

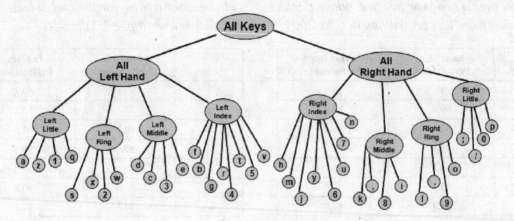

Figure 16. Touch-type hierarchy tree for transitions, adopted with permission from Ritzmann (2009)

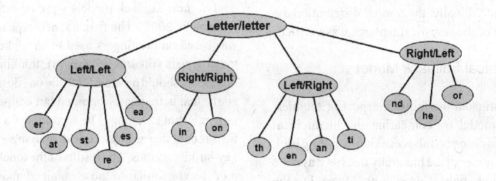

Figure 17. Identification accuracy versus outlier removal passes, adapted with permission from Villani (2006)

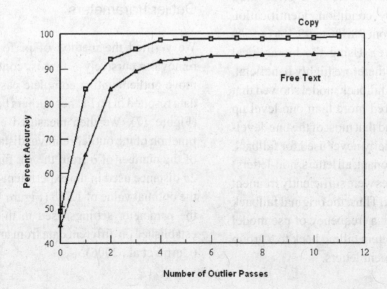

Figure 18. Identification accuracy versus outlier removal distance σ, adapted with permission from Villani (2006)

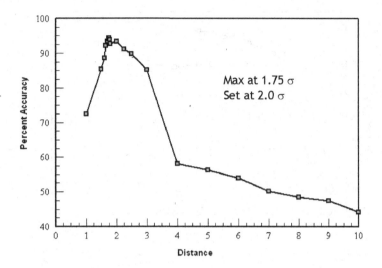

Figure 19. Identification accuracy versus enrollment samples, adapted with permission from Villani (2006)

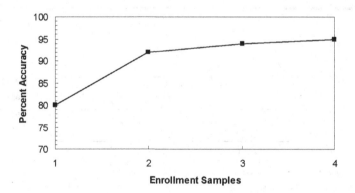

Number of Enrollment Samples

In order to check the sufficiency of the number of enrollment samples, we obtained accuracy as the number of enrollment samples varied from one to four (Figure 19). Because each participant supplied five data samples per quadrant, the leave-one-out procedure left a maximum of four enrollment samples to match against. The results indicate that two enrollment samples per user might suffice for this application.

Input Text Length

We obtained accuracy as a function of input text length (Figure 20). We found that our choice of 650 keystrokes was in the region where the curve levels off, but that reasonable accuracy can be obtained on shorter text lengths of about 300 keystrokes. The accuracy curve of the copy task is considerably smoother than that of the free text input, perhaps because all copy samples were of the same text but the free text samples were all of different texts.

Figure 20. Identification accuracy versus input text length, adapted with permission from Villani (2006)

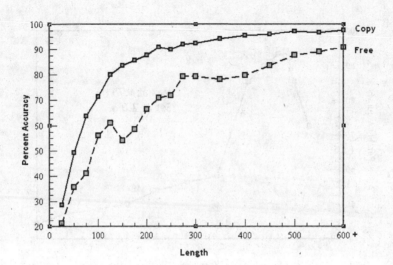

*Figure 21. Distributions of "**u**" duration times for each entry mode, adapted with permission from Villani (2006)*

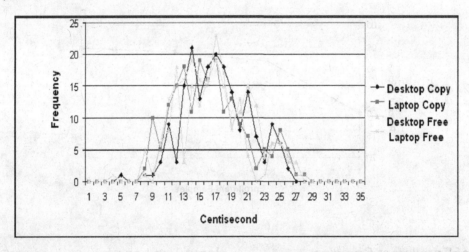

Probability Distributions of Statistical Features

We verified the normal distribution assumption for the duration times. Figure 21, for example, shows the distributions of the key-press durations for the letter **u** for each entry mode.

CONCLUSION AND FUTURE WORK

The results of this study are both important and timely as more people become involved in the applications of interest. Online test-taking is being used more frequently in both academic and business environments, and the test-takers need to be authenticated. And, as problems with the circulation of inappropriate (unprofessional, offensive, or obscene) e-mail become more prevalent, so does the need to identify the perpetrators. We also found that about 300 keystrokes (only four lines of text) yields sufficient accuracy in these applications, thereby reducing the text input requirement to less than half of that used in the experiments. Furthermore, because we eliminate long-duration outliers, there is no problem if the keyboard user pauses during text input for a phone call, a sip of coffee, or other reasons.

We found that the keystroke biometric can be useful for identification and authentication applications if two or more enrollment samples are available and if the same type of keyboard is used to produce both the enrollment and the questioned samples. The keystroke biometric was significantly weaker for the identification and authentication applications when enrollment and testing used different input modes (copy or free-text), different keyboard types (desktop or laptop), or both different input modes and different keyboard types. Additional findings include the degree of performance degradation as the number of participants increases and as the time interval between enrollment and testing increases.

The identification application of interest was to identify the sender of inappropriate email in a closed system of n people (1-of-n problem). Most such perpetrators will likely be novices not trying to disguise their typing, and not knowing that their keystrokes are being captured. For the studies described here, using first-choice accuracy as the evaluation criterion, we achieved high accuracies under ideal conditions – an average of 97.4% for the 36-participant experiments.

In this work we have applied the non-parametric, nearest-neighbor classifier to a multidimensional 239-feature problem. Because the error rate of the nearest-neighbor is limited to twice the Bayes rate as the quantity of data increases (Duda, Hart, & Stork, 2001), it is considered a robust technique and one that is often used in early work on a problem.

Obtaining ROC curves for this keystroke k-nearest-neighbor classifier resulted in some interesting findings. The k-nearest-neighbor procedure makes its classification decision by taking the majority of an odd number of the k nearest neighbors to the questioned (unknown) sample, and this method yielded high security at the sacrifice of low convenience in these keystroke experiments. For example, the 1-nearest-neighbor results in Table 4 yield an average FRR of 9.3% and average FAR of 2.6%, and the k-nearest-neighbor results for higher k were similar. The ROC curves, however, provide a full range of possible tradeoffs between FAR and FRR, and it is interesting that on the DeskCopy task an EER of approximately 2.7% is achieved by choosing a seemingly low threshold of $m=3$ out of the nearest 10 neighbors (Figure 13).

Although we appreciate the value of ROC curves in this work, we agree with Du & Chang (2007) that ROC curves should not be used exclusively. Most importantly, the ROC curve does not take into account the size of the database, and performance is known to decrease as the database is increased. Furthermore, the ROC curve cannot reflect the cost of classification, the failure-to-enroll rate, the template size, the recognition time, and the psychological factors of comfort, convenience, and acceptability.

Future work could also involve experiments using the system in an actual Internet security situation, like verifying the identity of online test takers. More sophisticated classification techniques might be explored, such as Support Vector Machines (SVM). Finally, although it is likely difficult to mimic another person's keystroke pattern, imposter performance might be investigated.

ACKNOWLEDGMENT

We thank the student teams in the masters-level projects course that contributed to this effort over the past several years.

REFERENCES

AdmitOne Security Inc. (2008). *Home*. Retrieved from http://www.admitonesecurity.com/

Bender, S. S., & Postley, H. J. (2007). *Key sequence rhythm recognition system and method* (U.S. Patent No. 7,206,938).

Bergadano, F., Gunetti, D., & Picardi, C. (2002). User authentication through keystroke dynamics. *ACM Transactions on Information and System Security*, *5*(4), 367–397. doi:10.1145/581271.581272

BioChec. (2008). *Home*. Retrieved from http://www.biochec.com/

Bolle, R., Connell, J., Pankanti, S., Ratha, N., & Senior, A. (2004). *Guide to biometrics*. New York: Springer.

Brown, M., & Rogers, S. J. (1993). User identification via keystroke characteristics of typed names using neural networks. *International Journal of Man-Machine Studies*, *39*(6), 999–1014. doi:10.1006/imms.1993.1092

Cha, S., & Srihari, S. N. (2000). Writer Identification: Statistical Analysis and Dichotomizer. In *Advances in Pattern Recognition - Proceedings of SPR and SSPR 2000* (LNCS 1876, pp. 123-132).

Choi, S.-S., Yoon, S., Cha, S.-H., & Tappert, C. C. (2004). Use of histogram distances in iris authentication. In *Image Analysis and Recognition – Proceedings of MSCE-MLMTA*, Las Vegas, NV (pp. 1118-1124). New York: Springer.

Curtin, M., Tappert, C., Villani, M., Ngo, G., Simone, J., St. Fort, H., et al. (2006). Keystroke biometric recognition on long-text input: A feasibility study. In *Proceedings of the International MultiConference of Engineers & Computer Scientists (IMECS)*, Hong Kong.

Du, Y., & Chang, C.-I. (2007). The problems of using ROC curve as the sole criterion in positive biometrics identification. In *Proceedings of SPIE 6579*.

Duda, R. O., Hart, P. E., & Stork, D. G. (2001). *Pattern Classification*. New York: Wiley.

Dunn, G., & Everitt, B. S. (2004). *An introduction to mathematical taxonomy*. Mineola, NY: Dover.

Gaines, H. F. (1956). *Cryptanalysis: A study of ciphers and their solution*. Mineola, NY: Dover.

Giot, R., El-Abed, M., & Rosenberger, C. (2009a). Keystroke dynamics with low constraints svm based passphrase enrollment. In *Proceedings of the IEEE International Conference on Biometrics: Theory, Applications, and Systems (BTAS 2009)*.

Giot, R., El-Abed, M., & Rosenberger, C. (2009b). GREYC keystroke: a benchmark for keystroke dynamics biometric systems. In *Proceedings of the IEEE International Conference on Biometrics: Theory, Applications, and Systems (BTAS 2009)*.

Gunetti, D., & Picardi, C. (2005). Keystroke analysis of free text. *ACM Transactions on Information and System Security*, *8*(3), 312–347. doi:10.1145/1085126.1085129

Jin, L., Ke, X., Manuel, R., & Wilkerson, M. (2004). Keystroke dynamics: A software based biometric solution. In *Proceedings of the 13th USENIX Security Symposium*.

Jurafsky, D., & Martin, J. H. (2000). *Speech and language processing*. Upper Saddle River, NJ: Prentice.

Leggett, J., & Williams, G. (1988). Verifying identity via keystroke characteristics. *International Journal of Man-Machine Studies, 28*(1), 67–76. doi:10.1016/S0020-7373(88)80053-1

Leggett, J., Williams, G., Usnick, M., & Longnecker, M. (1991). Dynamic identity verification via keystroke characteristics. *International Journal of Man-Machine Studies, 35*(6), 859–870. doi:10.1016/S0020-7373(05)80165-8

Monrose, F., Reiter, M. K., & Wetzel, S. (2002). Password hardening based on keystroke dynamics. *International Journal of Information Security, 1*(2), 69–83. doi:10.1007/s102070100006

Monrose, F., & Rubin, A. D. (2000). Keystroke dynamics as a biometric for authentication. *Future Generation Computer Systems, 16*(4), 351–359. doi:10.1016/S0167-739X(99)00059-X

Obaidat, M. S., & Sadoun, B. (1999). Keystroke dynamics based authentication. In Jain, A. K., Bolle, R., & Pankanti, S. (Eds.), *Biometrics: Personal Identification in Networked Society* (pp. 213–230). New York: Springer.

Peacock, A., Ke, X., & Wilkerson, M. (2004). Typing patterns: A key to user identification. *IEEE Security & Privacy, 2*(5), 40–47. doi:10.1109/MSP.2004.89

Revett, K. (2008). Keystroke dynamics. In *Behavioral biometrics: A remote access approach* (pp. 73–136). New York: Wiley. doi:10.1002/9780470997949.ch4

Ritzmann, M. (2009). *Strategies for managing missing or incomplete data in biometric and business applications.* Unpublished doctoral dissertation, Pace University, New York.

Rodrigues, R. N., Yared, G. F. G., Costa, C. R., Yabu-Uti, J. B. T., Violaro, F., & Ling, L. L. (2006). *Biometric access control through numerical keyboards based on keystroke dynamics (LNCS, 3832,* pp. 640–646).

Song, D., Venable, P., & Perrig, A. (1997). *User recognition by keystroke latency pattern analysis.* Retrieved from http://citeseer.ist.psu.edu/song97user.html

Srihari, S. N., Cha, S., Arora, H., & Lee, S. (2002). Individuality of Handwriting. *Journal of Forensic Sciences, 47*(4), 1–17.

Tappert, C. C., Villani, M., & Cha, S. (2009). Keystroke Biometric Identification and Authentication on Long-Text Input. In Wang, L., & Geng, X. (Eds.), *Behavioral Biometrics for Human Identification: Intelligent Applications* (pp. 342–367). Hershey, PA: IGI Global.

Villani, M. (2006). *Keystroke biometric identification studies on long text input.* Unpublished doctoral dissertation, Pace University, New York.

Villani, M., Tappert, C., Ngo, G., Simone, J., St. Fort, H., & Cha, H.-S. (2006). Keystroke biometric recognition studies on long-text input under ideal and application-oriented conditions. In *Proceedings of the Computer Vision & Pattern Recognition Workshop on Biometrics,* New York.

Woodward, J. D. Jr, Orlans, N. M., & Higgins, P. T. (2002). *Biometrics.* New York: McGraw-Hill.

Yoon, S., Choi, S.-S., Cha, S.-H., Lee, Y., & Tappert, C. C. (2005). On the individuality of the iris biometric. *Proc. Int. J. Graphics. Vision & Image Processing, 5*(5), 63–70.

Yu, E., & Cho, S. (2004). Keystroke dynamics identity verification – Its problems and practical solutions. *Computers & Security, 23*(5), 428–440. doi:10.1016/j.cose.2004.02.004

APPENDIX: SUMMARY OF THE 239 FEATURES

Table 1A.

Feature	Measure	Feature Measured	Feature	Measure	Feature Measured
1-2	μ & σ	dur all keystrokes	131-32	μ & σ	tran1 letter/non-letter
3-4	μ & σ	dur all alphabet letters	133-34	μ & σ	tran1 letter/space
5-6	μ & σ	dur vowels	135-36	μ & σ	tran1 letter/punct
7-8	μ & σ	dur vowels a	137-38	μ & σ	tran1 non-letter/letter
9-10	μ & σ	dur vowels e	139-40	μ & σ	tran1 shift/letter
11-12	μ & σ	dur vowels i	141-42	μ & σ	tran1 space/letter
13-14	μ & σ	dur vowels o	143-44	μ & σ	tran1 non-letter/non-letter
15-16	μ & σ	dur vowels u	145-46	μ & σ	tran1 space/shift
17-18	μ & σ	dur freq cons	147-48	μ & σ	tran1 punct/space
19-20	μ & σ	dur freq cons t	149-50	μ & σ	tran2 any-key/any-key
21-22	μ & σ	dur freq cons n	151-52	μ & σ	tran2 letter/letter
23-24	μ & σ	dur freq cons s	153-54	μ & σ	tran2 top cons pairs
25-26	μ & σ	dur freq cons r	155-56	μ & σ	tran2 top cons pairs th
27-28	μ & σ	dur freq cons h	157-58	μ & σ	tran2 top cons pairs st
29-30	μ & σ	dur next freq cons	159-60	μ & σ	tran2 top cons pairs nd
31-32	μ & σ	dur next freq cons l	161-62	μ & σ	tran2 vowel/cons
33-34	μ & σ	dur next freq cons d	163-64	μ & σ	tran2 vowel/cons an
35-36	μ & σ	dur next freq cons c	165-66	μ & σ	tran2 vowel/cons in
37-38	μ & σ	dur next freq cons p	167-68	μ & σ	tran2 vowel/cons er
39-40	μ & σ	dur next freq cons f	169-70	μ & σ	tran2 vowel/cons es
41-42	μ & σ	dur least freq cons	171-72	μ & σ	tran2 vowel/cons on
43-44	μ & σ	dur least freq cons m	173-74	μ & σ	tran2 vowel/cons at
45-46	μ & σ	dur least freq cons w	175-76	μ & σ	tran2 vowel/cons en
47-48	μ & σ	dur least freq cons y	177-78	μ & σ	tran2 vowel/cons or
49-50	μ & σ	dur least freq cons b	179-80	μ & σ	tran2 cons/vowel
51-52	μ & σ	dur least freq cons g	181-82	μ & σ	tran2 cons/vowel he
53-54	μ & σ	dur least freq cons other	183-84	μ & σ	tran2 cons/vowel re
55-56	μ & σ	dur all left hand letters	185-86	μ & σ	tran2 cons/vowel ti
57-58	μ & σ	dur all right hand letters	187-88	μ & σ	tran2 vowel/vowel
59-60	μ & σ	dur non-letters	189-90	μ & σ	tran2 vowel/vowel ea
61-62	μ & σ	dur space	191-92	μ & σ	tran2 double letters
63-64	μ & σ	dur shift	193-94	μ & σ	tran2 left/left
65-66	μ & σ	dur punctuation	195-96	μ & σ	tran2 left/right
67-68	μ & σ	dur punctuation period .	197-98	μ & σ	tran2 right/left
69-70	μ & σ	dur punctuation comma ,	199-200	μ & σ	tran right/right
71-72	μ & σ	dur punctuation apost '	201-02	μ & σ	tran2 letter/non-letter
73-74	μ & σ	dur punctuation other	203-04	μ & σ	tran2 letter/space

Continued on following page

Table 1A. Continued

Feature	Measure	Feature Measured	Feature	Measure	Feature Measured
75-76	μ & σ	dur numbers	205-06	μ & σ	tran2 letter/punct
77-78	μ & σ	dur other	2070-8	μ & σ	tran2 non-letter/letter
79-80	μ & σ	tran1 any-key/any-key	209-10	μ & σ	tran2 shift/letter
81-82	μ & σ	tran1 letter/letter	211-12	μ & σ	tran2 space/letter
83-84	μ & σ	tran1 top cons pairs	213-14	μ & σ	tran2 non-letter/non-letter
85-86	μ & σ	tran1 top cons pairs th	215-16	μ & σ	tran2 space/shift
87-88	μ & σ	tran1 top cons pairs st	217-18	μ & σ	tran2 punct/space
89-90	μ & σ	tran1 top cons pairs nd	219	%	shift
91-92	μ & σ	tran1 vowel/cons	220	%	caps lock
93-94	μ & σ	tran1 vowel/cons an	221	%	space
95-96	μ & σ	tran1 vowel/cons in	222	%	backspace
97-98	μ & σ	tran1 vowel/cons er	223	%	delete
99-100	μ & σ	tran1 vowel/cons es	224	%	insert
101-02	μ & σ	tran1 vowel/cons on	225	%	home
103-04	μ & σ	tran1 vowel/cons at	226	%	end
105-06	μ & σ	tran1 vowel/cons en	227	%	enter
107-08	μ & σ	tran1 vowel/cons or	228	%	ctl
109-10	μ & σ	tran1 cons/vowel	229	%	four arrow keys combined
111-12	μ & σ	tran1 cons/vowel he	230	%	sentence ending punct .?!
113-14	μ & σ	tran1 cons/vowel re	231	%	other punct
115-16	μ & σ	tran1 cons/vowel ti	232	%	left shift
117-18	μ & σ	tran1 vowel/vowel	233	%	right shift
119-20	μ & σ	tran1 vowel/vowel ea	234	%	left mouse click
121-22	μ & σ	tran1 double letters	235	%	right mouse click
123-24	μ & σ	tran1 left/left	236	%	double left mouse click
125-26	μ & σ	tran1 left/right	237	%	left shift to right shift
127-28	μ & σ	tran1 right/left	238	rate	input rate with pauses
129-30	μ & σ	tran1 right/right	239	rate	input rate w/o pauses

Chapter 4
A Six–View Perspective Framework for System Security:
Issues, Risks, and Requirements

Surya B. Yadav
Texas Tech University, USA

ABSTRACT

To secure information systems, the security risks and requirements must be clearly understood before the proper security mechanisms can be identified and designed. Today's security requirement specifications are generally incomplete and narrowly focused, which leads to ineffective security designs of information systems. The author asserts that multiple views—management, threat, resource, process, assessment, and legal—of information systems provides an opportunity for a better understanding of security risks and requirements. In this paper, the author proposes a six-view perspective of a system security framework to identify a more complete set of security risks and requirements. The proposed framework presents a synergistic view of the system security in which the author presents an extensive list of heuristics/ guidelines under each view, discussing security issues, risks, and requirements. Through a case study, the authors shows that a multiple view perspective of system security is effective in determining a more complete set of security requirements than the traditional approach of focusing on threats alone.

DOI: 10.4018/978-1-4666-0026-3.ch004

I. INTRODUCTION

The purpose of this paper is to propose a multi-view perspective framework for determining security requirements of an information system. The cyberspace age and Internet-based highly interactive environments are exposing more and more business operations and applications to the outside world (users, hackers, and compliance agencies etc.) as well as to the inside world (employees) (Savage, 2006). The complex business environment is necessitating a totally new view of system security. More and more security researchers and professionals (Straub, 1998; Dhillon, 2001; Levine, 2001; Whitman, 2005) have been recognizing that the system security should include not just the technical issues but also the other issues such as management, people, and process issues. There is high demand on businesses to deal with business process vulnerability, weakness in assessment and management activities, and legal requirements. This has increased the need for maintaining and securing a variety of information such as process, assessment, and legal information in addition to securing the traditional information about payroll and customers. Inadequate management structure, vulnerable business processes, or poor assessment criteria can have as much dire consequences as poor access controls, if not more. Since a system typically interacts with and is continuously exposed to the outside world (users, employees, hackers, etc.), one has to also be concerned with the ongoing assessment and management of system security. In order to develop a secure application, a complete picture of security risks and requirements should be understood before the proper security mechanisms can be identified and designed into the application. Secure application is an application that has been developed from the ground up with security mechanisms designed and built into it. In this paper we address three research questions: 1) What should security requirements be? 2) Can a scheme be devised to help identify a more complete set of security requirements that takes into account not only risks from standard threats but also risks from other sources such as process vulnerability, poor assessment, and inadequate policies? 3) How does the scheme help identify the security requirements and mechanisms? In answer to the first question, we argue that the scope of security in today's complex business environment is far broader and multi-faceted and we propose a more comprehensive view of security requirements. In answer to the second question, we develop a multiple-perspective framework to help identify a more complete set of security requirements. We then apply the framework to a case study to show that the framework helps identify a more complete set of security requirements.

Today's security requirement specifications are generally incomplete and narrowly focused. This results into an ineffective security design of an information system. In this paper we take a broader and a more synergistic view of system security. We assert that managers and system analysts need to look at the various aspects of system security simultaneously in order to have a more complete assessment of a situation and security needs. We propose a six-view perspective of system security that provides a more complete and unified depiction of different aspects of security while presenting an extensive list of heuristics and guidelines under each view. Under a unified view of system security, the analysis of security issues, risks, and requirements under each view is done within the context of all views. Each view of the perspective emphasizes and focuses on one aspect of system security. Each view also facilitates the identification of security requirements that must be met in order to address the issues under that view.

Section 2 discusses the current literature on system security. Section 3 presents the proposed six-view perspective of system security. Section 4 demonstrates the applicability of the six-view perspective of system security. The paper presents the contribution, limitation, and conclusion sections followed by the reference section.

II. CURRENT LITERATURE ON SYSTEM SECURITY

Security requirements determination is a major and a critical activity in designing any security system. Very scant attention has been given to the process of security requirements determination until recently. According to Gerber and Solms (Gerber, 2001), "Security requirements analysis is a fairly new process and certainly a lot of research needs to be done to determine the security require- ments of an organization…" Most of the work on system security has focused on technical issues. A recent review of IS security research presented by Dhillon and Backhouse (Dhillon, 2001) shows that most of the research on IS security has been done predominantly under the technical and function- alist preconceptions. They suggest that there is a need to use socio-organizational perspective and broaden the view of information system security issues (Dhillon, 2001). Mikko Siponen (Siponen, 2002), in his PhD dissertation on Designing Se- cure Information Systems and Software—Criti- cal evaluation of the existing approaches and a new paradigm, concludes that existing secure information system (SIS) design approaches lack a comprehensive modeling support. The lack of modeling support is evident at various stages of SIS design including the identification of security requirements stage. Here we review five extant methods (Fisher, 1984; Baskerville, 1988; Whit- more, 2001; BSI, 2002; and Whitman, 2005) for developing security systems and discuss their support for security requirements determination.

Approaches to Security Systems Development

Security systems development methods provide steps and guidelines to create and implement security systems for target systems (information systems). Table 1 shows a summary of the five methods. The second column contains the method steps for each extant method. The third column presents the extent of coverage each method gives to security requirements determination. The fourth column discusses guidelines, if any, included in the extant methods for identifying security requirements.

A brief discussion of the security design meth- ods follows.

Michael Whitman and Herbert Mattoro (Whitman, 2005) present a Security Systems Development Life Cycle (SecSDLC) which is based upon the Systems Development Life Cycle (SDLC) waterfall methodology. The SecSDLC methodology consists of investigation, analysis, logical design, physical design, implementation, and maintenance phases (Whitman, 2005). SecS- DLC has specific steps for documenting security policies, analyzing threats, and examining legal issues. Whitman (2005) presents several kinds of threats and assets. These threats and assets are very appropriate to pay attention to. The major- ity of threats relate to deliberate acts by hackers, viruses, acts of human error, and technical failures. However, a target system can be at risk from other sources of threat such as a poor security policy, a vulnerable business process, and inadequate assessment criteria. Whitman discusses threats and assets in detail but provides very few formal guidelines for identifying a comprehensive set of entities that may pose risks to a target system.

BS 7799.2:2002 (BSI, 2002; Cybertrust, 2005; Gamma, 2006) standard includes a process called Plan-Do-Check-Act (PDCA) to manage the life cycle of information security management sys- tems. The PDCA process consists of the follow- ing four steps (NSW, 2003a; Cybertrust, 2005; BSI, 2002):

- Plan—Establish the ISMS
  - Define the scope of the ISMS
  - Define the high-level ISMS policy
  - Determine approach to assessment
  - Identify the risks
  - Assess the risks

Table 1. Security design methods and their security requirements guidelines

Author(s)	Method and its Phases	Coverage of Security Requirements Determination	Guidelines for identifying security requirements
WhitMan & Mattoro 2005	Security Systems Development Life Cycle. 1. Investigation 2. Analysis 3. Logical Design 4. Physical Design 5. Implementation and Change	The first two phases deal with security requirements. Sub-steps include: 1. Documentation and analysis of existing security policies 2. Analyze current threats and controls 3. Examine legal issues 4. perform risk analysis	Different categories of threats such as acts of human error, compromises to intellectual properties, and technical failures are specified. Different kinds of legal, ethical and professionals issues are discussed. Various kinds of assets such as Employees, Nonemployees, Procedures, Information, and Software, are discussed. *Whitman and Mattoro provide one of the most extensive lists of threats and assets. However, these threats and assets do not cover all organizational resources and entities that may affect business interruptions. There is very little support in the form of guidelines to help identify security requirements.*
Whitmore 2001	Systematic Approach to Developing Security Architectures. 1. Develop business process model 2. Establish security design objectives 3. Select and enumerate security subsystems 4. Document conceptual security architecture Integrate security into the overall solution architecture	The first two phases deal with security design objectives.	Perils to IT process flows are specified. *Few guidelines are provided to identify information assets and security requirements. Guidelines are not comprehensive.*
BS 7799.2:2002	Plan-Do-Check-Act (PDCA) process. 1. Plan—Establish the information security management system (ISMS) 2. Do—Implement and operate the ISMS 3. Check—Monitor and review the ISMS 4. Act—Maintain and improve the ISMS	No direct discussion of security requirements steps. Security policies and risks are identified and assessed during the Plan phase. ISO/IEC 17799:2005 is used as a specification after the security requirements have been determined.	The PDCA process assumes that the security requirements are already known. *No guidelines for security requirements determination are provided.*
Baskerville 1988	Structured Security Analysis and Design. 1. Create physical model of the existing system 2. Produce a logical model of the existing system 3. Introduce controls into the logical model 4. Create new logical model of the new system 5. Add cross-reference to controls in each data dictionary entry	The security activities such as identify entities, identify risks, and identify controls are explicitly integrated into the Structured Systems Analysis and Design method.	Three risk classes—disclosure, modification, and destruction and the ideas of data and process controls are used to help identify security requirements. *Identification of entities is left to the Structured Analysis method which does not provide any guideline for identifying security-related entities. Guidelines are incomplete. Focus is mainly on data and process controls.*

Continued on following page

Table 1. Continued

Author(s)	Method and its Phases	Coverage of Security Requirements Determination	Guidelines for identifying security requirements
Fisher 1984	Data Control Life Cycle Methodology. 1. Identify Exposures 2. Assess Risk 3. Select Controls 4. Analyze Cost-Effectiveness	The first phase deals with security needs. The approach defines six groups of exposure of data—Accidental disclosure, Intentional disclosure, Accidental modification, Intentional modification, Accidental destruction, and Intentional destruction	Eleven data control points (CPs) are defined to help identify security requirements. A work flow diagram is marked with CPs. Each data is checked for six types of exposures at each data control point. *The identification process using data exposure and control point is quite extensive. However, it is physically-oriented [Baskerville 1988]. The guidelines are limited to only data exposure. They are technical in nature. The guidelines are not comprehensive.*

- Evaluate the options for the treatment of risks
- Select controls for the residual risks
- Prepare a Statement of Applicability (SOA)
- Do—Implement and operate the ISMS
  - Formulate a risk treatment plan
  - Implement the risk treatment plan
  - Implement controls selected
  - Implement training and awareness programs
  - Manage operations
  - Manage resources
  - Implement procedures
- Check—Monitor and review the ISMS
  - Execute monitoring procedures
  - Undertake regular reviews of the effectiveness of the ISMS
  - Review the level of residual risk and acceptable risk
  - Conduct internal ISMS audits at planned intervals
  - Undertake a management review of the ISMS on a regular basis and record actions and events that could have an impact on the effectiveness or performance of the ISMS
- Act—Maintain and improve the ISMS
  - Implement the identified improvements in the ISMS

- Take appropriate corrective and preventive actions
- Communicate the results and actions and agree with all interested parties
- Ensure that the improvements achieve their intended objectives

The PDCA process takes information security requirements as input and transforms them into a managed information security (BSI, 2002). The plan phase takes the information security requirements and defines a plan of the ISMS to be implemented. The "Select Controls for the residual risks" step of the Plan phase uses the ISO/IEC 17799:2005 (ISO 17799:2005 and Gamma, 2006) standard to select appropriate controls. It is important to point out that ISO/IEC 17799:2005 is used as a specification to select controls and not to identify assets and risks to those assets. The PDCA process is quite extensive but it does not have any specific guidelines to identify information security policies and other requirements (Eloff, 2003). We discuss the plan phase in more detail in Section 4. We use a modified version of the plan phase to illustrate our case-solution to the XYZ Association case.

James J. Whitmore (Whitmore, 2001) presents a method for designing secure solutions. He describes a systematic approach for defining, modeling, and documenting security functions.

Using Common Criteria as a basis, he proposes five interrelated security subsystems. These are (Whitmore, 2001):

1. Security audit subsystem
2. Solution integrity subsystem
3. Access control subsystem
4. Information flow control subsystem, and
5. Identity or credential subsystem.

James J. Whitmore's approach is for developing network security architectures. Once the security requirements have been identified, they can be mapped to the above mentioned security subsystems in order to come up with a security architecture for the system. This is a very important work for designing secure solutions. However, it does not address the identification and determination of security requirements as there are no guidelines. Also, the proposed security subsystems do not address the continuous security assessment and privacy issues.

Baskerville (Baskerville, 1988; Baskerville 1993) presents a structured security analysis and design method for information systems. The security analysis and design, as shown in Table 1, is done in parallel to Demarco's (DeMarco, 1979) Structured Analysis method. The integration of security analysis and design into the overall methods for developing systems is a very important concept. I believe that an integrated development method will be very useful and effective in designing secure systems. However, the structured security analysis and design method (Baskerville, 1988), in its current form, does not address the identification of all types of security requirements adequately.

Fisher (Fisher, 1984) presents, focusing on control points, a detailed method to identify data exposure and controls. The method also includes mapping data exposures to control points, assessing risks, and selecting controls. The method also discusses six major causes (i.e., people, hardware, software, communications, acts of God, and procedures) of data exposure (Fisher, 1984). The method, however, focuses mainly on data and uses the idea of a data control life cycle to identify data exposure control points along the flow of data. The method does not address exposure to other valuable organizational resources.

Vaidyanathan and Devraj (Vaidyanathan, 2003) present a five-factor framework for analyzing online risks in e-business. The suggested five factors are based upon the five new functions attributed to online B2B business. The five new functions are services, business models, processes, technologies, and fulfillment needs. The changed nature of these functions poses additional risks to online businesses. The function-based factors help in highlighting additional risks for online businesses. But these factors do not cover all aspects of a business. For instance, things such as legal, assessment, and management aspects of a business are not addressed by the framework. Furthermore, services and fulfillments are, in a way, subdivisions of the processes function.

The extant design methods have contributed to designing a system that can reduce security risks. However, the security-scope has been mainly limited to protecting data and/or physical assets. However, the scope of security in today's complex business environment is far broader and multi-faceted. We need to devise a way to cover all of today's business security needs.

III. SIX-VIEW PERSPECTIVE OF SYSTEM SECURITY: A UNIFIED FRAMEWORK

What should be the security requirements of a target system? How to protect a target system better? In order to answer these questions, we take a broader view of security requirements and address them in terms of overall business impact and the cost of business interruptions (Whitman, 2005). To better understand the overall security needs of a target system, we adopt the doctrine of

Table 2. Mapping between system characteristics and corresponding security views

Systems Theory and Open System Characteristics	Major Aspect of System (Security View)	Comments
Inputs—Energy, raw materials, etc.	Resource	Importation of energy, hiring of people
Outputs—products or outcomes	Resource	Producing products, product design, services
Through-Put—Transformation of resources	Process	Processes to transform one form of entity into another
Systems as Cycles of Events—Pattern of activities (structure)	Management	Forming up structures, administering structures
Negative Entropy—Storage of energy	Resource	Storing extra (additional) energy and other raw materials
The Steady State and Dynamic Homeostasis—Maintenance of steady state or equilibrium	Management	Achieving balance among subsystems and monitoring and controlling it
Information Input and Coding Process—Selective information about the environment	Resource	Information about the environment. Mechanism by which incoming information is accepted or rejected
Negative Feedback—Information feedback	Assessment	Information from outside and within in the form of negative feedback that enables a system to correct problems
Equifinality—Reaching the same final state from differing initial conditions and a variety of paths	Management	Setting up policies and plans
Differentiation—Elaboration and Specialization	Management	Development of specialized functions
Environment—Legal	Interaction—Legal	Interaction with government and other regulatory agencies
Environment—Other	Interaction—Threat	Interaction with other entities

expansionism (Ackoff, 1974), which posits that all things are part of larger wholes. Security of a target system should be viewed as part of the broader issue of business interruptions. We use open systems theory to look at different aspects of a target system. A secure system should be designed to support various types of security requirements. These security requirements arise due to several types of security issues and risks dealing with the various aspects of a target system. A target system has *processes* to carry out its activities; these processes use *resources*. The target system has to develop and establish a proper *structure* to support the processes. It interacts with its *environment* including the government and other regulatory agencies. The system also needs to continuously *assess* itself. These aspects—process, resource, structure, environment, and assessment give rise to different types of security issues, risks, and

requirements. In order to formalize the above discussed aspects, we treat the target system as an open system from the viewpoint of an analyst and manager. An open system has several characteristics. Using systems theory and concepts of open system characteristics, Table 2 shows a mapping between the target system characteristics and the corresponding security views of a system.

A key concept behind open systems is that of interdependent wholeness (Ackoff, 1974). This implies that every aspect of a system should be considered for possible protection and security. Each system characteristic relates to different activity and aspect of the system. For example, inputs and outputs refer to resources and we relate them to the resource aspect of the system. Through-put refers to the transformation of resources and it can be related the process aspect of the system. The comment column in Table 2 suggests the

Figure 1. SVPSS framework showing various views of system security

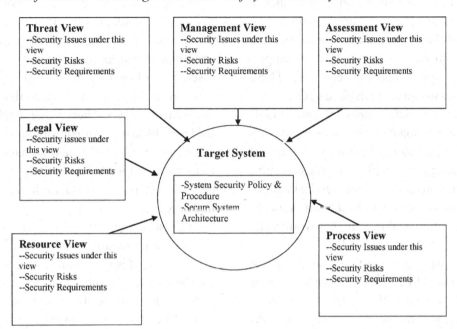

reason to associate each characteristic with a particular aspect of a system. Today's systems have to deal with complex regulatory requirements. Therefore a system has to pay serious attention to those requirements. Therefore, the complex environment has been divided into two categories—legal and other environment.

The security views suggested in Table 2 cover all characteristics of a target system. We propose, based upon the mapping shown in Table 2, the following six views of system security:

1. Threat view,
2. Management view,
3. Assessment view,
4. Legal view,
5. Resource view, and
6. Process view.

Each view covers, as mentioned earlier, one or more characteristics of a target system. We use the above views to propose a six-view perspective of target system security. The idea of using these various views is also borne out by the various

kinds of security related discussions in trade and practice literature. For example, an IBM brochure advertises about Security Assessment Services (IBM, 2005). Process engineering and manufacturing literature discusses the ideas of process security and process risk management. The idea of process security applies equally well to other types of organizations. Literature on regulation compliance emphasizes legal aspects of security.

Figure 1 pictorially shows a framework incorporating the six-view perspective of system security. We call this framework a "Six-View Perspective of System Security" (SVPSS) framework. Each rectangle in the SVPSS framework represents a view showing security issues, risks, and requirements, under that view.

The circle represents the target system that needs to be protected. It is shown in terms of its security policy and procedure as well as its secure system architecture. Arrows represent the influence of each view's overall security requirements on the target system's security policy, procedure, and architecture. Each of these views emphasizes a set of security issues and risks that give rise to a set of view-specific security requirements. These set of view-specific security requirements, in turn, should help determine functionalities that should be built into a secure system to support the security requirements of a company. These functionalities would be available to a person such as a company's 'Chief Security Information Officer'. These functionalities would help a person define, adjust, and monitor the security status of the system through a seamless interface. Appropriate mechanisms and services must be incorporated into the secure system to support the security functionalities. At this point, it is worthwhile to define security issues and risk.

Security issues are questions, situations, or events that should be thought about, addressed and possibly settled with regard to a system's security. Here we present security issues in terms of prodding questions that should be asked about a target system in order to elicit a more complete set of security requirements. Answers to these and other similar questions need not be the same for every target system. The answers to these questions would lead to a set of potential security risks specific to a target system. These potential security risks should then be assessed and appropriate security requirements identified in order to mitigate the risk. The main criterion to evaluate a particular security risk is the extent of its adverse impact on the target system.

Risk can be defined as "the possibility of loss or injury and the probability of such loss" (Loch, 1992). Risk assessment is the process of determining and evaluating security-related risks from internal and external threat sources. There are several methods discussed in the literature to assess risks (GAO, 1999; ASIS, 2003; Verdon, 2004). Most of these methods are very similar to each other and any of them can be used to assess risks. We will not discuss any risk assessment methods in this paper due to scope and space limitations. Every target system has limited resources to devote to system security. Therefore, determining security risks and prioritizing their

impact level is extremely vital to using valuable resources to combat risks effectively. We assert that a multi-view perspective of risk provides an opportunity for a more complete determination and assessment of security risks. Most of the existing work on security risk has focused almost entirely on threats to assets. There is not much attention paid to risks to other organizational entities such as process, assessment, and management. The framework of Figure 1 shows that there are several types of risks that should be identified and managed.

We discuss the issues, risks, general and functional security requirements under each of these views below. It is important to keep in mind that the discussion of security risks and requirements under each view are illustrative and general in nature. The framework enables an organization to 'see' and evaluate a more comprehensive set of system security requirements. The discussion does not imply that every target system must implement security mechanisms to tackle all the security requirements without regard to cost. Each security requirement's risk level and its cost should be evaluated for determining the appropriate actions.

3.1 Threat View of System Security

A threat is anything that can cause potential harm to information assets. The threat view focuses on identifying entities that may threaten the system security and coming up with requirements and mechanisms to protect the system from those threatening entities.

Issues under Threat Views

Threat issues arise in dealing with threats to system's security. We present security issues as prodding questions that should be identified and discussed when identifying security requirements of a specific company. The security threat issues include:

1. What is a security threat?
2. What are threat risks?
3. What are different types of security threats?
4. What are specific security threats under each type of security threats?
5. What are threat security needs (requirements) to deal with the specific security threats?
6. What should be threat security policy?
7. What should be secure system requirements to thwart each threat?
8. What are the appropriate security mechanisms to implement the secure system requirements?
9. What should be the Threat Secure subsystem Architecture to incorporate the security mechanisms?
10. How the Threat Secure subsystem should be embedded into the overall secure system architecture?

These issues are suggested as a basic set of questions that should be part of possibly a larger set of issues to be considered by a target system. Discussion of threat issues gives rise to threat risks and threat security requirements. The threat security requirements should be identified as per each security threat faced by a target system. There are various kinds of threats (Microsoft-TechNet, 2000; NSW, 2003b). In this paper we follow the threat guidelines as proposed in the Information Security Guideline of NSW Government (NSW, 2003b). The Information Security Guideline of the New South Wales (NSW) Government (NSW, 2003b) has compiled a very comprehensive list of various kinds of threats. These threats are categorized as environmental, deliberate, and accidental threats (NSW, 2003b). As an example, some of the deliberate threats are denial of service, eavesdropping, and malicious code.

Not every threat is obviously relevant to every situation. Furthermore, threats change as the environment changes; however, this does not obviate the need to be proactive and ever-vigilant about identifying threats and dealing with them effectively.

The identification of threats should be followed by the identification of security risks.

Security Risks under Threat View

All possible threat risks to a target system should be identified. Threat risks arise from the possible loss to assets from various kinds of threats mentioned above. Under this view, we consider risks from threats mainly to tangible assets. Intangible assets/resources are considered under the resource view. Threat risks include possible losses from natural disasters, deliberate threats such as sabotage and malice, and accidental threats such as operational staff errors. Some of the mechanisms to reduce such risks are:

- Equipment security
- Power supply security
- Data Backup
- Secured server room

The above list of mechanisms is included here to show, as an illustration, a correspondence between certain kinds of sources of risks and some of the possible security mechanisms.

Identification of security risks and their impact should be analyzed in order to prioritize and select appropriate risks for further treatment. The appropriate selection of threat risks should be followed by the appropriate selection of threat security requirements. These threat security needs of a target system must be supported by the secure system. As an illustration, some of the basic threat security requirements are listed below.

General (Basic) Security Needs (Requirements) under Threat View

There should be a threat security policy and plan to deal with internal as well as external threats. Some general requirements may include protection from natural disasters such as flood and fire as well as malicious and non-malicious threats.

Once the threat security needs of a target system have been determined, it is important to specify what functional requirements are required of a system to support the security needs. These functional requirements should be specified at a sufficiently detailed level so that most of them can be considered and at least partly supported through automated tools.

Functional Requirements under Threat View

A good disaster recovery plan should be implemented not only to protect infrastructures such as networks, servers, and software, but also data from disasters such as weather calamities, power failures, and equipment failures. Data should be copied and/or replicated and stored at a safe off site.

1. Functional requirements for data backup and storage:
    a. Backup data
    b. Verify backup-data
    c. Replicate data
    d. Verify replicated-data
    e. Store backup-data
2. Functional requirements to protect from malicious threats:
    a. Protect against Intrusion
        i.   Detect Intrusion
        ii. Prevent Intrusion
    b. Protect against Denial of Service
        i.   Thwart Flood Attack
        ii. Thwart Amplification Attack
        iii. Thwart Resource Depletion Attack
    c. Protect against Malicious Code
        i.   Thwart Buffer Overflow Attack
        ii. Thwart Unexpected Operator Attack
        iii. Thwart Access Control Discovery Attack

        iv. Thwart IP Address Discovery Attack
    d. Protect Against Eavesdropping
        i.   Encrypt Data
        ii. Decrypt Data
    e. Protect from non-malicious threats
    f. Protect against Operational Staff Errors
        i.   Verify and confirm input data and commands
        ii. Save Data periodically
    g. Protect against Technical Failures
        i.   Maintain Redundancy in system

Once the threat security needs of a target system have been determined, it is important to specify the functional requirements at a sufficiently detailed level. A list of functional requirements such as above can be used as a guideline as well as a check-list by analysts and managers.

3.2 Resource View of System Security

A resource is any IT and/or system asset that needs to be protected. This view focuses on identifying IT resources, security needs of the resources, and mechanisms to protect the IT resources.

Issues under Resource View

Resource issues arise in dealing with the protection of IT resources. These issues include:

1. What is an IT/system resource (asset)?
2. What are resource security risks?
3. What are different types of system resources that must be protected?
4. What are specific resources under each type of system resources?
5. What should be resource security policy?
6. What are resource security needs (requirements) to deal with the specific resource security?

7. What should be secure system requirements to protect each resource?
8. What are the appropriate security mechanisms to implement the secure system requirements?
9. What should be the Resource Secure subsystem Architecture to incorporate the security mechanisms?
10. How the Resource Secure subsystem should be embedded into the overall secure system architecture?

The resource-related security issues give rise to the identification of resource security requirements for various types of resources. Resources can be of different types. Resources managed by an operating system have been classified as hardware (physical) resources and software resources (Shittu, 2001). Hardware resources include processors, I/O devices, and memory, etc. Software resources include processes, files, and virtual memory, etc. (Shittu, 2001). A more recent view (Wiederrich, 2003) of infrastructure assets (resources) to be protected classifies resources under three main categories. These are:

1. Data,
2. Services, and
3. Communication.

These three categories do not include physical resources. However, these categories cover more resources than software resources (Shittu, 2001) as far as an information system is concerned. Whitman (Whitman, 2005) and the Information Security Guideline for NSW Government (NSW, 2003a) provide the most inclusive discussion of information assets. According to the Information Security Guideline, "An (information) asset is something that an organization (agency) values and therefore has to protect. Assets include all the information and supporting items that an agency requires to conduct its business" (NSW, 2003a). Information assets include information/data,

paper documents, software, physical equipment, services, people and their knowledge, and image and reputation of the organization (NSW, 2003a).

Security Risks under Resource View

Here we determine risks to resources. Resource risks arise from possible losses to information-related assets and resources. Risks include non-availability, compromised integrity, and disclosure of confidential resources. Mechanisms to reduce resource risks include:

- Data backup
- Access Control
- Security awareness training
- Intrusion detection
- Internet connection restriction

The identification of resource risks should be followed by the identification of resource security (protection) requirements. As an example, some of the basic resource security requirements are listed below.

General Security Requirements under Resource View

There should be a resource security policy and plan to protect target system's resources. Some of the general resource protection requirements include maintaining the confidentiality, integrity, availability, and reliability of resources.

Functional Requirements under Resource View

A secure system should provide functions (features) to help protect resources. Some examples of system functions for resource protection are given below.

1. Resource Availability Requirements
   a. Define Resource availability

b. Check Resource availability
c. Adjust Resource availability
d. Monitor Resource availability
e. Test Resource availability
2. Resource Confidentiality Requirements
    a. Define Resource confidentiality
    b. Check Resource confidentiality
    c. Adjust Resource confidentiality
    d. Monitor Resource confidentiality
    e. Test Resource confidentiality
3. Resource Integrity Requirements
    a. Define Resource integrity
    b. Check Resource integrity
    c. Adjust Resource integrity
    d. Monitor Resource integrity
    e. Test Resource integrity

3.3 Process View of System Security

The process view emphasizes secure methods and procedures used by a target system to realize its system security objectives. It is important to note that there is a difference between a secure process and a security process. A security process is a process used by a target system to develop and implement its security requirements. A secure process is a security process that is secure from security threats and intrusions. In general, a security process may or may not be secure.

Issues under Process View

Issues arise in dealing with the identification and securing of security processes. Issues under process view include:

1. What is a secure process?
2. What are security process risks?
3. What are different types of secure processes?
4. What are the specific processes under each type of secure process?
5. What should policies and plans are needed to secure processes?

6. What are the security requirements to protect each secure process?
7. What are the appropriate security mechanisms to implement the protection of security processes?
8. What should be the appropriate secure process subsystem architecture to incorporate the security mechanisms?
9. How should the secure process subsystem be built into the overall secure system architecture?

Risks under Process View

The identification of process risks is as important as the identification of resource and threat risks. Process risks relate to possible losses due to problems during the implementation of these processes. Problems can arise due to weak points in a process, vulnerabilities in the interface between the actors and the processes, and failures of processes. The literature on process control discusses various ways to reduce process risks. Some of the actions to minimize process risks include:

*   Establishing standards and following them in designing interfaces and steps of a process
*   Feed forward controls such as staff-training and scheduled process maintenance
*   Concurrent controls such as direct monitoring

Identification of process risks should be followed by the identification security requirements to reduce the impact of the identified process risks.

General Security Requirements under Process View

Policies and plans should be developed to secure processes. Some of the general security requirements are:

1. Develop secure processes for dealing with threats
2. Develop secure processes for protecting resources
3. Develop secure processes for managing legal and privacy requirements
4. Manage secure process integrity
5. Conduct audit of secure processes

Functional Requirements under Process View

Here we list functions that are required to help secure processes. Functional requirements under the process view can cut across several systems depending upon the level and scope of the process. Therefore, it is sometimes necessary to have a "secure process management system" that can enable management deal with security at a process level as opposed to a system level. Some of the functional requirements under process view include:

1. Develop Secure Process
    a. Define process policy
    b. Define process design standards
    c. Establish the start and the end of the process
    d. Establish flow of information through steps of the process
    e. Establish flow of control among the steps
    f. Identify weak points/steps of the process
    g. Rectify weak points/steps of the process
    h. Secure each steps of the process
    i. Link secure steps into secure processes
    j. Identify actors (entities) that perform the steps
    k. Identify items (resources) used by the process
    l. Design built-in mechanisms to collect appropriate data for auditing the process.

2. Manage Secure Process
    a. Review process policy
    b. Review process design standards
    c. Establish process ownership
    d. Separate duties of actors involved in a process
    e. Deal with terminations of actors promptly
    f. Control backup and recovery of a process
    g. Train users in the secure process
3. Audit Secure Process
    a. Verify data on a process
    b. Evaluate process
    c. Review process

3.4 Assessment View of System Security

The assessment of system security is an ongoing, continuous process. Continuous security assessment can be defined as an iterative review process to compare current (present) functions of security activities and outcomes against specific standards, as well as to yield a security assessment profile showing areas of conformance in which new procedures, training, or other methods of security improvement may be needed to comply with specific standards (Ryder, 2004). Security assessments can be conducted at various levels— from high-level reviews of the target system's policies and procedures to detailed technical level assessments of vulnerabilities.

Issues under Assessment View

An appropriate review process must be put in place to do an overall effective security assessment. Issues arise in determining review processes for assessing the effectiveness of various kinds of securities such as threats, resources, processes, and other securities. Issues under the assessment view include:

1. What is the continuous security assessment?
2. What are the security assessment risks?
3. What are different types of continuous security assessment?
4. What are the specific continuous assessments under each type of security assessment?
5. What should be the policy and plan for continuous security assessment?
6. What are the assessment requirements for each continuous security assessment?
7. What are the assessment mechanisms to implement assessment requirements?
8. What should be the appropriate security assessment subsystem architecture to incorporate the assessment mechanisms?
9. How should the security assessment subsystem be built into the overall secure system architecture?

Risks under Assessment View

The risks in assessment refer to the risks due to improper security assessments which can include losses due to inadequate and poor assessment criteria, inadequate assessment methods and procedures, lack of clarity and transparency in assessment methods, and lack of clear roles and responsibilities of assessment staffs (Millar, 2001). Security risks in assessment can arise due to incorrect assessment measure criteria, not being able to collect data on assessment measures, not responding to variations, and poor assessment methods. Some of the actions to minimize risks in assessment can include (Millar 2001):

- Establishing standards to be followed by the security assessment staff
- Establishing codes of practice including codes of conduct
- Establishing proper monitoring and management of assessment activities

The identification of assessment risks should be followed by the identification of security requirements to minimize these risks.

General Security Requirements under Assessment View

Policies and plans should be developed to provide guidelines for continuous security assessment. Some of the general security requirements under the assessment view include defining, measuring, and evaluating assessment policy, standards, and methods.

Functional Requirements under Assessment View

Here, we list functions that assist management in conducting continuous security assessment activities. Functions include:

1. Secure process assessment criteria requirements
   a. Define assessment criteria for assessing secure process
   b. Define measures for each criterion for assessing secure process
   c. Collect data on measures
   d. Evaluate the measures' effectiveness
2. Resource security assessment criteria requirements
   a. Define assessment criteria for assessing resource security
   b. Define measures for each criterion for assessing resource security
   c. Collect data on measures
   d. Evaluate the measures' effectiveness
3. Threat security assessment criteria requirements
   a. Define assessment criteria for assessing threat security
   b. Define measures for each criterion for assessing threat security
   c. Collect data on measures

d.   Evaluate the measures' effectiveness

4.   Security management assessment criteria requirements

   a.   Define assessment criteria for assessing the management of security.

   b.   Define measures for each criterion for assessing the management of security

   c.   Collect data on measures

   d.   Evaluate the measures' effectiveness

5.   Legal and privacy assessment criteria requirements

   a.   Define assessment criteria for assessing the legal and privacy security

   b.   Define measures for each criterion for assessing the legal and privacy security

   c.   Collect data on measures

   d.   Evaluate the measures' effectiveness

3.5 Management View of System Security

The term "security management" has been used in various ways in the literature (NetIQ, 2002; Caralli, 2003; Microsoft, 2005; and Altiris, 2005). According to Gartner Research, "enterprise IT security management focuses primarily on the tools, technologies and services that are needed by IT security operations to manage security devices and the security of IT infrastructure, applications and transactions" (Nicolett, 2002). Wikipedia (Wikipedia, 2005) defines security management as the set of functions (a) that protect telecommunications networks and systems from unauthorized access by persons, acts, or influences, and (b) that include many sub-functions, such as creating, deleting, and controlling security services and mechanisms; distributing security-relevant information; reporting security-relevant events; controlling the distribution of cryptographic keying material; and authorizing subscriber access, rights, and privileges. Both definitions cover security management quite well. Security management should be business-driven as opposed to technology-driven and it should encompass physical, technical, operational, and administrative controls.

Several trends such as mergers and acquisitions, hackers' attacks, rapid growth in e-business applications, and phenomenal growth in users have made the management of security very complex (NetIQ, 2002). Managing security is a dynamic and moving target. Target systems are facing new and complex challenges continuously in dealing with security management.

Issues under Management View

Security management issues arise in dealing with security policies and their implementation within the target system. Some of the security management issues are:

1.   What is security management?
2.   What are the security risks to management?
3.   What are different types of security management?
4.   What are the specific security management activities or tasks within each type of security management?
5.   What should be the security management policy and plan?
6.   What are the security requirements for each security management activities?
7.   What are the security management mechanisms to implement security management requirements?
8.   What should be the appropriate security management subsystem architecture to incorporate the security management mechanisms?
9.   How the security management subsystem should be built into the overall secure system architecture?

Security Risks under Management View

Management risks relate to the loss due to managerial inadequacies in the area of security. Every target system should be cognizant of the importance of a good security policy, accountability, monitoring, and remediation. Risks can arise due to poor and/or the lack of:

- Policy
- Accountability
- Administration
- Monitoring
- Remediation

Some of the mechanisms to reduce management risks include:

- Clearly defined policy
- Well defined accountability and codes of practice
- Transparent administration
- Monitoring standards
- Prompt remediation

General Security Requirements under Management View

General security management requirements include:

1. Establish Security Policy and Procedures
2. Establish Accountability
3. Administer Security
4. Monitor Security
5. Handle remediation

Functional Requirements under Management View

The functions under security management view enable management plan, control, and monitor security related activities in the target system. These functions include:

1. Establish Security Policy and Procedures
   a. Establish plan for overall security
   b. Establish plan for scanning
   c. Establish plan for auditing
      d. Establish plan for detecting intrusions
      e. Establish plan for defense in depth
      f. Establish plan for incident response
      g. Review security policy and procedures
2. Establish Accountability
   a. Establish plan for accountability
   b. Assign team/individuals for scanning
   c. Assign team/individuals for auditing
   d. Assign team/individuals for detecting intrusion
   e. Assign team/individuals for defending the perimeter and the network
   f. Assign team/individuals for incidence response
   g. Review accountability policy
   h. Refine accountability policy
3. Monitor Security
   a. Scan
   b. Audit
   c. Detect
   d. Evaluate
4. Administer Security
   a. Prevent incidents
   b. Respond to incidents
5. Handle Remediation
   a. Identify faulty policy
   b. Identify faulty mechanisms
   c. Take corrective action

3.6 Legal View of System Security

The legal view emphasizes privacy and legal security requirements. Privacy can be defined as the right of an individual to control personal information and not have it disclosed or used by others without permission (Braithwaite, 2005). Various privacy laws have been enacted throughout the world (Liberty Alliance Project, 2003). Some examples of U.S. privacy laws are The Graham-Leach-Bliley Act and The Health Information Portability and Accountability Act (HIPPA) (BBB, 2003; Liberty Alliance Project, 2003; U.S. Department of Health and Human Services, 2003a, 2003b). These privacy laws mandate legal security requirements that must be complied with. Legal security can be defined as a security process used to protect privacy and to comply with security laws.

Issues under Legal View

Privacy and legal-compliance issues arise when dealing with personal information. Some of these issues are:

1. What are legal issues?
2. What are privacy protection issues?
3. What are legal and privacy risks?
4. What are various kinds of laws that affect privacy?
5. What should be legal policy and plan?
6. What are the specific security requirements under each law?
7. What are the appropriate mechanisms to implement privacy and legal security requirements?
8. What should be the appropriate legal security subsystem architecture to incorporate the legal security mechanisms?
9. How should the legal security subsystem be built into the overall secure system architecture?

Security Risks under Legal View

Legal risks are the possibility of loss due to the violation of security and privacy laws, security-related legal uncertainties, and litigation. Legal uncertainties can arise from changing security laws and complex international transactions and contracts. Legal risks can be broadly classified as legal and privacy risks. Both types of security risks should be assessed and managed to avoid costly litigation and loss of business. Some of the controls to reduce legal risks include:

- Access policy
- Staff accountability for misuse of information
- Third-party auditing and oversight
- Operational rules for exchanging and sharing information among organizational units
- Legal consultants

Identification of legal risks should be followed by the identification of the security requirements needed to reduce the impact of the identified legal risks

General Security Requirements under Legal View

General security requirements under the legal view relate to privacy and security laws. The major general requirements are:

1. Enable Privacy
2. Comply with Privacy and Security Laws

Functional Requirements under Legal View

The functions under the legal view guide management in establishing privacy rules and complying with other security laws. These functions include:

1. Enable Privacy
   a. Establish rules for handling personal data
   b. Identify Personal Identifiable Information (PII)
   c. Establish proper access control for PII
2. Comply with Privacy and Security Laws
   a. Analyze legal risks for on-line environment
   b. Follow the information recording and retaining requirements to comply with privacy and security laws
   c. Comply with spam and other laws

IV. APPLICABILITY OF THE SIX-VIEW PERSPECTIVE SYSTEM SECURITY (SVPSS) FRAMEWORK

The SVPSS framework is multi-purpose and provides a comprehensive perspective of system security. The SVPSS framework is useful as a guide in many system security-related activities. Here, we discuss briefly the two most useful applications of the SVPSS framework. These are:

1. Determination of security risks, requirements, and mechanisms
2. Management of system security.

We discuss the above two usages next. The SVPSS framework is very useful during the security requirements analysis process. It is especially helpful in:

1. Identifying inventory of assets and threats to these assets.
2. Determining security requirements to deal with the threats.

The SVPSS framework does not propose that the same set of security requirements and mechanisms be applied in every situation. In fact, the identification and determination of security policies, requirements, and mechanisms depends upon the complexity and the size of the situation at hand. A thorough use of the SVPSS framework may not be always necessary. For example, if the system to be secured has a minimal impact on business operation, then there may not be a need to apply the framework in its totality.

We use a case study to validate the applicability and usefulness of the SVPSS framework. A case study approach is a reasonable way to validate the use of analysis and design methods/tools. Since the SVPSS framework is a security requirements analysis tool, its application to a case is an appropriate way to show its usefulness. Here, we not only show the use of the SVPSS framework to a case but also compare its use and solution to an already existing solution for the same case.

4.1 Determination of Security Risks and Requirements using SVPSS Framework

This framework is a useful guide for a systems analyst who is charged with identifying security risks and requirements of a target system. The various views under the framework remind an analyst that he or she should look at all aspects of system security and not just the threat or the resource aspect of security. The illustrative security issues, risks, and requirements under various views can act as a starting point to determine a set of specific security requirements for the target system under study. The SVPSS framework can be adapted in almost any security requirements determination process/method as a guide to help identify a comprehensive set of security risks, requirements, and mechanisms. For example, consider the Plan-Do-Check-Act (PDCA) process recommended by the AS/NZS 7799.2:2003 (BS, 2002) (NSW, 2003a) standard for developing an Information Security Management System (ISMS).

The security requirements are determined during the plan phase of the PDCA process. The plan phase consists of the following steps. The original steps have been modified to incorporate the SVPSS framework in the plan phase. The parts that have been changed are italicized and bolded.

- Define the ISMS scope and the target system's security policies *under each view using the SVPSS framework*
- Determine approach to risk assessment
- Identify and assess the risks *under each view using the SVPSS framework*
- *Identify security requirements to reduce each risk using the SVPSS framework*

Table 3. Comparison between the use of AS/NZS 7799.2:2003 and SVPSS framework

Case-Solution Comparison Criteria	Shrestha-solution Based upon AS/NZS 7799.2:2003	SVPSS-solution based upon SVPSS framework
Overall Approach Used	Uses the PDCA Process	Uses SVPSS framework within the PDCA process
Guidelines for the identification of Security Policies	Security Policy is emphasized but few guidelines	Provides multi-view checklist of several types of security policies
Guidelines for the Identification of risks	No systematic guidelines provided by AS/NZS 7799.2:2003	SVPSS framework provides guidelines by providing risk categories and heuristics
Guidelines for the identification of security requirements	Few systematic guidelines provided by AS/NZS 7799.2:2003	SVPSS framework provides guidelines and heuristics
Categories of Security Policies Identified	No clear categorization of policies	Several categories of policies
Types of Risks Identified	Focus is mainly on threats to assets	Multiple categories of risks
Types of Security Requirements Identified	Security requirements are not explicitly addressed. Risks are directly mapped to controls	Multiple categories of risks. Security requirements are explicitly addressed under each view. These requirements are then mapped to security mechanisms (controls)
Number of Sources of Risks	Six. The sources of risks are mainly threats.	Many sources of risks under various views. Six risks under threat; five risks under resource; two risks under legal; three risks under management; four risks under process; and five risks under assessment.

- Select preventive, mitigative, and other control objectives and controls (*mechanisms*) that will help manage these risks
- Prepare the statement of applicability (SOA)

The modified steps remind an analyst and enable him or her to take into account multiple views while identifying security risks and requirements. An application of SVPSS framework has been discussed by Yadav (Yadav, 2008).

The appendix A presents a case study to show the usefulness of the SVPSS framework in identifying security risks, requirements.

4.1.1 Discussion of the XYZ Association Case Solution

The appendix A shows an application of the SVPSS framework to the XYZ Association case. Amarottam Shrestha's case-solution referred here as the Shrestha-solution shows how to use the AS/NZS 7799.2:2003 standard to develop an ISMS for the XYZ Association. We used the same case to demonstrate the usability of the SVPSS framework. This enables us to compare our case-solution called the SVPSS-solution presented in appendix A with the Shrestha-solution (Shrestha, 2004) for the same case. We compare only the "Plan" phase of the solution because our focus is on determining security risks and requirements.

Table 3 presents the differences between the applications of AS/NZS 7799.2:2003 and the SVPSS framework. As Table 3 shows, the use of SVPSS enables us to identify several categories of security policies and more sources of risks and security requirements. Even though both case solutions are incomplete, it is obvious that the SVPSS-solution is more comprehensive in terms of the identification of security policies, risks, and requirements.

It is important to point out that even a limited case study shows clearly the advantage of the SVPSS framework. We chose this case study because there was an existing solution for the case. A more comprehensive case study would certainly be a better way to show the full potential of the SVPSS framework. However, such a case study would make this paper very lengthy and distract the paper from its main focus.

4.2 Management of System Security

The SVPSS framework provides a bird-eye view of system security. It highlights the need to see security from multiple angles. Management can use the framework as a guideline to make sure all aspects of security are taken care of. It can act as a central point of reference for initiating security-related policies and activities and cross-checking existing security-related policies and activities.

V. CONTRIBUTIONS OF THE SVPSS FRAMEWORK TO THE IS LITERATURE

This research has developed a design artifact (Hevner, 2004) in the form of a framework that can be used to analyze a broader and more complete view of system security. In today's world, information security needs must take into account the overall functioning of a business system. According to Whitman, "To address information security needs, each of the organization's communities of interest must address information security in terms of business impact and the cost of business interruptions, rather than focusing on security as a technical problem (Whitman, 2005)." The SVPSS framework enables analysts and managers to take a more inclusive view of system security. We believe that the SVPSS framework emphasizes a broader view of security by incorporating provisions to not only reduce the information security risk but also the business interruption risk. The framework is derived based upon the open systems view of a target system. Unlike the extant security design methods and standards, the SVPSS framework provides explicit guidelines to account for the security needs of each characteristics of a target

system during the security requirements analysis phase. More specifically,

1. We have proposed a synergistic and comprehensive framework for identifying security requirements of target system from multiple perspectives. The multiple perspectives allow us to identify a more complete set of security requirements. Very few extant design methods and standards provide such a systematic framework.
2. Each perspective provides heuristics/guidelines for identifying sources of security risks and requirements.
3. The SVPSS framework is easily adaptable to many security design methods.

Unlike an ad hoc checklist, the SVPSS framework provides systematic guideline for broadening the view of system security in today's complex business environment. Based upon the assumptions and activities underlying the second generation design methods (Baskerville, 1993), the SVPSS framework can be classified as a second generation security design tool. It can be easily incorporated into third/fourth generation security design methods [Baskerville, 1993]. In that sense, it can also be classified as a third/fourth generation security design tool [Baskerville, 1993].

VI. LIMITATIONS OF SVPSS FRAMEWORK

The SVPSS framework highlights the importance of looking at security from all aspects of a system. It includes heuristics/guidelines to help identify security risks and requirements that can account for most of the security threats and vulnerabilities. Even though the SVPSS framework has an extensive list of heuristics/guidelines, it does not include any method for applying the framework in a systematic way. However, it is quite easy to incorporate the framework in almost any extant security design methods. We modified the PDCA process to show the application of the SVPSS framework in Section 4.1. It will be worthwhile to develop a more integrative process to make use of the framework.

The paper does not address the security issues directly for Commercial off the Shelf (COTS) packages and applications; rather focusing on designing secure systems. However, the discussion of security issues and requirements are equally applicable when buying COTS.

VII. CONCLUSION AND FUTURE RESEARCH

We have presented a comprehensive perspective of system security. We have identified several security issues, risks, and security requirements under each view of system security. We believe that the six-view perspective of system security allows one to identify and determine a more complete set of security requirements that addresses many business security needs beyond the technical security needs. With each view emphasizing different aspects of a target system, one should be able to cover most of the security risks to be faced by a system. A more complete set of security requirements will enable designers come up with a better set of security mechanisms that should be included and implemented in a secure system. The SVPSS framework was applied to an existing case to demonstrate its usefulness in determining a more complete set of security requirements.

The field of system security is very dynamic and ever-expanding. Obviously, there are several research areas under system security. Here, we discuss some future research ideas that relate directly to our current paper. It would be useful to develop a "how-to" method to formally configure the SVPSS framework to suggest a set of security requirements and the corresponding security mechanisms for a situation. The development of a secure system architecture incorporating mecha-

nisms under multiple views of system security is an important research topic. Development of logical and specific archetypes would be another logical extension of the secure system architecture. The development of a method to design and implement secure systems is another research area. Extending the idea of secure system architecture to cover network systems would be extremely important research. The author is already pursuing several of the research ideas mentioned above.

VIII. REFERENCES

Ackoff, R. L. (1974). *Redesigning the Future*. New York: Wiley-Interscience.

Altiris. (2005). *System Security: A Comprehensive Approach*. Retrieved from http://wp.bitpipe.com/resource/org_950672243_424/SystemSecurityA-CompApproach_edp.pdf

ASIS. (2003). *General Security Risk Assessment Guideline*.

Australia. (2004). *AS/NZS 4360:2004 Risk Management*.

Baskerville, R. (1988). *Designing Information Systems Security*. New York: John Wiley & Sons.

Baskerville, R. (1993). Information Systems Security Design Methods: Implications for Information System Development. *ACM Computing Surveys*, *25*(4), 375–414. doi:10.1145/162124.162127

BBB. (2003). *A Review of Federal and State Privacy Laws*. Retrieved from http://www.bbbonline.org/UnderstandingPrivacy/library/fed_statePrivLaws.pdf

Braithwaite, W. R. (2005). *HIPPA Administrative Simplification: Practical Privacy and Security*. Retrieved from http://ehr.medigent.com/assets/collaborate/2005/04/02/eHI Privacy&Security Tutorial a.ppt

BSI. (2002). *Information Security Management—Part 2: Specification for Information Security Management Systems*. Retrieved from http://www.isaca-london.org/presentations/bs7799part2.pdf

Bump, C. (2005). *Data Security: Translating Legal Requirements into Internal Policies*. Retrieved from http://www.privacyassociation.org/docs/sum05/10-3D-Bump.pdf

Caralli, R., & Wilson, W. (2003). *The Challenges of Security Management*. Retrieved from http://www.cert.org/archive/pdf/ESMchallenges.pdf

Centers for Medicare & Medicaid Services (CMS). (2002). *CMS Information Security Risk Assessment (RA) Methodology-Version #1.1*. Baltimore, MD: Department of Health & Human Services.

Cybertrust. (2005). *Adopting BS 7799-2:2002—practical, Achievable Security*. Retrieved from http://www.Cybertrust.com.

DeMarco, T. (1979). *Structured Analysis and System Specification*. New York: Yourdon Press.

Dhillon, G., & Backhouse, J. (2001). Current Directions in IS Security Research: towards socio-organizational perspectives. *Information Systems Journal*, *11*(2), 127–153. doi:10.1046/j.1365-2575.2001.00099.x

Eloff, J., & Eloff, M. (2003). Information Security Management—A New Paradigm. In. *Proceedings of SAICSIT, 2003*, 130–136.

Fisher, R. P. (1984). *Information Systems Security*. Englewood Cliffs, NJ: Prentice-Hall.

Gamma. (2006). *History of 27000*. Retrieved from http://www.gammassl.co.uk/bs7799/history.html

Gamma. (2006). *IS 17799*. Retrieved from http://www.gammassl.co.uk/bs7799/

GAO. (1999). *Information Security Risk Assessment—Practices of Leading s. Accounting and Information Management Division*. Washington, DC: United States General Accounting Office.

Gerber, M., & von Solms, R. (2001). From Risk Analysis to Security Requirements. *Computers & Security*, *20*(7), 577–584. doi:10.1016/S0167-4048(01)00706-4

Hevner, A., March, S. T., Park, J., & Ram, S. (2004). Design Science Research. *Management Information Systems Quarterly*, *28*(1), 75–105.

IBM. (2005). *IBM Security Assessment Services*. Retrieved from http://www-935.ibm.com/services/au/igs/pdf/ibm-security-assessment-services.pdf

ISO/IEC 17799. (2005). *Information technology - Security techniques - Code of practice for information security management*. Retrieved from http://www.iso.org/iso/en/prods-services/popstds/informationsecurity.html

Levine, D. S. (2001). One on One with Charles Cresson Wood of InfoSecurity Infrastructure. *Techbiz Online*. Retrieved from http://sanfrancisco.bizjournals.com/sanfrancisco/stories/2001/10/15/newscolumn7.html

Liberty Alliance Project. (2003). *Privacy and Security Best Practices*. Retrieved from http://ehr.medigent.com/assets/collaborate/2005/04/03/final_privacy_security_best_practices.pdf

Loch, K. D., Carr, H., & Warkentin, M. E. (1992). Threats to Information Systems: Today's Reality, Yesterday's Understanding. *Management Information Systems Quarterly*, 173–186. doi:10.2307/249574

Microsoft. (2005). *Service Management Functions—Security Management*. Retrieved from http://www.microsoft.com/technet/itsolutions/cits/mo/smf/mofsmsmf.mspx

Microsoft-TechNet. (2000). *Security Threats*. Retrieved from http://www.microsoft.com/technet/security/bestprac/bpent/sec1/secthret.mspx#EGAA

Millar, J. (2001). *Quality in Teaching & Learning Framework and Current Risks to Quality and Action Plan.* Retrieved from http://www.ecu.edu.au/GPPS/acad_secret/assets/ctlc/011204agn.pdf

Net, I. Q. (2002). *Enterprise Security: Moving from Chaos to Control with Integrated Security Management.* Retrieved from http://download.netiq.com/CMS/WHITEPAPER/NetIQ_WP_EnterpriseSecurity.pdf

Nicolett, M., & Easley, M. (2002). *The Emerging IT Security Management Market.* Retrieved from http://www.dataquest.com/resources/110800/110845/110845.pdf

NSW. (2003a). *Information Security Guideline for NSW Government – Part 1 Information Security Risk Management.* Retrieved from http://www.albany.edu/acc/courses/ia/inf766/nswinfosecriskmanagementpt11997.pdf

NSW. (2003b). *Information Security Guideline for New South Wales (NSW) Government - Part 2 Examples of Threats and Vulnerabilities.* Retrieved from http://www.oict.nsw.gov.au/content/2.3.17-Security-Pt2.asp

Ryder, R. (2004, February). *Connecticut Part C Stakeholders' Meeting.* Paper presented at the CASE Seminar, Clearwater, FL.

Savage, M. (2006). Protect what's Precious. *Information Security Magazine*, 23-28.

Shittu, H. (2001). *Resource Protection Mechanisms: Implementations in Operating Systems.* Retrieved from http://www.genixcorp.com/papers.html

Shrestha, A. (2004). *Information Security Management System (7799) for an Internet Gateway.* Retrieved from http://www.sans.org/reading_room/whitepapers/iso17799/1454.php

Siponen, M. (2002). *Designing Secure Information Systems and Software.* Unpublished doctoral dissertation, University of Oulu, Finland.

Straub, D. W., & Welke, R. J. (1998). Coping with Systems Risk: Security Planning Models for Management Decision Making. *Management Information Systems Quarterly*, 22, 441–469. doi:10.2307/249551

The Open Group. (2000). *Open Group Technical Standard—Authorization (AZN) API.* Retrieved from http://www.opengroup.org/onlinepubs/9690999199/toc.htm

UB. (2003). *Understanding the .NET Code Access Security.* Retrieved from http://www.codeproject.com/dotnet/UB_CAS_NET.asp

U.S. Coast Guard. (2003). *Marine Operations Risk Guide.* Retrieved from http://www.uscg.mil/hq/g-m/nmc/ptp/morg.pdf

U.S. Department of Defense. (1996). *Goal Security Architecture, Vol. 6, Version 3.0.* Retrieved from http://www2.umassd.edu/swarchresearch/tafim/v6.pdf

U.S. Department of Health and Human Services. (2003a). Health Insurance Reforms: Security Standards. *Federal Register*, 68(38).

U.S. Department of Health and Human Services. (2003b). *Summary of the HIPPA Privacy Rule.* Retrieved from http://www.hhs.gov/ocr/privacysummary.pdf

Vaidyanathan, G., & Devaraj, S. (2003). A Five Framework for analyzing Online Risks in E-Businesses. *Communications of the ACM*, 46(12), 354–361. doi:10.1145/953460.953522

Verdon, D., & McGraw, G. (2004). Risk Analysis in Software Design. *IEEE Security & Privacy*, 2(4), 79–84. doi:10.1109/MSP.2004.55

Whitman, M. E., & Mattoro, H. J. (2005). *Principles of Information Security* (2nd ed.). Thomson Course Technology.

Whitmore, J. J. (2001). A Method for Designing Secure Solutions. *IBM Systems Journal*, *40*(3), 747–768.

Wiederrich, S. (2003). *Enterprise Security—Workshop and Assessment.* Paper presented at the Microsoft Business Technology Symposium.

Wikipedia. (2005). *Security Management.* Retrieved from http://en.wikipedia.org/wiki/Security_management

Yadav, S. B. (2008). SEACON: An Integrated Approach to the Analysis and Design of Secure Enterprise Architecture-Based Computer Networks. *International Journal of Information Security and Privacy*, *2*(1), 1–25.

APPENDIX A

Application of the SVPSS Framework

We apply the SVPSS framework to the XYZ Association case authored by Amarottam Shrestha (Shrestha, 2004) for the SANS Institute. The XYZ Association is located in Australia. Amaorttaam Shrestha used the XYZ Association case to demonstrate the use of PDCA (Plan, Do, Check, Act) process based upon the AS/NZS 7799.2:2003 (NSW, 2003a; Gamma, 2006; Cybertrust, 2005) standard in developing an information security management system (ISMS) for the XYZ Association. We will refer to the case-solution developed by Amarottam Shrestha (Shrestha, 2004) as the Shrestha-solution. The rationale to select the XYZ association case is as follows:

1. The XYZ association case has been developed by a third person. It is a good size case.
2. A solution for the case already exists. The well known PDCA process was used to arrive at the solution for the case. The solution was developed by a third person.
3. An existing solution for the case allows for a comparison with the new solution for the same case.

We follow the Shrestha-solution very closely in order to compare our case-solution with the Shrestha-solution. We follow the same overall process and make similar assumptions as made by the Shrestha-solution (Shrestha, 2004). We will refer to the Australian privacy and legal laws whenever necessary. We follow the PDCA process to apply the SVPSS framework.

Only the Plan phase is relevant to our illustration. The security requirements are determined during the Plan phase of the PDCA process. Therefore, we limit our case illustration to the Plan phase only. As discussed in Section 4.1, the Plan phase with the modified steps is used to discuss the XYZ Association case.

These steps are followed iteratively. The initial ISMS scope and security policy are, for example, refined subsequently after assessing the risks.

ISMS Scope and Security Policy

Here, we establish the scope of ISMS and define the security policy. As per the original case study, the Internet gateway of the XYZ Association is selected as the target system for developing the ISMS. The ISMS scope is specified in detail by Amarottam Shrestha (Shrestha, 2004).

The security policy should address the following policy areas as per the six views of the SVPSS:

- Threat security policy
- Resource security policy
- Process security policy
- Security assessment policy
- Legal security policy
- Security management policy

For the Internet gateway, threat security policy would focus on principles dealing with vulnerabilities and a defense system against various types of threats—natural disasters, viruses, and hackers, etc. The resource security policy will include principles dealing with the availability, confidentiality, and integrity of the XYZ Association resources such as data, Internet services, and the Internet gateway infrastructure. The process security policy will specify rules and guidelines to develop secure processes dealing with the Internet gateway—processes such as email service, member's hosting, and remote access service, etc. The security assessment policy will be used to develop assessment standard, criteria, and measures for evaluating security assessment activities such as email service and web hosting assessment. The legal security policy will include rules to deal with privacy and legal laws affecting email, web hosting, and other membership data. The security management policy will include a plan for the overall security of the Internet gateway and guidelines for administering and monitoring Internet gateway security.

Risk Assessment Approach

We will follow the risk management methodology based upon the Australian and New Zealand Standard AS/NZS 4360:2004 (Australia, 2004) and the risk assessment (RA) methodology suggested by the Centers for Medicare & Medicaid Services (CMS) (CMS, 2002). The following risk assessment steps are adapted from the AS/NZS 4360:2004:

- Establish the Context (Identify assets)
- Identify Risks.
- Analyze risks
- Evaluate risks
- Treat risks
- Monitor and review

We provide a brief description of the above steps. Please refer to AS/NZS 4360:2004 (Australia, 2004) and CMS (CMS, 2002) for more details.

Establishment of Context

This step involves determining the context in which the target system operates. It covers understanding the strategic, the organizational, and the risk management contexts. It includes the determination of assets and setting the risk evaluation criteria for each asset. Here, we will focus on the later two activities—identification of assets and determination of risk evaluation criteria.

Identification of Assets

The SVPSS framework suggests that assets/resources be examined from six perspectives. The various perspectives facilitate the job of identifying a more complete set of assets. The XYZ Association's assets under various views are listed in Table A1. This is obviously not a list of all assets. The purpose of the case study is to illustrate the use of the SVPSS framework and not present a complete solution.

Table 1. List of assets /resources for XYZ association under various views

Views	Assets	Description
Threat	1. Physical location 2. Operation 3. Internet Gateway Infrastructure	These assets are more of a physical nature.
Resource	1. Technical Expertise 2. XYZ Association's Internet Services 3. XYZ Association Data	These resources/assets are more of intangible nature
Legal	4. Compliance to the Privacy Act 1988, as Amended 2000 5. Compliance to the Spam Act 2003	Being in compliance is an intangible asset of a company
Management	6. Policy 7. Accountability Guidelines	Policy and accountability guidelines are intangible but important assets to be maintained by the management
Process	8. Process Steps 9. Process Control 10. Process Interface	Process Steps, Process Control, and Process Interface are important parts of a process structure.
Assessment	11. Assessment Criteria 12. Assessment Method 13. Assessment Standards	Assessment Criteria, Assessment Method, and Assessment Standards are important ingredients of effective security assessment activities. Inappropriate and inadequate assessment criteria, for example, can lead to missed conformance

Risk Evaluation Criteria

Here, the XYZ Association management should specify acceptable level of security risks. We assume that a risk level of "Low" is considered acceptable to the XYZ Association, and any risk level of "Medium" or higher will require treatment (control) to reduce it to an acceptable level (Shrestha, 2004).

Identification of Risks

Here we identify risks to assets that could lead to adverse effects to the XYZ Association. According to the AS/NZS 4360:2004 security management standard, the emphasis is on determining what, where, when, why, and how something could happen (Australia, 2004). The identified risks under this step are listed under the "Sources of Risk" column in the risk register shown in Table A.3. A security risk register is a tabular representation of details about identified risks and security requirements for reducing those risks. A security risk register can be used to document the outputs of the risk assessment process.

Risk Analysis

We use the same risk analysis method as used by Amarottam Shrestha (Shrestha, 2004) and described by the Centers for Medicare & Medicaid Services (CMS) (CMS, 2002). For each source of risk in the risk register, we estimate its likelihood of occurrence and the consequence (impact) if the risk materializes. The levels of likelihood of occurrence are Negligible, Very Low, Low, Medium, High, Very High, and Extreme. The levels of severity of impact (consequence) are Insignificant, Minor, Significant, Damaging, Serious, and Critical. In Table A.3, fire has a likelihood estimate of low and a consequence estimate of critical. A risk level is then computed based upon the likelihood of occurrence and its impact. It is defined as:

$$RiskLevel =$$
$$LikelihoodofOccurrenceLevel * Impact\ Severity\ Level$$

The above formula computes a set of risk levels that are used to evaluate a risk.

Risk Evaluation

Risk levels, based upon the above formula, are Nil, Low, Medium, High, Critical, and Extreme (CMS, 2002). These risk levels are used to determine the level of a particular risk. For example, as shown in Table A.3, the resultant risk level of fire is computed as High. The risk level can be given a numerical value to specify its rating. A numerical value is assigned to a risk level as shown in Table A2 (Shrestha, 2004).

A priority level of a risk can then be computed based upon its risk rating. We subtract the acceptable risk level rating of a risk from its risk rating to determine its priority level. The formula for the priority level is given below:

Table 2. Risk rating table

Risk Level	Numerical Rating
Nil	0
Low	1
Medium	2
High	3
Critical	4
Extreme	5

$$Priority\ Level =$$
$$Risk\ Level\ Rating - Acceptable\ Risk\ Level\ Rating$$

For example, as shown in Table A.3, the risk priority level of fire is 2, given an acceptable risk level of low. The higher the number the higher is the priority rating of a risk.

Risk Treatment (Selection of Security Requirements and Mechanisms (Controls) for Managing Risks)

Once the priority levels are determined, appropriate security requirements and mechanisms should be identified to reduce the risk level of a risk to its acceptable level. Table A.3 shows the needed security requirements and mechanisms. Security requirements and mechanisms are recommended for every risk with priority level 1 and above. The requirements and the mechanisms are based upon the SVPSS framework. As mentioned earlier, Table A.3 is presented as an illustration and it does not show all possible risks.

Other related topics such as classification of security mechanisms, ISMS management structure, a detailed description of security policies, and statement of applicability (SOA) are not covered here due to space and other limitations.

The above case solution demonstrates the usefulness of the SVPSS framework. It provides better structure and guidelines to identify assets and possible risks to those assets. An extensive set of security requirements and mechanisms help analyst select appropriate measures for reducing risks under various security views.

Figure 2. Table A3. Risk register showing showing security risks and requirements under various views

Views	Assets	Sources of Risk	Threat Likelihood Estimate	Consequence, if the threat is realized	Resultant Risk Level	Acceptable Risk Level	Risk Priority Level	Security Requirements
Threat	Physical location	Fire	Low	Critical	High	Low	2	1. Protect against fire 2. Backup Data 3. Store backup-data remotely
		Earthquake	Very Low	Damaging	Low	Low	0	
	Internet Gateway Infrastructure	Wrong Configuration of the Security Enforcing Device	Low	Damaging	Medium	Nil	2	1. Monitor resource integrity 2. Check Resource integrity 3. Adjust resource integrity
	Operation	Technical Failure	Medium	Minor	Low	Low	0	
		Power failure	Low	Minor	Low	Low	0	
		Operational Staff Error	High	Significant	High	Nil	3	1. Verify and confirm input data and commands 2. Save data periodically
	XYZ Associations Internet Services	Critical Network Device Failure	Low	Significant	Medium	Low	1	1. Check resource availability 2. Monitor resource availability 3. Maintain redundancy in system
		Denial of Service Attack from the Internet	Very High	Significant	High	Low	2	1. Protect against Denial of Service 2. Protect against intrusion 3. Protect against malicious code
Resource	XYZ Association Data	Hackers from the Internet	Low	Serious	High	Nil	3	1. Monitor resource integrity 2. Check Resource integrity 3. Adjust resource integrity 4. Monitor resource confidentiality 5. Check resource confidentiality 6. Adjust resource confidentiality
		Insider Attack	Low	Significant	Medium	Nil	2	1. Monitor resource integrity 2. Check Resource integrity 3. Adjust resource integrity 4. Monitor resource confidentiality 5. Check resource confidentiality 6. Adjust resource confidentiality
	Technical expertise	Loss of Key Personnel	Medium	Significant	Medium	Low	1	1. Protect from loss of key personnel
Legal	Compliance to the Privacy Act 1988, as Amended 2000	Violation of National Privacy Principles	Medium	Damaging	High	Nil	3	1. Establish rules for handling personal data 2. Identify Personal Identifiable Information (PII) 3. Establish proper access control for PII
	Compliance to the Spam Act 2003	Violation of Spam Code of Practice	High	Minor	Medium	Low	1	1. Analyze legal risks for on-line environment 2. Comply with the Spam Act of 2003

Figure 2 continued

Views	Assets	Sources of Risk	Threat Likelihood Estimate	Consequence if the threat is realized	Resultant Risk Level	Acceptable Risk Level	Risk Priority Level	Security Requirements
Management	Policy	Inadequate Policy	Low	Serious	High	Nil	3	1. Identify faulty policy 2. Take corrective action 3. Establish security policy and procedures 4. Review security policy and procedures 5. Monitor security
	Accountability Guidelines	Vague Accountability for Individuals	Medium	Damaging	High	Nil	3	1. Review accountability policy 2. Refine accountability-assignment
		Lack of Accountability Standards	Low	Significant	Medium	Nil	2	1. Review accountability policy 2. Review accountability standards 3. Establish accountability standards
	Process Steps	Poorly defined Process Steps	Very Low	Damaging	Low	Nil	1	1. Evaluate process 2. Rectify weak points/steps of the process 3. Secure each steps of the process 4. Train users in the secure process
Process	Process Control	Lack of Staff Training	Medium	Damaging	High	Nil	3	1. Train users in the secure process 2. Review secure process
		Lack of Monitoring	High	Minor	Medium	Low	1	1. Review process 2. Establish process ownership 3. Separate duties of actors involved in the process 4. Train users in the secure process 5. Review process policy
	Process Interface	Lack of Interface Design Standards	Low	Significant	Medium	Low	1	1. Review process policy 2. Review process design standards 3. Evaluate process

Figure 2 continued

Views	Assets	Sources of Risk	Threat Likelihood Estimate	Consequence, if the threat is realized	Resultant Risk Level	Acceptable Risk Level	Risk Priority Level	Security Requirements
Assessment	Assessment Criteria	Inadequate Criteria	Medium	Significant	Medium	Low	1	1. Evaluate assessment criteria 2. Define assessment criteria 3. Define measures for each criterion 4. Collect data on measures 5. Evaluate the measures' effectiveness
		Vague Criteria	Medium	Significant	Medium	Low	1	1. Evaluate assessment criteria 2. Define assessment criteria 3. Define measures for each criterion 4. Collect data on measures 5. Evaluate the measures' effectiveness
	Assessment Method	No Assessment Method	Low	Significant	Medium	Nil	2	1. Define assessment method 2. Train users in assessment
		Inadequate Assessment Training	Low	Significant	Medium	Low	1	1. Train users in assessment 2. Evaluate assessment policy
	Assessment Standards	Inadequate Standards	Low	Significant	Medium	Low	1	1. Evaluate assessment policy 2. Define assessment standards 3. Train users in assessment

This work was previously published in International Journal of Information Security and Privacy, Volume 4, Issue 1, edited by Hamid Nemati, pp. 61-92, copyright 2010 by IGI Publishing (an imprint of IGI Global).

Chapter 5
Are Online Privacy Policies Readable?

M. Sumeeth
University of Alberta, Canada

R.I. Singh
University of Alberta, Canada

J. Miller
University of Alberta, Canada

ABSTRACT

This paper examines the question of are on-line privacy policies understandable to the users of the Internet? This examination is undertaken by collecting privacy policies from the most popular sites on the Internet, and analyzing their readability using a number of readability measures. The study finds that the results are consistent regardless of the readability measure utilized. The authors also compare their findings with the results from previous studies. The authors conclude that, on average, privacy policies are becoming more readable. However, these policies are still beyond the capability of a large section of Internet users, and roughly 20% of the policies require an educational level approaching a post-graduate degree to support comprehension.

1. INTRODUCTION

Human readable privacy policies are widely used in websites as they allow users to interpret privacy policies without machine intervention. An important factor in these policies is their readability. The Federal Trade Commission (FTC) describes a privacy policy to be a comprehensive description of: a domain's collection of user-related informa-

tion, located on a website that may be accessed by clicking on a hyperlink (Federal Trade Commission, 1998).

The Graham Leach Bliley Act (GLBA), states that policies must be "clear and conspicuous". GLBA's privacy requirements state "organizations or institutions should post a notice that is reasonably understandable and designed to call attention to the nature and significance of the information in the notice" (Anton, 2004). Hence,

DOI: 10.4018/978-1-4666-0026-3.ch005

privacy policies are examined for their coherence, readability and information they convey to users.

Klare defines readability as "the ease of understanding or comprehension due to the style of writing." (Klare, 1963). This definition focuses on the writing style of privacy policies. Similar emphasis on writing style and clarity is mentioned by Hargis et. al. (1998). The SMOG readability formula defines readability as: "the degree to which a given class of people find certain reading matter compelling and comprehensible."(McLaughlin, 1969). This definition stresses the interaction between the text and a class of readers of known characteristics such as reading skill, prior knowledge, and motivation. Perhaps, Dale and Chall provided the most comprehensive definition of readability:

The sum total (including all the interactions) of all those elements within a given piece of printed material that affect the success a group of readers have with it. The success is the extent to which they understand it, read it at optimal speed, and find it interesting. (Dale, 1949).

The focus of most readability definitions is on clarity, ease-of-readability, and level of comprehension. However, the question of are current privacy policies published on websites meeting these requirements has received limited attention. These policies are usually long and unstructured documents that are difficult for users to read and understand. Lack of clarity and understanding of privacy policies has resulted in several privacy-related complaints. Hence, we urgently need more research, which initially assesses the readability of these policies; and if they are found it be deficient, research to improve their readability.

The remainder of this paper seeks to address this first research question and is structured as follows: Section 2 covers some legal issues regarding privacy policies. Section 3 briefly outlines the requirements of a readability policy. Section 4 introduces the approaches used to estimate read-

ability in this study. Section 5 reviews previous empirical research on this topic; and Section 6 introduces the study's experimental design and analyses the principally results from our study. Section 7 provides a comparison of the results from our study (Section 6) against previous results (Section 5). And Section 8 concludes the paper.

2. PRIVACY POLICIES: THEIR REQUIREMENTS AND RESTRICTIONS

An overview of privacy policies would seem to be the first order of business at hand. To start with, are privacy policies likely to be read? And then there are also questions about legalities, user characteristics and privacy policies. Readability is an issue to be addressed as well as the contents of an ideal privacy policy. These issues and other will be explored further in this section.

Regarding how probable is it that a privacy statement gets read; is easy to bring forth anecdotal evidence when it comes to speculating how likely privacy statements are to be read. Far more difficult is to find empirical evidence on the subject. In a study of 2,468 adult US internet users, it was found that reading rates are linked to several factors. One factor is the concern for privacy. Another is positive ideas about the understandability of the notice. Related to this are higher degrees of trust in the privacy notice. (Milne & Culin, 2004). The reader is referred to Milne and Culin (2004) for further reading.

A literature review was conducted to find out the implications of a privacy policy being legally and contractually binding. A contract can contain almost anything; the question is if it is enforceable. And therein lies the starting point of the literature search, namely what laws apply to privacy in which countries. Generally speaking there are two levels of law governing privacy: legal jurisdictional laws and sectoral laws. Legal jurisdictional laws relate to the "laws of the land" and sectoral laws "govern the usage of sensitive information within a given industrial sector". (Reay et al., 2009) Numerous nations including Canada, USA, the EU, Australia and Japan have enacted some sort of legislation regarding privacy. Legally binding thus has different meaning in different jurisdictions

Interestingly, a number of commonalities between nations emerge when examining legalities. Reay et al., (2009) shows that web sites do not even masquerade to follow all privacy laws in their legal jurisdiction.

Another study quotes an eminent article on privacy that defines privacy as the "right to be left alone". This article was written in 1890 and published in the Harvard Law Review. Clearly privacy has remained an unresolved legal issue for the past 120 years. The article goes on to examine the privacy policies of the Fortune 50 US companies. What is interesting here is that many studies use the most popular websites on the Internet; this study uses the 50 largest US companies. US privacy legislation follows the line of fair information practices, though the study found that at one point the law lacked any "aggressive enforcement". The new subset of internet sites was interestingly enough, found to follow the results of popular web sites surveyed over time. Thus the reader can infer that two quite different web site subsets produced overall the same results. (Peslak, 2005)

Fitting user characteristics, Internet use, and privacy policies together is more complicated than one might think. Consider the use of mobile devices; is a privacy policy appropriate on the desktop appropriate for a tiny device where one has to pay a near premium for Internet access? Add to this the fact that mobile devices are mostly used in an unsteady manner in environments that are less than optimal for concentration. Nonetheless (Singh et al, 2010) have explored the question how much comprehension drops moving from the desktop to the mobile device and if this makes the privacy policies in their current format utterly worthless.

Adding to the difficulty of comprehending privacy policies on the mobile device are limited screen size, display resolution, font size, paging and color support; all these factors affect readability. No standards exist for input devices on mobile systems among manufacturers; standards for users with disabilities seems a long way off. A mobile device is used in a mobile environment that is shaky and does not support reading physiology i.e. the way we have learned to read. Furthermore, it is in the mobile device users' interests to reduce pricey internet access costs, it is in the internet providers interests to maintain profits.

All is not lost. Singh et al (2010) point out that while natural language privacy statements are unlikely to ever succeed in the mobile world other graphical options hold solid promise. A format based on a method used by the UK Food Standards Agency using a "signpost" format that uses a graphic based on a set of traffic lights for food labelling. Such a graphic is cross cultural in the mobile world and equally important represents the minimal amount of information in a picture format. Initial trials suggest that this method was understandable, promote easier comprehension, and articulate. On inspection, such a format far better supports reading physiology especially in a mobile environment.

In regards to readability, is it totally defined from the point of view of the end user? Remember that the end user was only a reader before they became a computer user. Readability formulas came into play long ago in areas such as Journalism and Advertising Studies before they appeared in Software Engineering. So the safe bet is to say "yes" to this question.

From a legal point of view, it seems all one needs to be aware of are legal jurisdictional laws and sector laws. Ultimately, manual business processes are based on societal laws and so should automated processes. Regarding these processes Brodie et al, (2005) did a survey followed by an interview of thirteen select respondents. Most of the interview sessions were based on a scenario given by the respondent that concerned the Personal Information (PI) flow through their organization. The participants stated that protecting PI requires an intricate approach. Amongst the facets that must be addressed by the organization are how to create an implementable privacy policy, educate the people who work with the policy and make sure they are aware of its importance, clarify where PI is stored and used in their business processes and then develop and implement manual and technical procedures for the policies they have developed. (Brodie et al, 2005).

Has anyone explored the relationship between the contents of a web site's privacy statement and its readability? Readability is fundamentally a human trait and the issue represents a tough challenge for Human Computer Interface namely how to present a great deal of complex and critical information to a user without overpowering them. (Jensen & Potts, 2004a). Reay et al., (2007) state that according to an analysis of online privacy statements less than half of total Internet users lack the education to correctly comprehend the legal jargon used or even technologies used in the process (e.g. cookies) (Raey et al., 2007)

Reading comprehension levels are related to educational acquirement and in order to reach the general population of the US, research says that effective communication has to be targeted at the 6-8th grade level (NCES, 1992). At the very least privacy policies are unnecessarily long, forcing readers to read lengthy passages of text that has very unlikely changed since the last time they visited the site. (Jensen & Potts, 2004a). More troubling is the practice of assuming that access implies consent. In order to access the privacy statement the user has to access the home page and then the privacy page. This implies a no win situation where the user must accept the privacy policy in order to access it. In a survey of 64 current policies by Jenson and Potts (2004a), all of them contained statements to this effect.

An ideal privacy policy should be based on legal principles agreed upon by countries involved.

US Fair Information Practices (FIP) are based on a subset of Organization for Economic Development (OECD) guidelines. The OECD consists of 30 member countries. In the US, Fair Information Practices form the basis of their privacy laws and consists of five principles.

- Notice: Businesses must tell consumers what data they collect on consumers and how they intend to use it
- Choice: Consumers should be allowed to complain if their data is misused
- Access: Consumers should have access to their information and the right to make corrections
- Integrity/Security: Businesses are obligated to protect the collection and storage of consumer information
- Redress/ Enforcement: Real enforcement is needed to ensure that businesses follow their policies

It is the intention of the above principles that informed choices and enforced action is part of privacy policies in the area where they have jurisdiction.

3. REQUIREMENTS OF HUMAN READABLE POLICIES

There is a need to improve current web design to help Internet users better navigate through, and comprehend, these policies; and to create and increase users' awareness about privacy while on the Internet. The following four aspects are seen as important for human readable policies: (Bolchini, 2004):

- Content: The language used in privacy policies is often difficult for users to understand. They usually contain a fair amount of technical and legal details. The lack of specific domain knowledge handicaps users from quickly understanding the content and potential issues in submitting their personal data.

- Structure: Different websites use different templates and structures to convey privacy practices to users. This can be confusing for users who generally look for specific information at a particular place in policies. For example, some websites may include legal information at the beginning of the policy, while others may start by explaining the strategy and technology used to protect information. Others organize their policy's content with a list of frequently asked questions (FAQ's). The lack of standard templates, structure and organization of information leads to poor readability.

- Navigation: The navigational structure of most present-day policies is independent of their context of use; they neither cater to an individual user's needs nor provide facilities to customized user-specific (policy) information. All users navigating the website will have to consider the entire document. Regardless of what the user is looking for or doing on the site, the policy always contains the same information and in the same order. To reach and retrieve such information from a privacy policy, users must navigate the site across several web pages. Although the user is interested in specific information, they must carefully read the entire document most of which may not be

of any relevance to the described context of use.

- Accessibility: The accessibility of privacy policies can also be less than ideal. The link to the privacy document is often difficult to spot, many times being designed as a recurrent pattern (perhaps implemented in a frame), in small font at the very bottom of the page. Even if it is accessible from every page of the site, it is not customized with regard to the content of any specific page.

Addressing these aspects is important to better educate users and enhance the readability of privacy information. Furthermore, the readability level of policies must cater to the education levels of online Internet population.

3.1 Readability and Literacy Level of Internet Users

There is a strong correlation between user literacy, education and income (NTIA, 2002). As computers and Internet access are still relatively expensive, online user population seem to have an above average education and literacy rate. Table 1 provides a relation between education levels and Internet usage in the US. Notice that a larger proportion (roughly 50%) of the US adult population has an education at the high school-level. This, however, constitutes a smaller percent (around 25%) of the online Internet population.

Table 1. Relation between education levels and Internet usage in the US. (Jensen & Potts, 2005, NTIA02)

Education Level	General Population (% of total population)	Internet Population (% of online population)
Less Than High School	15.5	3.8
High School/GED	32.4	24.5
Some College/Associates	25.6	30.5
Bachelors Degree	17.7	26.6
Beyond Bachelors Degree	9.2	14.6

Table 2. A forecast of Internet user penetration in various countries (adapted from IWS, 2008)

	2008	2009	2010	2011
US	193.9	200.1	206.2	211.3
% population	66.6%	68.1%	69.6%	70.6%
Canada	22.6	23.3	24.1	24.8
% population	67.1%	68.5%	70.3%	71.9%
Australia	14	14.4	14.8	15.3
% population	68.0%	69.2%	70.8%	72.5%
China	181.2	206.6	227.3	245.5
% population	13.6%	15.4%	16.9%	18.1%
India	41.5	50.6	60.7	71.6
% population	3.6%	4.3%	5.1%	6.0%
Japan	90.9	92.5	94.0	95.5
% population	71.4%	72.7%	73.9%	75.1%
S. Korea	36.5	37.2	37.8	38.4
% population	74.2%	75.3%	76.2%	77.3%
France	33.4	35.8	37.5	38.9
% population	54.5%	58.2%	60.9%	62.9%
Germany	44.1	47.2	49.8	52.1
% population	53.5%	57.4%	60.5%	63.4%
Italy	31.4	32.7	35.4	36.2
% population	54%	56.3%	60.9%	62.4%
Spain	20.1	21.5	22.7	24
% population	49.6%	53.1%	56.0%	59.1%
U.K.	39.1	42.3	44.2	45.0
% population	64.2%	69.2%	72.1%	73.2%

A large number of Internet users have at least a college level education.

A forecast of Internet user penetration in different countries is provided in Table 2. It can be seen that the percentage of Internet users in developed countries is far higher than the developing countries. This disparity in the penetration can be attributed to the education and literacy rate. With an understanding of the population's literacy rate, we can examine the readability of present-day privacy policies.

Table 2 provides a forecast of the number of Internet users between 2008 and 2011. It is interesting to note that the Internet user population is expected to significantly increase over this short period. Clearly, the authors of privacy policies need to be aware of this explosion in the Internet population as it will have a profound impact of literacy levels and hence demand a reconsideration of their privacy policies. This change of population will clearly impact the readability of these policies; hence readability in this context is a "moving target" and demands that this issue is re-examined on a regular basis as the readability of privacy policies may experience detrimental ageing effects.

4. READABILITY EVALUATION METHODS

Two methods are commonly used to evaluate readability of text documents: readability formulas (Chall, 1988; Davison 1984; Klare, 1975) and the cloze test (Taylor, 1953; Coleman, 1963). Readability formulas are statistical-based methods that offer objective evaluation of privacy policies. Readability formulas are useful for benchmarking readability scores. Authors can use them to get a quick feedback and amend their writing. Cloze test evaluation, on the other hand, is subjective. It requires authors to interact with target audience to get a feedback on their writing. It tests readers' domain knowledge and language comprehension. Cloze test evaluation is extremely expensive in terms of time and effort, and hence is only commonly used in extreme highe value situations or were extremely small sample sizes are acceptable.

Readability formulas measure comprehension of text passages and evaluate them in terms of grade-level. A comprehensive survey of readability formulas can be found in (Klare, 1977; Bormuth, 1966). Several new formulas have been developed over the years, some for general applications and others for evaluating specific materials. Readability formulas are used in evaluating documents written in various fields such as business (Stevens, 1992), legal, health (Eysenbach, 2002). Recent works by (Hochhauser, 2002; Jensen & Potts, 2004a) have focused on evaluating the readability of privacy policies. In this paper, we shall address the following research questions:

- Has the readability of policies changed over time? Are present-day policies are more or less readable than those in the past? We address this first aspect a thorough numerical comparison of our study with those of Hochhauser (2002); Anton et al. (2004) and Jensen and Potts (2004b, 2005) .

- Do the widely used formulas concur on the readability of present-day privacy policies? Formulas differ in the way they measure readability. We shall study if the evaluation of policies using different formulas result in a similar conclusion.

- Are current day privacy policies readable to current and future Internet populations?

Basically, readability formulas capture essential characteristics that correlate highly with reading-ease (or difficulty). For example, the formulas account for the following underlying features of text that plays a role in determining readability:

- Average sentence length, length of words;
- Number of prepositional phrases per 100 words;
- Number of different hard words not in the Dale-Chall list;
- Number of affixes (prefix and suffix), personal words; and
- Number of syllables, monosyllables.

Klare and others (Klare, 1975; Bormuth, 1966; Dale; 1949; Flesch, 1974) have noted that the complexity of words and sentences are the essential features determining readability; complex sentence structures and abstract words are harder to comprehend than text with simple sentences and common words.

4.1 Readability Formulas

Some of the widely used formulas include: the Flesch readability score (FRES), the Flesch grade level (FGL), the Dale-Chall index, the Fog index, the Fry graph, and the SMOG grading formula.

Flesch Readability Score (FRES)

This is perhaps the most widely (Flesch, 1974) used readability metric; it is commonly used to

Table 3. Mapping FRES to readability "levels"

FRES	Readability
0-29	Very Difficult
30-49	Difficult
50-59	Fairly Difficult
60-69	Standard
70-79	Fairly Easy
80-89	Easy
90-100	Very Easy

Table 4. DCI to grade level translation

DCI	Grade Level
4.0-5	1-4
5-5.9	5-6
6-6.9	7-8
7-7.9	9-10
8-8.9	11-12
9-9.9	13-15
10+	16+

evaluate the readability of school texts, legal documents and insurance policies. The formula for FRES is given by

$$FRES = 206.835 - (1.015)\left(\frac{words}{sentences} - ASL\right) - (84.6)\left(\frac{syllables}{words} - ASW\right)$$

where words, sentences, syllables, ASL and ASW denote the number of words, sentences, syllables, average syllables per word, and average sentence length in words respectively. FRES lies between 0 and 100, where higher values denote greater readability. From the formula, we can notice that longer sentences and words result in a lower FRES. The FRES mapping to readability "levels" is shown in Table 3.

Flesch Grade Level (FGL)

The FGL provides a grade level required for comprehending text documents. The formula for computing FGL is given by

$$FGL = (0.39 * ASL) + (11.8 * ASW) - 15.59.$$

The FGL index lies between 1 and 21, where a lower grade denotes easier text. FGL, like FRES, depends on average sentence length and word length; longer sentences and words results in higher FGL.

Dale-Chall Index (DCI)

The Dale-Chall index is similar to FRES and FGL in a sense that it accounts for sentence length and word complexity. However, word complexity in DCI is measured based on whether each word is in a list of acceptable words. The following formula is used to compute DCI

$$DCI = 0.1579 * PDW + 0.0496 * ASL + 3.6365$$

PDW denotes the percentage of "difficult" words ("difficult words" are defined as not appearing in the Dale-Chall word-list[1]). DCI is flexible, in the sense that, the word-list can accommodate new words. The translation of Dale-Chall index to grade level is given in Table 4.

Fog Index (FI)

The Fog Index is similar to FGL, but instead of counting all of the syllables in a word, it accounts the percentage of words with more than three syllables. The formula to calculate the Fog index is given by

$$FI = \left(0.4 * ASL + 100 * \left(\frac{complex\ words}{words}\right)\right),$$

where complex words denotes the number of words with greater than three syllables. The Fog index maps directly to grade-level.

SMOG Index (SMOG)

SMOG index is simpler and faster to compute than other readability formulas. The formula to compute the SMOG index is given by

$$SMOG = \left(3 + \sqrt{pollysyllable\ count}\right),$$

where the polysyllable count is the number of words of three or more syllables. A translation from thr SMOG index to grade-level is provided in Table 5. Generally, a grade level of six or less is targeted.

Fry Graph

The Fry graph consists of the average length of sentences (on the y-axis) mapped against average number of syllables (on the x-axis). For a given text-passage, the average sentence-length and average number of syllables are marked on the Fry graph. The intersection determines the readability level of the text passage. This is illustrated in Figure 1.

5. PREVIOUS INVESTIGATIONS

Relatively few investigations have focused on the evaluation of privacy polices using readability formulas; at this point of time, the authors are only aware of three published surveys:

- Jensen and Potts (2004b; 2005) evaluated the accessibility, usability and readability of websites' privacy policies primarily for health organizations. Jensen and Potts (2005)

Table 5. SMOG index to grade-level translation (adapted from SRC, 2008)

SMOG Grade	Educational Level
0 – 6	low-literate
7	junior high school
8	junior high school
9	some high school
10	some high school
11	some high school
12	high school graduate
13 – 15	Some college
16	university degree
17 – 18	post-graduate studies
19+	post-graduate degree

also contains evaluations for several "popular" sites;
- Anton et. al. (2004) measured readability of privacy documents including Legal Disclaimers and Terms of Use; and
- Hochhauser (2002) used readability formulas to analyze the privacy policies of financial institutions.

Jensen and Potts Study

Jensen and Potts (2004b) note that a lack of standardization and regulatory bodies has resulted in significant variations among privacy policies in terms of language used and the information policies convey. To overcome this, standardization procedures and bodies are slowly emerging; for example, the Health Insurance Portability and Accountability Act (HIPAA) (2008), the Gramm-Leach-Bliley Act (GLBA) (Federal Trade Commission, 2008b), the Children's Online Privacy Protection Act (COPA) (Federal Trade Commission, 2008a), and so forth.

Before posting the policies online, the policies have to undergo a certification process. The standardization bodies enforce consistency among policies and require certain minimum information

Figure 1. Fry graph depicting readability levels

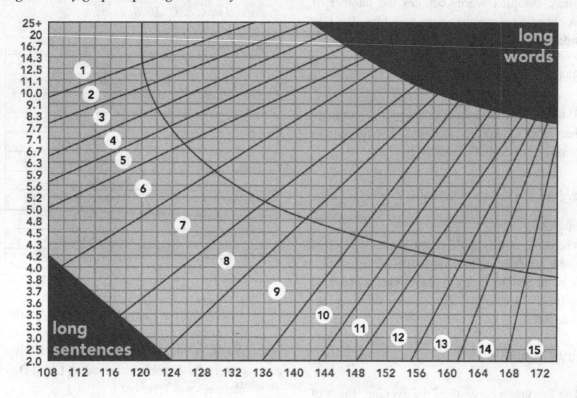

to be present in the policies. The main focus of (Jensen & Potts, 2004a) was to evaluate whether such a standardization procedure, specifically the HIPAA process, meets the needs of users such as accessibility, readability, and content. The study undertaken in (Jensen & Potts, 2004a) involved the evaluation and comparison of policies before and after the certification process. 18 health sector companies were chosen for the study, the companies were from an earlier study by Anton et. al. (Anton, 2002). The authors considered two readability formulas for evaluating websites' policies: the Flesch Readability Score (FRES) and the Flesch Grade Level (FGL). Their results are tabulated in Table 6. From Table 6 we see that, on average, privacy polices are difficult to read. The following general conclusions were drawn on the readability of privacy policies (Jensen & Potts, 2004b):

- The readability score (FGL) is lower than the average education level of Internet users (14.4) but higher than that of the US population (13.5). The policy with the maximum FGL (17.96) requires an education level of post graduation. The minimum score was 11.50. It was concluded that a large percentage of the population are unlikely to comprehend the majority of online privacy policies.

- The readability of health care policies after HIPAA did not show any significant improvements. The average value of the FRES and FGL readability estimates changed from 36.5 and 13.4, to 35.5 and 14.03 respectively. The authors therefore concluded that certification and enforcements brought about by HIPAA did not considerably affect readability.

Table 6. Readability of health-care sites (adapted from Jensen & Potts, 2004a)

Site Name	July 2001			September 2003		
	Words	Flesch Score	Grade	Words	Flesch Score	Grade
AETNA	806	39.4	14.2	802	37.3	14.14
AFLAC	1930	30.4	14.98	2160	26.4	15.37
BCBS	638	40.2	15.2	716	37.2	14.98
CIGNA	875	45.2	10.70	1115	42.2	11.50
EHealthInsurance	1546	23.1	15.35	2113	29.9	14.03
Kaiser Permanente	689	32.0	14.11	4678	40.5	13.45
OnlineHealthPlan	1390	31.9	13.83	N/A		
CornerDrugStore	1906	37.6	12.98	N/A		
DeestinationRx	1925	38.7	13.20	1871	36	13.46
Drugstore	1499	38.7	13.75	2139	37.8	14.12
Eckerd	1340	35.5	14.02	6404	34	16.24
HealthAllies	1025	34.5	13.81	1414	29.3	14.94
HealthCentral	1283	41.1	13.10	675	38.5	13.31
IVillage	3382	28.9	15.89	3681	26.2	16.21
PrescriptionOnline	753	33.8	12.69	N/A		
PrescriptionsByMail	1082	39.9	12.90	706	36.8	12.65
Bayer	760	40.9	13.10	953	41.4	13.6
Glaxo	448	39.5	12.60	396	37.9	13.19
Lilly(Eli)	507	40.4	13.60	1014	35.2	14.76
Novartis(Ciba)	1340	39.7	13.50	1366	36.5	13.68
Pfizer	393	41.1	12.10	331	35.8	12.39
Pharmacia	957	38.7	13.08	N/A		
Average	1203.4	36.5	13.45	1807.4	35.5	14.03
Standard Deviation	1216	5.1	1.16	1613.7	4.7	1.26

In Jensen and Potts (2005), these authors provide the same estimates for many of the health-oriented web-sites from (Jensen & Potts, 2004a); in addition, theyt provide readability estimates for a large number of "popular" sites, these are shown in Table 7.

Anton et al. Study

A similar study undertaken by Anton et. al. (2004) involved the evaluation and comparison of policies before and after the HIPAA process. 9 health sector companies were chosen for the study. Two sets of privacy documents were used: pre-HIPAA policies included policies prior to summer 2000 and post-HIPAA set included policies dated September 2003 or later. FRES and FGL scores were computed on the two sets, the results are given in Table 8.

Anton et. al. showed that the readability of most chosen sample-policies decreased after the HIPAA process. The average FGL increased nearly one grade-level from 13.3 to 14.2 and average FRES decreased from 39.6 to 34.9. The authors concluded that HIPAA process has resulted in less readable healthcare policies.

Table 7. Readability of Popular Sample (adapted from Jensen & Potts, 2005)

Website	Words	FRES	FGL	Website	Words	FRES	FGL	Website	Words	FRES	FGL
AOL	1101	34.2	14.8	Classmates	3542	33.9	14.57	Walmart	2098	45.2	12.07
MSN	6222	41.5	13.18	Weather Channel	2510	32.5	14.84	United Online	4403	29.7	14.04
Yahoo	3651	37.9	12.49	Overture	1641	31	14.20	News Corp.	2098	15.6	17.96
Ebay	5216	36.5	13.66	eUniverse	1099	22.2	17.14	Travelocity	403	26.3	14.53
Google	657	45.7	11.68	Vivendi	1729	26.9	16.02	Gannett Sites	No common policy		
Terra Lycos	5522	34.7	13.96	Verizon	2090	34	12.79	Dell	2274	45.4	11.87
About	2173	35.0	13.94	EA Online	2984	31.4	14.84	America Greeting	3693	40	12.85
Amazon	2427	37.8	14.67	Expedia	4362	28.7	14.60	Earthlink	1788	28.5	15.7
Gator	1786	31.1	15.01	SBC	4693	35.2	12.97	HP	3301	34.5	13.44
Symantec	2215	38.6	12.99	ATT	1946	28.7	12.54	NY Times	3472	46.2	12.23
Excite	3298	31.2	15.39	Sony Online	3948	30	16.88	Orbitz	3308	40.2	13.34
Viacom	No Common policy			Monster Property	2752	34.6	14.82	McAfee	2160	33.9	13.03
Info Space	2033	34.2	13.76	iVillage	3681	26.2	16.2	Adobe	2417	30.8	15.17
Walt Disney	3170	44.5	11.7	Ask Jeeves	1256	34.6	14.25	Trip Network	No common policy		
CNET	1723	36	13.26	Weatherbug.com	3461	29.4	15.2	Buy.com	5773	39.6	13.38
Real.com	4306	36.4	13.6	Dealtime	868	43.7	12.68	NFL Internet	2708	33.7	14.27
				Cox Enterprise	1755	22.7	17.4	Comcast	1158	35.9	14.21
								Average	2806	34.2	14.2
								Std. Dev.	1345	6.5	1.5

Hochhauser Study

Hochhauser (2002) studied the readability of 34 privacy policies taken from the financial sector; these results are provided in Table 9. The average values for FRES and FGL were found to be 34 and 15.6. Hochhauser (2002) showed that a grade level of greater than 13 was required to read these policies. FRES evaluation of policies resulted in most policies as "difficult" to read and the others as "very difficult" Furthermore, it was noted that a significant percentage of the policies required readers to have an education level at a bachelor's degree. Therefore, the author concluded that nearly half of the US Internet population does not have the required reading education level to comprehend policies.

CONCLUSION

The research to date has focused on evaluating FRES and FGL scores of privacy policies. A thorough analysis based on other metrics such

Table 8. Pre-HIPAA and post-HIPAA analysis of privacy policies (adapted from Anton, 2004)

Website	FRES		FGL	
	Pre	Post	Pre	Post
AETNA	42.8	33.6	13.4	14.2
AFLAC	30.4	33.7	15	14.2
CIGNA	43.9	35.7	10.9	14
Destination-Rx	40	35.4	12.9	14.7
Drugstore.com	39.1	38.4	13.6	14.4
Health Central	39.5	33	12.5	14.7
Glaxo	39.5	35.4	12.5	14.4
Novartis	-	34.4	16.7	14.9
Pfizer	41.8	-	11.8	12.4
Average	39.6	34.9	13.3	14.2
Std. Dev.	4.11	1.70	1.731	0.737

Table 9. Readability of financial privacy policies (adapted from Hochhauser, 2002)

Financial Privacy Notice	FRES (60 recommended)	FGL (8 recommended)	Financial Privacy Notice	FRES	FGL
Anchor Bank	Difficult/43	14	Provident Financial Group	Difficult/35	15-16
Washington Mutual	Difficult/42	14	Mellon Financial Services	Difficult/35	15-16
FDS	Difficult/42	14	USbancorp	Difficult/35	15-16
Discover Card	Difficult/42	14-15	Macy's	Difficult/34	16
ePacific	Difficult/41	14	Bank One	Difficult/34	15-16
Postal Credit Union	Difficult/39	14-15	Cascade Bank	Difficult/34	15-16
Key	Difficult/38	15	Fleet Boston Financial	Difficult/33	16
May National Bank	Difficult/38	15	Household Bank	Difficult/33	16
Providian Bank	Difficult/38	15	Wells Fargo	Difficult/33	16
Bank of America	Difficult/37	15	Exxon Credit Card	Difficult/31	16
Synovus	Difficult/37	15-16	People's Bank	Difficult/31	16-17
Sears	Difficult/36	16	California Federal Bank	Very Difficult/30	16
Target (Retailers National Bank)	Difficult/36	15	Chase	Very Difficult/30	16-17
Capital One	Difficult/35	16	Union Bank of CA	Very Difficult/29	16
State Farm	Difficult/35	15-16	PNC Bank	Very Difficult/28	Graduate School
National City Bank	Difficult/35	15	Marquette Bank	Very Difficult/27	Graduate School
American Express	Very Difficult/27	Graduate School	Webster Bank	Very Difficult/25	Graduate School
Wachovia	Very Difficult/25	16	Countrywide Loans	Very Difficult/24	Graduate School
			Average	Difficult/34	15.6
			Std. Dev.	5.073	N/A

as Dale-Chall, SMOG, FI, and Fry graphs is still lacking. Note that these formulas reveal different aspects of readability of privacy policies. In addition, the results investigate privacy policies pre-dating 2005, no serious undertaking have examined the current state of readability of privacy policies on the Internet.

In browsing the previous three studies, one might infer a relationship between the type of website (e.g. financial) and its policies regarding privacy. As a clarification, there is no relationship between a web site and its privacy policies. At best, there is only a tendency. For example, all-encompassing laws apply to all bodies in a legal jurisdiction but transferring data between legal jurisdictions is a judicially problematic issue. (Reay et al., 2009)

6. READABILITY EVALUATION METHODOLOGY FOR THIS STUDY

6.1 Website Selection

For our study, we selected websites based on user traffic from Alexa's list (ALEXA, 2008). Alexa (ALEXA, 2008) collects web-traffic statistics using their software installed on millions of computers across the world. Web traffic statistics are based on a value calculated from reach and page views. Reach indicates the number of users accessing a web domain; while page views are the number of unique pages viewed by visitors. Traffic rank is based on an average taken over a few months time. The top 50 websites were chosen from Alexa's list of 500 most visited websites for February 2008 (ALEXA, 2008). The list of websites used for this study is provided in Table 10. A few websites had policies located on different websites. For example, Yahoo Geocities had a part of its privacy policy on Geocities website while the rest was available from Yahoo's website. In such cases policy information located on different websites were combined.

6.2 Analysis

The results for the average number of words, average number of sentences and FRES and FGL are provided in Table 10. For the 50 most visited websites, the average number of words and sentences in a policy are around 2022.6 and 89.26. The average FGL and FRES are found to be 12.91 (standard deviation = 2.31) and 43.50 (standard deviation = 9.16) respectively.

The average FGL obtained in our analysis is lower than both the education level of the Internet (14.4) and the US population (13.6). However, it is important to note that nearly 20% of the policies have an FGL greater than the education level of the US population. MySpace.com has the highest FGL (18.4) and Mininova the least FGL (7.3).

Based on FRES, Mininova was the easiest policy to read (67.6) while Wordpress was the most difficult (21.3). Further, the average FRES (43.50) indicates that the privacy policies are classified as difficult to comprehend[2].

To compare scores of different readability formulas, we use Pearson correlation analysis. In addition, we shall provide a graphical scatter plot and corresponding least-squares analysis to show linear dependence between readability scores. To compare three or more readability scores we use principal component analysis.

Results of correlation analysis of FRES and FGL data are provided in Table 11

The correlation between the FRES and FGL scores resulted in a negative correlation coefficient of 0.9190. The negative correlation indicates that inverse relation between FRES and FGL, i.e., a larger FRES (easy) corresponds to a lower FGL score.

A scatter plot (and least squares line regression line) capturing the correlation is illustrated in Figure 2.

The results of Dale-Chall evaluation of policies are provided in Table 12. Notice that the average Dale-Chall index is 7.58. This corresponds to a grade level between 9 and 10. It is worth noting

Table 10. FRES and FGL scores of privacy policies

Websites	Word	Sentences	FRES	FGL	Websites	Words	Sentences	FRES	FGL
Yahoo	1431	120	51	9.1	BBC	2433	124	61.8	9.5
Google	1867	74	36.3	14.5	AOL	3435	157	54.5	11.1
Windows Live	1346	59	45.9	12.5	LiveJournal	2460	95	34.9	14.8
Youtube	1523	63	45.9	12.9	Wordpress	747	29	21.3	16.7
MSN	6217	286	53.6	11.2	Flickr	394	29	60.6	8.2
MySpace	1612	53	33	18.4	Sendspace	746	42	51.8	10.4
Facebook	3480	140	40.3	13.8	Apple	2313	94	39.7	13.8
Wikipedia	1607	84	52.6	10.8	Adobe	3547	115	34.3	16.1
Hi5	1949	75	42.4	13.8	Badoo	1720	82	49.7	11.5
Orkut	1105	49	48.7	12.1	Bebo	2448	110	49.6	11.9
Rapidshare	293	9	35.1	15	MediaFire	582	26	41.5	13
Blogger	2316	96	39.6	13.7	Mininova	1779	126	67.6	7.3
Megaupload	285	14	43.7	12.2	Google UK	1867	74	36.3	14.5
Friendster	1995	70	43.4	14.3	Yahoo Geocities	1676	149	53	8.7
Photobucket	2007	84	42.3	13.3	Multiply	2129	81	42.3	13.9
CNN	1737	61	37.5	15.1	SourceForge	3402	161	34.5	13.7
Fotolog	1250	57	44.7	12.5	ISOhunt	144	7	40.3	12.8
Microsoft	3694	142	40.3	14.1	LinkedIn	2662	118	45.1	12.6
Ebay	2198	96	39.6	13.4	PartyPoker	2716	121	44.1	12.7
Skyrock	9656	330	41.9	14.7	Mozilla	1436	69	31.2	14.1
Bestbuy	1177	40	30	16.4	Dell	2339	97	39.7	13.7
Amazon	2761	146	43.7	11.9	Miniclip	753	32	36.3	14
IMDB	2036	93	44	12.6	EasyShare	384	22	58.3	9.5
Dailymotion	601	23	50.1	12.8	Webshots	1876	117	51.9	10
Megavideo	976	33	25.8	17	Average	2022.6	89.26	43.50	12.91
					Std. Dev.	1571.6	61.93	9.16	2.31
					Minimum	144	7	21.3	7.3
					Maximum	9656	330	67.6	8.4

Table 11. Correlation analysis on FRES and FGL scores

Pearson correlation (r)	-.9190
Coefficient of determination (r2)	.8445
Significance of correlation	p < .0001

Figure 2. Correlation between FRES and FGL across 50 privacy policies

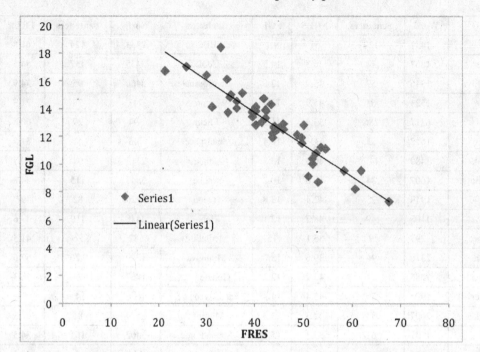

that the average grade level obtained by using DCI is lower than the FGL (12.91). The grade level average (9-10) is well below the education level of the Internet population (14.4) and the US population (13.5). According to Dale-Chall index, AOL has a high readability with a score of 6.37 that corresponds to a grade level of 7-8. On the other hand, Wordpress is the most difficult (8.31) that requires a grade level between 11 and 12 to comprehend policy.

The results of SMOG and FI evaluation of policies are also provided in Table 12. The average SMOG and FI scores are 14.06 and 16.36 respectively. This indicates that the readers require a college degree to comprehend policies. The most difficult policy, according to SMOG and FOG indices, is Wordpress that requires a postgraduate degree. The most readable based on SMOG (FI as well) is Flickr; for which only a high school education level is sufficient.

It is important to analyze the correlation between the scores. Recall that the Dale-Chall

readability formula is a function of two factors: word complexity as measured by Dale-Chall list and average sentence length. The SMOG index is a function of the number of polysyllables. While both the formulas measure readability, they do not have a variable in common, i.e., there is no direct relation between the two readability formulas. A correlation analysis of DCI and SMOG scores is provided in Table 13.

A correlation plot in Figure 3 illustrates that Dale-Chall and SMOG indices are positively correlated, i.e., an increase in SMOG corresponds to increase in Dale-Chall index. The Pearson correlation coefficient between Dale-Chall and SMOG data sets is found to be 0.930 and the p-value indicates that the results are statistically significant.

A relation between results of FGI, SMOG, DCI, and FI scores is analyzed using principal component analysis (PCA). This technique extracts relevant "relational" information from several data-sets. It reduces complex data sets to

Table 12. Dale-Chall, SMOG and FI scores of the sample privacy policies

Websites	Dale-Chall	SMOG	FI	Websites	Dale-Chall	SMOG	FI
Yahoo	7.027	11	12	BBC	6.78	12.1	13.4
Google	7.66	14.6	17.2	AOL	6.85	12.5	14.2
Windows Live	7.75	14.5	16.8	LiveJournal	8.06	15.5	18.4
Youtube	7.08	13.2	15.4	Wordpress	9.31	17.7	21.5
MSN	7.19	13.2	15.1	Flickr	6.07	9.8	10
MySpace	7.95	15.8	19.4	Sendspace	7.23	12.7	14.2
Facebook	7.83	14.9	17.5	Apple	7.84	14.9	17.5
Wikipedia	6.96	12.4	13.8	Adobe	8.019	16	19.7
Hi5	7.69	14.8	17.5	Badoo	6.98	12.7	14.3
Orkut	7.03	13	14.9	Bebo	7.25	13.4	15.4
Rapidshare	7.91	15.9	19	MediaFire	8.04	14.9	17.4
Blogger	7.47	14.1	16.4	Mininova	6.47	10.6	11.2
Megaupload	7.54	13.7	15.6	Google UK	7.66	14.6	17.2
Friendster	7.08	13.6	16.7	Yahoo Geocities	6.92	10.7	11.5
Photobucket	7.82	14.7	17.3	Multiply	7.78	15	17.8
CNN	7.85	15.4	18.6	SourceForge	8.09	14.8	17.2
Fotolog	7.75	14.3	16.5	ISOhunt	7.91	14.3	16.6
Microsoft	7.75	14.9	17.7	LinkedIn	7.46	13.8	16
Ebay	7.78	14.5	16.9	PartyPoker	7.52	14	16.1
Skyrock	7.77	15.3	18.6	Mozilla	8.94	16.1	19.2
Bestbuy	8.53	16.9	20.6	Dell	7.78	14.7	17.2
Amazon	7.63	13.5	15.4	Miniclip	8.37	15.7	18.5
IMDB	7.43	13.7	15.7	EasyShare	6.97	12.1	13.3
Dailymotion	7.18	13.7	16.2	Webshots	7.11	12.1	13.3
Megavideo	8.36	16.6	20.2	Average	7.58	14.06	16.36
				Std. Dev.	0.5929	1.66	2.46

Table 13. Correlation analysis on SMOG and DCI scores

Pearson correlation (r)	.9390
Coefficient of determination (r2)	.8817
Significance of correlation	p < .001

Figure 3. Correlation between Dale-Chall and SMOG across 50 privacy policies

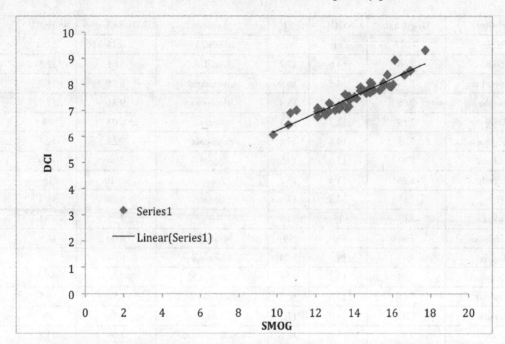

Table 14. The variance-covariance matrix

5.34	3.59	5.45	1.09
3.59	2.75	4.07	0.91
5.45	4.07	6.07	1.32
1.09	0.91	1.32	0.35

Table 15. Eigen decomposition and the corresponding Eigenvectors

0.6027	.7626	0.2275	0.0582
.4362	-.4129	-.0243	-.7992
.6533	-.3525	.4150	.5261
.1401	-.3517	-.8806	.2850

lower dimensions to capture simplified structure that under lie the data sets. Results of PCA of FGL, SMOG, FI and DCI are provided next. The variance-covariance matrix is given in Table 14.

The diagonal elements provide the variance and the non-diagonal elements represent the co-variance. The Eigen decomposition resulted in the following Eigenvalues: (14.1058, 0.3745, 0.0358, 0.0079) and the corresponding Eigenvectors are given in Table 15.

The Eigenvector corresponding to the highest Eigenvalue is the principal component. In the above case, the largest Eigenvalue is 14.1 and therefore the principal component is (.6027, .4362, .6533, .1410). This captures the underlying pattern

among different data sets: the principal component (Eigenvector) denotes the direction and the Ei-genvalue denotes the magnitude. Graphically, this can be seen as a line of least-squares. Note that the other Eigenvalues are very small when com-pared to 14.1, and hence these secondary values can be dismissed as insignificant. Therefore, the analysis shows that all of the significant informa-tion is contained in the association between the techniques. A plot of average number of syllables vs. average number of sentences is given in Fig-ure 4. This result is mapped onto a Fry graph. The Fry graph evaluation of the privacy policies is illustrated in Figure 5. The chart provides the age-level (translates to grade-level) required for

Figure 4. A plot of average number of syllables vs. average number of sentences

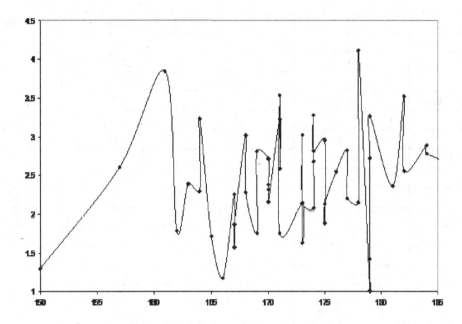

Figure 5. Fry graph for evaluating readability of privacy policies

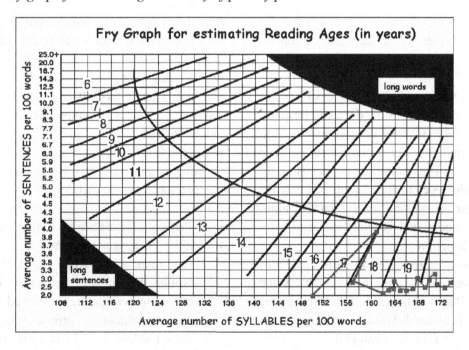

comprehending the policies. Results indicate that a minimum education at eleventh grade level is required. Based on Fry graph evaluation, a grade level between 12-14 (average) is essential for comprehension.

Table 16. A comparison study with (Hochauser, 2002; Jensen & Potts, 2004a, 2005; Anton, 2004)

		Average	Std. Dev	Min/Max
Our study (2008)	FRES	43.50	9.16	21.3/67.6
	FGL	12.91	2.3	7.3/18.4
	Words	2022.59	1571.57	144/9656
Jensen & Potts (2004b)	FRES	35.5	4.7	26.2/42.2
	FGL	14.3	1.26	11.5/16.24
	Words	1807	1613	331/6404
Jensen & Potts (2005)	FRES	34.2	6.5	15.6/46.2
	FGL	14.5	1.5	11.68/17.96
	Words	2806	1345	403/6222
Anton (2004)	FRES	34.9	1.7	33/38.4
	FGL	14.2	0.73	12.4/14.9
	Word	N/A	N/A	N/A
Hochhauser (2002)	FRES	34	N/A	22/43
	FGL	15.6	N/A	14/17
	Words	N/A	N/A	N/A

Evaluation of policies using different readability formulas resulted in the following conclusions:

- The average grade level scores of policies when evaluated using different formulas were quite close. In general, results indicated that an average grade level between 12 and 14 is essential to comprehend policies. However, the results differed in terms of their distribution, maximum and minimum grade-level requirements and standard deviation.
- Statistical correlation analysis confirmed an inverse correlation between FRES and FGL. It also indicated high positive correlation between different readability formulas: SMOG, FI, DCI and FGL.

7. A COMPARISON STUDY

We shall now address the question: whether the readability of privacy policies has improved over time. To study this question, we provide a numerical comparison of FRES and FGL results of our work with those of Hochhauser (2002) conducted in 2001, Anton et al. (2004) conducted in 2004 and Jensen and Potts (2004b) conducted in 2004. Table 16 provides a comparison of statistical values such as averages, standard deviation, and minimum (maximum) scores.

Several aspects are worth noting from the comparison provided in Table 16.

- Privacy policies are becoming more readable: There is a constant decrease in FGL (and increase in FRES) scores over years. Notice that in 2001 privacy policies required an average grade-level education of 15.6 for readability purposes. This requirement reduced to 14.21 in 2004 and further to 12.91 in 2008.

An independent t-test was used to support this finding. Two sets of data-sets were chosen for the test: 2004 readability estimates of policies (Jensen & Potts, 2004b) and readability estimates of our study (2008). Both data-sets satisfy the normality assumption required for such parametric testing. The results of thr t-test are given in Table 17.

The t-test results in Table 17 indicate that the means of 2004 and 2008 readability estimates are distinct and the results are highly statistically significant.

- Efforts in making policies more readable: The maximum FGL has increased over the years. In 2001, maximum FGL was around 17, which increased to 17.96 and 18.4 in 2004 and 2008 respectively. Minimum FGL on the other hand has decreased over time. In 2001, minimum FGL was around 14, which decreased to 11.68 and 7.3 in 2004 and 2008 respectively. This indicates that while some efforts are being made to address readability, a few others have not considered readability..
- Increase in variance of readability scores: Notice that the standard deviation of FGL scores has increased from 1.5 in 2004 to 2.3 in 2008 (equivalently FRES from 6.5 to 9.16).. Readability among policies differ more today than those in the past.
- Privacy policies are getting shorter: In 2004, the average number of words in a policy was around 2806. This has reduced considerably to an average of 2022 words

per policy in 2008. The data for 2001 is not available.

A comparison of estimates of individual web-sites' policies for 2004 and 2008 are provided in Table 18. From the FGL scores we can note that the readability of AOL, MSN, and Yahoo have improved significantly over time; EBay's policy has not changed much; and the readability of Google, Adobe, and Dell have become more difficult to comprehend.

8. DISCUSSION AND CONCLUSION

We have provided an analysis of the readability of privacy policies based upon readability formulas.

Table 17. Summary of t-test results

		2004	2008
Samples		47	50
Average		34.2	43.5
Ave2004 – Ave2008		-9.32	
t		-5.79	
degree of freedom		95	
P	one-tailed	<.0001	
	two-tailed	<.0001	

Table 18. Comparison of estimates of individual policies for 2004 and 2008

	2004		2008	
	FRES	**FGL**	**FRES**	**FGL**
AOL	34.2	14.8	54.5	11.1
MSN	41.5	13.18	53.6	11.2
Yahoo	37.9	12.49	51	9.1
Ebay	36.5	13.66	39.6	13.4
Google	45.7	11.68	36.3	14.5
Adobe	30.8	15.17	34.3	16.1
Dell	45.4	11.87	39.7	13.7

The 50 most visited websites were taken from Alexa's list are investigated. A wide variety of websites ranging from news, file sharing, game, financial, to social networking were chosen. Since these sites receive large number of visitors, they require highly "readable" policies.

We used the widely used readability formulas such as FRES, FGL, Dale-Chall, Fog, Fry graph and SMOG to evaluate privacy policies. Several results are worth noting:

- Privacy policies are getting shorter with time. This trend will however saturate, as minimum amount of information must be conveyed by policies.
- While FGL scores indicate a decrease in average grade level requirement over the years, FRES evaluation still terms policies as "difficult" to read.
- Evaluation based on FGL, DCI, FI, SMOG, Fry graph indicate that an average grade level of 12-14 is at least required to comprehend these policies.
- Present-day readability-average is lower than: the average education level of US population and the Internet population. This was however not the case at least until 2004.
- Readability formulas suggest that roughly 20% of the policies require a post-graduate degree.
- Pearson correlation analysis indicates that a high inverse correlation exists between FRES and FGL. Correlation analysis also suggests that Dale-Chall and SMOG are positively correlated.

In conclusion, on average, privacy policies are getting more readable. However, the population of the Internat is also changing and the population's average reading ability is set to decline. Content providers need to be aware of this and must take steps to ensure that their policies remain accessability to the Internet populations of the future.

REFERENCES

ALEXA. (2008). *Top 100 most visited websites*. Retrieved from http://www.alexa.com/ site/ds/ top_sites?ts_mode=lang&lang=en

Anton, A. I., Earp, J. B., Qingfeng, H., Stufflebeam, W., Bolchini, D., & Jensen, C. (2004). Financial privacy policies and the need for standardization. *IEEE Security & Privacy*, *2*(2), 36–45. doi:10.1109/MSECP.2004.1281243

Bormuth, J. R. (1966). Readability: A new approach. *Reading Research Quarterly*, *1*, 79–132. doi:10.2307/747021

Brodie, C., Karat, C., & Karat, J. (2005). Usable Security and Privacy: A Case Study of Developing Privacy Management Tools. In *Proceedings of the Symposium on Usable Privacy and Security (SOUPS '05)*. New York: ACM Digital Library.

Chall, J. S. (1988). The beginning years. In Zakaluk, B. L., & Samuels, S. J. (Eds.), *Readability: Its past, present, and future*. Newark, DE: International Reading Association.

Coleman, E. B., & Blumenfeld, P. J. (1963). Cloze scores of nominalization and their grammatical transformations using active verbs. *Psychological Reports*, *13*, 651–654.

Dale, E., & Chall, J. S. (1949). The concept of readability. *Elementary English*, 26-23.

Davison, A. (1984). Readability formulas and comprehension. In *Comprehension instruction: Perspectives and suggestions*. New York: Longman.

Eysenbach, G., Powell, J., Kuss, O., & Sa, E. R. (2002). Empirical studies assessing the quality of health information for consumers on the World Wide Web: a systematic review. *Journal of Amer).icican Medcial Association*, *287*(20), 2691–2700. doi:10.1001/jama.287.20.2691

Federal Trade Commission. (1998). *Privacy online: A report to congress, June 98*. Retrieved from http://www.ftc.gov/reports/privacy3/

Federal Trade Commission. (2008a). *Children Online Privacy Act (COPA)*. Retrieved from http://www.ftc.gov/ogc/coppa1.htm

Federal Trade Commission. (2008b). *The Gramm-Leach Bliley Act*. Retrieved from http://www.ftc.gov/privacy/privacyinitiatives/glbact.html

Flesch, R. (1974). *The art of readable writing*. New York: Harper

Hargis, G., Hernandez, A. K., Hughes, P., Ramaker, J., Rouiller, S., & Wilde, E. (1998). *Developing quality technical information: A handbook for writers and editors*. Upper Saddle River, NJ: Prentice Hall.

HIPAA. (2008). *Health insurance portability and accountability act of 1996*. Retrieved from http://www.cms.hhs.gov/HIPAAGenInfo/Downloads/HIPAALaw.pdf

Hochhauser, M. (2002). The effects of HIPAA on research consent forms. *Patient Care Management, 17*(5), 6–7.

IWS. (2008). *Highest Internet Penetration Rate*. Retrieved from http://www.internetworldstats.com/top25.htm

Jensen, C., & Potts, C. (2004a). Privacy Policies as Decision-Making Tools: A Usability Evaluation of Online Privacy Notices. In *Proceedings of ACM Conference on Human Factors in Computing Systems: CHI 2004* (pp. 471-478).

Jensen, C., & Potts, C. (2004b). *Privacy Policies Examined: Fair Warning or Fair Game*. Georgia Tech.

Jensen, C., & Potts, C. (2005). Privacy Practices of Internet Users: Self-report versus Observed Behavior. *International Journal of Human Computer Studies*.

Klare, G. R. (1963). *The Measurement of Readability*. Ames, IA: Iowa State University Press.

McLaughlin, G. H. (1969). SMOG grading - a new readability formula. *Journal of Reading, 22*, 639–646.

Milne, G. R., & Culnan, M. J. (2002). Using the Content of Online Privacy Notices to Inform Public Policy: A Longitudinal Analysis of the 1998–2001 U.S. Web Surveys. *The Information Society, 18*(5), 345–360. doi:10.1080/01972240290108168

Milne, G. R., & Culnan, M. J. (2004). Strategies for Reducing Online Privacy Risks: Why Consumers Read (or Don't Read) Online Privacy Notices. *Journal of Interactive Marketing, 18*(3), 15–29. doi:10.1002/dir.20009

NCES. (1992). *The National Adult Literacy Survey*. Retrieved from http://www.informatics-review.com/FAQ/reading.html

NTIA. (2002). *National Telecommunications and Information Administration. A Nation Online: How Americans Are Expanding Their Use of the Internet*. Retrieved from http://www.ntia.doc.gov/ntiahome/dn/

Peslak, A. (2005). Internet Privacy Policies: A Review and Survey of the Fortune 50. *Information Resources Management Journal, 18*, 29–41.

Reay, I., Dick, S., & Miller, J. A. (2009). *Large-scale empirical study of online privacy policies: stated actions vs. legal obligations*. ACM Transactions on the Web.

Reay, I. K., Beatty, P., Dick, S., & Miller, J. (2007). A survey and analysis of the P3P protocol's agents, adoptions, maintenance, and future. *IEEE Transactions on Dependable and Secure Computing, 4*(2), 151–164. doi:10.1109/TDSC.2007.1004

Singh, R. I., Sumeeth, M., & Miller, J. (2010). Evaluating the Readability of Privacy Policies in Mobile Environments. *International Journal of Mobile Human Computer Interaction*.

SRC. (2008). *SMOG Readability Calculator.* Retrieved from http://www.harrymclaughlin. com/SMOG.htm

Stevens, K. T., & Stevens, K. C. (1992). Measuring the Readability of Business Writing: The Cloze Procedure vs. Readability Formulas. *Journal of Business Communication*, *29*, 367–382. doi:10.1177/002194369202900404

Taylor, W. (1953). Cloze procedure: A new tool for measuring readability. *The Journalism Quarterly*, *30*, 415–433.

ENDNOTES

1. To address some of the shortcomings of FRES, Dale and Chall came up with a word-list, 80% of which are familiar to 4th grade students.
2. The translation of FRES scores to readability was provided in Table 3.

This work was previously published in International Journal of Information Security and Privacy, Volume 4, Issue 1, edited by Hamid Nemati, pp. 93-116, copyright 2010 by IGI Publishing (an imprint of IGI Global).

Chapter 6
Protecting User Privacy Better with Query l–Diversity

Fuyu Liu
University of Central Florida, USA

Kien A. Hua
University of Central Florida, USA

ABSTRACT

This paper examines major privacy concerns in location-based services. Most user privacy techniques are based on cloaking, which achieves location k-anonymity. The key is to reduce location resolution by ensuring that each cloaking area reported to a service provider contains at least k mobile users. However, maintaining location k-anonymity alone is inadequate when the majority of the k mobile users are interested in the same query subject. In this paper, the authors address this problem by defining a novel concept called query l-diversity, which requires diversified queries submitted from the k users. The authors propose two techniques: Expand Cloak and Hilbert Cloak to achieve query l-diversity. To show the effectiveness of the proposed techniques, they compare the improved Interval Cloak technique through extensive simulation studies. The results show that these techniques better protect user privacy.

1. INTRODUCTION

With rapid advances in wireless communication and wide spread of location positioning systems, *Location-Based Services* (LBS) are becoming increasingly popular. Mobile users can send queries, such as "where is the nearest gas station?" or "where is the closest women clinic?", to service providers and get query results back. These queries are called location-based queries, because they typically consist of a location, usually the location of the query issuer, and a question. There are a lot of challenges to answer this type of query for mobile users. One of the challenges is how to protect user's privacy. As we can see, to get a query result, one has to provide a location as well as a query question to the service provider, which

DOI: 10.4018/978-1-4666-0026-3.ch006

raises a privacy concern if the service provider is not trustworthy.

Many studies have been done to address this challenge (Gruteser and Grunwald, 2003; Gedik and Liu, 2005; Mokbel et al., 2006; Chow and Mokbel, 2007; Bamba et al., 2008; Xu and Cai, 2007, 2008). Most existing solutions assume a three tier architecture, in which mobile users first send the location and query information to a trusted anonymizer server, then the anonymizer server performs some cloaking procedure to enlarge the query's location into a region, finally forwards that region to a service provider. Typically, the goal of this cloaking procedure is to enforce location k-anonymity. That is, the cloaked region must contain at least (k-1) other users, such that an adversary can only link the cloaked query to the actual query issuer with $\frac{1}{k}$ probability. To protect against a *query sampling attack* (Chow and Mokbel, 2007), techniques have been proposed to ensure that all users included in the same cloaked region must report this region as their cloaked region.

Enforcing k-anonymity alone is not sufficient to ensure privacy. Let us consider a scenario, in which all users from a cloaked region are interested in the same type of service such as the location of a special club. In this case, even an adversary cannot link an individual query back to a specific user, it is still known to the adversary that all the users in the cloaked region have inquired about that special club. While this example depicts an extreme case, in reality, it is not uncommon that users from the same cloaked region request only a limited number of services. Consequently, an adversary can still infer that some user has issued a query on a certain service with a high probability. This kind of attack is referred to as *query homogeneity attack* (Xiao et al., 2008), and renders the existing k-anonymity model vulnerable. To counter this kind of attack, we modify the l-diversity concept (Machanavajjhala et al., 2006),

originally proposed for the relational database domain, and apply it in LBS domain to protect query contents. The key idea is to ensure that for all queries sharing the same cloaked region, their query contents must be different enough, such that the probability of linking a query to its original issuer is less than some pre-defined threshold.

In this paper, we first formally define the problem, and then propose two cloaking techniques that can counter against query homogeneity attack. Both of these techniques first divide the whole terrain into grid cells. Their space partitioning schemes, however, are different. The first technique starts from the center cell, and gradually expands over the space in all directions in search for a good way to partition the space. In contrast, the second technique first maps the two-dimensional grid space into a one-dimensional line of grid cells using a space filling curve, and then sequentially scans these cells to find the best partitioning strategy. We will describe these techniques in details later, and give simulation results to show that they are significantly better than the improved Interval Cloak technique (Gruteser and Grunwald, 2003).

The contributions we make in this paper can be summarized as follows:

- To the best of our knowledge, we are the first to use the l-diversity concept to address the query homogeneity attack.
- We consider a new anonymization criteria: $\langle k,l \rangle$-sharing region, and propose two cloaking techniques to partition the space using this new criteria.
- We conduct extensive simulation studies to evaluate the proposed techniques.

The remainder of this paper is organized as follows. We first discuss related work in Section 2. The preliminary and some definitions are then presented in Section 3 to facilitate further discussion. The two proposed cloaking techniques are introduced in Section 4, followed by the simulation study in Section 5. Finally, we conclude this paper in Section 6.

2. RELATED WORK

In this section, we discuss the two concepts: *k*-anonymity and *l*-diversity in relational databases and their applications in location-based services.

2.1 *k*-Anonymity and *l*-Diversity in Relational Databases

In a relational database, to publish data (such as censor or medical data) to support third-party data mining applications, it is important to prevent an adversary from linking the published data back to an individual. One obvious solution is to remove the *identifiers* such as a person's name and social security number for each published record. However, this is not enough since there still exist so-called *quansi-identifiers* such as age, height, zip code, etc., which can be used to infer a person's identify. To address this problem, the *k*-anonymity concept is proposed in Sweeney (2002), Samarati (2001). The key idea is to make a record indistinguishable from other (*k*-1) records with the same set of quansi-identifier. All the records sharing the same set of quansi-identifier form an *anonymization set*, and the size of this set should be larger than or equal to *k*. There are mainly two techniques in achieving *k*-anonymity: through *suppression* or *generalization*. Suppression means to remove the quansi-idenfiers, while generalization is to replace the quansi-idenfiers with more general terms, for example, replacing a person's age with a range.

Recently, it was pointed out in Machanavajjhala et al.(2006) that maintaining *k*-anonymity alone is not sufficient. In each anonymization set, the number of distinct sensitive values is more important than the size of the set, namely, *k*. To address this concern, a new notion called *l*-diversity is proposed in Machanavajjhala et al.(2006), which requires each distinct sensitive value in an anonymization set to be well represented; and two different metrics are introduced to measure the representativeness. This scheme uses an algorithm based on the technique used in LeFevre et al.(2005) to generate anonymization sets meeting both *k*-anonymity and *l*-diversity properties. More recently, a linear algorithm is introduced in Xiao and Tao(2006) to generate anonymization sets meeting the *l*-diversity requirement. In Ghinita et al.(2007), the multidimensional quansi-identifers are mapped into one dimension to solve the *k*-anonymity and *l*-diversity problems. In Ghinita et al.(2008), the authors solved the privacy problem for datasets with high dimensions.

2.2 *k*-Anonymity and *l*-Diversity in Location-Based Services

Location k-anonymity has been studied quite extensively in the location-based services community. The idea is similar to that in relational database. Given a location-based query, there is a trusted anonymizer server to cloak the location of the query issuer into a region, with the requirement that there are at least (*k*-1) other users in that cloaked region.

Most of existing researches focus on designing an efficient cloaking algorithm to achieve location *k*-anonymity. The Interval Cloak technique, based on the quad tree structure (Finkel and Bentley, 1974), is proposed in Gruteser and Grunwald (2003). Given a query, the algorithm recursively divides the area into quadrants, and checks the quadrant where the query is located to see if the quadrant contains more than *k* users. If it does not contain at least *k* users, the quadrant's parent is used as the cloaked region. In Gedik and Liu (2005), the Clique Cloak algorithm is presented, in which a set of users are combined to form a graph clique, and these users form an anonymization set. In Mokbel et al.(2006), a system called Casper is introduced, which uses a pyramid data structure to quickly find a cloaking box. In Chow and Mokbel (2007), the distinction between location k-anonymity and query k-anonymity is made, where the latter is to assure that the cloaked region for a query should also be shared by other (k-1) queries as their cloaked region. In Bamba et al.(2008), grid based approaches are investigated to achieve location k-anonymity and location l-diversity, where the location l-diversity is proposed to ensure that the query issuer cannot be identified from l different physical locations (such as buildings and postal addresses).

The aforementioned techniques focus on how to cloak a query location, but ignore the protection of query content. The latter was considered recently in Xiao et al.(2008), in which queries were divided into two types: *sensitive* and *insensitive*. For an anonymization set, which includes both sensitive and insensitive queries, the percentage of sensitive queries shall not exceed a certain threshold to protect privacy. A Partition-Enumeration tree (PE-tree) structure is proposed in Xiao et al.(2008) to facilitate the cloaking process. This technique has a few drawbacks. First, since the PE-tree has to store each mobile user's location, given that location updates are frequent in typical location-based applications, the maintenance cost for the tree could be very high. Second, queries are divided into sensitive and insensitive types, but how to define a query as a sensitive one is quite subjective. A sensitive query to one user might be deemed as insensitive to another user.

This paper is an extension of our previous work (Liu et al., 2009). We extend the original paper in a number of ways. First, a new cloaking algorithm is proposed and compared with the existing cloaking algorithms. Secondly, more extensive simulation studies are conducted.

3. PRELIMINARIES

In this section, we first introduce the system architecture, then go over some properties that are important for privacy-preserving applications,

including the novel $\langle k,l \rangle$-sharing region property, finally, we present the goal for anonymization techniques.

3.1 System Architecture

We consider a system consisting of a large number of mobile users, a trusted anonymizer server, and one or more service providers, as illustrated in Figure 1. Mobile users send location-based queries to the anonymizer server using an authenticated and encrypted wireless connection. An LBS query typically includes a user ID, the location of the user, a time stamp, and service-specific information. After receiving a query from a mobile user, the anonymizer server first decrypts the message, then performs a cloaking operation, which typically consists of the following two steps: (1) replace the user ID with a pseudo-identifier, (2) cloak the query location into a region. Finally, the anonymizer server forwards the cloaked (anonymized) query without its exact location (i.e. with the enlarged region only) to the selected service provider. Upon receiving an anonymized query, the service provider answers the query and sends the result back to the anonymizer server. The anonymizer server then refines the result and forwards the refined result to the mobile user.

3.2 Privacy-Preserving Properties

However, one obvious problem with the above approach is that if the query issuer is the only user residing in the cloaked region, an adversary can easily link the query to the query issuer, and makes the effort to protect query's actual location useless. To fix this problem, the following property is necessary for a cloaked region.

- (k-anonymity region) This property requires that for a cloaked region, it must contain at least k different mobile users. Therefore, the adversary can only link the

Figure 1. System architecture

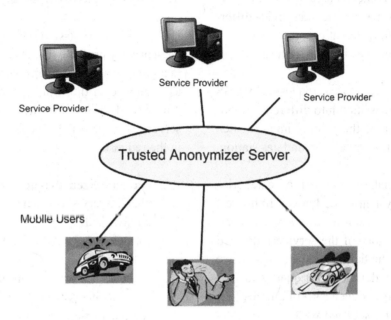

cloaked query to the query issuer with probability $\frac{1}{k}$.

Nevertheless, as pointed out in Chow and Mokbel (2007), when the locations of mobile users are revealed to adversaries, even with the k-anonymity region property, the adversary can still use *query sampling attack* to link a cloaked query back to the query issuer. To counter this type of attack, Chow and Mokbel (2007) identified the following property.

- **(k-sharing region)** This property states that the cloaked region contains at least k users, and this region is also reported by at least k of these users as their cloaked region.

One special case with this property is that for a cloaked region with more than k users, all users report this region as their cloaked region. As we can see, the k-sharing region is a stronger requirement than the k-anonymity region. Even when all users' locations are known to an adversary, since

there are at least k-different queries originated from the same cloaked region, the adversary still only has $\frac{1}{k}$ probability to link a query back to the query issuer. Based on the analysis presented in paper Chow and Mokbel (2007), among existing techniques, only the techniques proposed in Kalnis et al.(2007) and Gedik and Liu (2005) have the k-sharing region property.

However, if the number of distinct services requested by users residing in the same k-sharing region are small, in this scenario, even though a query cannot be linked back to a specific user, the adversary can deduce with high probability that some users are interested in some service. This type of attack is called *query homogeneity attack*. To counter this type of attack, we need to assure that among the queries submitted by users from the same k-sharing region, the requested services are different enough.

In other words, for a group of queries sharing the same cloaked region, the group should possess enough query diversity to stand query homogeneity attack. However, how to define and measure query diversity becomes a challenge. Inspired by the fact that yellow page companies divide different businesses into different categories, we also divide different services into categories.

- **(Category)** The services requested by LBS queries are classified into different categories according to the point of interest, such as restaurant, hospital, bar, and gas station.

We assume that the number of categories available in the system is pre-known. In the rest of this paper, when we refer to query category, we mean the category of the service requested by a query. With the definition for category, we have the following definition for query entropy.

(Query Entropy) Given a set of queries $\{q\}$, with each query q associated with a query category c, then the percentage that a query category c_i is requested can be computed as $p_i = \dfrac{|\{q \mid q.c = c_i\}|}{|\{q\}|}$. Then query entropy is calculated as:

$$query\ entropy = -\sum p_i \log p_i. \qquad (1)$$

- **(Query *l*-diversity)** This property means that for a set of queries $\{q\}$, given an integer l, the query entropy is equal to or greater than $\log l$.

Finally, we define a new property, called $\langle k,l \rangle$-sharing region, which takes k-anonymity and query l-diversity into consideration.

- **($\langle k,l \rangle$-sharing region)** This property is more restrictive than the k-sharing region property. Besides the restrictions imposed by the k-sharing region, this property also requires that among all queries submitted by users from this region, they must possess the query l-diversity property.

3.3 Anonymization Goal

In the system, we assume that each mobile user has a privacy profile, which specifies the requirement on privacy. The profile is a two-tuple $\langle k,l \rangle$, as explained in the following definition. When a user sends a query to the trusted anonymizer server, he/she also includes his/her privacy profile in the request.

- **(Personalized Privacy Query)** A personalized query sent from a user to the trusted anonymization server has the following format: $\langle id, \langle k,l \rangle, \langle t,x,y \rangle, C \rangle$, in which the *id* is the unique id assigned to the user, $\langle k,l \rangle$ is the user's privacy profile, with k as the number of users required in the k-sharing region, while l indicating the requirement for query l-diversity, $\langle t,x,y \rangle$ specifies the time and location where the query is issued, and C is the content of the query (with the type of service specified).

After the anonymizer server receives a personalized query, it performs the cloaking operation to obtain a cloaked query, and sends the cloaked query to the service provider.

- **(Cloaked Query)** A cloaked query has the following format: $\langle id', t, MBR, C \rangle$, where *id'* is the pseudo-identifier for the query, t is the time stamp, *MBR* is minimal bounding rectangle for the cloaked region, and C is the content of the query.

The goal of an anonymization algorithm is to find regions with the $\langle k,l \rangle$-sharing region property, and the identified region satisfies the $\langle k,l \rangle$ requirements for all users in the region. Formally, denote a personalized query as q, and its cloaked version as q', and the whole set of cloaked queries at any given time t as Q, and the goal of an anonymization algorithm is to find a Q' for each q, such that:

$$Q' \subset Q \wedge \forall \{q'_i, q'_j\} \in Q', q'_i.MBR =$$
$$q'_j.MBR \wedge \forall q' \in Q', \left(|Q'| \geq q.k \wedge Q'.entropy \geq \log q.l \right)$$

4. CLOAKING ALGORITHMS

In this section, we first discuss data structure used on the anonymizer server, then present the two proposed cloaking algorithms.

4.1 Data Structure

The whole terrain is divided into grid cells, where each cell is a square with size α. For each query received at every time unit, the anonymizer server records the query information, including the query issuer's id, location, $\langle k, l \rangle$ profile, and content. Also, for each cell, we keep the following aggregated variables for queries belonging to the cell: (1) A counter n to keep the total number of queries at current time unit. (2). A variable k_{spec} to store the maximum of all k's, among all query's privacy profile. (3). Similarly, a variable l_{spec} to store the maximum of all l's. (4). A signature, as described below.

- **(Signature)** Each cell keeps a bit vector, called *signature*, to indicate category information for all the queries in the cell. Recall that for each submitted query, from the content C, we can map the query into a certain category. Assume that the maximum number of category available is cat_{max}, then the vector is a cat_{max} bit vector. For each cell, if it covers a query with category i, the vector's ith bit is set to 1, otherwise, it is set to 0. Given a signature *sig*, we refer to the number of one's in *sig* as its cardinality, denoted as *sig.card*.
- **(Signature Union)** A union of two signatures is defined as the bit union for the two bit vectors of the two signatures.

In other words, if the ith bit of either signature is 1, the resultant bit vector also has 1 at the ith bit; if both signatures have 0 at the ith bit, then the resultant bit vector has 0 at that bit. Note that a union of two signatures is still a signature. This union operation is useful when multiple cells are merged into one area, in order to obtain the signature for the combined area, we can simply compute the union of the signatures.

Note that for a given area, if the cardinality of the area's signature is equal to l, the maximum query entropy of this area is obtained only when the distribution of query categories are uniform, and the maximum is $\log l$. Therefore, to test if an area meets the query l-diversity requirement, we can compare the cardinality with l first. Only if the cardinality is greater than or equal to l, there is a need to calculate the area's entropy.

4.2 Expand Cloak

In this section, we introduce the first proposed cloaking algorithm, named as Expand Cloak.

Algorithm 1 depicts the Expand Cloak algorithm. The algorithm starts with a *for* loop to examine every cell in the area. The examine order can be linear, starting from the bottom-left cell and moving to right and top, or be spiral, from the center of the area. We prefer the latter, noticing that usually more mobile users are around the center area than the boundary area.

First, we check if the cell is already cloaked (lines 2-4). If yes, the algorithm moves to the next cell. Then we initialize the *area* variable using the cell c (line 5). We call the Check Area Validity algorithm as shown in Algorithm 2, with the details to be discussed later. If the area meets its privacy requirement, we then create a new cloaked region for this area/cell, and label this area/cell as cloaked (lines 6-10), then move to the next cell. Otherwise, we start to check the area's neighbor cells. If all neighbor cells are already cloaked or none of the neighbor cell contains a query, we give up in cloaking this area (lines 13-15). Then

Algorithm 1. Expand cloak

```
1: for each cell c do
2: if c is already cloaked then
3: Continue;
4: end if
5: area ←{c}; {Initialization}
6: if CheckAreaValidity(area) then
7: Create a cloak region for area;
8: Label area as cloaked;
9: Continue;
10: end if
11: while area is not cloaked do
12: N C ←area's neighbor cells that are not
            cloaked;
13: if N C == Ø || ∀cᵢ ∈ N C, ci .n == 0 then
14: Continue; {Do not cloak this area}
15: end if
16: result ←Ø; {To store candidate neighbor cells}
17: for each cell ci in N C do
18: tempArea ←area ∪ ci;
19: if CheckAreaValidity(tmpArea) then
20: result ←result ∪ ci ;
21: end if
22: end for
23: if result ! = Ø then
24: cp ←the cell in result with the fewest
            queries;
25: Create a cloak region for area ∪ cp ;
26: Label area and cp as cloaked;
27: else
28: cp ←the cell in N C with the most queries;
29: area ←area ∪ cp
30: end if
31: end while
32: end for
```

Algorithm 2. Check area validity

```
CheckAreaValidity(area)
Input: an area consists of one or more cells
Output: true or false
1: kact ←0; {actual number of queries for the area}
2: kspec ←0; {specified maximum k for the area}
3: sig ← Ø; {signature}
4: lspec ←0; {specified maximum l for the area}
5: for each cell c in area do
6: kact ←kact + c.n;
7: kspec ←max(c.kspec, kspec);
8: sig ←sig _ c.signature;
9: lspec ←max(c.lspec, lspec);
10: end for
11: if kact ≥ kspec then
12: if sig.card ≥ lspec then
13: entropy ←calculate the area's entropy;
14: if entropy ≥ log lspec then
15: return true;
16: end if
17: end if
18: end if
19: return false;
```

Figure 2. Illustrations for Expand Cloak and Hilbert Cloak

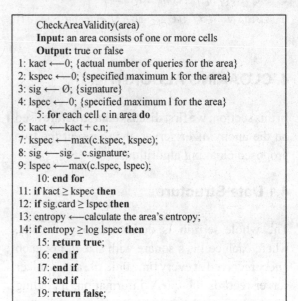

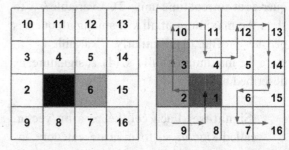

we examine each of the area's neighbor cell by calling the Check Area Validity algorithm (lines 17-22). If after a neighbor cell is unioned with the area, the updated area meets the privacy requirement, that neighbor cell is saved into the *result*. If the *result* is not empty (line 23), we pick the cell with the fewest queries to form a new cloaked region with the *area* (lines 24-26), otherwise, the cell with the most queries is picked to form an updated *area* (lines 28-29), and the while loop is executed again.

The input to Algorithm 4.2 is an area consisting of multiple cells. The goal is to examine if the input area can meet the privacy requirement. First,

we initialize some variables (lines 1-4). Then, we iterate through each cell in the *area* to update these variables (lines 5-10).After that, we check if the area meets the *k*-anonymity requirement, if yes, then we use the cardinality of the signature union to check if the area could potentially meet the *l*-diversity requirement. Finally, we compute the actual entropy for the area and compare it with the specified entropy to determine if the area meets both privacy requirements (lines 11-18).

We demonstrate the Expand Cloak algorithm using an example. Figure 1 shows the space divided into 16 cells, with each cell assigned a cell ID. The data stored in cells from 1 to 9 are detailed

Table 1. Data in cells

Cell ID	n	kspec	lspec	signature	query count
1	3	6	3	0011	{0, 0, 2, 1}
2	3	3	2	0011	{0, 0, 1, 2}
3	2	3	2	1100	{1, 1, 0, 0}
4	4	3	2	1100	{3, 1, 0, 0}
5	0	0	0	0000	{0, 0, 0, 0}
6	3	4	2	1100	{2, 1, 0, 0}
7	1	4	3	0001	{0, 0, 0, 1}
8	0	0	0	0000	{0, 0, 0, 0}
9	0	0	0	0000	{0, 0, 0, 0}

in Table 1, where n, k_{spec}, l_{spec}, and *signature* have the values as specified in Section 4.1. For the ease of explanation, we assume there are only four types of query categories, therefore, each *signature* is a four-bit vector. The *query count* indicates the number of queries for each query category. For example, Cell 1 has 3 queries, with the specified k_{spec} and l_{spec} as 6 and 3, respectively. There are two queries belonging to the third category and one query belonging to the fourth category, as a result, the *signature* is 0011.

Suppose we want to cloak Cell 1 (the dark shaded cell in the middle). First, we check if the cell by itself can meet the privacy requirement. Since there are only 3 queries in Cell 1, and less than the k_{spec}, expansion is needed. The algorithm checks all the surrounding eight cells and filters out cells 3, 5, 7, 8, 9 out immediately due to the small number of queries. In the next step, the algorithm checks the cardinality of the signature unions, which then eliminates Cell 2 because the signature union shows that there are two types of query categories and cannot meet the *l*-diversity privacy requirement. Till now, the cells left are Cell 4 and Cell 6. After we calculate the entropies for the two combined area {Cell 1, Cell 4}, and {Cell 1, Cell 6}, the results show that both combined areas satisfy the privacy requirement. Then, the algorithm decides to merge Cell 6 with Cell 1 to form a new cloaked region, since Cell 6 has

fewer queries. Fig. 1 shows Cell 1 and Cell 6 form a new cloaked region, all the other examined cells are decorated with stripes.

For the Expand Cloak technique, there are two scenarios when queries from certain cell cannot be successfully cloaked. The first scenario is that all neighbor cells are empty, so the algorithm considers that the cell (or area) is an isolated cell (or area) and gives up on it. The second scenario is that the cell is very close to the boundary of the whole space, which also makes it difficult to find suitable neighbor cells to merge with. In Section 5, we use a metrics called *Relative Success Rate* to measure the percentage of these two scenarios occurring.

4.3 Hilbert Cloak

The proposed Expand Cloak technique starts from one cell, and expands to both horizontal and vertical directions. Because all neighbor cells must be checked and evaluated before the algorithm can make a decision, the computation cost could be high. To remedy this problem, we propose to use space filling curve to design a cloaking algorithm. Hilbert curve is a type of space filling curve. In Figure 1, we show a 4×4 hilbert curve, which can map a two dimensional space into one dimension, thus save us from expanding toward two directions.

Here we present the second proposed cloaking algorithm, Hilbert Cloak, as shown in Algorithm 3. Hilbert Cloak first sorts the cells based on its Hilbert curve value (line 1). Then, for each cell, the algorithm checks if it is already cloaked or empty (lines 3-5). If not, it examines the cell to see if the cell by itself meets the privacy requirement. If yes, a cloaked region is created and the cell is labeled as cloaked (lines 8-12). If not, the next cell (based on Hilbert Curve order) is included into the *area* (lines 13-14), then the updated *area* is checked again using the while loop until a satisfying region is found.

We use the same example from the previous section to illustrate Hilbert Cloak algorithm. The algorithm starts from Cell 9. Based on Table 1, both Cells 9 and 8 are empty and thus skipped. The next cell is Cell 1, which does not meet the privacy requirement by itself. Then the next cell, Cell 2, is merged with Cell 1 to form an *area*. However, the signature union check indicates that the merged area is still not good enough. Then, the next cell, Cell 3, is added into the *area*, which passes the validity test. Therefore, Cells 1, 2, and 3 form a cloaked region, shown in Fig. 1 as shaded cells.

4.4 Discussions

The degree of query *l*-diversity is measured using the entropy concept, which has been pointed out as being too restrictive DBLP:conf/icde/Machanavajjhala GKV06. Note that since the proposed techniques are orthogonal to the method used to define diversity, our techniques can work with other methods with straightforward modifications.

For *k*-anonymity in relational databases, it has been shown in Meyerson and Williams (2004) that the optimal *k*-anonymization problem of relations is *NP*-hard. The problem studied in this paper, involving one more parameter *l*, therefore, is also very difficult. The two proposed techniques cannot guarantee that the optimal solutions can be found, nevertheless, as demonstrated by the simulation study, the performances are acceptable in practice.

Algorithm 3. Hilbert Cloak

```
 1: Sort the cells using Hilbert Curve values;
 2: for each cell c do
 3:   if c is already cloaked ||c.n == 0 then
 4:     Continue;
 5:   end if
 6: area ⟵ {c}; {Initialization}
 7:   while area is not cloaked do
 8:     if CheckAreaValidity(area) then
 9:       Create a cloaked region for area;
10:       Label area as cloaked;
11:       Break;
12:     end if
13:   cn ⟵ the next cell;
14:   area ⟵ area ∪ cn ;
15: end while
```

For queries that cannot be cloaked in the Expand Cloak technique, typically due to the lack of neighboring queries, we can insert some dummy queries to help cloak the queries (Kido et al., 2005).. As what to be shown in the simulation study, the percentage of queries not being cloaked is quite low, which means the number of dummy queries needs to be generated is also small.

5. PERFORMANCE STUDY

In this section, we study the effectiveness and scalability of the proposed cloaking techniques using simulation studies. First, we introduce the performance metrics employed in our study, then cover the experimental setup, finally, we present the detailed simulation results.

5.1 Performance Metrics

In this section, we introduce the list of performance metrics used in the performance study.

The first measure is *Query Anonymization Time* (*QAT*), which measures the run-time efficiency of a cloaking technique. However, the *QAT* only shows how fast a technique runs, to evaluate the quality of the generated cloaked regions, other performance metrics are called for. The following metrics are employed to gauge the anonymization quality.

The second measure is called *Query Success Rate* (*QSR*), which indicates the percentage of queries whose locations are successfully cloaked into regions. A good cloaking technique should have a *QSR* very close to one. Should this number be equal to one, it means that the technique cloaks all queries successfully.

Another measure is *Relative Anonymization Area* (*RAA*). *RAA* is defined as the ratio of the sum of the sizes of all anonymization areas to the size of the entire system area, where an anonymization area is defined as the minimal bounding rectangle of a cloaked region, which consists of one or multiple cells. This metrics is quite important. Recall that in the three tier architecture (Figure 1), after query locations are cloaked into regions, the anonymizer server needs to send the region information to service providers. The smaller the size of a region, the lighter workload imposed on service providers.

As discussed in Section 3, when an user issues a query, a personal privacy profile is specified by a tuple $\langle k,l \rangle$. Given an anonymization area, the ideal scenario is that the area should meet the privacy requirements for all users included in the area, but without exceeding the requirements by too much. To measure this effect, we can use the *Relative Anonymity Level* (*RAL*), which is defined as follows:

$$RAL = \frac{k_{act}}{k_{spec}} * \frac{e_{act}}{e_{spec}} \qquad (2)$$

where k_{act} is the actual number of queries in a cloaked region, and k_{spec} is the maximum of the specified k among all queries in the cloaked region, similarly, e_{act} is the actual query entropy for queries in the region, and e_{spec} is the calculated entropy using the maximum of the specified l among all queries in the cloaked region.

In a word, to evaluate a cloaking technique, all the above four metrics should be taken into consideration. A good cloaking technique must behave well in all the metrics.

5.2 Experimental Setup

The Brinkhoff data generator DBLP:journals/geoinformatica/Brinkhoff02 is used to generate moving objects on the map of oldenburg, Germany. The outputs of the data generator are saved into files, which are then read by our simulator. In the initialization phase of the simulation, every moving object specifies a personal privacy profile $\langle k,l \rangle$. If we denote k_{max} and l_{max} as the supported maximum k and l of the system, respectively, then in each object's privacy profile, k is a randomly selected value in the range of $[1, k_{max}]$, and l is randomly selected from $[1, l_{max}]$. Each object issues a location-based query inquiring about a randomly chosen query category. The anonymizer server then cloaks the queries for all objects using the proposed cloaking techniques.

The simulation is implemented in Java, and the running environment is a desktop computer with Intel Pentium 3.06GHz CPU and 2G memory, running a Linux operation system. In the experiments, we vary different parameters, as listed in Table 2, to study the efficiency and scalability of the proposed cloaking techniques. If not otherwise specified, the experiment takes the default values. For each parameter setting, the simulation is run with different input trace files for 100 times, and the averaged results are reported.

5.3 Experimental Results

In this section, we first study the effects of varying the number of cells n_{cell}, then measure the performance of the techniques by varying k_{max} and l_{max}, finally, we study the scalability of the proposed techniques by varying the number of moving queries n_q and the number of query categories n_{cat}.

Table 2. Simulation parameters

Parameter	Description	Value Set	Default Value
n_{cell}	Number of cells	{64, 256, 1024, 4096}	1024
k_{max}	Maximum of allowed k	{10, 20, 30, 40, 50}	20
l_{max}	Maximum of allowed l	{2, 4, 6, 8 10}	4
n_q	Number of queries	{1000, 2000, 3000, 4000, 5000}	2000
n_{cat}	Number of categories for queries	{10, 20, 30, 40, 50}	20

Figure 3. Varying number of cells

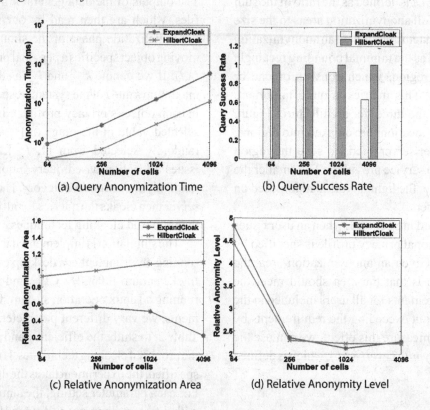

(a) Query Anonymization Time

(b) Query Success Rate

(c) Relative Anonymization Area

(d) Relative Anonymity Level

5.3.1 Varying Number of Cells

Since the whole terrain is divided into grid cells, we want to study the effect of grid cell size on the system performance. Note that a small grid cell size means a large number of cells. The total number of cells is varied from 64 to 4096, with the results shown in Figure 3.

In Figure 3, the effect on *QAT* is studied. Please note that the vertical axis is in logarithmic scale.

The plot shows that more cells mean longer anonymization time for both techniques. This is as expected, as more computations are necessary when cell size becomes smaller. The plot also shows that Expand Cloak technique runs slower than Hilbert Cloak, due to the expensive cell-expanding operations.

From Figure 3, we learn that the *QSR* of Hilbert Cloak is always one, which means all queries can be successfully cloaked. However, the Expand

Cloak technique experiences variations. Initially, the QSR increases as the number of cells increases, but if there are too many cells, the rate starts to drop. This can be explained as follows. When the number of cells is small (i.e. the size of a grid cell is large), the cloaked region is also large, which leads to over-anonymization, as shown in Figure 3. As a result, it adds difficulty for some cells (especially boundary ones) to find neighbor cells to form a cloaked region. As n_{cell} increases, more boundary cells can be successfully cloaked, which leads to an improved QSR. However, if there are too many cells, cell size becomes very small, then some cells can not find non-empty neighbor cells to be combined with, which also leads to the drop of the success rate.

In Figure 3, we studied the effect of n_{cell} on RAA. The results show that as n_{cell} increases, the RAA for Expand Cloak decreases while the RAA for Hilbert Cloak increases. This is because that for the Expand Cloak technique, smaller cell size can lead to smaller cloaked region; however, for the Hilbert Cloak technique, due to the one-dimensional nature of the Hilbert Curve, there are many overlappings among different cloaked regions. As a result, the more cloaked regions, the more overlapped space there are, which explains the RAA increases as the cell size gets smaller. Figure 3 shows that both techniques give a relatively low anonymity level. When n_{cell} increases, the RAL drops, which is more desirable.

5.3.2 Varying *k* and *l*

In this section, we evaluate the proposed techniques by varying the other two important factors: the user defined k and l. Furthermore, the Interval Cloak technique DBLP:conf/mobisys/GruteserG03 described in Section 2, is modified to generate cloaked regions meeting the $\langle k,l \rangle$-sharing region requirement. The proposed techniques are then compared against the improved Interval Cloak technique.

In Figure 4, we study the effects of varying k_{max} from 10 to 50. Recall that the user specified k in k-anonymity is randomly selected from the range $[1, k_{max}]$. In Figure 4, the plot shows that as k_{max} increases, the QAT increases. This is quite reasonable since a larger k_{max} means that the user defined k would be larger, which then requires more cell-expanding operations. Interestingly, the Hilbert Cloak technique seems to be immune to the k_{max} changes. This is because we only need to scan the grid cells to determine cloaked regions. A larger k_{max} leads to a larger cloaked region, however, the overall execution time is not affected. Also quite interestingly, the Interval Cloak technique demands less execution time as k_{max} increases, which is due to the fact that the Interval Cloak technique is a top-down approach, a larger k_{max} means larger cloaked regions and fewer number of iterations.

Figure 4 shows that all three techniques have high QSR, and the RAA increases with the increase of k_{max}. Among the three techniques, the Expand Cloak technique incurs the smallest anonymization area size, while the Hilbert Cloak technique requires the largest anonymization area size. This is because the Expand Cloak technique calculates a cloaked region using cell expanding technique, which can reduce the including of unnecessary dead space. On the other hand, since Hilbert Cloak relies on the one-dimensional Hilbert Curve, the cloaked regions have a lot of overlapping, which leads to a large anonymization area.

Figure 4 measures the RAL for the three techniques. The plot shows that both Expand Cloak and Hilbert Cloak have smaller RAL compared to Interval Cloak, which indicates that the cloaked regions meet the user defined requirement better. On the contrary, Interval Cloak has a much larger RAL, the result of creating unnecessarily large regions.

In Figure 5, we vary l_{max} from 2 to 18, and study its effect on the cloaking techniques.

First of all, Figure 5 shows that as l_{max} increases, both Expand Cloak and Hilbert Cloak

Figure 4. Varying k in k-anonymity

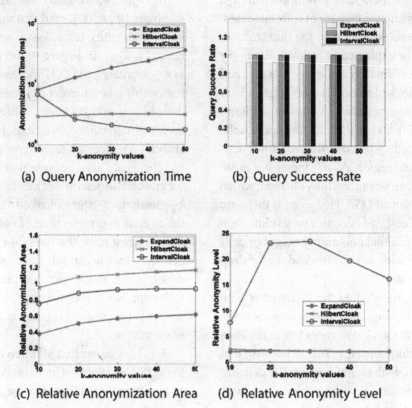

(a) Query Anonymization Time

(b) Query Success Rate

(c) Relative Anonymization Area

(d) Relative Anonymity Level

incur longer computation time, however the anonymization time for Interval Cloak decreases. When l_{max} increases, for the Expand Cloak technique, to find a cloaked region for a given cell, more neighboring cells must be examined and included to meet the l-diversity requirement, which explains why the anonymization time is longer. However, for the Hilbert Cloak technique, the increase in anonymization time is mainly due to the cost in calculating query entropy. When the l is getting larger, the cost for calculating query entropy is also higher. Interestingly, the time needed for Interval Cloak decreases, which is because Interval Cloak stops after a few iterations. This leads to larger cloaked regions when compared to the other two techniques, as we will see from the *RAL* metrics.

Figure 5b, Figure 5c, and Figure 5d compare the quality of the three cloaking techniques. Fig-

ure 5b tells us that all three techniques have high *QSR*, and Figure 5c again shows that the Expand Cloak technique leads to cloaked regions with the smallest size, similar to the results obtained when varying k_{max}. In Figure 5d, we find out that although Interval Cloak do well in terms of the two performance metrics: *QSR* and *RAA*, it actually over-anonymizes many queries, as demonstrated by the high *RAL* values.

We also observe that when l_{max} is increased from 14 to 18, the *QAT* for Expand Cloak experiences a sharp increase. This is because the default number for the total available number of query is 20, when l_{max} is getting larger and close to 20, it becomes very difficult to find a region that can meet the privacy requirement. As a result, it takes longer to cloak queries, and the resultant cloaked regions are larger. This impact is also observed

Figure 5. Varying l in l-diversity

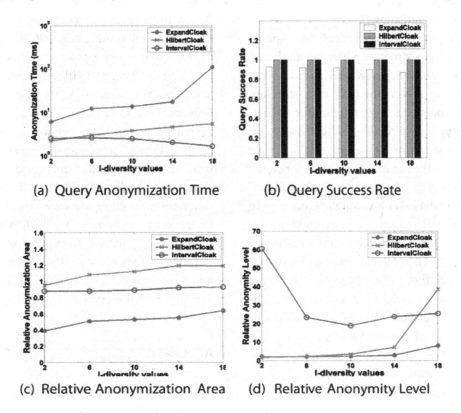

(a) Query Anonymization Time (b) Query Success Rate

(c) Relative Anonymization Area (d) Relative Anonymity Level

Figure 6. Scalability study by varying number of queries and query categories

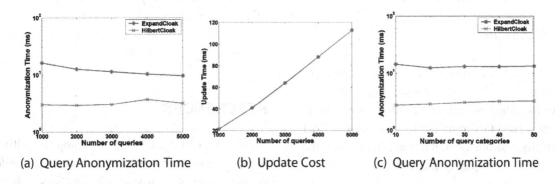

(a) Query Anonymization Time (b) Update Cost (c) Query Anonymization Time

from the sharp raise in *RAL* and the drop in *QSR* when l_{max} is increased from 14 to 18.

5.3.3 Scalability Study

In this section, we study the scalability of the proposed techniques, with results shown in Fig-

ure 6. First, in Figure 6a, we vary the number of queries from 1000 to 5000 and measure its effect on anonymization time. The plot shows that the effect on the Hilbert Cloak technique is very small. However, the Expand Cloak technique incurs less anonymization time with the increase of queries, this is because the more queries in each grid cell, the less cell-expanding is necessary, which reduces the overall anonymization time.

Second, Figure 6b measures the time to update the grid-based data structure when the number of queries increases. When new queries are sent to the anonymizer server, the grid data structure needs to be updated accordingly. In our simulation, the grid data structure is kept as an in-memory data structure. As we can see, the update cost is linear to the number of queries. Since the grid-based index is a flat structure, it has advantage over a tree-based index, which requires more expensive operations to maintain its tree structure.

Third, we increase the total number of query categories from 10 to 50 and study its impact on anonymization time. The obtained results are shown in Figure 6c, which shows that both techniques are not sensitive to the number of query categories. For the Expand Cloak technique, when the number of categories is increased from 10 to 20, the anonymization time drops slightly, indicating that it is easier to find cloaked regions due to more available query categories. However, after that point, while the number of categories keeps increasing, the effect is not noticeable.

5.3.4 Discussion

Please note that although the Expand Cloak technique needs longer time when compared to the other two, the time actually needed is only a few milliseconds. Given that it has the lowest *RAA* and a close-to-one *QSR*, it has advantage over the other two techniques in practice.

6. CONCLUSION

In privacy-aware mobile information system, it is important for a cloaking technique to hide both user locations and the content of the issued queries. Existing techniques typically only focus on anonymizing user locations. In this paper, we first proposed to use both location k-anonymity and query l-diversity to better protect user privacy. A new property called $\langle k,l \rangle$-sharing region was then identified as the guide to design new cloaking algorithms. This property was used to design the Expand Cloak and Hilbert Cloak techniques to achieve both location k- anonymity and query l-diversity. To assess their performance, we also designed an improved version of the original Interval Cloak technique (Gruteser and Grunwald, 2003) to handle query l-diversity. The simulation results indicate that Expand Cloak generates cloaked regions with smaller size and lower *Relative Anonymity Level*, while Hilbert Cloak is faster but leads to larger cloaked regions. Both techniques are significantly better than the improved Interval Cloak technique in providing user privacy protection.

ACKNOWLEDGMENT

This material is based upon work partially supported by the National Science Foundation under Grant Numbers CNS-0917082. Any opinions, findings, and conclusions or recommendations expressed in this materials are those of the authors and do not necessarily reflect the views of the National Science Foundation.

REFERENCES

Bamba, B., Liu, L., Pesti, P., & Wang, T. (2008). Supporting anonymous location queries in mobile environments with privacygrid. In *Proceeedings of WWW 2008* (pp. 237-246).

Brinkhoff, T. (2002). A framework for generating network-based moving objects. *GeoInformatica*, *6*(2), 153–180. doi:10.1023/A:1015231126594

Chow, C.-Y., & Mokbel, M. F. (2007). Enabling private continuous queries for revealed user locations. In. *Proceedings of SSTD*, *2007*, 258–275.

Finkel, R. A., & Bentley, J. L. (1974). Quad trees: A data structure for retrieval on composite keys. *Acta Informatica, 4*, 1–9. doi:10.1007/BF00288933

Gedik, B., & Liu, L. (2005). Location privacy in mobile systems: A personalized anonymization model. In *Proceedings of ICDCS, 2005,* 620–629.

Ghinita, G., Karras, P., Kalnis, P., & Mamoulis, N. (2007). Fast data anonymization with low information loss. In *Proceedings of VLDB, 2007,* 758–769.

Ghinita, G., Tao, Y., & Kalnis, P. (2008). On the anonymization of sparse high-dimensional data. In *Proceedings of ICDE, 2008,* 715–724.

Gruteser, M., & Grunwald, D. (2003). *Anonymous usage of location-based services through spatial and temporal cloaking.* Paper presented at MobiSys 2003.

Kalnis, P., Ghinita, G., Mouratidis, K., & Papadias, D. (2007). Preventing location-based identity inference in anonymous spatial queries. *IEEE Transactions on Knowledge and Data Engineering, 19*(12), 1719–1733. doi:10.1109/TKDE.2007.190662

Kido, H., Yanagisawa, Y., & Satoh, T. (2005). Protection of location privacy using dummies for location-based services. In *Proceedings of the ICDE Workshops* (p. 1248).

LeFevre, K., DeWitt, D. J., & Ramakrishnan, R. (2005). Incognito: Efficient full-domain k-anonymity. In *Proceedings of SIGMOD, 2005,* 49–60.

Liu, F., Hua, K. A., & Cai, Y. (2009). *Query l-diversity in location based services.* Paper presented at the International Workshop on Privacy-Aware Location-based Mobile Services (PALMS).

Machanavajjhala, A., Gehrke, J., Kifer, D., & Venkitasubramaniam, M. (2006). l-diversity: Privacy beyond k-anonymity. In *Proceedings of ICDE 2006* (p. 24).

Meyerson, A., & Williams, R. (2004). *On the complexity of optimal k-anonymity* (pp. 223–228). PODS.

Mokbel, M. F., Chow, C.-Y., & Aref, W. G. (2006). *The new casper: Query processing for location services without compromising privacy* (pp. 763–774). VLDB.

Samarati, P. (2001). Protecting respondents' identities in microdata release. *IEEE Transactions on Knowledge and Data Engineering, 13*(6), 1010–1027. doi:10.1109/69.971193

Sweeney, L. (2002). k-anonymity: A model for protecting privacy. *International Journal of Uncertainty. Fuzziness and Knowledge-Based Systems, 10*(5), 557–570. doi:10.1142/S0218488502001648

Xiao, X., & Tao, Y. (2006). Simple and effective privacy preservation. In *VLDB 2006* (pp. 139–150). Anatomy.

Xiao, Z., Xu, J., & Meng, X. (2008). *p-sensitivity: A semantic privacy-protection model for location-based services.* Paper presented at the International Workshop on Privacy-Aware Location-Based Mobile Services (PALMS 2008).

Xu, T., & Cai, Y. (2007). *Location anonymity in continuous location-based services* (p. 39). GIS.

Xu, T., & Cai, Y. (2008). *Exploring historical location data for anonymity preservation in location-based services.* Paper presented at INFOCOM.

This work was previously published in International Journal of Information Security and Privacy, Volume 4, Issue 2, edited by Hamid Nemati, pp. 1-18, copyright 2010 by IGI Publishing (an imprint of IGI Global).

Chapter 7

Globalization and Data Privacy:
An Exploratory Study

Robert L. Totterdale
Robert Morris University, USA

ABSTRACT

Global organizations operate in multiple countries and are subject to both local and federal laws in each of the jurisdictions in which they conduct business. The collection, storage, processing, and transfer of data between countries or operating locations are often subject to a multitude of data privacy laws, regulations, and legal systems that are at times in conflict. Companies struggle to have the proper policies, processes, and technologies in place that will allow them to comply with a myriad of laws which are constantly changing. Using an established privacy management framework, this study provides a summary of major data privacy laws in the U.S., Europe, and India, and their implication for businesses. Additionally, in this paper, relationships between age, residence (country), attitudes and awareness of business rules and data privacy laws are explored for 331 business professionals located in the U.S and India.

INTRODUCTION

As companies extend their operations into multiple geographies around the world, the need for understanding and complying with data privacy laws and regulations in a myriad of jurisdictions has become critical to avoid penalties, fines, loss of reputation, and possible imprisonment. Since over 90% of business records today are in electronic form (Morelli, 2007) understanding what types of content must be secured, how long it must be retained, when it should be destroyed, how it should be secured, and what limitations exist for transferring the content both within and between companies has become very complex. This complexity arises because some geographies

DOI: 10.4018/978-1-4666-0026-3.ch007

have strict laws, others have no or limited laws in place relating to data privacy, and yet others have implemented regulations for only specific types of content, or only to address certain industries or groups (Holder & Grimes, 2007; Perkins & Markel, 2004).

Where data privacy laws do exist, differences have been seen in how data privacy is defined, what is considered to be personally identifiable information, and what obligations a company or individual has to meet the requirements of the law (Barnes, 2006). This is further complicated by the existence of case law, state or municipal law, federal law, or constitutional provisions in each geography that may be applicable to certain aspects of how the information about an individual was captured, transferred, or stored in that geography. Penalties for failure to comply also differ between geographies, with some jurisdictions having little enforcement, while others levy fines and penalties that have been into the millions of dollars (Davies, 2008).

The importance of data privacy to companies is reflected in the literature, and is confirmed by the large number of organizations in the legal, accounting, and consulting fields that provide services, training, and education on the topic. In addition, a number of technology providers offer software, hardware, and network security devices that can play a significant role in meeting compliance needs (Anonymous, 2009a, 2009b; Musthaler, 2008; Totterdale, 2008). However, even with the availability of services and technologies to support compliance along with the implementation of "best practices" in an organization, a partner in a major international law firm argues that "there will always be failures-...." Additionally, Segrio Pedro, a managing director of PWC cites recent survey results from his organization that revealed that "most organizations (54% of respondents) do not know where personal data is collected, transmitted or stored" (Anonymous, 2009d).

This study provides a summary of major data privacy laws in the U.S., Europe, and India. Each

of these countries is a major contributor in global commerce or outsourcing services. In addition, through survey research of 331 professionals who were assigned to one of two technology projects located in the U.S. and India, attitudes toward and awareness of business policies and data privacy laws were assessed. The purpose of the analysis was to explore whether differences in attitudes and awareness existed based on the home geography (i.e. country) of the participants, the project team to which they were assigned, their ages, and their frequency of use of electronic content. These differences were explored through the following research questions:

R1. Do awareness and attitudes differ based on project assignment (i.e. Project 1 or 2)?

R2. Do awareness and attitudes differ based on participant ages?

R3. Do awareness and attitudes differ between U.S. and Indian residents?

R4. Do awareness and attitudes differ for frequent users of electronic content versus infrequent users?

The findings from this research provide insights to differences in attitudes and awareness that may be useful in implementing new business practices to improve compliance and/or minimize business risk.

LITERATURE REVIEW AND COMPANY BACKGROUND

The importance of data privacy has long been recognized in law by many countries, states, and municipalities from around the world (Stephens, 2007). However, the various legal systems today are rarely consistent in their definition of terms, the obligations imposed on individuals and organizations, and the remedies for failure to comply with their respective laws (Perkins & Markel, 2004). Significant laws have been implemented, such as the European Data Directive of 1998 that have provided a framework for attempting to harmonize data privacy laws across their member states and to encourage other countries to adopt a similar platform. Although held out to be an example of a comprehensive approach to achieving data privacy, this legislation itself is currently being questioned as to its adequacy in meeting privacy needs in today's highly complex technological environment.

Privacy Framework

To help gain an understanding of data privacy and its implications for businesses, a privacy framework developed by Earp, Anton, and Jarvinen (2010) has been adapted for use in this paper. This framework provides for evaluating privacy from various organizational perspectives including legal, technical, business rules, social norms, and contractual norms. As depicted in Figure 1, the legal perspective establishes the context for privacy, and serves to constrain the other perspectives. Since social and contractual norms are often embodied within business rules, they are not separately addressed in this paper.

Legal Perspective: Privacy and Personally Identifiable Information

An important element of the legal perspective is to understand how privacy is defined. Although there are many definitions of what constitutes privacy, O'Reilly (2008) suggested that it can be defined as "the ability to exclude others from seeing your personally sensitive information" and as such is "an exclusion of others without your individual consent to disclosure" (p. 2). Standler (1997) argued that privacy is "the expectation that confidential personal information disclosed in a private place will not be disclosed to third parties … where information can be broadly interpreted to include "facts, images, or disparaging opinions" (p. 1). In addition, a report by Linklaters (2009b),

Figure 1. Privacy framework

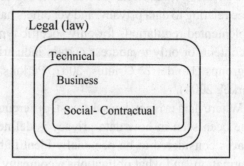

an international law firm, indicated that even after 10 years since the inception of the Data Protection Directive in Europe, there is still debate over what is considered personal data.

In 1995, the member states of the European Union (now totaling 27 members) adopted the EU Data Protection Directive (95/46/EC) that applied to the collecting, recording, using and storing of *personal data* or personally sensitive information which was defined as "any information relating to an identified or identifiable natural person" (European Union, 1995). Examples of personal data included name, height and weight, medical records, blood type, ID numbers, ethnic origin, income, credit and loan records, employee files, disciplinary actions, and social status. Personal data did not include any information that was publically available; such as job title, telephone number, or address (Perkins & Markel, 2004). However, with the continued evolution of technology, the EU Working Party 29 in April of 2008, issued an opinion that interpreted personal information to include several other types of data processed by search engines including actual search queries from users, IP addresses of users, and cookies (Van Eecke & Truyens, 2008; Swartz, 2008). This opinion is evidence that as technology changes occur, new laws are often enacted, or existing laws are interpreted in reaction to these changes.

Unfortunately for global commerce, there is no one common definition of privacy or personally identifiable information that has been universally adopted. In addition to varying definitions of privacy, countries, states, and local governments have implemented a number of laws that afford different degrees of protection. Laws specific to the United States, Europe, and India are included in the following paragraphs.

Legal Perspective: United States

"In the United States, informational privacy protections are provided by an assortment of federal and state constitutional law, statutory provisions, and judicially determined case law" (Gindin, 1997, p. 14). The right of privacy is not specifically guaranteed by the constitution, although some protections can be found in the first and fourth amendments. U.S. industry has also developed certain privacy practices and policies that have resulted in self regulation in lieu of specific guidance from the courts and legislative bodies (Stephens, 2007). The following paragraphs summarize key protections provided by state and federal law.

Cases, such as *Katz v. United States,* confirmed Fourth Amendment rights relating to a reasonable expectation of privacy in communications. A military court in 1995, citing the Katz decision, found that there was also a reasonable expectation of privacy relating to email communications (Gindin, 1997). Through the Privacy Protection Act of the First Amendment, privacy limits have been cited relating to the governmental seizure of publishers' work product materials. Since anyone posting messages on the Internet can be considered a "publisher," the protections from this Act would apply.

Early privacy legislation can be seen in the Privacy Act of 1974 that protects information about U.S. Citizens captured in records maintained by federal agencies. However, when the Act was enacted, compromises "left the statue encumbered, as a bureaucratic paperwork exercise oriented to paper files, limited to the systems of records" (O'Reilly, 2008, p. 4). Also, the Act applied only to federal agencies and did not address the broader issue of both domestic and international entities.

Other legislative efforts have focused on specific issues or industries such as health records in 1996 (HIPAA) and obligations of financial services companies (Graham Leach Bliley Act, 1999). With respect to health records, HIPAA limits the circumstances under which personally identifiable health information may be released to individuals or entities (Holder & Grimes, 2007). For financial services companies, the Graham Leach-Bliley Act of 1999 restricts how customer financial data can be shared within and between institutions, and imposes certain duties on the financial institutions regarding the safekeeping of the data. Other federal legislation from the Federal Trade Commission has made it an unfair practice under section 5 of the FTC Act to hold personal data without providing adequate security (Gilbert, 2008).

In addition to federal law, a number of states have passed laws dealing with various aspects of information privacy. As an example, California in 2002 enacted SB 1386 that requires notification if personal information has been disclosed (Holder & Grimes, 2007), restricts use of social security numbers, and requires financial institutions to obtain permission before sharing personal information with nonaffiliated companies (Stephens, 2007). Similar laws dealing with notification have been enacted in several states including Arkansas, Connecticut, Florida, Georgia, Illinois, Indiana, Montana, Nevada, Texas, and Washington (Paez & Galil, 2005). Further, Bennett and Paez (2009) found that an increasing number of states in the U.S. actively regulate how and when organizations must protect personal information, and that 33 states have "adopted laws restricting or prohibiting the collection, use, or disclosure of social security numbers by private entities" (p. 2). Additionally, they suggest that "because the scope and underlying requirements of each state law differ, organizations must separately evaluate their potential obligations under each state law" (p. 3).

Recent legislation enacted in 2008 in Massachusetts and Nevada, significantly expand a continuing trend of increasing regulation of- and potential liability relating to- the business use of individuals' personal information (Kirkland & Ellis, 2008). In Massachusetts, personal information is defined as "a person's name in combination with a Social Security number, drivers license, state ID number, or financial account, credit card, or debit card" (p. 2). The law is not limited to businesses with a physical presence in the state, which has serious implications for companies throughout the U.S. The law requires that companies adopt a written information security program that meets approximately 14 standards and that they implement a computer security program that meets eight defined requirements. In contrast to the Massachusetts law, the Nevada law has a narrower definition of personal information in that it only applies to customers.

Legal Perspective: Europe

Adding further complexity for organizations that do business and maintain personal information globally, a number of countries as well as the European Union have implemented laws that reflect their views on privacy and the ability of an organization to move personal information from one geographic location to another (Dowling, 2007). Summarized below is information relating to laws enacted by the EU, and various European countries which are major trading partners with the U.S.

A significant piece of legislation relating to data privacy enacted by the European Union is the 1998 Directive on Data Protection (95/46/EU) (European Union, 1995). This legislation, which has formed the basis for many countries' privacy laws, provides for a continent wide standard of protection for all European citizens. The law requires that personal data be managed such that it

is collected for specified and legitimate purposes, and not processed further, that it is relevant and not excessive for the purpose collected, that it is accurate and updated as necessary, and that it is kept in a form that permits identification of data subjects for no longer than necessary (Stephens, 2007). Further, the law prohibits the direct transfer of data to other countries unless those countries provide adequate protection for the data. The U.S. is not considered compliant. In Europe, "there is a presumption that the government actively engages in efforts to protect individual rights" (O'Reilly, 2008, p. 11). The directive was aimed at the multitude of laws that would negatively affect the common market within the EU especially, where trans-border data flows were involved. Further legislation was adopted by the EU in 2002 concerning the processing of personal data and the protection of privacy in the electronic communications standard. This e-privacy directive introduces restrictions on "unsolicited communications" by email and SMS (Morrison & Foerster, 2008).

In addition to the broad coverage provided by the European Data Directive, each of the member states in the EU is expected to have their own local data protection legislation. Although there is some consistency between the various country laws such as the Spanish Organic Law 12/1999 (Azin-Khan, Nicholson, Liotta, & Hodgkinson, 2008), the German Federal Data Protection Act, the French Data Protection Act, and the U.K.'s Data Privacy Act (1998) (Warren & Oppenheim, 2004), differences exist relating to the scope of the legislation, penalties, and enforcement actions (Linklaters 2009a; Davies, 2008).

Although the EU Directive is seen by many as being one of the most comprehensive laws relating to data privacy, the Information Commissioner's Office (ICO) in the U.K. believes that the European Data Protection law needs to be modernized to meet the technological and social challenges of the 21st century (Anonymous, 2008). The ICO suggests that the current law is out of date and fails to meet challenges relating to transfer of personal information across borders, and the huge growth in personal information on line. In addition to a study commissioned by the ICO to address these issues, the European Commission is planning a study to consider changes to the law.

Since the EU does not believe that the existing legal framework in the U.S. provides adequate protection for personal information, a US. Safe Harbor Agreement (between the EU and the U.S.) has been implemented where organizations signing the agreement certify that they have implemented some number of the practices required by the EU and can therefore be considered compliant (Barnes, 2006). Although this mechanism has in most cases allowed commerce to continue, and has been viewed as compliant by EU members, concerns remain about the adequacy of this agreement to insure proper levels of privacy. Other options for permitting the transfer of protected personal data outside of the EU include the adoption of Binding Corporate Rules (BCRs), and the adoption of Model Clauses. With respect to BCRS, they allow a multinational organization to establish its own internal rules, provided that they meet European data protection law requirements. The adoption of these rules, however, does increase a company's potential liability by increasing the rights of data subjects to enforce their rights. Conversely the "model clauses" are "pre-approved" clauses by the European data authorities for use in data transfer contracts. The adoption of Model Clauses requires that the company adopting the clauses submit to European laws, provides for private rights of enforcement by individuals, and subject the company to audits by the European Data Protection Authorities (Tanenbaum & Echegoyen, 2007).

Legal Perspective: India

In addition to conducting business with European countries, many U.S. companies outsource IT and business functions to India which hosts billions of dollars of outsourcing business, and employs several hundred thousand employees in this area

(Kumaraguru & Cranor, 2006). Although India has successfully claimed a significant share of the offshore business process outsourcing (BPO market), concerns exist about the level of data protection afforded by their legal system (Dalal, 2009). There is no omnibus data security law in the country; however, constitutional and legislative provisions that are applicable to data protection and security (Holder & Grimes, 2007; Freshfields Bruckaus Deringer, 2008) do exist. Under Article 21 of the constitution, the Supreme Court recognized a right to privacy although the extent and nature remains in question. Similarly, protections are provided for freedom of speech in Article 19, but also without much definition or specificity. There are also some provisions in the Information Technology Act of 2000 which deals with breach of confidentiality and privacy, however "this section falls woefully short of providing specificity needed for effective regulation" (p. 702). After eight years, in December of 2008, amendments to the 2000 Act were incorporated and passed into Bill 2008. This bill unfortunately has received criticism from multiple corners, including from the IT Secretary Singh that declared "the ministry would shortly come up with fresh regulations to be added to the bill" (Anonymous, 2009c). Other Indian statues such as the Indian Penal Code, 1860, the Consumer Protection Act, 1986 and the Copyright Act of 1972 also indirectly protect the disclosure of personal data (White & Case, 2007). However, compared to other more comprehensive privacy laws in the EU and other countries, improvements are necessary (Kumaraguru & Cranor, 2006).

Business Perspective

Having assessed the legal perspective of the privacy framework, the next dimension to examine is the business perspective, which includes business implications of the legal perspective, business relationships, cultural aspects, and policies. For organizations that transact business globally, or outsource all or portions of their transaction processing to other countries, a critical business implication is the need to understand local and federal laws relating to data privacy, and their impact on the capture and transfer of data between countries (Perkins & Markel, 2004). The failure to properly protect personal information, or to comply with privacy laws, has resulted in large fines such as the $2.25 Million CVS settlement regarding the loss of credit card, medical records, and social security numbers (Pereira, 2009), and the £980,000 fine levied against the Nationwide Building society for failing to have effective systems and controls to manage its information security risks (Clifford Chance, 2007).

Because organizations must deal with a complex network of legal systems, and must manage increasingly large databases of business content, the marketplace has responded by having professional service firms (legal, consulting, and accounting) offering assistance in the area of data privacy, and by having technology solutions introduced to help manage and control risk. A review of web sites of the top 10 International Law firms as cited in the American Lawyer in October 2008, found that all of the firms provided legal services relating to data privacy, provided publications and newsletters on the topic to their clients, and often times provided briefings and seminars. These service providers are representative of the "contractual" dimension of the business perspective.

Culture, another key element of a business organization, has been shown to "affect a populations attitudes toward privacy" (Kumaraguru & Cranor, 2006). In a study conducted by Hofstede and Hofstede (2005) involving over 72 countries dealing with national culture, individuals were found to be influenced by multiple cultures, including organizational, gender, social class, industry, and occupational. In Hofstede's study, India was identified as a collectivist society where individuals have more trust and faith than individuals in individualist societies such as the United States (Totterdale, 2009). This level of trust suggests perhaps less concern over the use of personal information and general privacy concerns. Another study of 407 Indians, conducted in 2004 by Kumaraguru and Cranor (2006), focused on individual's attitudes and awareness of privacy in India. Findings from this study suggested that there was less concern and awareness of privacy among Indians than among Americans based on survey results.

In addition to attitudes and awareness, Stephens (2005) argues for the need for global baseline retention policies, enterprise wide consistency of retention policies, and compliance with international retention laws. These business rules, an integral part of the business perspective, must deal with the many laws and regulations that exist around the globe, and must be understood by the employees of an organization.

Technical Perspective

The final dimension of the privacy framework to be addressed relates to technology. As technology has become pervasive in society and business, solutions to improve security and protect privacy have been introduced. At the same time, the growth of the use of technology to support large global databases, advances in data mining, computer networking, wireless computing, near real time availability of information, and ubiquitous computing, has introduced the need for complex trade-offs between policy and technology functionality (Agre & Rotenberg, 1998).

With respect to technology solutions in the marketplace, organizations such as Opentext, IBM, EMC, Oracle, and SAP all offer technology solutions that can assist in securing and managing content within an organization (Anonymous, 2009a, 2009b, Clifton, Kantarcioglu, & Vaidya, 2002; Totterdale, 2008). In addition, a recent data privacy application from SAP and Cisco "uses real time network monitoring of business policies and controls" to flag and prevent data security breaches (Musthaler, 2008). Other privacy enhancing technologies include capabilities such as "public-key cryptographic methods" for controlling access to sensitive information (Agre & Rotenberg, 1998, p. 4).

The professional services organization participating in this research utilized a number of collaboration tools and technologies including SharePoint Services, Outlook, Lotus Notes and Clearcase/Clearquest to secure and manage their electronic content. Security rules and password protection was implemented to restrict access where appropriate and consistent with business requirements (Totterdale, 2009).

A final element of the technology perspective relates to its adoption in an organization. Earlier research by Davis (1989) identified perceived usefulness and ease of use as the primary components of a technology acceptance model. The dimensions of privacy and security have subsequently been explored by other researchers to assess their effects on customer attitudes and adaptation. In a study conducted by Jahangir and Begum (2007) in e-banking, security, and privacy were found to be positively related to customer attitudes toward the adoption of a technology and customer adaptation.

Summary

As previously discussed, organizations must understand the laws (legal perspective) in all of the geographies that they operate, and must implement business policies and processes (business perspective) and technologies (technology perspective) to adhere to numerous legal systems and business needs. Through focus group feedback and survey research, this study assesses whether attitudes and awareness of business rules and laws vary between projects, countries, and age groups. In the next section of this report, attitudes and awareness of business policies and laws relating to privacy by individuals in a global professional services firm are examined.

METHODOLOGY

This study is based on survey and focus group data obtained from a global professional services firm during a two week period in October and November of 2008. The data used for this analysis represents a subset of survey results gathered from a broader survey instrument that focused on the capture and storage of electronic content. The purpose of this study was to determine if attitudes and awareness regarding data privacy and company policies differed between younger and older professionals, between professionals located in the U.S. and India, and between two project teams that have staffing in both India and the U.S. In addition, the research was intended to assess if differences in attitude and awareness existed between frequent users of electronic content and those who used it infrequently, or not at all.

Given the size of the organization participating in the research, and the need to capture information both quickly and economically, a survey was used for data collection. The survey was cross sectional where the data was collected at one point in time and was administered on-line through Zoomerang, an Internet survey tool.

Population and Demographics

The professional services organization had over 100,000 employees at the time the research was conducted. Executives from the firm agreed to have six of their project teams or groups made up of a total of 1,985 personnel participate in the study. This convenience sample, which included multiple age groups and geographies, was considered to be representative of the broader organization. Since the email addresses of the 1,985 participants were known, a single stage sampling procedure was used and 100% of the population was sent the link to the electronic survey instrument. The survey tool captured 785 responses across multiple geographies. These responses were then filtered to include only participants from India and the U.S.

Table 1. Survey questions

Type	Description	Perspective
Attitude With respect to electronic content in the company, it is important that:	Q1. All client related documents are properly filed within a collaboration tool. Q2. All emails that reference a client are properly filed within a collaboration tool.	Technology
Attitude It is important to properly categorize electronic content in order to:	Q3. Comply with local laws Q4. Meet long term records mgmt and retention needs. Q5. Comply with company policies and procedures. Q6. Secure information to restrict access.	Legal Business Business Business
Awareness Relating to electronic content that I work with:	Q7. I am aware of local laws and regulations relating to data privacy. Q8. I am aware of company policies and procedures relating to confidentiality	Legal Business
Frequency of Use How often do you use collaboration tools to save, edit, or access the following:	Q9. Documents Q10. Email	N/A

that were assigned to either 'project one' or 'project two' (actual names removed for confidentiality reasons). A total of 331 responses were included in this analysis. Each of the two teams selected for inclusion in this study provided application development and on-going system maintenance for a different client of the organization.

Survey Instrument

A survey instrument was constructed to gather demographic data including a participant's country of residence, age, and project team assignment as well as information relating to technology use, attitudes, and awareness. Survey questions were developed from a series of focus group meetings that included approximately 35 individuals from the population to be surveyed. Once the survey document was developed, it was tested on seven individuals to insure that the questions were understood and that the results were consistent with focus group feedback.

The specific questions included in the survey are shown in Table 1. The phrase "properly filed" represents that content which accurately identifies the client, project, folder/sub folder, and security

rules necessary for the retrieval and management of the content. Each survey question has been related to the privacy framework previously discussed.

The questions included in the survey were designed to capture attitudes about the importance of properly categorizing electronic content as well as information about a participant's awareness of local privacy laws. Two final questions relating to how often a participant works with electronic content were included to provide a basis for determining if differences existed in attitudes between frequent and infrequent users. After defining the survey questions, the next step in the development of the survey instrument was to define the response categories or scales to gather information from the participants. All "importance" questions used a five-point Likert-like scale with valid responses of "Don't Know", "Disagree", Somewhat Disagree", "Somewhat Agree", and "Agree." For frequency of use responses, a five point Likert-like scale consisting of "Not at All," "Seldom," "Occasionally," "Often and Frequently" was used. Age groupings used in the survey included <26, 26-30, 31-36, 37-47, and 48 or more.

Table 2. Recoding of variables

Variable	Original Response	Recoded Response
Age	<26	Younger
	27-30	Younger
	31-36	Older
	37-47	Older
	48 or older	Older
Importance/Awareness	Don't Know	Disagree
	Disagree	Disagree
	Somewhat Disagree	Disagree
	Somewhat Agree	Agree
	Agree	Agree
Frequency	Never	Infrequently
	Monthly	Infrequently
	Weekly	Infrequently
	Daily	Frequently
	More than Once a Day	Frequently

As previously indicated, a separate case, or subset of the data was selected within the analysis tool to include only participants from the U.S. and India who worked on one of two projects included in the broader survey. Participants from the U.S. and India were selected since they represented two very different legal systems and cultures yet shared a common company culture, and had a sufficient number of respondents to conduct a meaningful analysis.

Four independent variables (age, geography, project, and frequency of use) were evaluated separately against the dependent variables (importance questions and awareness questions) in the analysis. Recoding of the variables was performed as shown in Table 2 to facilitate the analysis of the data.

Upon closing the survey process, survey feedback was downloaded from Zoomerang and imported into SPSS for reporting and analysis. SPSS was used to generate frequency distributions for the survey responses, and was also used to perform independent sample t-tests to determine if differences in attitudes and awareness levels existed for the age groups, geographies, projects, and usage groups included in the analysis.

RESULTS

From the survey process, 331 respondents self identified themselves as being assigned to either project one or project two, and claimed their residence to be either in the United States or India. This group is the focus of the results and discussion that follows in this section. Descriptive statistics that summarize responses for each of these variables is provided in Table 3.

In addition to country and project variables, information was gathered regarding the ages of

Table 3 Country and project frequencies

Country	Count	%	Project	Count	%
India	135	41	Project One	211	64
U.S.	196	59	Project Two	120	36
Total	331	100	Total	331	100

the participants (i.e. those <=30 and those over 30 years of age). From the responses, 172 participants or 52% indicated that they were less than or equal to 30 years old, while 159 or 48% indicated that they were over 30 years of age. Table 4 summarizes these results.

Other variables that were used in the analysis related to the frequency with which respondents indicated that they saved, edited, or accessed email or electronic documents. Table 5 summarizes the results regarding electronic documents, while Table 6 summarizes the results for email.

With respect to documents, 62% of the respondents (204) said that they did so frequently, while 38% or 127 respondents, indicated that they did so infrequently. Lastly, regarding saving, editing or accessing email, 65% or 216 respondents indicated that they did so frequently, while 35% or 115 respondents indicated that they did so infrequently. Using t-tests for assessing potential differences in means between two groups, each of these variables are evaluated against a series of questions that deal with attitudes and awareness of respondents relating to data privacy, compliance, and security.

As shown in Figure 2, a high percentage (>70%) of respondents indicated their agreement on the importance of properly filing content to meet records management requirements, to secure the

Table 4. Age of participants

Age	Count	%
<=30	172	52
Over 30	159	48
Total	331	100

Table 5. Frequency of saving, editing, or accessing electronic documents

Frequency	Count	%
Frequently saved, edited, or accessed	204	62
Did not frequently save, edit or access	127	38
Total	331	100

Table 6. Frequency of saving, editing, or accessing email

Frequency	Count	%
Frequently saved, edited, or accessed	216	65
Did not frequently save, edit or access	115	35
Total	331	100

Figure 2. Response summary –importance (N=331)

Attitudes- Importance	Don't Know	%	Disagree	%	Neutral	%	Agree	%
Q1. Properly File Documents	0	0	33	10	71	22	227	68
Q2. Properly File Emails	0	0	65	20	84	25	182	55
Q3. Comply with Local Laws	26	8	19	6	61	18	225	68
Q4. Meet Records Mgmt Needs	11	3	14	4	49	15	257	78
Q5. Comply W/Company Policies	15	5	13	4	52	16	251	75
Q6. Secure Info to Restrict Access	13	4	17	5	49	15	252	76

Table 7. Response Summary – Awareness (N=331)

Awareness	Don't Know	%	Disagree	%	Neutral	%	Agree	%
Q7. Aware of Laws-Data Privacy	0	0	33	10	52	16	246	74
Q8. Aware of company policy relating to confidentiality	0	0	9	3	36	11	286	87

content, and to comply with company policies (i.e. business perspective). In contrast, only 68% agreed on the importance of properly categorizing content to comply with local laws (i.e. legal perspective), 55% agreed it was important to properly file emails, and 68% agreed on the importance of properly filing electronic documents.

In addition to survey responses on the importance of laws, security, and business policies, respondents indicated their agreement that they were aware of local laws relating to data privacy 74% of the time and that they were aware of company policies relating to confidentiality 87% of the time (Table 7). Although respondents indicated high levels of awareness and importance relating to laws and policies relating to data privacy, security, and confidential information; approximately 40% (Figure 3) agreed that they would not file or categorize certain types of content because of concerns about these same factors.

After obtaining and summarizing survey responses, t-tests were performed to assess if differences in responses existed between countries, age groups, project teams, and usage groups (i.e. those who work with electronic content frequently versus infrequently). The null hypothesis for each of these tests was that there were no dif-

ferences in mean responses between the groups and each of the survey questions relating to importance and awareness. The findings for t-tests are grouped below for each of the research questions.

R1. Do awareness and attitudes differ based on project assignment?

With the exception of Q1 regarding properly filing documents, and Q2 regarding the proper filing of emails, the null hypothesis cannot be rejected. This finding suggests that there were no significant differences in means for Q3-Q8 between Project One and Project Two, and thus, that attitudes and awareness regarding laws, policies and security were similar. However, respondents from Project Two ($M = 2.47$, $SD = .744$) agreed less often than did the participants of Project One ($M = 2.65$, $SD = .608$), $t(329) = -2.48$, $p < .014$ on the importance of properly filing electronic documents. Conversely, for Q2, relating to the importance of properly filing emails, Project One ($M = 2.45$, $SD = .731$) was more likely than Project Two ($M = 2.18$, $SD = .857$) to agree on its importance, $t(329) = -3.143$, $p < .002$.

Figure 3. Response summary – reasons for not filing content

Reasons for Not Filing Content	Disagree	%	Neutral	%	Agree	%
Concerns About Security	96	29	99	30	136	41
Concerns About Legality	91	27	102	31	138	42
Material Is Personal	107	32	103	31	121	37
Material Is Highly Confidential	68	20	115	35	148	45
Violating a Company Policy	87	26	112	34	132	40

Table 8. Significant effects-country

Question	Country	Statistics		Perspective
Q1 Documents	U.S. India	*M*=2.49, *SD*=.727 *M*=2.73, *SD*=.539	*t*(329)=-3.215, p<.001	Technology
Q2 Email	U.S. India	*M*=2.13, *SD*=.837 *M*=2.67, *SD*=.584	*t*(329)=-6.505, p<.001	Technology
Q7. Awareness Law	U.S. India	*M*=2.58, *SD*=.736 *M*=2.73, *SD*=.507	*t*(329)=-2.079, p<.038	Law

R2. Do awareness and attitudes differ based on participant ages?

No significant effects were found for age, except for Q2, relating to the importance of properly filing email. The null hypothesis cannot be rejected for the other questions (Q1, Q3-Q8) relating to attitudes and awareness. With respect to the importance of properly filing emails (Q2), younger respondents (M= 2.48, SD = .745) were more likely than older respondents (M= 2.21, SD=.814) to agree on its importance, t(329)= 3.135, p<.002.

R3. Do awareness and attitudes differ between U.S. and Indian residents?

Significant effects were found relating to an individual's home country relating to the perceived importance of properly filing electronic documents (Q1) and emails (Q2) as well as regarding their awareness of local laws relating to data privacy (Q7). For the other questions (Q3-Q6, Q8), the null

hypothesis cannot be rejected since no significant differences were found. As shown in Table 8, for Q1, Q2, and Q7, the Indian respondents were more likely than the U.S. respondents to agree on the importance of properly filing documents and emails and on their awareness of laws relating to data privacy.

R4. Do awareness and attitudes differ for frequent users of electronic content versus infrequent users?

Each respondent's usage (i.e. creating, accessing or editing content) of electronic content was captured in order to determine if their usage characteristics (frequent vs. infrequent) was related to their attitudes and awareness, as defined in the survey questions.

As shown in Figure 4, frequent users of electronic content were more likely than infrequent users to be aware of local laws regarding data privacy and to agree on the importance of properly filing electronic documents. In addition, frequent

Figure 4. Frequent document users

Question	Usage-Documents	Statistics		Perspective
Q1 Documents	Infrequently. Frequently	*M*=2.47, *SD*=.733 *M*=2.66, *SD*=.612	t(329)=-2.469, p<.014	Technology
Q4. Records	Infrequently. Frequently	*M*=3.56, *SD*=.842 *M*=3.74, *SD*=.611	t(329)=-2.202, p<.028	Business
Q5. Company Policies	Infrequently. Frequently	*M*=3.49, *SD*=.899 *M*=3.72, *SD*=.657	t(329)=-2.654, p<.008	Business
Q6. Secure Content	Infrequently. Frequently	*M*=3.43, *SD*=.922 *M*=3.76, *SD*=.601	t(329)=-3.999, p<.001	Business
Q7. Awareness Law	Infrequently. Frequently	*M*=2.48, *SD*=.754 *M*=2.75, *SD*=.565	t(329)=-3.638, p<.001	Law

Figure 5. Frequent email users

Question	Usage (Email)	Statistics		Perspective
Q1 Documents	Infrequently.	$M=2.41$, $SD=.748$	$t(329)=-3.601 p<.001$	Technical
	Frequently	$M=2.68$, $SD=.598$		
Q2 Email	Infrequently.	$M=2.12$, $SD=.839$	$t(329)=-3.984$, $p<.001$	Technical
	Frequently	$M=2.48$, $SD=.734$		
Q4. Records	Infrequently.	$M=3.51$, $SD=.852$	$t(329)=-2.914$, $p<.004$	Business
	Frequently	$M=3.75$, $SD=.612$		
Q5. Company Policies	Infrequently.	$M=3.48$, $SD=.930$	$t(329)=-2.627$, $p<.009$	Business
	Frequently	$M=3.71$, $SD=.649$		
Q6. Secure Content	Infrequently.	$M=3.45$, $SD=.939$	$t(329)=-3.187$, $p<.002$	Business
	Frequently	$M=3.73$, $SD=.621$		
Q7. Awareness Law	Infrequently.	$M=2.49$, $SD=.765$	$t(329)=-3.213$, $p<.001$	Law
	Frequently	$M=2.73$, $SD=.574$		

users agreed more often on the importance of filing content to meet records management requirements, to comply with company policies and to the importance of properly securing electronic content. The null hypothesis was rejected for Q1, Q4, and Q5-Q7.

Similar to the findings for frequent users of electronic documents, significance was found for frequent users of email. As shown in Figure 5, frequent email users were more likely than infrequent users to agree on the importance of properly filing document and emails. In addition, frequent email users, were more likely to agree on the importance of properly categorizing content to meet records management needs, to be compliant with company policies, and to properly secure content. A final area of significance observed was that frequent email users were more likely to be aware of laws relating to data privacy.

CONCLUSION

Global organizations must comply with a multitude of laws and legal systems in the various countries in which they operate. Customer, employee, and supplier information in these organizations are increasingly being subjected to data privacy laws. These laws place obligations on companies to obtain consent for collecting information, to require security practices be in place to protect it, to report on any losses or unauthorized disclosures, to keep it for a limited time, and to prohibit the transfer of information across geographic boundaries. Failure to comply with these laws can result in fines, penalties, and imprisonment.

In order to reduce their risks and improve compliance, organizations must implement policies, procedures, and technologies (business and technology perspective) that can help to secure content that is captured, delete it when it is no longer required, and categorize it for storage and retrieval purposes. This implementation must become part of the culture and be incorporated into training programs and corporate communications

Table 9. Variable summary – questions resulting in statistically significant differences

Variable	Q1	Q2	Q3	Q4	Q5	Q6	Q7	Q8
Project (One/Two)	■	■						
Age (Younger/Older)		■						
Country(U.S/India)	■	■					■	
Frequent/Infrequent	■	■		■	■	■	■	

that raise awareness levels about legal obligations and the importance of properly and legally handling personally identifiable information (legal perspective). Companies must also consider where content is stored (i.e. which countries) if they are unable to comply with laws relating to the movement of information across borders. In addition, when creating large databases or data mining applications that may contain personal information, technologies may need to be considered that can restrict or prohibit the retrieval of that information.

For the organization that participated in this study, over 87% of the respondents indicated an awareness of company policies relating to confidentiality, while 74% reported an awareness of local laws and regulations. In addition, over 70% of respondents in the survey "agreed" on the importance of properly categorizing electronic content to comply with local laws, to meet long-term record's needs, to comply with company policies, and to restrict access. These findings suggest the organization has broadly communicated the need for security and confidentiality of information throughout their project teams. Although high levels of awareness were observed in the survey responses, almost 40% of the respondents also indicated that they would not file/categorize certain content because of concerns over privacy, security, or confidentiality. This may reflect concerns about the ability of the technology to properly protect and limit access to highly confidential content.

As summarized in Table 9, differences existed in attitudes toward the proper filing of electronic content (i.e. documents and emails) between the projects, age groups, countries, and frequency of use groups assessed in the study. Of the variables considered, the frequency of use factor was observed to be most significant, where frequent users of electronic content were more likely to recognize the importance of compliance, confidentiality, and security more often than those who worked with electronic content infrequently. This group was also more likely to be aware of local laws. However, no significant differences were found for any of the groups relating to the awareness of company policies on confidentiality, indicating a high level of consistency between the groups on this question.

With respect to the awareness of data privacy laws, the Indian respondents were more likely than the U.S. respondents to indicate that they were aware of local laws. Reasons for this variation cannot be determined from the data, and suggest the need for further exploration. The frequent users of electronic content were also more likely than the infrequent users to claim awareness of local laws. This may indicate that they have received more training or communications on the laws as part of their work activity, or may reflect other variables not examined in this research.

Limitations, Recommendations, and Significance

The data analysis for this study was limited in scope to only participants from two large projects from a professional services firm located in India and the U.S., and as such the results cannot be generalized to other projects or countries. In addition, although the survey questions were designed to capture awareness and attitudes relating to data privacy, they lacked details about specific laws and definitions of what constitutes personally identifiable information. The research also did not attempt to quantify whether individuals actually categorize and file electronic content in a manner that is compliant with both laws and company policies. These limitations suggest opportunities for further research and exploration to gain a better understanding of data privacy policies and practices, and how they are implemented in a global organization.

Since significant differences were found between countries regarding both attitudes and awareness of local laws, additional data collection should be considered to include other geographies such as China, and the various countries in Europe. In addition, studies could be performed to assess compliance of categorization practices by examining actual content and comparing it to legal and internal policy requirements.

The findings that differences existed in attitudes and awareness of laws relating to data privacy and confidentiality, provide valuable insights to global organizations that need to be considered as they attempt to improve their compliance with laws from around the world. The fact that not all respondents were aware of laws and internal policies indicate that further work is required to communicate this information to the entire employee base. In addition, since significant differences between frequent and infrequent users existed, opportunities exist to minimize risk in the organization by improving their awareness of local laws and to change their attitudes about the importance of security, policies, confidentiality, and compliance. Lastly, since participants indicated that they would sometimes not properly file electronic content because of security or confidentiality concerns, an opportunity exists for the company to examine their current technologies and business practices to determine if improvements can be made to minimize or eliminate these concerns and to improve compliance.

REFERENCES

Agre, P., & Rotenberg, M. (1998). *Technology and Privacy: The New Landscape*. Boston: MIT Press.

Anonymous. (2008, July 7). ICO: UK privacy watchdog spearheads debate on the future of European Privacy Law. *M2 Presswire*.

Anonymous. (2009a). Axis Technology, LLC; Axis Technology Unveils Breakthrough Data Masking Platform to Help Companies Ensure Compliance with New Federal and State Privacy Standards. *Managed Care Weekly Digest,*32.

Anonymous. (2009b). EMC Corporation; Healthcare Organizations Deploy RSA Solutions to Improve Privacy and Efficiency of Patient Care. *Managed Care Weekly Digest*, 50.

Anonymous. (2009c). *Indian Information Technology Act, 2000 in Doldrums*. Retrieved from http://www.webnewswire.com/node/450791

Anonymous. (2009d, July 10). Understanding Ops Key To Effective Data Privacy. *Operations Management*.

Azin-Khan, R., Nicholson, J., Liotta, A., & Hodgkinson, D. (2008, May). New Spanish Regulations Tighten Up Data Protection Requirements. *Privacy & Data Security Law Journal*.

Barnes, M. E. (2006). Falling Short of the Mark: The United States Response to the European Union's Data Privacy Directive. *Northwestern Journal of International Law & Business*, 27(1), 171.

Bennett, S., & Paez, M. (2009). *Protecting Social Security Numbers: Federal Legislation in Sight*. Retrieved from http://www.jonesday.com/pubs/pubs_detail.aspx?pubID=S5920

Clifford Chance. (2007). *Theft of Laptop Results in 980,000 Fine*. Retrieved from http://www.cliffordchance.com/expertise/Publications/details.aspx?FilterName=@URL&contentitemid=11704

Clifton, C., Kantarcioglu, M., & Vaidya, J. (2002). *Defining Privacy for Data Mining*. Retrieved from http://cimic.rutgers.edu/~jsvaidya/pub-papers/ngdm-privacy.pdf

Dalal, P. (2009). *Data Protection Regulations in India*. Retrieved from http://www.legalnewsandviews.blogspot.com/2009/04/data-protection-regulations-in-india-html

Davies, J. (2008). Does Europe need a single law on what staff can do in cyberspace? *People Management, 14*(8).

Davis, F. D. (1989). Perceived Usefulness, Perceived Ease of Use, and User Acceptance of Information Technology. *Management Information Systems Quarterly, 13*(3), 20. doi:10.2307/249008

Dowling, D. (2007). *European Union Data Protection Law and US-Based Multinational Banks: A Compliance Primer*. New York: White & Case LLP. Retrieved from http://www.whitecase.com/publications_09012007_1/

Earp, J., Anton, A., & Jarvinen, O. (2002). *A Social, Technical, and Legal Framework for Privacy Management and Policies*. Paper presented at the Americas Conference on Information Systems.

European Union. (1995). *Directive 95/46/EC of the European Parliament*. Retrieved from http:europa.eu.int/comm/internal_market/privacy/index_en.htm

Freshfields Bruckhaus Deringer. (2008). *Data privacy protection across Asia*. Retrieved from http://www.freshfields.com/practices/intellectual/publications/?year=2008

Funk, J. A., & Toher, J. P. (2004). Big Brother Is Watching: A Survey of the Regulatory Landscape Impacting Outsourcing Transactions. *Law Journal Newsletters, 2*(3).

Gilbert, F. (2008, February). Hot Issues in Cyberspace: Critical Information Privacy and Security Issues. *The Practical Lawyer*.

Gindin, S. (1997). *Lost and Found in Cyberspace-Informational Privacy in the Age of the Internet*. Retrieved from http://www.info-law.com/lost.html

Hofstede, G., & Hofstede, G. J. (2005). *Cultures and Organizations: Software of the Mind*. New York: McGraw-Hill.

Holder, J. T., & Grimes, D. E. (2007). Government Regulated Data Privacy: The Challenge for Global Outsourcer. *Georgetown Journal of International Law, 38*(3), 16.

Jahangir, N., & Begum, N. (2007). Effect of Perceived Usefulness, Ease of Use, Security and Privacy on Consumer Attitude and Adaptation in the Context of E-Banking. *Journal of Management Research, 7*(3).

Kirkland & Ellis. (2008). *New Laws Significantly Regulate Business Practices Relating to Personal Information*. Retrieved from http://www.kirkland.com/siteFiles/Publications/044FFB8745AE1B2ED379DF50D8897FD2.pdf

Kumaraguru, P., & Cranor, L. (2006). Privacy in India: Attitudes and Awareness. In *Privacy Enhancing Technologies* (LNCS 3856, pp. 243-258).

Linklaters. (2009a). *Data Protection 2009- Current Issues in Privacy and Data Protection*. Retrieved from http://www.linklaters.com/pdfs/seminars/dpconference2009.pdf

Linklaters. (2009b). *Technology Media and Communications*. Retrieved from http://www.linklaters.com/TMTnews/index.asp?issuestoryid=4014&languageid=1&opendivs=,16

Morelli, J. (2007). Hybrid filing schemes: the use of metadata signposts in functional file plans. *Records Management Journal, 17*(1), 17. doi:10.1108/09565690710730679

Morrison-Foerster. (2008). *European Law & Regulations: A survival guide for technology companies.*

Musthaler, L. (2008, November 10). New approach to a network-based data privacy application. *Network World.*

O'Reilly, J. (2008). Don't Stick Your Head in the Sand. *Vital Speeches of the Day, 74*(6), 9.

Paez, M., & Galil, Y. (2005). *New York Enacts Data Security and Notification Law.* Retrieved from https://extranet.jonesday.com/pubs/pubs_detail.aspx?pubID=S2813

Pereira, J. (2009). Corporate News: CVS to Pay $2.25 Million In Privacy Case. *Wall Street Journal,* p. B.4. Retrieved from http://proquest.umi.com/pqdweb?did=1647569251&Fmt=7&clientId=2138&RQT=309&VName=PQD

Perkins, E., & Markel, M. (2004). Multinational data-privacy laws: an introduction for IT managers. *IEEE Transactions on Professional Communication, 47*(2), 85–94. doi:10.1109/TPC.2004.828207

Standler, R. (1997). *Privacy Law in the USA.* Retrieved from https://www.rbs2.com/privacy.htm

Stephens, D. O. (2007). Protecting Personal Privacy in the Global Business Environment. *Information Management Journal, 41*(3).

Swartz, N. (2008). EU Panel: Delete Search Info Sooner. *Information Management Journal, 42*(4).

Tanenbaum, W. A., & Echegoyen, R. (2007, September). Getting a Grip on European Data Transfers. *New York Law Journal.*

Totterdale, R. L. (2008). Enterprise content management- A usability study. *Issues in Information Systems,* IX.

Totterdale, R. L. (2009). *Exploring Barriers to the Categorization of Electronic Content in a Global Professional Services Firm.* Pittsburgh: Robert Morris University.

Van Eecke, P., & Truyens, M. (2008, June). Recent Events in EU Internet Law. *Journal of Internet Law.*

Warren, A., & Oppenheim, C. (2004). Integration of Roles? Implementing New Information Laws in UK Public Organizations. *Journal of Information Science, 30*(48), 48–59. doi:10.1177/0165551504041678

White & Case. (2007). *Data Privacy.* Retrieved from http://www.whitecase.com/presentations/dataprivacy/

This work was previously published in International Journal of Information Security and Privacy, Volume 4, Issue 2, edited by Hamid Nemati, pp. 19-35, copyright 2010 by IGI Publishing (an imprint of IGI Global).

Chapter 8
Security Issues for Cloud Computing

Kevin Hamlen
The University of Texas at Dallas, USA

Murat Kantarcioglu
The University of Texas at Dallas, USA

Latifur Khan
The University of Texas at Dallas, USA

Bhavani Thuraisingham
The University of Texas at Dallas, USA

ABSTRACT

In this paper, the authors discuss security issues for cloud computing and present a layered framework for secure clouds and then focus on two of the layers, i.e., the storage layer and the data layer. In particular, the authors discuss a scheme for secure third party publications of documents in a cloud. Next, the paper will converse secure federated query processing with map Reduce and Hadoop, and discuss the use of secure co-processors for cloud computing. Finally, the authors discuss XACML implementation for Hadoop and discuss their beliefs that building trusted applications from untrusted components will be a major aspect of secure cloud computing.

INTRODUCTION

There is a critical need to securely store, manage, share and analyze massive amounts of complex (e.g., semi-structured and unstructured) data to determine patterns and trends in order to improve the quality of healthcare, better safeguard the nation and explore alternative energy. Because of the critical nature of the applications, it is important that clouds be secure. The major security challenge with clouds is that the owner of the data may not have control of where the data is placed. This is because if one wants to exploit the benefits of using cloud computing, one must also utilize the resource allocation and scheduling provided by clouds. Therefore, we need to safeguard the data in the midst of untrusted processes.

DOI: 10.4018/978-1-4666-0026-3.ch008

The emerging cloud computing model attempts to address the explosive growth of web-connected devices, and handle massive amounts of data. Google has now introduced the MapReduce framework for processing large amounts of data on commodity hardware. Apache's Hadoop distributed file system (HDFS) is emerging as a superior software component for cloud computing combined with integrated parts such as MapReduce. The need to augment human reasoning, interpreting, and decision-making abilities has resulted in the emergence of the Semantic Web, which is an initiative that attempts to transform the web from its current, merely human-readable form, to a machine-processable form. This in turn has resulted in numerous social networking sites with massive amounts of data to be shared and managed. Therefore, we urgently need a system that can scale to handle a large number of sites and process massive amounts of data. However, state of the art systems utilizing HDFS and MapReduce are not sufficient due to the fact that they do not provide adequate security mechanisms to protect sensitive data.

We are conducting research on secure cloud computing. Due to the extensive complexity of the cloud, we contend that it will be difficult to provide a holistic solution to securing the cloud, at present. Therefore, our goal is to make increment enhancements to securing the cloud that will ultimately result in a secure cloud. In particular, we are developing a secure cloud consisting of hardware (includes 800TB of data storage on a mechanical disk drive, 2400 GB of memory and several commodity computers), software (includes Hadoop) and data (includes a semantic web data repository). Our cloud system will: (a) support efficient storage of encrypted sensitive data, (b) store, manage and query massive amounts of data, (c) support fine-grained access control and (d) support strong authentication. This paper describes our approach to securing the cloud. The organization of this paper is as follows: In section 2, we will give an overview of security issues for cloud. In section 3, we will discuss secure third party publication of data in clouds. In section 4, we will discuss how encrypted data may be queried. Section 5 will discuss Hadoop for cloud computing and our approach to secure query processes with Hadoop. The paper is concluded in section 6.

SECURITY ISSUES FOR CLOUDS

There are numerous security issues for cloud computing as it encompasses many technologies including networks, databases, operating systems, virtualization, resource scheduling, transaction management, load balancing, concurrency control and memory management. Therefore, security issues for many of these systems and technologies are applicable to cloud computing. For example, the network that interconnects the systems in a cloud has to be secure. Furthermore, virtualization paradigm in cloud computing results in several security concerns. For example, mapping the virtual machines to the physical machines has to be carried out securely. Data security involves encrypting the data as well as ensuring that appropriate policies are enforced for data sharing. In addition, resource allocation and memory management algorithms have to be secure. Finally, data mining techniques may be applicable to malware detection in clouds.

We have extended the technologies and concepts we have developed for secure grid to a secure cloud. We have defined a layered framework for assured cloud computing consisting of the secure virtual machine layer, secure cloud storage layer, secure cloud data layer, and the secure virtual network monitor layer (Figure 1). Cross cutting services are provided by the policy layer, the cloud monitoring layer, the reliability layer and the risk analysis layer.

For the Secure Virtual Machine (VM) Monitor we are combining both hardware and software solutions in virtual machines to handle problems such as key logger examining XEN developed at

Figure 1. Layered framework for assured cloud

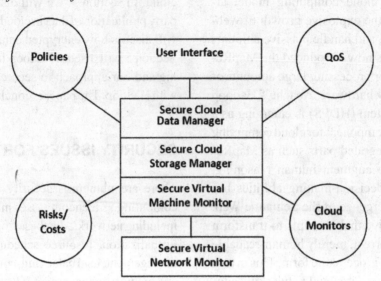

the University of Cambridge and exploring security to meet the needs of our applications (e.g., secure distributed storage and data management). For Secure Cloud Storage Management, we are developing a storage infrastructure which integrates resources from multiple providers to form a massive virtual storage system. When a storage node hosts the data from multiple domains, a VM will be created for each domain to isolate the information and corresponding data processing. Since data may be dynamically created and allocated to storage nodes, we are investigating secure VM management services including VM pool management, VM diversification management, and VM access control management. Hadoop and MapReduce are the technologies being used. For Secure Cloud Data Management, we have developed secure query processing algorithms for RDF (Resource Description Framework) and SQL (HIVE) data in clouds with an XACML-based (eXtensible Access Control Markup Language) policy manager utilizing the Hadoop/MapReduce Framework. For Secure Cloud Network Management, our goal is to implement a Secure Virtual Network Monitor (VNM)

that will create end-to-end virtual links with the requested bandwidth, as well as monitor the computing resources. Figure 2 illustrates the technologies we are utilizing for each of the layers.

This project is being carried out in close collaboration with the AFOSR MURI project on Assured Information Sharing and EOARD funded research project on policy management for information sharing. We have completed a robust demonstration of secure query processing. We have also developed secure storage algorithms and completed the design of XACML for Hadoop. Since Yahoo has come up with a secure Hadoop, we can now implement our design. We have also developed access control and accountability for cloud.

In this paper, we will focus only on some aspects of the secure cloud, namely aspects of the cloud storage and data layers. In particular, (i) we describe ways of efficiently storing the data in foreign machines, (ii) querying encrypted data, as much of the data on the cloud may be encrypted and (iii) secure query processing of the data. We are using Hadoop distributed file system for

Figure 2. Layered framework for assured cloud

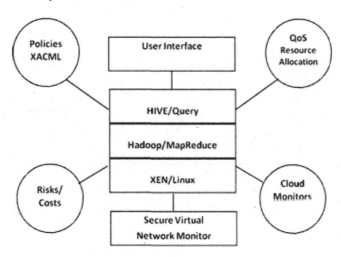

virtualization at the storage level and applying security for Hadoop which includes an XACML implementation. In addition, we are investigating secure federated query processing on clouds over Hadoop. These efforts will be described in the subsequent sections. Subsequent papers will describe the design and implementation of each of the layers.

THIRD PARTY SECURE DATA PUBLICATION APPLIED TO CLOUD

Cloud computing facilitates storage of data at a remote site to maximize resource utilization. As a result, it is critical that this data be protected and only given to authorized individuals. This essentially amounts to secure third party publication of data that is necessary for data outsourcing, as well as external publications. We have developed techniques for third party publication of data in a secure manner. We assume that the data is represented as an XML document. This is a valid assumption as many of the documents on the web are now represented as XML documents. First, we discuss the access control framework proposed in Bertino (2002) and then discuss secure third party publication discussed in Bertino (2004).

In the access control framework proposed in Bertino (2002), security policy is specified depending on user roles and credentials (see Figure 3). Users must possess the credentials to access XML documents. The credentials depend on their roles. For example, a professor has access to all of the details of students while a secretary only has access to administrative information. XML specifications are used to specify the security policies. Access is granted for an entire XML document or portions of the document. Under certain conditions, access control may be propagated down the XML tree.

For example, if access is granted to the root, it does not necessarily mean access is granted to all the children. One may grant access to the XML schema and not to the document instances. One may grant access to certain portions of the document. For example, a professor does not have access to the medical information of students while he has access to student grade and academic information. Design of a system for enforcing access control policies is also described in Bertino (2002). Essentially, the goal is to use a form of view modification so that the user is authorized to see the XML views as specified by the policies. More research needs to be done on role-based access control for XML and the semantic web.

Figure 3. Access control framework

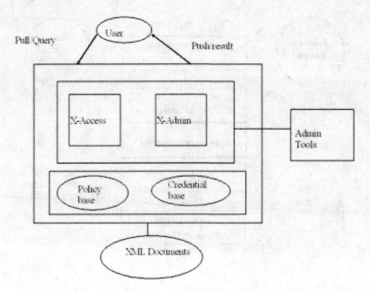

In Bertino (2004), we discuss the secure publication of XML documents (see Figure 4). The idea is to have untrusted third party publishers. The owner of a document specifies access control polices for the subjects. Subjects get the policies from the owner when they subscribe to a document. The owner sends the documents to the Publisher. When the subject requests a document, the publisher will apply the policies relevant to the subject and give portions of the documents to the subject. Now, since the publisher is untrusted, it may give false information to the subject. There-fore, the owner will encrypt various combinations of documents and policies with his/her private key. Using Merkle signature and the encryption techniques, the subject can verify the authenticity and completeness of the document (see Figure 4 for secure publishing of XML documents).

In the cloud environment, the third party publisher is the machine that stored the sensitive data in the cloud. This data has to be protected and the techniques we have discussed above have to be applied to that authenticity and completeness can be maintained.

Figure 4. Secure third party publication

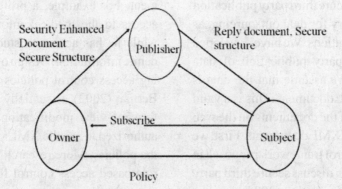

ENCRYPTED DATA STORAGE FOR CLOUD

Since data in the cloud will be placed anywhere, it is important that the data is encrypted. We are using secure co-processor as part of the cloud infrastructure to enable efficient encrypted storage of sensitive data. One could ask us the question: why not implement your software on hardware provided by current cloud computing systems such as Open Cirrus? We have explored this option. First, Open Cirrus provides limited access based on their economic model (e.g., Virtual cash). Furthermore, Open Cirrus does not provide the hardware support we need (e.g., secure co-processors). By embedding a secure co-processor (SCP) into the cloud infrastructure, the system can handle encrypted data efficiently (see Figure 5).

Basically, SCP is a tamper-resistant hardware capable of limited general-purpose computation. For example, IBM 4758 Cryptographic Coprocessor (IBM) is a single-board computer consisting of a CPU, memory and special-purpose cryptographic hardware contained in a tamper-resistant shell, certified to level 4 under FIPS PUB 140-1. When installed on the server, it is capable of performing local computations that are completely hidden from the server. If tampering is detected, then the secure co-processor clears the internal memory. Since the secure coprocessor is tamper-resistant, one could be tempted to run the entire sensitive data storage server on the secure co-processor. Pushing the entire data storage functionality into a secure co-processor is not feasible due to many reasons.

First of all, due to the tamper-resistant shell, secure co-processors have usually limited memory (only a few megabytes of RAM and a few kilobytes of non-volatile memory) and computational power (Smith, 1999). Performance will improve over time, but problems such as heat dissipation/power use (which must be controlled to avoid disclosing processing) will force a gap between general purposes and secure computing. Another

Figure 5. Parts of the proposed instrument

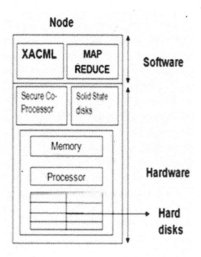

issue is that the software running on the SCP must be totally trusted and verified. This security requirement implies that the software running on the SCP should be kept as simple as possible. So how does this hardware help in storing large sensitive data sets? We can encrypt the sensitive data sets using random private keys and to alleviate the risk of key disclosure, we can use tamper-resistant hardware to store some of the encryption/decryption keys (i.e., a master key that encrypts all other keys). Since the keys will not reside in memory unencrypted at any time, an attacker cannot learn the keys by taking the snapshot of the system. Also, any attempt by the attacker to take control of (or tamper with) the co-processor, either through software or physically, will clear the co-processor, thus eliminating a way to decrypt any sensitive information. This framework will facilitate (a) secure data storage and (b) assured information sharing. For example, SCPs can be used for privacy preserving information integration which is important for assured information sharing.

We have conducted research on querying encrypted data as well as secure multipart computation (SMC). With SMC protocols, one knows about his own data but not his partner's data since the data is encrypted. However, operations can be

Figure 6. Hadoop Distributed File System (HDFS architecture)

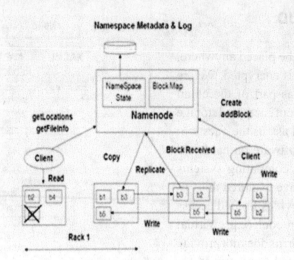

performed on the encrypted data and the results of the operations are available for everyone, say, in the coalition to see. One drawback of SMC is the high computation costs. However, we are investigating more efficient ways to develop SMC algorithms and how these mechanisms can be applied to a cloud.

SECURE QUERY PROCESSING WITH HADOOP

Overview of Hadoop

A major part of our system is HDFS which is a distributed Java-based file system with the capacity to handle a large number of nodes storing petabytes of data. Ideally a file size is a multiple of 64 MB. Reliability is achieved by replicating the data across several hosts. The default replication value is 3 (i.e., data is stored on three nodes). Two of these nodes reside on the same rack while the other is on a different rack. A cluster of data nodes constructs the file system. The nodes transmit data over HTTP and clients' access data using a web browser. Data nodes communicate with each other to regulate, transfer and replicate data.

HDFS architecture is based on the Master-Slave approach (Figure 6). The master is called a Namenode and contains metadata. It keeps the directory tree of all files and tracks which data is available from which node across the cluster. This information is stored as an image in memory. Data blocks are stored in Datanodes. The namenode is the single point of failure as it contains the metadata. So, there is optional secondary Namenode that can be setup on any machine. The client accesses the Namenode to get the metadata of the required file. After getting the metadata, the client directly talks to the respective Datanodes in order to get data or to perform IO actions (Hadoop). On top of the file systems there exists the *map/reduce engine*. This engine consists of a Job Tracker. The client applications submit map/reduce jobs to this engine. The Job Tracker attempts to place the work near the data by pushing the work out to the available Task Tracker nodes in the cluster.

Inadequacies of Hadoop

Current systems utilizing Hadoop have the following limitations:

1. **No facility to handle encrypted sensitive data:** Sensitive data ranging from medical

records to credit card transactions need to be stored using encryption techniques for additional protection. Currently, HDFS does not perform secure and efficient query processing over encrypted data.

2. **Semantic Web Data Management**: There is a need for viable solutions to improve the performance and scalability of queries against semantic web data such as RDF (Resource Description Framework). The number of RDF datasets is increasing. The problem of storing billions of RDF triples and the ability to efficiently query them is yet to be solved (Muys, 2006; Teswanich, 2007; Ramanujam, 2009). At present, there is no support to store and retrieve RDF data in HDFS.

3. **No fine-grained access control**: HDFS does not provide fine-grained access control. There is some work to provide access control lists for HDFS (Zhang, 2009). For many applications such as assured information sharing, access control lists are not sufficient and there is a need to support more complex policies.

4. **No strong authentication:** A user who can connect to the JobTracker can submit any job with the privileges of the account used to set up the HDFS. Future versions of HDFS will support network authentication protocols like Kerberos for user authentication and encryption of data transfers (Zhang, 2009). However, for some assured information sharing scenarios, we will need public key infrastructures (PKI) to provide digital signature support.

System Design

While the secure co-processors can provide the hardware support to query and store the data, we need to develop a software system to store, query, and mine the data. More and more applications are now using semantic web data such as XML and RDF due to their representation power especially for web data management. Therefore, we are exploring ways to securely query semantic web data such as RDF data on the cloud. We are using several software tools that are available to help us in the process including the following:

- **Jena:** Jena is a framework which is widely used for solving SPARQL queries over RDF data (Jena). But the main problem with Jena is scalability. It scales in proportion to the size of main-memory. It does not have distributed processing. However, we will be using Jena in the initial stages of our preprocessing steps.

- **Pellet:** We use Pellet to reason at various stages. We do real-time query reasoning using pellet libraries (Pellet) coupled with Hadoop's map-reduce functionalities.

- **Pig Latin**: Pig Latin is a scripting language which runs on top of Hadoop (Gates, 2009). Pig is a platform for analyzing large data sets. Pig's language, Pig Latin, facilitates sequence of data transformations such as merging data sets, filtering them, and applying functions to records or groups of records. It comes with many built-in functions, but we can also create our own user-defined functions to do special-purpose processing. Using this scripting language, we will avoid writing our own map-reduce code; we will rely on Pig Latin's scripting power that will automatically generate script code to map-reduce code.

- **Mahout, Hama**: These are open source data mining and machine learning packages that already augment Hadoop (Mahout) (Hama) (Moretti, 2008).

Our approach consists of processing SPARQL queries securely over Hadoop. SPARQL is a query language used to query RDF data (W3C, *SPARQL*). The software part we will develop is a framework to query RDF data distributed over Hadoop (New-

Figure 7. System architecture for SPARQL query optimization

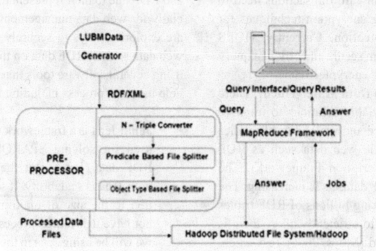

man, 2008; McNabb, 2007). There are a number of steps to preprocess and query RDF data (see Figure 7). With this proposed part, researchers can obtain results to optimize query processing of massive amounts of data. Below we discuss the steps involved in the development of this part.

- **Pre-processing:** Generally, RDF data is in XML format (see Lehigh University Benchmark [LUBM] RDF data). In order to execute a SPARQL query, we propose some data pre-processing steps and store the pre-processed data into HDFS. We have an N-triple Convertor module which converts RDF/XML format of data into N-triple format as this format is more understandable. We will use Jena framework as stated earlier, for this conversion purpose. In Predicate Based File Splitter module, we split all N-triple format files based on the predicates. Therefore, the total number of files for a dataset is equal to the number of predicates in the ontology/taxonomy. In the last module of the pre-processing step, we further divide predicate files on the basis of the type of object it contains. So, now each predicate file has specific types of objects in it. This is done with the help of the Pellet library. This pre-processed data is stored into Hadoop.

- **Query Execution and Optimization:** We are developing a SPARQL query execution and optimization module for Hadoop. As our storage strategy is based on predicate splits, first, we will look at the predicates present in the query. Second, rather than looking at all of the input files, we will look at a subset of the input files that are matched with predicates. Third, SPARQL queries generally have many joins in them and all of these joins may not be possible to perform in a single Hadoop job. Therefore, we will devise an algorithm that decides the number of jobs required for each kind of query. As part of optimization, we will apply a greedy strategy and cost-based optimization to reduce query processing time. An example of greedy strategy is to cover the maximum number of possible joins in a single job. For the cost model, the join to be performed first is based on summary statistics (e.g., selectivity factor of a bounded variable, join triple selectivity factor for three triple patterns. For example, consider a query for LUBM dataset: "List all persons who are alumni of a particular university." In SPARQL:

```
PREFIX rdf: <http://www.
w3.org/1999/02/22-rdf-syntax-ns#>
PREFIX ub: <http://www.lehigh.
edu/~zhp2/2004/0401/univ-bench.owl#>
SELECT ?X WHERE {
?X rdf:type ub:Person .
<http://www University0.edu>
ub:hasAlumnus ?X }
```

The query optimizer will take this query input and decide a subset of input files to look at based on predicates that appear in the query. Ontology and pellet reasoner will identify three input files (underGraduateDegreeFrom, masterDegreeFrom and DoctoraldegreeFrom) related to predicate, "hasAlumns". Next, from type file we filter all the records whose objects are a subclass of Person using the pellet library. From these three input files (underGraduateDegreeFrom, masterDegreeFrom and DoctoraldegreeFrom) the optimizer filters out triples on the basis of <http://www.University0. edu> as required in the query. Finally, the optimizer determines the requirement for a single job for this type of query and then the join is carried out on the variable X in that job.

With respect to secure query processing, we are investigating two approaches. One is rewriting the query in such a way that the policies are enforced in an appropriate manner. The second is query modification where the policies are used in the "where" clause to modify the query.

Integrate SUN XACML Implementation into HDFS

Current Hadoop implementations enforce a very coarse-grained access control policy that permits or denies a principal access to essentially all system resources as a group without distinguishing

amongst resources. For example, users who are granted access to the Namenode (see Figure 6) may execute any program on any client machine, and all client machines have read and write access to all files stored on all clients. Such coarse-grained security is clearly unacceptable when data, queries, and the system resources that implement them are security-relevant, and when not all users and processes are fully trusted. Current work (Zhang, 2009) addresses this by implementing standard access control lists for Hadoop to constrain access to certain system resources, such as files; however, this approach has the limitation that the enforced security policy is baked into the operating system and therefore cannot be easily changed without modifying the operating system. We are enforcing more flexible and fine-grained access control policies on Hadoop by designing an In-lined Reference Monitor implementation of Sun XACML. XACML (Moses, 2005) is an OASIS standard for expressing a rich language of access control policies in XML. Subjects, objects, relations, and contexts are all generic and extensible in XACML, making it well-suited for a distributed environment where many different sub-policies may interact to form larger, composite, system-level policies. An abstract XACML enforcement mechanism is depicted in Figure 7. Untrusted processes in the framework access security-relevant resources by submitting a request to the resource's Policy Enforcement Point (PEP). The PEP reformulates the request as a policy query and submits it to a Policy Decision Point (PDP). The PDP consults any policies related to the request to answer the query. The PEP either grants or denies the resource request based on the answer it receives. While the PEP and PDP components of the enforcement mechanism are traditionally implemented at the level of the operating system or as trusted system libraries, we propose to achieve greater flexibility by implementing them in our system as In-lined Reference Monitors (IRM's). IRM's implement runtime security checks by in-lining those checks directly into the binary code of untrusted processes.

Figure 8. XACML enforcement architecture

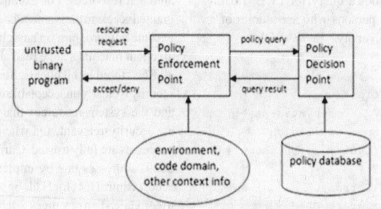

This has the advantage that the policy can be enforced without modifying the operating system or system libraries. IRM policies can additionally constrain program operations that might be difficult or impossible to intercept at the operating system level. For example, memory allocations in Java are implemented as Java bytecode instructions that do not call any external program or library. Enforcing a fine-grained memory-bound policy as a traditional reference monitor in Java therefore requires modifying the Java virtual machine or JIT-compiler. In contrast, an IRM can identify these security-relevant instructions and inject appropriate guards directly into the untrusted code to enforce the policy.

Finally, IRM's can efficiently enforce history-based security policies, rather than merely policies that constrain individual security-relevant events. For example, our past work (Jones, 2009) has used IRMs to enforce fairness policies that require untrusted applications to share as much data as they request. This prevents processes from effecting denial of service attacks based on freeloading behavior. The code injected into the untrusted binary by the IRM constrains each program operation based on the past history of program operations rather than in isolation. This involves injecting security state variables and counters into the untrusted code, which is difficult

to accomplish efficiently at the operating system level (Figure 8).

The core of an IRM framework consists of a *binary-rewriter*, which statically modifies the binary code of each untrusted process before it is executed to insert security guards around potentially dangerous operations. Our proposed binary-rewriter implementation will be based on SPoX (Security Policy XML) (Hamlen, 2008), which we developed to enforce declarative, XML-based, IRM policies for Java bytecode programs. In order to provide strong security guarantees for our system, we will apply automated software verification technologies, including type and model-checking, which we have previously used to certify the output of binary-rewriters (Hamlen, 2006; DeVries, 2009). Such certification allows a small, trusted verifier to independently prove that rewritten binary code satisfies the original security policy, thereby shifting the comparatively larger binary-rewriter out of the trusted computing base of the system.

Strong Authentication

Currently, Hadoop does not authenticate users. This makes it hard to enforce access control for security sensitive applications and makes it easier for malicious users to circumvent file permission checking done by HDFS. To address these issues, the open source community is actively working to integrate Kerberos protocols with Hadoop (Zhang, 2009). On top of the proposed Kerboros protocol, for some assured information applications, there may be a need for adding simple authentication protocols to authenticate with secure co-processors. For this reason, we can add a simple public key infrastructure to our system so that users can independently authenticate with secure co-processors to retrieve secret keys used for encrypting sensitive data. We can use open source public key infrastructure such as the OpenCA PKI implementation for our system (OpenCA).

SUMMARY AND CONCLUSION

In this paper, we first discussed security issues for cloud. These issues include storage security, middleware security, data security, network security and application security. The main goal is to securely store and manage data that is not controlled by the owner of the data. Then we focused on specific aspects of cloud computing. In particular, we are taking a bottom up approach to security where we are working on small problems in the cloud that we hope will solve the larger problem of cloud security. First, we discussed how we may secure documents that may be published in a third party environment. Next, we discussed how secure co-processors may be used to enhance security. Finally, we discussed how XACML may be implemented in the Hadoop environment as well as in secure federated query processing with SPARQL using MapReduce and Hadoop.

There are several other security challenges including security aspects of virtualization. We believe that due to the complexity of the cloud, it will be difficult to achieve end-to-end security. However, the challenge we have is to ensure more secure operations even if some parts of the cloud fail. For many applications, we not only need information assurance but also mission assurance.

Therefore, even if an adversary has entered the system, the objective is to thwart the adversary so that the enterprise has time to carry out the mission. As such, building trust applications from untrusted components will be a major aspect with respect to cloud security.

REFERENCES

W3C. (n.d.). *SPARQL*. Retrieved from http://www.w3.org/TR/rdf-sparql-query

Bertino, E. (2002). Access Control for XML Documents. *Data & Knowledge Engineering, 43*(3).

Bertino, E. (2004). Selective and Authentic Third Party Distribution of XML Documents. *IEEE Transactions on Knowledge and Data Engineering, 16*(10). doi:10.1109/TKDE.2004.63

DeVries, B. W., Gupta, G., Hamlen, K. W., Moore, S., & Sridhar, M. (2009). ActionScript Bytecode Verification with Co-Logic Programming. In *Proceedings of the ACM SIGPLAN Workshop on Programming Languages and Analysis for Security (PLAS)*.

Gates, F., Natkovich, O., Chopra, S., Kamath, S. M., Kamath, P., Narayanamuthry, S. M., et al. (2009). Building a High-Level Dataflow System on top of Map-Reduce: The Pig Experience. In *Proceedings of the Thirty-Fifth International Conference on Very Large Data Bases (VLDB) (Industrial, Applications and Experience Track)*, Lyon, France.

Hadoop. (n.d.). Retrieved from http://hadoop.apache.org

Hama. (n.d.). Retrieved from http://cwiki.apache.org/labs/cloudsglossary.html

Hamlen, K. W., & Jones, M. (2008). Aspect-Oriented In-lined Reference Monitors. In *Proceedings of the ACM SIGPLAN Workshop on Programming Languages and Analysis for Security (PLAS)*.

Hamlen, K. W., Morrisett, G., & Schneider, F. B. (2006). Certified In-lined Reference Monitoring on. NET. In *Proceedings of the ACM SIGPLAN Workshop on Programming Languages and Analysis for Security (PLAS)*.

IBM. (2004). *IBM PCI cryptographic coprocessor*. Retrieved from http://www.ibm.com/security/cryptocards.

Jena. (n.d.). Retrieved from http://jena.sourceforge.net

Jones, M., & Hamlen, K. W. (2009). Enforcing IRM Security Policies: Two Case Studies. In *Proceedings of the IEEE Intelligence and Security Informatics Conference (ISI)*.

Lehigh University Benchmark (LUBM). (n.d.). Retrieved from http://swat.cse.lehigh.edu/projects/lubm

Mahout. (n.d.). Retrieved from http://lucene.apache.org/mahout/

McNabb, A., Monson, C., & Seppi, K. (2007). MRPSO: MapReduce particle swarm optimization. In *Proceedings of the 9th annual conference on genetic and evolutionary computation (GECCO 2007)* (p. 177). New York: ACM Press.

Moretti, C., Steinhaeuser, K., Thainer, D., & Chawla, N. (2008). Scaling Up Classifiers to Cloud Computers. In *Proceedings of the IEEE ICDM*.

Moses, T. (Ed.). (2005, February). eXtensible Access Control Markup Language (XACML) Version 2.0. *OASIS Standard*. Retrieved from http://docs.oasis-open.org/xacml/2.0/access_control-xacml-2.0-core-spec-os.pdf

Muys, A. (2006). *Building an Enterprise-Scale Database for RDF Data*.

Newman, A., Hunter, J., Li, Y. F., Bouton, C., & Davis, M. (2008). In *Proceedings of a Scale-Out RDF Molecule Store for Distributed Processing of Biomedical Data Semantic Web for Health Care and Life Sciences Workshop (WWW 2008)*.

Open, C. A. *Implementation*. (n.d.). Retrieved from http://www.openca.org/projects/openca/

Pellet. (n.d.). Retrieved from http://clarkparsia.com/pellet

Ramanujam, S., Gupta, A., Khan, L., & Seida, S. (2009). R2D: Extracting relational structure from RDF stores. In *Proceedings of the ACM/IEEE International Conference on Web Intelligence*, Milan, Italy.

Smith, S., & Weingart, S. (1999). Building a high-performance, programmable secure coprocessor. *Computer Networks*, *31*, 831–860. doi:10.1016/S1389-1286(98)00019-X

Teswanich, W., & Chittayasothorn, S. (2007). A Transformation of RDF Documents and Schemas to Relational Databases. *IEEE Pacific Rim Conferences on Communications, Computers, and Signal Processing*, 38-41.

Zhang, K. (2009). *Adding user and service-to-service authentication to Hadoop*. Retrieved from https://issues.apache.org/jira/browse/HADOOP-4343

This work was previously published in International Journal of Information Security and Privacy, Volume 4, Issue 2, edited by Hamid Nemati, pp. 36-48, copyright 2010 by IGI Publishing (an imprint of IGI Global).

Chapter 9
Global Information Security Factors

Garry White
Texas State University - San Marcos, USA

Ju Long
Texas State University - San Marcos, USA

ABSTRACT

The Internet has changed security and because the Internet is borderless, security threats are now on a global scale. In this paper, the authors explore the global nature of information security from the perspectives of corporate professionals. Through an empirical study with corporate professionals, who have first-hand information security knowledge, the authors confirm that the proposed knowledge topics are relevant toward a comprehensive understanding of information security issues. Analyzing the empirical data, the authors found two global security factors: business protection of data and government/social issues.

INTRODUCTION

Globalization, through the Internet, has allowed knowledge sharing and collaborations across countries, judicial boundaries. It makes information security more challenging and an issue for corporations. The Internet allows hackers and other criminals to roam the Internet, evading law enforcement by moving from country to country (Jung et al., 2001). Because of the global nature

of the Internet, hackers and criminals can cause information security breaches from anywhere on the globe.

For instance, Symantec (2008) reported that 56% of the worldwide denial-of-service attacks were targeted towards the U.S. Most of these attacks were traced to sources outside the U.S. Symantec (2008) also reported 43% of worms (a type of malicious code) originated in Europe, Middle East, and Africa and 42% of spam detected worldwide originated outside the United States. Clearly, the information security risks

DOI: 10.4018/978-1-4666-0026-3.ch009

have brought numerous challenges to business practices. The risk factors in international trade and the complications in bringing buyers and sellers together in a mutually trustworthy environment were close to insurmountable (DuBois, 2004). To address these information security challenges, a comprehensive understanding of the global nature of the information security is crucial.

In addition, information security is a multidisciplinary field (Cresson-Wood, 2004; Gritzalis et al., 2005; Cegielski, 2008). It is a field that involves the social aspects of legal and ethical issues (Himma, 2008). A wide range of educational experiences are required for information security professionals (Todd & Vickers, 2003). Information security professionals need knowledge of management, business administration, ethics, sociology, and political science, E-Commerce, software assurance, fault-tolerance and survivability, etc. (Hentea et al., 2006).

Therefore, we argue that a multidisciplinary body of knowledge and skills are needed for a comprehensive understanding of information security. Casey (2006) indicated that expertises in information security, digital forensics, penetration testing, reverse engineering, programming, and behavioral profiling are required. We propose the framework of the global information security topics include: information systems and computer science political science because of security regulations and policies cross national boundaries, criminal justice, and business knowledge.

This paper looks at what corporate practitioners think they need to know in order to better understand the issues of global information security. The theoretical model and topics used were developed from a previous research paper, Long & White (2010).

From these global information security topics, what knowledge factors can be determined? In this research, we set to explore the global factors and topics that are relevant to the corporate information security issues. Based on an empirical survey of 36 corporate professionals, our goal is to find a common set of global factors that the practitioners all regard as essential in understanding the global perspectives of information technology.

The purpose of this paper is not to discuss what global information security is, or how to meet the global information security challenges. Rather, we focus the research on empirically determine what knowledge base that the practitioners are considered as invaluable in global information security field.

Our research results provide a foundation for the development and adoption of a global information security infrastructure. Our study will also provide guidance to career development and to corporate management that focus on global information security infrastructure.

The following sections provide the theory background, propose our research framework, data collection process, and discussion of the research results. The last section discusses implications and future research directions.

LITERATURE REVIEW

Global Nature of Information Security

Internet has enabled the information exchange across judicial national boundaries, without the limit of customs, time differences, or language. It also attracts criminals to the cyber space because of its borderless feature. Criminals only need a computer and an Internet connection to be able to roam freely between the countries, covering their tracks along the way. However, this borderless feature of the virtual world also makes fighting with the criminal especially difficult. It is slow and tedious, and many times, almost impossible, to police the virtual world across national borders and jurisdictions (Ferrell, 2004). Laws from different nations are not fully compatible. Data sharing between the law enforcement agencies from different nations are not sufficient. Certain activities are permissible in one country but not in another. Each set of laws reflects the nations' own political and economic interests and their legal systems (Oz, 1994). Without an international treaty on fighting cyber crimes, it will be up to the countries to apply their own, quite different laws (Powers, 2008). There are some early efforts in establishing such an international treaty. For example, the European Union adopted a directive requiring spammers to obtain the consumer's consent before sending unsolicited commercial e-mail (Saunders, 2002, Himma, 2008). However, these are still very early efforts.

Moreover, the countries that are weak in the law enforcement area are often the origins of the cyber crimes (Williams, 2001). Because of the lack of specific statute or case laws in these countries, many legal problems become evident in facing the new challenges from the cyber crimes (Powers, 2008). The notorious "I Love You" virus is a good example. The origin of the virus was identified as from the Philippine. However, because Philippine had yet to have any law to prosecute the kind of cyber crime at that time, the attacker was never punished for the damages he had done (Sofaer & Goodman, 2006). The recent data on information security breach also shows the global nature of cyber crimes. For instance, 60% of the phishing activity on the Internet originated from Russia (Symantec, 2008). Countries other than the U.S. originated almost 70% of the cyber crimes in 2005 (Symantec, 2006). This shows that criminals in global cyber space have very high mobility to roam among various countries that have weak enforcement capacity and seek out digital safe havens for their crimes (Symantec, 2008).

Another specific challenge in global information security is enforcing the law beyond the jurisdictional boundaries. It often requires the close collaboration and coordination among the law enforcement agencies of countries involved (Deflem & Shutt, 2008). The cross border nature of the global information security makes such collaboration and coordination especially challenging (Calkins, 2000). Often, the myriad jurisdictions make the prosecution of the cyber crimes very complicated (Powers, 2008).

Global Information Security and Its Impact on the Business World

The global information security has become increasingly complex. Its impact in the business world has received more focus because cyber crimes and attacks have become more serious and organized. These attacks make the vulnerabilities in business security ever more evident (Rasmussen, 2003, Gerber & von Solms, 2008).

While the global perspective in information security becomes important, the competition in the business world also shifts from a national scope to an international scope (Karimi & Konsynski, 1991). A global information technology platform allows multinational companies to compete and collaborate across different countries (Stephens, 1999). The free flow of information has become one of the most essential requirements for the economic growth of any organization (Oz, 1994). Such free flow of information are especially challenging for information security in the global platform, which constantly requires the exchange of data among different countries and international organizations (Rudraswamy & Vance, 2001). Moreover, In the countries where the broadband connectivity is new or is rapidly expanding, Internet Service Providers (ISPs) may be more focused on meeting growing demands than on ensuring that adequate security measures are in place (Symantec, 2008). Often in these countries, users and administrators are also less likely to be familiar with these security measures. In these countries, law enforcement and legislation may also be lacking (Symantec, 2008). However, these countries are often the ones that companies are eager to expand to, which makes fighting against the information security threats for the companies going global ever more challenging.

The differences in IT security environments across different countries can be very damaging even for the best intentioned organizations trying to integrate operations (DuBois, 2004). For companies to secure their business practice and data exchange in the global plat, a close coordination and collaboration in information security is critical (Reidenberg, 2000). However, such collaboration is still in its early stage. A series of problems, including geographic distance, the cultural, administrative and economic distance that separates the world's trading partners, needs to be addressed (Ghemawhat, 2001). This is especially true to information security. For instance, the definition of personal data varies from nation to nation, as does the regulatory agencies governing them (Connolly, 2000, Rudraswamy & Vance, 2001).

To address the information security issues in the corporate world, an in-depth understanding of global components in information security is crucial. For instance, how can the current international events affect a multinational corporation's security interests? However, the global perspectives have been lacking in this area (White & Long, 2007).

We specifically focus on information security issues that are most relevant to business practices, especially accounting and finance fields. These fields are increasingly becoming the primary targets of cyber crimes. They are especially vulnerable in defending against the security threats. The damages induced by the cyber crimes to these business fields are also especially devastating, often costing businesses substantial financial losses (Jung et al., 2001). This is particularly true to the companies engaging in e-commerce, such as online shopping and Internet banking, security breaches can result in huge amount of financial loss, particularly if credit card information or banking details are exposed (Symantec, 2008).

Because of the close relationship between information security and internal control, and the corollary relevance of information security for Sarbanes-Oxley compliance (Walters, 2007), the information security has become very relevant

to accounting professionals. Similarly, in the finance and banking industry, if the information security breach succeeds, it often brings the cyber criminals huge amount of financial benefits, thus making this field particularly a focus for cyber attacks (Symantec, 2008). For instance, 90% of all phishing attacks were in the financial sector in 2008 (Symantec, 2008). The attacks are also increasing in an exponential rate, for instance, in the second half of 2007, the number of potential banking Trojan infections increased 86% from the previous reporting period (Symantec, 2008).

In the above sections, we reviewed the theories in the existing literature the importance of having a global perspective in understanding information security. We also reviewed how global information security is especially important to the corporate world. In the next section, we will discuss our research method and data analysis results.

METHOD

To determine what the knowledge factors are, a survey instrument from a prior study (Long & White, 2010) was used to determine the relevancy of ten international security topics in the corporate world. The participants are requested to rate each of the issues on a five-point Likert Scale. Each survey item was rated by selecting Strongly Relevant (+2), Relevant (+1), Undecided/Neutral/No Opinion (0), NOT Relevant (-1), or Strongly NOT Relevant (-2). The ten issues are as follows:

1. Introduction on international information security risks.
2. International sources and techniques of cyber-crime and cyber-terrorism
3. Information & privacy laws from foreign countries and how they differ.
4. Various measures and technologies that different governments and foreign agencies are using in fighting international cyber-crime and how they differ.

Figure 1. Topics mapped to various disciplines: This framework presents the topics from knowledge disciplines we wish to study (Long & White, 2010). From these topics, the knowledge factors will be determined through factor analysis.

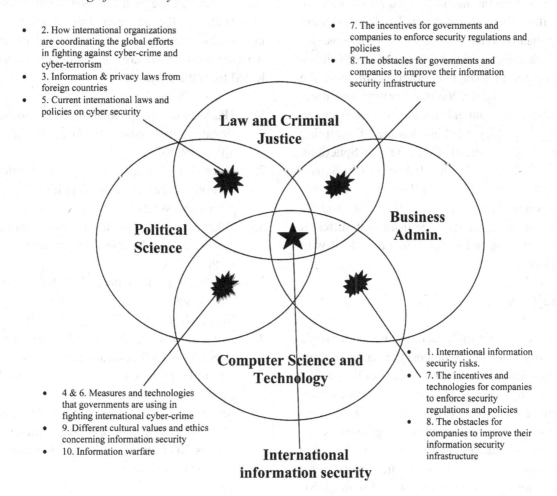

5. Current international laws and policies on cyber security and how these laws are enforced in different countries.

6. How international organizations, such as U.N. and E.U. are coordinating the global efforts in fighting against cyber-crime and cyber-terrorism

7. The incentives for governments and companies of developing nations to enforce security regulations and policies.

8. The obstacles for governments and companies of developing nations to improve their information security infrastructure.

9. Different cultural values and ethics concerning information security.

10. Introduction on information warfare.

Validation of Issues from Prior Study

To validate the issues as related to information security, a prior study (Long & White, 2010) administered the survey to 116 faculty and graduate students from Finance, Management, Accounting, Economics, Computer Information Systems, Criminal Justice, Political Science, and Computer Science departments at a central Texas university.

They were asked to indicate the how relevant the international issues are to information security.

A correlation matrix showed all issues were significantly related at the .01 level (2-tail). Item #9 appeared to have the lowest correlations.

A factor analysis was used to ensure the items are related to a single component. In doing the factor analysis, the Varimax method was used. The Scree Plot did indicate only one component. The Kaiser-Meyer-Olkin Measure of Sampling was .878. And the Bartlett's Test of Sphericity was significant at .001 level (Approx. Chi-Square 714.812, df 45). All ten items loaded into the single component. However, items #9 and #10 had the lowest loading values. One dealt with different culture values and ethics. The other dealt with warfare.

Subjects

Subjects for this study came from a university's advisory board for a computer information systems department, officers and members of the professional organization Association of Information Technology Professionals (AITP). There were 36 participants. A prior study, using business and security executives, had a similar sample size (Johnson, 2009). In this study the subjects were corporate members who must deal with global information security issues. Over a third of the subjects did experience an international security issue in the last 3 years. And 34 of the 36 indicated the importance of understanding international security issues for those in the working world.

Demographics: Background Knowledge in Information Security

We also examine the background knowledge the subjects have in the information security filed. Almost 80% have taken a course dealing with information security. And 48% believed at least 60% of information security attacks come from

outside the U.S.A. These professionals have a background with security and believe that most security attacks are of the international nature. They believe that understanding international information security issues is important for the working world. Here are the demographics collected from the subjects:

1. Has your company experienced an international security issue in the last 3 years?
   YES 35% NO 65%
2. Have you taken a course that had an information security component in it?
   YES 79% NO 21%
3. What percentage of information security attacks do you believe come from outside of the U.S.A.:
   < 20% 20% - 40% 40% - 60% 60% - 80% > 80%
   Respondents: 6% 12% 33% 33% 15%
4. How important is the understanding of the international information security issues for you to be prepared for the working world (Table 1)?
   Score +1.35: Where +2 is Strongly Relevant, +1 is Relevant, 0 is No Opinion, -1 is NOT Relevant, and -2 is Strongly NOT Relevant.

RESULTS

Reliability

The Cronbach's Alpha was used to check reliability of the responses. This measure indicates the different respondents had different opinions. The survey was not confusing and had no multiple interpretations. For the 10 items, the Cronbach's Alpha was .839. There was a large internal consistency of the items in the survey.

Relevance of International Information Security Issues

One of the main objectives of this study is to examine how relevant our respondents rank the main issues of global information security. The participants are requested to rate the relevance of each of the issues on a five-point Likert scale, including Strongly Relevant (+2), Relevant (+1), Undecided/Neutral/No Opinion (0), NOT Relevant (-1), or Strongly NOT Relevant (-2). All issues were negatively skewed and each topic was significantly different ($p < .01$) from a normal distribution for relevance based on One-Sample Kolmogorov-Smirnov Tests. As shown in Table 2, all of the 10 proposed issues are regarded as relevant by our respondents.

We also compared and ranked the relative relevance of each of the issues. As shown in Figure 2, the highest ranked topic by the 36 respondents was topic #2, sources and techniques of global cyber-rimes and cyber terrorism. The second ranked topic was topic #1, introduction on international information security risks. The third ranked topic was topic #10, information warfare. These issues are very relevant to businesses. Such attacks could disrupt business operations.

The bottom three issues (#8,6,7) involved developing nations and international organizations; entities less relevant to business operations and more relevant to political science and criminal justice.

Factor Analysis

A factor analysis was used to determine if the items are related to a single or multiple components. In doing the factor analysis, the Varimax method was used to ensure factors were uncorrelated. The Scree Plot and Rotated Component Matrix indicated two components.

The KMO Bartlett's Test indicated sampling was adequate and the factor model was appropriate ($p < .001$). This very low p value result shows the robust and the profound effect with only 36 subjects. The factors extracted accounted for a fare/middling amount of variance (Figure 3).

The first issue, I1 "Introduction on international information security risks," had a loading

Table 1. Answers to question 4

		Frequency	Percent
Valid	0	2	5.6
	1	19	52.8
	2	15	41.7
	Total	36	100.0

Table 2. Frequencies of relevance by each issue

Issue	Strongly Not Relevant	Not Relevant	Neutral	Relevant	Strongly Relevant
1	0	1	1	20	14
2	0	0	1	19	16
3	0	2	5	20	9
4	0	0	5	24	7
5	1	0	5	23	7
6	1	3	6	19	7
7	0	4	6	21	5
8	1	3	4	21	7
9	0	1	4	21	10
10	0	0	4	21	11

Figure 2. Rank and mean score of each item

Score	Item	Issue
1.42	2.	International sources and techniques of cyber-crime and cyber-terrorism
1.31	1.	Introduction on international information security risks.
1.19	10.	Introduction on information warfare.
1.11	9.	Different cultural values and ethics concerning information security.
1.06	4.	Various measures and technologies that different governments and foreign agencies are using in fighting international cyber-crime and how they differ.
1.00	3.	Information & privacy laws from foreign countries and how they differ.
0.97	5.	Current international laws and policies on cyber security and how these laws are enforced in different countries.
0.83	8.	The obstacles for governments and companies of developing nations to improve their information security infrastructure.
0.78	6.	How international organizations, such as U.N. and E.U. are coordinating the global efforts in fighting against cyber-crime and cyber-terrorism
0.75	7.	The incentives for governments and companies of developing nations to enforce security regulations and policies.

value of less than .5 suggesting that it not be included in any factor. Yet, this issue was the second highest relevant issue (1.31). Since the loading value is sensitive to sample size and its loading into the second factor was almost doubled for the first factor, we included the first issue in the second factor.

The overall theme for Factor 1 appears to be the social/political management from culture and governments. International laws, how such laws are enforced, international governments and organizations, and culture have less impact on businesses as compared to Factor 2 as show by the relevance average of items. This factor appears to be more suited for those with a political science or law enforcement background. The focus is on the society.

Factor 1: Social/Political management (culture & governments)
Relevance average of items .89

5. Current international laws and policies on cyber security and how these laws are enforced in different countries.
6. How international organizations, such as U.N. and E.U. are coordinating the global efforts in fighting against cyber-crime and cyber-terrorism
7. The incentives for governments and companies of developing nations to enforce security regulations and policies.
8. The obstacles for governments and companies of developing nations to improve their information security infrastructure.

9. Different cultural values and ethics concerning information security.

The overall theme for Factor 2 appears to be the techniques/operations technologies that will protect data. Risks, privacy laws, cyber-crime, and information warfare directly impact a business. This factor appears to be more suited for those with a business administration background. The focus is on the business.

Factor 2: Risks and Attacks (protection of data) Relevance average of items 1.20.

1. Introduction on international information security risks.
2. International sources and techniques of cyber-crime and cyber-terrorism
3. Information & privacy laws from foreign countries and how they differ.
4. Various measures and technologies that different governments and foreign agencies are using in fighting international cyber-crime and how they differ.
10. Introduction on information warfare.

DISCUSSION

The Internet is borderless. It is easy to roam from country to country via the computer. Threats can come from any country around the globe. And the protection of data varies from nation to nation, as well as agencies governing them (Connolly, 2000; Rudraswamy & Vance, 2001). These national differences create havoc in global organizations (DuBois, 2004). This paper attempted to address this havoc by looking at what perspectives business professionals have with global information security issues.

This research has shown that all corporate professionals in this study agreed that global information security issues are relevant to their businesses. Based on our empirical data, this global perspective of business professionals

Figure 3. KMO and Bartlett's Test and Rotated Component Matrix

KMO and Bartlett's Test

Kaiser-Meyer-Olkin Measure of Sampling Adequacy.		.782
Bartlett's Test of Sphericity	Approx. Chi-Square	134.232
	df	45
	Sig.	.000

Rotated Component Matrix[a]

	Component	
	1	2
I1	.259	**.461**
I2	.111	**.760**
I3	-.034	**.698**
I4	.381	**.711**
I5	**.608**	.500
I6	**.672**	.305
I7	**.866**	.046
I8	**.889**	.029
I9	**.742**	.251
I10	.159	**.690**

Extraction Method: Principal Component Analysis.

Rotation Method: Varimax with Kaiser Normalization.

a. Rotation converged in 3 iterations.

could be categorized into two factors; what they have little or no control (government/culture) and what they have full control (data protection from attacks and risks).

The first factor covers culture & governments (Social/Political). These are the external infrastructures (environment) businesses must operate in. Such areas include international laws, regional laws, and regional ethics. Businesses have no control over these external infrastructures. Still these issues have an indirect impact on business operations, policies, and risks. The relevance average of these items was .89.

The second factor covers techniques/operations technologies to protect business data from attacks due to cyber warfare and cyber crime. Such areas impact corporate policies and business risks directly. Compared with the first topic, these issues impact the internal infrastructures more than external ones. Businesses usually have more control over these internal infrastructures. The relevance average of these items was 1.20.

These two components cover the external environment (society) and internal data protection (business) areas of global information systems. Conceptually this makes sense, a business works in an environment. The literature separates the social and business aspect of global security. In academia, these areas are looked at as different disciplines. This supports the notion that global information security is multidiscipline.

From Figure 1, the external environment covers Political Science, Law and Criminal Justice. The internal data protection covers Business Administration, Computer Science and Technology. These are the two knowledge factors for global information security.

It is interesting to note the issues that businesses have more control are more relevant to the businesses. However, business professionals do see the importance of the factors that are related to external infrastructures, such as the impact on information security from different judicial boundaries.

There are the problems of cultural, administrative and economic differences between judicial boundaries (Ghemawhat, 2001). Global collaboration in global information security is critical to secure data flows between judicial boundaries (Reidenberg, 2000). This requires both businesses and governments working together Global information security is critical to both businesses and governments.

These two knowledge components can have an impact on corporate structure and management. Corporations would have two distinct areas to manage; internal protection of data and external dealings with government/society. This requires two different areas of knowledge and skills. One area would involve the technical skills and procedures to insure data security on a global scale. Management would be at the operational and tactical levels of the business. The other area would involve legal knowledge of foreign countries. Management would be at the strategic level of the business.

These two knowledge components can also have an impact on educators. Two distinct curriculum would be business information systems (BIS) and political science (PS). The BIS curriculum would cover risk, techniques/technologies of attack, and privacy issues a corporation must consider. The PS curriculum would cover laws of other countries, foreign infrastructures, international organizations, and cultural values.

CONCLUSION

Changes in technologies have moved the business world to a global scope (Karimi & Konsynski, 1991). Today, multinational companies have developed a global information integration infrastructure that crosses national borders and time zones (Stephens, 1999; Rudraswamy & Vance, 2001). Security is going global.

This study showed professionals from the corporate world believe global information security is relevant to the business operation. However, they see it as two components; technologies to protect data from attack (business focus) and social/political factors (society focus) that mainly influence the information security externally. Although both these two components are relevant, it appears that protecting data is more relevant than external cultural/governments policies to the business professionals. This suggests two distinctive issues in the field of global information security: business security and culture/political policies. Although managers can control corporate infrastructures, they tend to have less control on international political infrastructures. Therefore, corporate professionals focus more on the issues that directly protect and impact business data and operations rather than political issues.

REFERENCES

Cegielski, C. G. (2008). Toward the Development of an Interdisciplinary Information Assurance Curriculum: Knowledge Domains and Skill Sets Required of Information Assurance Professionals. *Decision Sciences Journal of Innovative Education*, 6(1), 29–49. doi:10.1111/j.1540-4609.2007.00156.x

Cresson-Wood, C. (2004). Why Information Security is Now Multi-Disciplinary, Multi-Departmental, and Multi-Organizational in Nature. *Computer Fraud & Security*, 1, 16–17. doi:10.1016/S1361-3723(04)00019-3

Dash, J. (2001). Schools Push Soft Skills for Info Security Majors. *Computerworld*, 35(6), 24.

Deflem, M., & Shutt, J. E. (2008). Law enforcement and computer security threats and measures. In Bidgoli, H. (Ed.), *Global perspectives in information security: legal, social, and international issues*. New York: Wiley.

DuBois, F. (2004). Globalization Risks and Information Management. *Journal of Global Information Management*, 10(1), 1–5.

Ferrell, K. (2004, September 22). Cybercrime Spins Out Of Control. *TechWeb.com*.

Gerber, M., & von Solms, R. (2008). Information security requirements – Interpreting the legal aspects. *Computers & Security*, 27(5-6), 124–135. doi:10.1016/j.cose.2008.07.009

Ghemawat, P. (2001). *Distance still matters: The hard reality of global expansion*. Harvard Business Review.

Gritzalis, D., Theoharidou, M., & Kalimeri, E. (2005). Towards an Interdisciplinary InfoSec Education Model. In *Proceedings of the 4th IFIP World Conference on Information Security Education*, Moscow Russia (pp. 22-35).

Hentea, M., Dhillon, H., & Dhillon, M. (2006). Towards Changes in Information Security Education. *Journal of Information Technology Education*, 5, 221–233.

Himma, K. E. (2008). Legal, social, and ethical issues of the internet. In Bidgoli, H. (Ed.), *Global perspectives in information security: legal, social, and international issues*. New York: Wiley.

Irvine, C. E., Chin, S-K., & Frincke, D. (1998). Integrating Security Into the Curriculum. *IEEE Computer*, 25 -30.

Jayaratna, N. (1993). Research Notes: Information Systems as Social Systems: Research at the LSE. *International Journal of Information Management*, 13(4), 299–301.

Johnson, A. (2009). Business and Security Executives Views of Information Security Investment Drivers: Results from a Delphi Study. *Journal of Information Privacy & Security*, 5(1), 3.

Jung, B., Han, I., & Lee, S. (2001). Security Threats to Internet: A Korean Multi-industry Investigation. *Information & Management*, 38(8), 487–498. doi:10.1016/S0378-7206(01)00071-4

Karimi, J., & Knsynski, B. (1991). Globalization and information management strategies. *Journal of Management Information Systems*, 7(4), 7–26.

Long, J., & White, G. (2010). *On the Global Knowledge Components in an Information Security Curriculum – A Multidisciplinary Approach*. Education & Information Technologies.

Milberg, S., Smith, J., & Burke, S. (2000). Information privacy: Corporate management and national regulation. *Organization Science*, 11(1), 35–57. doi:10.1287/orsc.11.1.35.12567

Oz, E. (1994). Barriers to international data transfer. *Journal of Global Information Management, 2*(2), 22–29.

Powers, D. M. (2008). Cyberlaw: the major areas, development, and information security aspects. In Bidgoli, H. (Ed.), *Global perspectives in information security: legal, social, and international issues*. New York: Wiley.

Rasmussen, M. (2003). *Analyst Report: IT Trends 2003 – Information Security Standards, Regulations and Legislation.* Retrieved from http://www.csoonline.com/analyst/report721.html

Reidenberg, J. R. (2000). Resolving conflicting international data privacy rules in cyberspace. *Stanford Law Review, 52*(5), 1315–1367. doi:10.2307/1229516

Rudraswamy, V., & Vance, D. A. (2001). Transborder data flows: Adoption and diffusion of protective legislation in the global electronic commerce environment. *Logistics Information Management, 14*(1/2), 127–136. doi:10.1108/09576050110362717

Saunders, C. (2002). *EU Oks spam ban, online privacy rules, Internet News.* Retrieved from http://www.internetnews.com/IAR/article.php/1154391

Sofaer, A. D., & Goodman, S. E. (2006). *Cyber Crime and Security. The Transnational Dimension.* Palo Alto, CA: Hoover Institution.

Stephens, D. (1999). The globalization of information technology in multinational corporations. *Information Management Journal, 33*(3), 66–71.

Symantec. (2006). *Trends for July 05–December 05, Volume IX.* Retrieved from https://enterprise.symantec.com/enterprise/whitepaper.cfm

Symantec. (2008). *Trends for July 07–December 07, Volume XIII.* Retrieved from http://eval.symantec.com/mktginfo/enterprise/white_papers/b-whitepaper_internet_security_threat_report_xiii_04-2008.en-us.pdf

Teer, F. E., Kruck, S. E., & Kruck, G. (2007). Empirical Study of Students' Computer Security - Practices/Perceptions. *Journal of Computer Information Systems, 3*(105).

Theoharidou, M., & Gritzalis, D. (2007). Common Body of Knowledge for Information Security. *IEEE Security & Privacy, 5*(2), 64–67. doi:10.1109/MSP.2007.32

Todd, J., & Vickers, K. (2003). Developing High-Tech Entrepreneurs: A Multidisciplinary Strategy. *Decision Sciences Journal of Innovative Education, 1*(2), 317–320. doi:10.1111/j.1540-4609.2003.00027.x

Walters, L. M. (2007). A Draft of an Information Systems Security and Control Course. *Journal of Information Systems, 21*(1), 123–148. doi:10.2308/jis.2007.21.1.123

White, G., & Long, J. (2007). *Thinking Globally: Incorporating an International Component in Information Security Curricula.* Information Systems Education Journal.

Williams, P. (2001). Organized Crime and Cybercrime: Synergies, Trends, and Responses. *Global Issues (Washington, D.C.), 6*(2).

Zuckerman, A. (2001). Order in the courts? *World Trade, 14*(9), 26–29.

Chapter 10
The Integrated Privacy Model:
Building a Privacy Model in the Business Processes of the Enterprise

Munir Majdalawieh
American University of Sharjah, UAE

ABSTRACT

This paper discusses the challenges that faced in the "DigNet" age in terms of privacy and proposes a framework for privacy protection. This framework is integral in ensuring that personal data protection is impeded part of business processes of any systems that are involved in collecting, disseminating, and accessing an individual's data. The cooperation and partnership between nations in passing privacy laws is essential and requires some building blocks. In this paper, the author argues that the building blocks should be integrated into the business processes and take into consideration three main domains: governments' legislation, entity's policies and procedures, and data protection controls. The proposed conceptual framework helps organizations develop data protection in their business processes, assess the privacy issues in their organization, protect the interests of their customers, increase their value proposition to customers, and make it easier to identify the impact of privacy on their business.

DOI: 10.4018/978-1-4666-0026-3.ch010

INTRODUCTION

In the digital and Internet "DigNet" age, a private, public, not-for-profit organizations, and individuals are utilizing the Internet by interacting with their suppliers, customers/clients (online users) or citizens and in most cases they collect and use the personal data for a variety of purposes. The purposes of processing personal data include, but not limited to, buying or selling goods or services; paying fines; banking services; employment's services; and even when browsing the Internet. When sensitive personal data (bank records, credit card, religious beliefs, political allegiances, travel records, sexual orientation, health, race, membership of past organizations) are being processed, extra controls must be applied. How to protect privacy rights in the "DigNet" age has been a recurring problem since the inception of the Internet. Clarkson et al. (2009) indicate that individuals in the "DigNet" age are not aware that information about their personal lives and preferences is being collected by Internet companies and other online users without even getting the permission to do so. The online marketers are willing to pay a very high price to those who are willing to sell them such information. Because of these concerns and the possibility of lawsuits based on privacy laws, online businesses post on their web sites a privacy policy statement disclosing how personal data obtained from their online users will be used and how the organization will protect and use their online users personal data. But, is this enough to protect the privacy of individuals? And even more important, is this enough to provide online users with assurance that their personal data is protected? Who can guarantee that an organization is meeting its obligation of protecting the online user's personal data? The "Privacy Statement" is not static, it may change to adapt new laws or when the organization changes its business structure. In such cases, which policy applies to which online user's personal data and in which territory?

Pirim et al. (2008) argue that privacy has been empirically studied in the information technology research from an organizational context. They added that from a general individual perspective privacy has not been addressed in relation to Information Technology. Furthermore, privacy has not been researched or investigated from business process management perspective and the current literature has shown lack of a well defined methodology for integrating security and privacy into business processes (Anderson & Rachamadugu, 2008). Privacy has a huge impact on the business survival of all companies conducting business online.

Online users are skeptical when it comes to privacy and the Internet in general and online business in specific. The impact of privacy on online businesses is very significant. Teifke (2003) believes that the impact of the potential loss of privacy takes on a whole new meaning when we look at the issue from the perspective of our individual companies. A 2005 poll conducted by Web Design Directory (2005) indicated that 62 percent of the 1000 adults surveyed are worried their personal data could be stolen online. A joint study by TNS and TRUSTe (2008) found that lack of transparency may factor into privacy concerns that online customers have. Among the 1,015 interviewers, 71 percent of the participants are aware that their browsing information may be collected by a third party for advertising purposes. The percent did not change much for the same survey in 2009 (TNS and TRUSTe). This indicates that the online users are aware of the privacy issues and the challenges that they are facing when conducting business or just browsing on the Internet. As such many online businesses are missing huge amount of growth because they are not giving enough assurance to the online users that their personal data is protected. Teifke (2003) concluded that "protecting privacy is good for the bottom line, and not protecting it could be catastrophic."

Private and public organizations need to conduct, at least annually, a thorough analysis of privacy implications to identify problems and provide solutions before they develop and impact their business. Online users need to be able to trust that online businesses are using their personal data in care and they do not violate their privacy and misuse their personal data. Most of the enterprise online businesses are providing a privacy statement on their online website to provide the users with some assurance about how the company will protect and use their personal data. Is the "Privacy Statement" enough to gain the trust of the users? Is "Privacy Statement" is a legally binding contract? Who can guarantee that the organization is meeting its obligation of protecting the user's private data? The "Privacy Statement" is not static, it may change to adapt new laws or when the company changes its business structure. In such cases, which policy applies to which online user's personal data and in which territory?

Based on all of these concerns, this paper proposes an advanced business-centric personal data management system (ABC-PDMS). ABC-PDMS is a framework based on integrating the personal data privacy into the business processes of the enterprise. Such framework gives much more assurances to the online user that his/her data is protected and the organization is treating his/her data as per the "Privacy Statement". Such integration will ensure that the online user will be involved in the processing of his/her own data. It is similar to the usage of software acquired by a company. In this case, it is the responsibility of the organization to ensure that usage of the software is compliance with the license agreement with the software provider. More over this integration will help organizations to develop some mechanisms to ensure continuous compliance with any new privacy laws in very effective and efficient manner.

In the following sections, I will discuss the current status of privacy related to information and communications of personal data, followed by a discussion of data protection in the enterprise. Then, I discuss the results and limitations of the study. Next the implications for practice and future research are presented. Finally, the conclusion of the study will be presented.

ANALYSIS OF THE CURRENT STATUS OF PRIVACY

Privacy is a shared responsibility between the online business that is processing the personal data, the user who is providing the data, and the government in which the entity is operating. The entity responsibility is to establish policies and procedures related to personal data privacy and to provide control mechanisms to ensure that these policies and procedures are maintained. Controls should be established to ensure that the data is accurate and secure when it is in processing (DIP), in transmission (DIT), and at rest (DAR). Controlling DIP includes: collecting data, organizing, altering, adapting, retrieving, combining, and erasing or destroying the data. Controlling DIT includes: transmitting, sharing, and disclosing the data. Controlling DAR includes: holding or keeping data on file on storage without doing anything to or with it.

The individual's responsibility is somewhat limited to provide his/her data to a legitimate entity and to use the Internet tools to protect his/her data and privacy (EPIC, n.d.) when is possible. But is this enough to maintain individual's privacy? The obvious answer is no since we are operating in a "DigNet" age, users have no control on the data they provided voluntarily or involuntarily to others over the net. It is the responsibility of the government to issue and to enforce data protection legislation. Recently there has been an increased concern over the status of data protection laws in specific countries. But the issue is beyond the boundaries of a specific country. The data could be collected in one country, accessed from another country, and yet distributed to other countries.

The focus so far for practitioners and researchers in addressing the issue of privacy is in protecting personal data, providing tools for end users to manage their data (IPEC), providing a policy statement, and satisfying the law requirements imposed by the government's privacy legislations.

Privacy

Privacy means different things to different people. The definitions of privacy vary widely according to concept, context and environment. In general, privacy means the right to an individual to be left alone and the right to be free of unreasonable personal intrusion by government, individuals, or institutions. Privacy concerns exist way before the "DigNet" age. Wistin (1967) defined privacy as the individual's right to determine or control the distribution of their information, including how it is collected, used and distributed, to whom it is provided, and to what extent it is released.

Smith (2000) defines privacy as "the desire by each of us for physical space where we can be free of interruption, intrusion, embarrassment, or accountability and the attempt to control the time and manner of disclosures of personal information about ourselves." According to PrivacyInternational (2003) the concept of data protection has been fused with privacy, which interprets privacy in terms of personal information management. Privacy can be divided into four separate but related concepts: Information privacy, Privacy of communications, Territorial privacy, and Bodily privacy (PrivacyInternational, 2003). In this paper the focus is on the privacy of information and communications. Privacy of information involves the establishment of rules governing the (DIP), (DIT), and the (DAR) of personal data. Privacy of communication covers the security and privacy of retrieving data from databases through applications within the enterprise or outside the enterprise such as e-mail and other forms of communication.

The increase in privacy concerns in the "DigNet" is well documented (Lwin, Wirtz, &

Williams, 2007; Ashworth & Free, 2006; Peslak, 2005a, 2005b, 2006, 2007; Milne, 2000; Thomas & Maurer, 1997; McCrohan, 1989). Such concern is shared among individuals, organizations, and governments. The growing capabilities in the "DigNet" are to collect, process, use data, and convert it to information. Such capabilities forced individuals, organizations, and governments to study a balance between privacy and participation (Westin, 1967). Individuals would like to participate in the "DigNet" activities, but they are very concerned about their privacy and how organizations are handling the processing of their information. Organizations and governments would like to have more users to participate in the "DigNet" activities to increase their sales of products and services and to help them make the right decisions based on accurate data. To accomplish this goal, they are working very hard to provide users with some assurances about the protection of their data and privacy. How to balance between these two conflicting activities is what I propose in this paper.

The Internet makes it very simple to collect, share, transmit, sort, file, access information comparing with the complexity of the manual process that exists before the "DigNet" era. Online businesses are using such capabilities to develop their databases and to collect much personal data about their online users or potential users to be used for future marketing campaigns. Even more, a $26 could buy you a social security number online in a matter of hours, which is often enough to gain much more information as you need about someone (Teifke, 2003).

Organizations are using several techniques to collect data about individuals. For example, the majority of organizations monitor which web sites their workers visit, as well as employee e-mail, instant messages, message boards, and blogs. Web sites can learn the identities of their visitors if the visitors voluntarily register at the site to purchase or obtain a free product or service. Web sites can also capture data about visitors without their knowledge using cookie, web bug, and spyware programs. Such data is very valuable to companies and marketers. Marketers would like to know the behavior of these individuals, what they buy, what they are interested in, and where they came from. Such information becomes very valuable to these organizations when they are accurate, precise, and complete. More dangerously, when such data gets in the hands of intruders in which they use such information to harm the individual financially or physically.

Privacy Protection Laws

In many countries around the world, governments established laws to protect and govern the privacy of individuals. In most cases the government has a "privacy" agency to monitor and evaluate the private and public companies to ensure compliance with its legislations. In the United States (U.S.) which relies on industry-specific legislation, privacy of citizens is protected primary by the constitution in addition to many U.S. federal and state laws, regulations, directives, and acts that set forth the principles for handling personal information in such areas as credit reporting, financial records, education records, newspaper records, search engines records, and electronic transaction records. The Privacy Act of 1974 is considered to be the father of all privacy laws since it sets the foundation of regulating how the federal government agencies can collect, use, and disclose an individual's data and information. Many other laws including: Electronic Communications Privacy Act of 1986, Computer Matching and Privacy Protection Act of 1988, Computer Security Act of 1987, Driver's Privacy Protection Act of 1994, and E-Government Act of 2003 established to protect the privacy of individuals (Laudon & Traver, 2008). Laudon and Traver (2008) indicate that most of the U.S. federal privacy laws apply only to the federal government and regulate very few areas of the private sector.

Based on the "Recommendation Concerning and Guidelines Governing the Protection of Privacy and Transborder Flows of Personal Data" issued by the Organization for Economic Cooperation and Development (OECD, 1980) the European Union (E.U.) has issued a comprehensive privacy legislation with certain guidelines. The legislation is referred to the European Directive on Data Protection. The directive regulates the processing of personal data within the E.U. and includes requirement such as the registration of databases for the personal data, and in some instances prior approval from the consumers before personal data processing may begin. Such requirements in the directive have huge positive impact on the development of personal data management systems. Such systems should utilize the directive's principles throughout the system development life cycle. In addition, the directive required countries in E.U. to cease to share data considered the subject matter of protection to any third country unless they adhere to similar laws. Though there are commercial interests behind these guidelines, very few countries within the E.U. can stay away from these guidelines and other countries must adhere to these guidelines if they want to do business in any E.U. country.

E.U. is a head of the U.S. in recognizing the need for a global policy that will ensure data protection for consumers conducting business online. The OECD Guidelines is considered to be the reference point for regulatory arrangements on the Protection of Privacy and Transborder Flows of Personal Data (Clarke, 2000). The U.S. Department of Commerce in consultation with the E.U. developed a "safe harbor" framework to comply with European privacy laws and to provide a streamlined means for U.S. organizations to comply with the Directive.

Canada and Australia adopted several laws described as a "co-regulatory model." Under these laws, companies representing the industry develop rules for the protection of data that are enforced by the industry and overseen by a "privacy" agency.

Furthermore, in January 1, 2004 the Canada's federal government's personal privacy protection legislation was enforced. This legislation is based on the Personal Information Protection and Electronic Documents Act (PIPEDA). As a result, companies started getting their "privacy" practices in order to be compliant with the law or they will face potentially damaging consequences (Williams, 2003). Organizations conducting business in Canada are required to comply with the PIPEDA 10 principles (Williams, 2003). PEPEDA legislation includes elements drawn from the OECD principles and Canada has gone further than the OECD's guidelines by adopting and enforcing these principles (Millar, 2006).

In general, most of these laws established several principles in which every organization must meet the obligations declared in these principles. Failing to comply with these principles could have serious implications including: audit of the organization's privacy practices, public reports about the audit's findings, litigation in the federal courts with the prospect of fines, sanctions, and/or criminal liability, and substantial legal and privacy compliance costs.

The principles governing the OECD's recommendations for protection of personal data include collection limitation, data quality, purpose specification, use limitation, security safeguards, openness, individual participation, and accountability (Clarke, 2000). These principles will be discussed in more detail later on in this paper since they are part of the proposed ABC-PDMS framework. These principles are considered to be complete and when the United States agrees to go by these guidelines and apply them in the U.S. and to any organization conducting business in the U.S., they will be considered universal standards.

Privacy Policy Statement

Organizations are aware of the government's legislations regarding Privacy Acts. To protect their interest, organizations post on their web sites a privacy policy statement placed solely for compliance purposes. A privacy policy statement is a legal document that discloses some or all of the ways an online business collect, uses, disseminates, and manages a client/customer's data. Despite governments' regulation requirements for privacy policy statements, there does not seem to be a universal standard formats and contents for privacy policy statements (Gazaleh, 2008). The exact contents of a privacy policy statement will depend upon the requirements of government's or governments' applicable laws and the organization's own policies. For example, one study noted that the levels of non-compliance in the privacy policy statements to the United Kingdom (U.K.) and E.U. privacy laws were substantial (Jamal, 2005).

In order to allow online businesses to retain flexibility over the use of the data they acquired from their online users, they intentionally make the privacy policy statement vague (Milne, 2000). Moreover, organizations make the privacy policy statements very difficult to understand and the comprehension of 80% of U.S. privacy policy statements required a university level education (Pollach, 2005). For these reasons and others, less than 50% of online users read the privacy statements (Laudon & Traver, 2008) although, the vast majority of them claim they are concerned about privacy. As such, the revenue impact on line businesses is huge. According to a survey of 5,000 US customers released by Gartner (2008) about 39% say they have made a change to their online shopping behavior due to worries about their personal data being stolen. The result of the survey mentioned in the report "2008 Data Breaches and Financial Crimes Scare Consumers Away," also reveals that 59% of those who have changed behavior say they have cut online shopping. Of those, 30% say they shop less online and 28% say they abandon a session if redirected to another web site to enter payment information. 71% say they are more cautious about where they purchase online, 67% more careful about entering personal and financial information on web sites and 15% say they have stopped shopping on the web completely. To regain the consumers' confidence, organizations need to change their behavior towards the management of the users' personal data. Integrating the ABC-PDMS in the company's enterprise business processes will give it a very strong personal data management value proposition since it will help the company to increase customer base, increase revenues, increase market share, and improve customer/client retention levels. To achieve all of these benefits, any business process in the enterprise must interact with the ABC-PDMS at anytime the business process is required to process personal data.

Jamal (2005) concluded in his study that respondents clearly felt that privacy statements were not 'fit for purpose' and the real use of a privacy policy statement may even be counter-productive to generating web-based trust. The integration of the privacy policy statement in the ABC-PDMS is essential since it will provide that level of confidence from the online users' point of view and at the same time will positively impact the trust between the online users and the online businesses. Such trust will be established overtime since the online user will provide consent in the form of acknowledgement that s/he has read and accepted the contents of the privacy policy statement and will be forced to respond to messages sent by the online businesses that hold his/her personal data when the data is being processed.

Most of the governments' legislations related to personal data protection required that organizations to publish a privacy statement in their web sites. For example, as part of the PIPEDA legislation, organizations are required to publish a privacy statement explaining their data collecting practices (Clement et al., 2008). OECD legislation also required as part of the Openness principles from organizations to make the privacy policy statements clear, concise, and conspicuous to consumers (Kobsa, 2007).

Privacy Protection Solutions

As mentioned earlier, privacy protection is the responsibility of the online business that is processing the personal data, the person who is providing the data, and the government in which the entity is operating. In addition to legislation, several tools are available for online customers to protect their privacy when they interact with online businesses. EPIC provides comprehensive privacy-enhancing tools to secure and protect privacy on the user's web browser computer. Many of these tools are used for encrypting e-mail, files and folders; for preventing client machines from accepting cookies; by disabling the monitoring and recording the sites visited; and by detecting and eliminating spyware and web bug programs.

There are now tools to help users determine the kind of personal data that can be extracted by Web sites. The Platform for Privacy Preferences Project known as (P3P) enables Web sites to develop their privacy statements in a standard format through an interactive Privacy Policy Editor that can be retrieved automatically and interpreted easily by user agents. P3P user agents will allow users to be informed of site practices (in both machine- and human-readable formats) and to automate decision-making based on these practices when appropriate. Thus users need not read the privacy policies at every site they visit (W3C, n.d.). P3P works only between members of the WWW consortiums who have translated their privacy policy into P3P format. Furthermore P3P provides mechanisms for users to trust the web site that they are visiting, but this trust is associated with the first visit. P3P does not provide any mechanisms for users to be informed by the company when they use their data later on.

The Honorable Karen Evans (OMB, 2007) in her statement before the committee on government reform, U.S. House of Representatives indicated that Security and privacy should be developed within the same responsibilities and programs. They are separate pieces of the same puzzle.

Personally identifiable information is an example of what to protect, while security is a program for how to protect it. Government agencies continuously are developing several programs and enhancing their strategy for addressing security and privacy challenges. Federal Information Security Management Act (FISMA, 2006) report reveals modest success in meeting several key privacy performance measures including: program oversight (all agencies report having a privacy official who participates in privacy compliance activities), Privacy Impact Assessments (PIAs) for applicable systems, and Systems of Records Notices (SORNs) focusing on developed, published, and maintained systems that contain personally identifiable information.

In 2006, several U.S. federal agencies reported high profile data security breaches involving Personal Identifiable Information (PII). During Clay Johnson's (OMB, 2007) testimony before the Committee on Oversight and Government Reform, she described the inter-relationship between security and privacy programs by indicating that personally identifiable information is an example of what to protect, while security is a program for how to protect it.

OMB (2007) issued policy M 07-16, "Safeguarding Against and responding to the Breach of Personally Identifiable Information," which directs federal agencies to develop and implement a risk-based breach notification policy, while ensuring proper safeguards are in place to protect the personally identifiable information. This is evidence of how even government bodies are looking at privacy only as an inter-related to security and not addressing the real problem to measure the success of integrating these policies and programs in the business processes of organizations to develop the right strategies related to privacy.

Although these solutions can be very effective to protect individual's data, they are looked at only from security and safeguard dimension. By continuing focus on security and safeguard

mechanisms will shift the responsibility from management to the technical department. So, a company will focus on the technical solutions and let go of the business and legislation requirements.

DATA PROTECTION SOLUTIONS IN THE ENTERPRISE

The right of individual's to determine and control the processing of their data is an issue that researchers and practitioners have been struggling in proposing and implementing. Governments are asking organizations to be compliant with the "privacy" laws by doing combinations of the following actions: appoint a "privacy" officer, conduct a "privacy impact assessment" to determine the type of information collected, create and implement a "Privacy Policy" to govern the organization's processing of personal information, and develop training programs for employees (OMB, 2003). As such organizations must develop a practical framework to comply with the "Privacy" laws established in the countries they do business in, or the cost of business risk will be very high on these organizations.

Before I discuss the proposed framework, it is useful to briefly review the traditional approaches to personal data protection systems.

Traditional Personal Data Management Systems

The business processes related to data processing implementation is the basis for the interactions shown in Figure 1 between the operational, management, and information processes of the enterprise (Gelinas, 2004). These processes should work together to accomplish the goal of an enterprise organization to maintain the privacy of individual's conducting business with.

As shown in Figure 1, in dark lines, is the flow of activities related to individual data protection procedures and policies within the traditional

Figure 1. A Logical Model of a traditional personal data management system

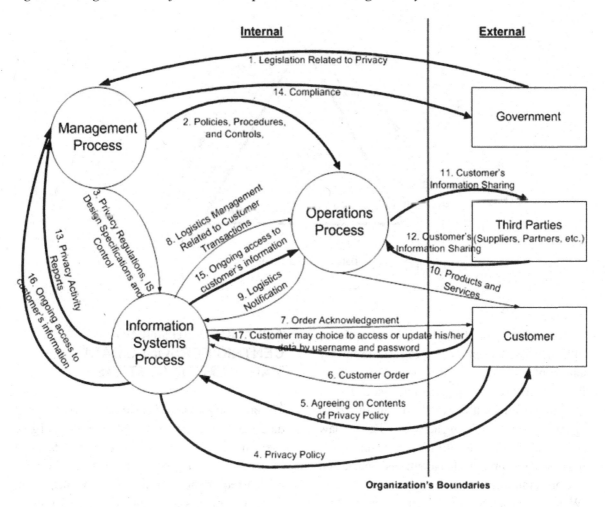

personal data management system (TPDMS). As an example, such data will be collected from a customer/client when s/he buys a product or a service from such a company. Most of the companies today are using the traditional personal data management systems (TPDMS) to claim that they are protecting the privacy of individuals. The essence of the TPDMS is for the customer/client to trust that the company will treat his/her data with care as per its "Privacy Statement". The company's management sets the privacy policies and controls and it is responsible for monitoring and evaluating the privacy activities to ensure that they are compliant with the government privacy legislations. A customer upon ordering products

or services visits the company's Web site through the information systems process, reads the privacy statement, and provides personal data to fulfill the requirements of accepting the term and conditions of the company's "Privacy Policy". A customer/client usually will be provided with a username and password to access his/her account in case he/she wants to update their data records. Beyond this, the customer has no control on the processing of his/her data. In some cases the company could decide to share the customer's data with other third parties or to use the data internally for marketing or sales purposes or even worse, some employees could access the data for personal gains.

Figure 2. The Three Domains of the ABC-PDMS

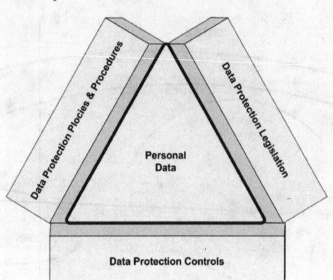

For example, E-Trade and in compliance with the U.S. Patriot Act posted the following statement in its Web site: "Important information about procedures for opening a new account: To help the government fight the funding of terrorism and money laundering activities, Federal law requires all financial institutions to obtain, verify, and record information that identifies each person who opens an account." The statement continued: "What this means for you: When you open an account, we will ask for your name, address, date of birth, and other information that will allow us to identify you. We may also utilize a third-party information provider for verification purposes and/or ask for a copy of your driver's license or other identifying documents." Such policy indicates to the customer/client that if you want to do business with E-Trade you need to say good bye to your privacy, because the company will share your information with the government, seek more information about you from third parties, and they may share your information with other third parties. In the following section I will discuss the approach to personal data management system.

ADVANCED BUSINESS-CENTRIC PERSONAL DATA MANAGEMENT SYSTEMS

The proposed advanced business-centric personal data management system (ABC-PDMS) will give users more control on the usage of their data and give organizations more control to fulfill the compliance requirements from their own policies and the government's legislations. Before I present the framework I need to build some foundation concepts and I will start with the data protection in the enterprise.

The ABC-PDMS Three Domains and Their Privacy Services

Data protection in the ABC-PDMS is built on three main domains: data protection legislation (government-regulation), data protection policies and procedures (self-regulation), and data protection controls (self-regulation). Figure 2 demonstrates the relationship between these three domains in relationship to personal data. Each domain consists of its own principles (Privacy Services). The privacy services are routines that interact with the internal, external, and the personal data store for processing.

The *data protection legislation domain* is built on what has been known as the universe data privacy regulation principles (privacy services) that many governments are adopting as part of their data privacy legislations. These principles (Williams, 2003) are: Authority (Consent), Collection Limitation (Limiting), Data Quality Principle (Accuracy), Purpose Specification Principle (Purpose), Use Limitation Principle (Processing), Security Safeguards (Security), Openness (Openness), Individual Participation (Access), Challenges Compliance (Compliance), and Accountability (Accountability).

The *data protection policies and procedures domain* is built on the universe data protection principles (privacy services) outlined above in addition to several resources addressed this issue (Aston, 2001; P3P). These privacy services include: What, Why, How, and Who (WWWW); Security and Safeguard (Security); Publicly Available Information (Public); Subject Consent (Consent); Sensitive Data (Sensitive); Right of Access to Data; (Access) and Retention of Data (Retention).

The *data protection controls domain* is built on many available procedures, tools and techniques to secure an individual's data. These services include: Data Collection (Collection), Data Accessibility (Accessibility), Data Dissemination (Dissemination), Data Accuracy (Accuracy), Data at Rest (DAR), Data in Processing (DIP), and Data in Transmission (DIT). Organizations should develop and deploy controls to protect data collection, data accessibility, data dissemination, and data accuracy. In addition controls should be established to protect data at rest, data while in processing, and data while in transmission. It is the management responsibility to ensure that these controls are sufficient to meet the government privacy legislations and to meet the organization's goals and objectives.

In ABC-PDMS, the elements of each domain should be integrated in every business process of the enterprise. Such integration guarantees that the company is providing a customer/client with a clear privacy statement in which it is linked to the data protection legislation domain, the data protection policies and procedures domain, and the data protection controls domain. In such, the data protection legislation principles are covered in the policies and procedures of the enterprise and the data protection controls are a manifestation of both the data protection legislation and the data protection policies and procedures (see Figure 3). Moreover the customer/client will have complete control when s/he submits his/her data, updating the data, or anytime the host organization is attempting to use the data internally or externally.

In the ABC-PDMS system, the framework integrates the three domains into the organization's business processes. Such integration will allow the system to communicate with the customer/client each time the company processes his/her data by getting acknowledgement from the user to accept such processing. Such a system will help organizations retain their online users and maximize the joint venture returns with other business partners without sacrificing the privacy commitments that the organization made with the customer/client.

The ABC-PDMS interacts with internal processes and external entities. The main two external entities are a customer/client or any third party requests data about a customer/client record. In the ABC-PDMS the customer/client is in control of his/her data through any activity the company is conducting using the customer/client data. The company must receive an approval from the customer/client anytime access to his/her data is processed. ABC-PDMS shifts the control from trusting the organization that collecting and processing the personal data as they wish to practice the right of online users to determine or control the distribution of their data, including how it is collected, used and distributed, to whom

Figure 3. The Privacy Services (Principles) of the Three Domains of the ABC-PDMS

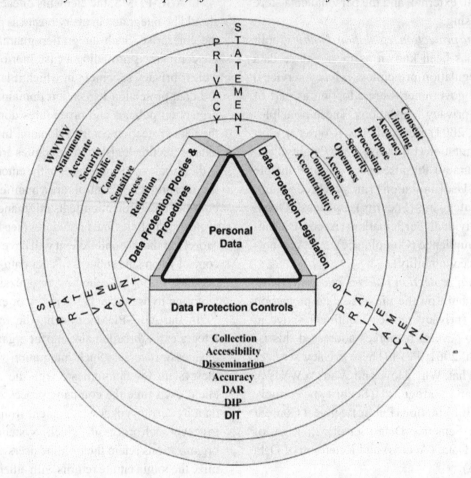

ABC-PDMS Five Processes

As shown in Figure 4 the ABC-PDMS consists of five main processes (represented by the bubbles) to manage and control the flow of personal data. The five processes are: Receive Privacy Statement, Collect Data, Access Data, Accurate Data, and Disseminate Data. These processes interact amongst themselves and with external entities (represented by the rectangles) at the same time. External entities are providers and recipients of data inputs and outputs to and from the ABC-PDMS respectively, which in a typical setting includes online users (data provider) and third parties (interested in accessing personal data). Such interactions are briefly described below.

As its name indicates, the *receive* privacy statement process is responsible of presenting the "Privacy Statement" to the customer/client and receive the acknowledgement from the customer/client that s/he has read the statement and agreed upon the contents. The privacy statement is a data flow input parameter between the ABC-PDMS and the client/customer. The receive privacy statement process is the switch gate to other processes. When the customer/client acknowledged that s/he has read and agreed upon the contents of the statement, the other processes will be activated to process the personal data of his/her

it is provided, and to what extent it is released (Westin, 1967).

Figure 4. Logical DFD for the ABC-PDMS

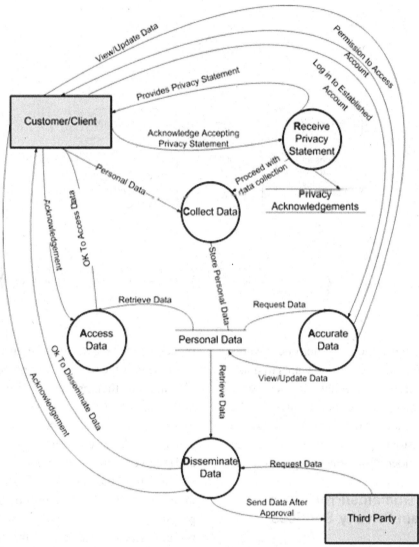

records. The acknowledgement by the client/customer will be recorded in a privacy acknowledgement data store. The second process is the *collect* data process. It is responsible for collecting the personal data from a customer/client after receiving the acknowledgement and stores the data into the personal data store. The next process is the *access* data process. It is responsible for communicating with the customer/client at any situation when any other process within the organization request data from the personal data

store. This process will ensure that an approval from the customer/client who owns the data is obtained before the process can release the data. The next process is the *disseminate* data process. This process will be activated when any external entity request data or information about individuals. The process will seek getting approval from the customer/client to send the data to the external entity and will not release the data until it receives the approval from the customer/client. The last process is the *accurate* data process. It

Figure 5. The Receive process with its privacy services

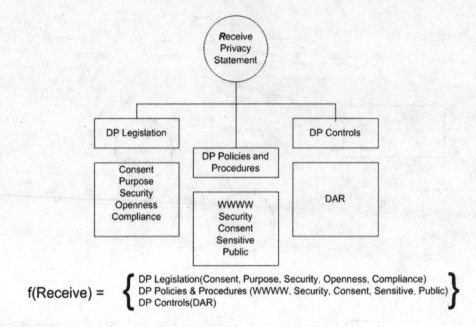

$$f(Receive) = \left\{ \begin{array}{l} \text{DP Legislation(Consent, Purpose, Security, Openness, Compliance)} \\ \text{DP Policies \& Procedures (WWWW, Security, Consent, Sensitive, Public)} \\ \text{DP Controls(DAR)} \end{array} \right\}$$

will be invoked when the customer/client wants to access his/her data in case s/he wants to make any changes or check his/her data. In such a case he/she will be able to make any changes to the data. The organization will have some control to not allow the customer/client to delete some data that will help in identifying the customer/client.

ABC-PDMS Domains/Processes and their Main Privacy Services

The five processes discussed above should be integrated with the three main domains of the ABC-PDMS. By focusing on the business processes the organization will decide starting in the initiation phase of the system development which privacy services within each domain/process required to be part of which business process. This model will give management more control on personal data activities to ensure the compliance with the government's legislation and their own policies and procedures. The "Policy Statement" will be maintained and will reflect how the organization is handling data as part of the actual business

processes of the enterprise. Figures 5 through 9 illustrate how the five business processes, the three domains, and their privacy services are integrated in the ABC-PDMS.

The receive privacy statement (receive) process is responsible for communicating with the client and receive acknowledgement from the client that s/he has read the statement and they agreed on the contents of it. The receive process has consent, purpose, security, openness, and compliance privacy services as part of the DP legislation domain. These services should be developed and activated for this domain to ensure compliance with the government legislations' related to privacy. Also, the receive process has WWWW, security, consent, sensitive, and public privacy services as part of the DP policies and procedures domain. These services should be developed and activated for this domain to ensure compliance with the organization's policies and procedures. In addition, the receive process has DAR privacy services as part of the DP controls domain.

The collect data (collect) process is responsible for collecting the personal data from the

Figure 6. The Collect Process with its Privacy Se

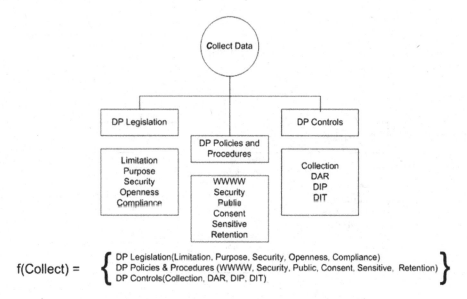

$$f(Collect) = \left\{ \begin{array}{l} \text{DP Legislation(Limitation, Purpose, Security, Openness, Compliance)} \\ \text{DP Policies \& Procedures (WWWW, Security, Public, Consent, Sensitive, Retention)} \\ \text{DP Controls(Collection, DAR, DIP, DIT)} \end{array} \right\}$$

client and store the data into the personal data store. The collect process has limitation, purpose, security, openness, and compliance privacy services as part of the DP legislation domain. These services should be developed and activated for this domain to ensure compliance with the government legislations' related to privacy. Also, the collect process has WWWW, security, public, consent, sensitive, and retention privacy services as part of the DP policies and procedures domain. These services should be developed and activated for this domain to ensure compliance with the organization's policy and procedures. In addition, the collect process has collection, DAR, DIP, and DIT privacy services as part of the DP controls domain.

The accurate data (accurate) process is responsible for responding to a client request when he/she wants to make any changes to his/her own data. The accurate process has accuracy, security, openness, and compliance privacy services as part of the DP legislation domain. These services should be developed and activated for this domain to ensure compliance with the government legislations' related to privacy. Also, the accurate process has accuracy, security, and retention

privacy services as part of the DP policies and procedures domain. These services should be developed and activated for this domain to ensure compliance with the organization's policies and procedures. In addition, the collect process has accuracy, DAR, and DIP privacy services as part of the DP controls domain.

The access data (access) process is responsible for communicating with the client when any other process in the enterprise requests any personal information about the client and it should receive acknowledgement from the client before it releases any information to that process. The collect process has access, security, openness, and compliance privacy services as part of the DP legislation domain. These services should be developed and activated for this domain to ensure compliance with the government legislations' related to privacy. Also, the collect process has WWWW, security, access, public, and retention privacy services as part of the DP policies and procedures domain. These services should be developed and activated for this domain to ensure compliance with the organization's policy and procedures. In addition, the collect process has

Figure 7. The Accurate Process with its Privacy Services

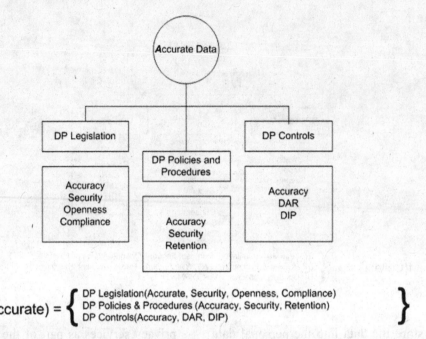

$$f(Accurate) = \left\{ \begin{array}{l} \text{DP Legislation(Accurate, Security, Openness, Compliance)} \\ \text{DP Policies \& Procedures (Accuracy, Security, Retention)} \\ \text{DP Controls(Accuracy, DAR, DIP)} \end{array} \right\}$$

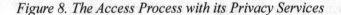

Figure 8. The Access Process with its Privacy Services

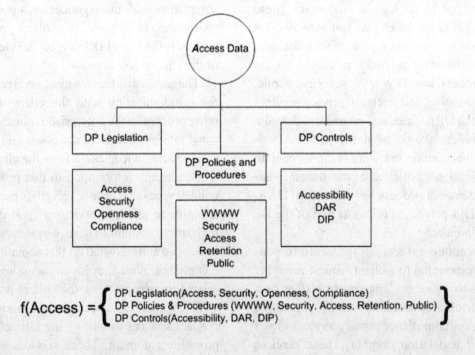

$$f(Access) = \left\{ \begin{array}{l} \text{DP Legislation(Access, Security, Openness, Compliance)} \\ \text{DP Policies \& Procedures (WWWW, Security, Access, Retention, Public)} \\ \text{DP Controls(Accessibility, DAR, DIP)} \end{array} \right\}$$

accessibility, DAR, and DIP privacy services as part of the DP controls domain.

The disseminate data (disseminate) process is responsible for responding to any external entity that requests information about a client (Figure

Figure 9. The Disseminate Process with its Privacy Services

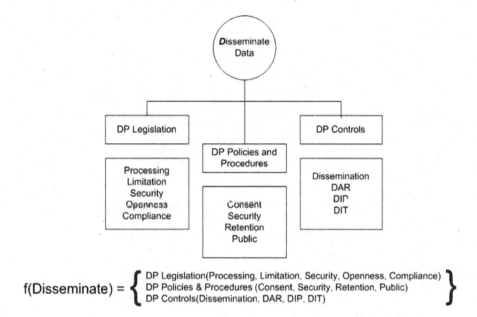

9). The process will seek acknowledgement from the client before releasing any information. The disseminate process has processing, limitation, security, openness, and compliance privacy services as part of the DP legislation domain. These services should be developed and activated for this domain to ensure compliance with the government legislations' related to privacy. Also, the disseminate process has consent, security, retention, and public privacy services as part of the DP policies and procedures domain. These services should be developed and activated for this domain to ensure compliance with the organization's policy and procedures. In addition, the disseminate process has dissemination, DAR, DIP, and DIT privacy services as part of the DP controls domain.

INTEGRATING THE ABC-PDMS IN THE ENTERPRISE

The five processes of the ABC-PDMS and the privacy services associated with its domains should be developed during the analysis, design, and implementation phases of the system development life cycle. The ABC-PDMS should be enabled and integrated in each business process of the enterprise that interacts with the personal data store. Such integration required a closer look on the impact from strategic perspective of the new system on the organization's business. New technologies based on m-commerce associated with personal digital assistants (PDAs) and Smartphones have become so popular that companies can integrate their capabilities in more efficient method in the ABC-PDMS to reach and communicate with their online users. With such integration, the management team will ensure that the organization is compliant with legislation laws and its own policies and procedures. Moreover, the organization will develop a trust with its online users by ensuring that their personal data is protected and they have full control of the usage of their own data. As a result, such system will increase online users confidence and increase the penetration rate of customers doing business with such an entity.

Figure 10. Integrating O2C into ABC-PDMS

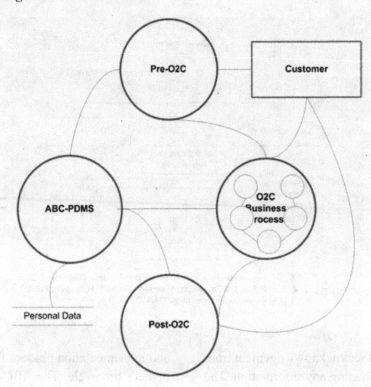

The ABC-PDMS system will be the interface with the customer/client through the organization enterprise business processes. Such integration will guarantee that one centralized business process will be responsible for such interaction. The O2C will be used as an example to validate and demonstrate how the ABC-PDMS integration takes place (see Figure 10).

The Order-to-Cash (O2C) business process helps companies to measurably improve and manage their O2C end-to-end processing life cycle. The O2C spans multiple steps including: order fulfillment, shipping & delivery, invoicing & billing, and payment. According to Wipro (2008), customer experience in the O2C process is perceived through 4 key requirements: choice, predictability, flexibility, and cost. A product/service company needs to deliver these requirements to meet customer/client perception. Today, most organizations are focusing on enhancing such process from operational aspects to increase

the effectiveness and the efficiency of the life cycle. The main driven factors are related to direct gains in revenues and market share. The integration of the ABC-PDMS into such process will help organizations to meet these goals in addition to gain new online users and retain the online users by satisfying them when it comes to controlling their personal data. Integrating ABC-PDMS into the O2C process will be established by introducing three phases of O2C: Pre-O2C, O2C, and Post-O2C.

The pre-O2C phase is very important since it presents a level of confidence by the customer/client that the personal data collection process will be controlled per the company's "Privacy Statement". In this phase, a new client/customer will be introduced to the "receive" and "collect" processes of the ABC-PDMS. This will guarantee that the personal data will be collected in compliance with the government legislation, policies and procedures of the company, and the control mechanisms established in the organization. The client/customer will acknowledge (via e-mail and m-commerce capabilities) the reading and approving of the privacy statement and provide his/her personal information accordingly. The collected data will be stored in the personal data file for future usage. A returning client/customer will be introduced to an updated privacy statement in case the statement has been updated to receive his/her approval, otherwise the returning client/customer will be handled to the O2C process. The O2C process will be activated and interact with the client/customer as per the steps defined above. Any personal data processing during the O2C order fulfillment, shipping & delivery, invoicing & billing, and payment will be handled to the ABC-PDMS to ensure compliance with company's own policies and procedures.

In the post-O2C phase, a customer/client will have control on the usage of his/her data by integrating the "accurate", "access", and "disseminate" processes into the data management system. So, a client/customer will be able to log into his/her account to make any changes, will be engaged in any dissemination of his/her information, and be informed and getting his/her acknowledgement in case the company plans to send his/her information to a third party.

IMPLICATIONS FOR PRACTICE AND FUTURE RESEARCH

As per the results of the surveys mentioned earlier in this paper, it is clear that online customers are not happy about how governments and organizations are treating their personal data. Also, organizations are missing huge opportunity to gain the trust of such individuals to help in increasing their sales and customer satisfaction. The proposed framework will increase the trust of customers in the way organizations and governments are dealing with their data and will help in increasing the customer confidence and in turn increase the sales of online

products and services and participation on online activities. As such, the proposed framework will have a crucial effect on practice. From a strategic perspective, the ability of the organization to integrate the ABC-PDMS into their overall business strategy is important for the success factors in adopting and deploying the solution. As such, the implications of the integration of the ABC-PDMS on organization from a strategic perspective need to be examined. Further work should attempt to show how integration methods of privacy into the business processes used in this study is appropriate across all business processes of the enterprise. One area for research is to develop business process controls for the ABC-PDMS. Such control will provide assurance about the quality of the data collection process and the accuracy process. Control systems enable management to meet this responsibility. For example, for the U.S. government agencies to be compliant with FISMA, Personal Identifiable Information (PII) controls should be developed in the ABC-ADMS to prevent the storage of data that can be used to uniquely identify an individual or can be used with other data sources to uniquely identify a single person. This framework has not been empirically tested as it is a conceptual method and future research in this area is needed to test the framework. Moreover, the sciences of design methodology (Hevner et al., 2004; Hevner, 2007) with its three cycles to information systems research could be adopted to present the framework. In such environment, several design evaluation methods could be used to evaluate the framework. Despite this limitation the framework can yield rich representations of the personal data privacy with its main domains, processes, and privacy services.

CONCLUSION

The importance of personal data protection is putting a heavy weight on both governments and organizations to come up with convincing solutions to customers that their data is protected and will be used only for the purpose it has been collected for in addition to provide the customers with full control of their own data. In line with this requirement, I have argued in this paper that personal data protection should be integrated in the business processes of the enterprise and control development should be integrated within systems development for process-centric personal data management system. The lack of an established approach and methodologies for the personal data protection has a huge effect on the number of customers involving in conducting business on the Internet. I have attempted a modest effort in this paper by proposing an integration of personal data into the business processes of the enterprise. Though conceptual developments in this paper have been limited to requirements analysis, they could easily be extended to cover system design and implementation as well. The approach used in this paper was simply modest and illustrative and it will have a positive impact on the body of knowledge for the study of privacy mainly in the area of personal data protection. Several authors (Kokolakis et al., 2000; Carnaghan, 2006) propose different modeling and design techniques to support a more rigid integration between process-centric systems that can be used for the ABC-PDMS.

REFERENCES

W3C. (n.d.). *The Platform for Privacy Preferences Project (P3P): Enabling smarter Privacy Tools for the Web*. Retrieved November 7, 2010, from http://www.w3.org/P3P/

Anderson, J., & Rachamadugu, V. (2008). *Managing Security and Privacy Integration across Enterprise Business Process and Infrastructure*. Paper presented at the IEEE International Conference on Services Computing.

Ashworth, L., & Free, C. (2006). Marketing Dataveillance and Digital Privacy: Using Theories of Justice to Understand Consumers' Online Privacy Concerns. *Journal of Business Ethics*, *67*(2), 107–123. doi:10.1007/s10551-006-9007-7

Aston University. (2001). *Data Protection Policy*. Retrieved November 7, 2010, from http://www1.aston.ac.uk/EasySiteWeb/GatewayLink.aspx?alId=6607

Carnaghan, C. (2006). Business Process Modeling Approaches in the Context of Process Level Audit Risk Assessment: an Analysis and Comparison. *International Journal of Accounting Information Systems*, 170–204. doi:10.1016/j.accinf.2005.10.005

Clarke, R. (2000). *Beyond the OECD Guidelines: Privacy Protection for the 21st Century*. Retrieved November 8, 2010, from http://www.rogerclarke.com/DV/PP21C.html

Clarkson, K., Miller, R., Gaylord, J., & Cross, F. (2009). *Business Law Text and Cases, Legal, Ethical, Global, and E-commerce Environment* (11th ed.). Mason, OH: South-Western, Cengage Learning.

Clement, A., Ley, D., Costantino, T., Kurtz, D., & Tissenbaum, M. (2008). The PIPWatch Toolbar: Combining PIPEDA, PETs and market forces through social navigation to enhance privacy protection and compliance. In *Proceedings of the 2008 IEEE International Symposium on Technology and Society*.

EPIC. (n.d.). *EPIC Online Guide to Practical Privacy Tools*. Retrieved November 7, 2010, from http://epic.org/privacy/tools.html

FISMA. (2006). *FY2006 Report to Congress on Implementation of the Federal Information Security Management Act of 2002*. Retrieved November 7, 2010, from http://www.whitehouse.gov/omb/inforeg/reports/2006_fisma_report.pdf

Gartner. (2008). *2008 Data Breaches and Financial Crimes Scare Consumers Away.* Retrieved November 7, 2010, from http://www.internetretailing.net/news/data-theft-concerns-beginning-to-hit-internet-shopping-volumes

Gazaleh, M.(2008). Online Trust and Perceived Utility for Consumers of Web Privacy Statements: UK Overview – WBS.

Gilinas, U., Sutton, S., & Fedorowics, J. (2004). *Business Process and Information Technology.* Mason, OH: Thomson South-Western.

Hevner, A. (2007). A Three Cycle View of Design Science Research. *Scandinavian Journal of Information Systems, 19*(2), 87–92.

Hevner, A., & March, S., J. P., & Ram, S. (2004). Design Science Research in Information Systems. *Management Information Systems Quarterly, 28*(1), 75–105.

Jamal, K. (2005). Enforced Standards Versus Evolution by General Acceptance: A Comparative Study of E-Commerce Privacy Disclosure and Practice in the United States and the United Kingdom. *Journal of Accounting Research, 43,* 73–96. doi:10.1111/j.1475-679x.2004.00163.x

Kobsa, A. (2007). Privacy-enhanced personalization: Multi-pronged strategies are needed to reconcile the tension between personalization and privacy. *Communications of the ACM, 50*(8), 24–33. doi:10.1145/1278201.1278202

Kokolakis, S. A., Demopoulos, A. J., & Kiountouzis, E. A. (2000). The Use of Business Process Modeling in Information Systems Security Analysis and Design. *Information Management & Computer Security, 8*(3), 107–116. doi:10.1108/09685220010339192

Laudon, K. C., & Traver, C. G. (2008). *E-Commerce, Business, Technology, Society* (4th ed.). Upper Saddle River, NJ: Pearson International.

Lwin, M.O., Wirtz, J., & Williams, J.D. (2007). Consumer online privacy concerns and responses: a power-responsibility equilibrium perspective. *Journal of the Academy of Marketing Science.*

Millar, S. A. (2006). Privacy and security: Best practices for global security. *Journal of International Trade Law and Policy, 5*(1), 36–49. doi:10.1108/14770020680000539

Milne, G. R. (2000). Privacy and ethical issues in database/interactive marketing and public policy: a research framework and overview of the special issue. *Journal of Public Policy & Marketing, 19,* 1–6. doi:10.1509/jppm.19.1.1.16934

Office of Management and Budget (OMB). (2003). *OMB Guidance for Implementing the Privacy Provisions of the E-Government Act of 2002.* Retrieved November 7, 2010, from http://www.whitehouse.gov/omb/memoranda_m03-22/

Office of Management and Budget (OMB). (2007). *Statement of the Honorable Karen Evans Administrator for Electronic Government and Information Technology Office of Management and Budget Before the Committee on Government Reform U.S. House of Representatives.* Washington, DC: Executive Office of the President.

Organization for Economic Cooperation and Development (OECD). (1980). *Guidelines Governing the Protection of Privacy and Transborder Flows of Personal Data.* Retrieved November 7, 2010, from http://www.oecd.org/document/18/0,3343,en_2649_34255_1815186_1_1_1_1,00.html

Peslak, A. R. (2005a). Privacy Policies: A Framework and Survey of the Fortune 50. *Information Resources Management Journal, 18*(1), 29–41.

Peslak, A. R. (2005b, April). Privacy Policies of the Largest Privately Held Companies – A Review and Analysis of the Forbes Private 50. In *Proceedings of ACM SIGMIS Conference 2005*, Atlanta, GA.

Peslak, A. R. (2006). Current Privacy Issues and Factors: Development and Analysis. *Journal of Information Technology Impact*, *6*(3), 171–186.

Peslak, A. R. (2007). Progress in Internet Privacy Policies: a Review and Survey of US Companies from 1998 through 2006. In Khosrow-Pour, M. (Ed.), *Emerging Information Resources Management and Technologies* (*Vol. 6*). Hershey, PA: Idea Group Inc.

Pirim, T., James, T., Boswell, K., Reithel, B., & Barkhi, R. (2008). An empirical Investigation of an Individual's Perceived need for Privacy and Security. *International Journal of Information Security and Privacy*, *2*(1), 42–53.

Pollach, I. (2005). A Typology of Communicative Strategies in Online Privacy Policies: Ethics, Power and Informed Consent. *Journal of Business Ethics*, *62*(3), 221–235. doi:10.1007/s10551-005-7898-3

PrivacyInternational. (2003). *Privacy and Human Rights 2003: Overview*. Retrieved November 7, 2010, from http://www.privacyinternational.org/survey/phr2003/overview.htm

Smith, R. E. (2000). *Ben Franklin's Web Site: Privacy and Curiosity from Plymouth Rock to the Internet*. Privacy Journal.

Teifke, L. (2003). *The Importance of Privacy*. Retrieved November 7, 2010, from http://www.bankersonline.com/vendor_guru/alltel/alltel_privacy.html

Thomas, R. E., & Maurer, V. G. (1997). Database marketing practice: protecting consumer privacy. *Journal of Public Policy & Marketing*, *16*, 147–155.

TNS & TRUSTe. (2008). *Internet users' knowledge, attitudes and concerns about behavioral targeting and its implications on their online privacy*. Retrieved November 7, 2010, from http://www.truste.org/about/press_release/03_26_08.php

Web Design Directory. (2005). *Consumers Fret About Online ID Theft But Still Don't Protect Themselves*. Retrieved November 7, 2010, from http://www.designdir.net/newsst_1440.html

Williams, A. (2003). *Privacy Matters – Why You Need to Pay Attention Now*. Retrieved November 7, 2010, from http://www.dww.com/?page_id=1060

Wipro. (2008). *Improving Order-To-Cash Cycle*. Retrieved November 7, 2010, from http://www.wipro.com/pace/pdf/order2cash_in_telecom_mmi_a_nov08_073.pdf

This work was previously published in International Journal of Information Security and Privacy, Volume 4, Issue 3, edited by Hamid Nemati, pp. 1-21, copyright 2010 by IGI Publishing (an imprint of IGI Global).

Chapter 11
Policy Enforcement System for Inter-Organizational Data Sharing

Mamoun Awad
UAE University, UAE

Latifur Khan
The University of Texas at Dallas, USA

Bhavani Thuraisingham
The University of Texas at Dallas, USA

ABSTRACT

Sharing data among organizations plays an important role in security and data mining. In this paper, the authors describe a Data Sharing Miner and Analyzer (DASMA) system that simulates data sharing among N organizations. Each organization has its own enforced policy. The N organizations share their data based on trusted third party. The system collects the released data from each organization, processes it, mines it, and analyzes the results. Sharing in DASMA is based on trusted third parties. However, organizations may encode some attributes, for example. Each organization has its own policy represented in XML format. This policy states what attributes can be released, encoded, and randomized. DASMA processes the data set and collects the data, combines it, and prepares it for mining. After mining, a statistical report is produced stating the similarities between mining with data sharing and mining without sharing. The authors test, apply data sharing, enforce policy, and analyze the results of two separate datasets in different domains. The results indicate a fluctuation on the amount of information loss using different releasing factors.

DOI: 10.4018/978-1-4666-0026-3.ch011

1. INTRODUCTION

Data sharing among organizations has become a critical research topic. Sharing data among organization is governed by the sharing policies maintained and enforced by the organizations rules and by the government laws. As a result of that, the amount of information used, in any certain sharing scenario among organizations, is smaller than or equal to the whole information maintained in all such organizations.

In our previous paper we discussed our Policy-based Information Sharing System (Kumar, Khan, & Thuraisingham, 2008). In this current paper we extend our previous research by examining how much information information is lost by enforcing policies. There has always been a dichotomy between information sharing and policy enforcement. However none of the previous work has focused on information loss. The work we are discussing in this current paper is the first attempt to our knowledge on computing the information loss. This will give guidance to those who have a need to share information securely.

In this current work we study the effect of information hiding on the amount of knowledge obtained using standard machine learning techniques. Hiding information is represented by the policies and regulations enforced by the organization. We introduce the *releasing factor* measure that indicates the percentage of attributes an organization releases to the total number of attributes such organization has. For mining the shared data, we consider Association Rule Mining.

It is important to point out that, in this study, we assume that all organizations are trusted parties. However, each organization abides by its policies and rules in order to release data. For each organization, we develop sharing policies that govern what kind of data an organization can release. For example, a medical organization, can release information about blood pressure and temperature of patients. However, it cannot release type of illness each patient has.

Also, we try to simulate a realistic scenario of data partitioning. For example, for a specific entity, such as patient, one organization, such as the hospital, might have attributes/fields about the patient medications. However, for another organization, such as insurance companies, such fields are missing. We consider three different partitioning of the attributes, namely, horizontal, vertical, and hybrid partitioning. In horizontal partitioning, we simulate the scenario in which one organization has all fields/attributes about some entities. In vertical partitioning, an organization knows all entities, however, it has some of the fields/attributes about each. In hybrid partitioning, we assume horizontal and vertical knowledge about entities and attributes/fields, i.e., some entities are known totally or partially by some organizations. Notice that data partitioning is related to the layout of the data (see Section 2 for details). *It is also important to point out that we assume that there is a fixed set of attributes/fields about entities.*

After partitioning the dataset, we assume a centralized trust broker, which requests the information from different parties and mines the data. When the broker requests data from an organization x, organization x will apply its policy first, and then send a compliant data, with x policy, to the broker (see Figure 1).

The process of mining shared data among organizations poses several challenges related to the automation of data sharing. First, data disclosure might not be possible because organizations are limited to their sharing policy, i.e., an organization might not release all the data that it has because, for example, of privacy issues. Next, data reprocessing as a result of discrepancies of the format, representation, scales, etc. of the data among organizations. Finally, human intervention to resolve issues such as mapping data from one organization data base to another. That is because it is possible that two attributes have the same names, however, different meaning and vice versa.

Figure 1. Communications between the broker and an organization

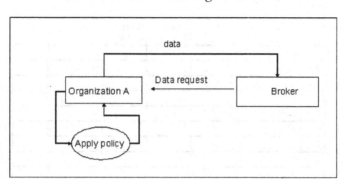

In this study, we randomly partition the data (using three schemes, namely, horizontal, vertical, and hybrid partitioning) among N organizations. In order to resolve the issue of data disclosure, we create several test cases with increasing releasing factor. For example, we create 25 test cases 1, 2, 3, 4, ...,25 and applied releasing factors 1, 4, 8, 12, ...,100 for each test case, respectively. We do not try to solve the problem of mismatch in the formatting of the data among organizations; however, we introduce an xml based framework that can be extended later to handle such mismatch.

The paper is organized as follows. Section 2 presents the data partitioning schemes we use. Section 3 presents the enforcement and application of policies. Section 4 shows results and comparisons. Section 5 summarizes the paper and outlines some future work. Our user manual is given in the Appendix. For details on assured information sharing we refer to Thuraisingham (2008). For a discussion of data mining we refer to Thuraisingham (1998).

2. DATA PARTITIONING

In this section, we describe and explain the different schemes of partitioning data. Since we do not have real time shared data, we try to partition a dataset among *N* imaginary organizations.

2.1 Type of Partitioning

There are several ways to share the data. The data is distributed among different organizations with three different scenarios.

2.1.1 Horizontal Partitioning

In the horizontal partitioning an organization has all records/information about some entities (such as persons). Figure 2 presents an example of such partitioning in which we have four organizations sharing information about persons. The first row in Figure 2 shows the name of attributes/fields about people, for example, here we have the following attributes: SSN, data of birth, credit history, annual income, occupation, and auto insurance company. The rest of the rows represent records about different persons. Notice that each organization has all the attributes/fields about some persons; however, it lacks information about other persons in the dataset. Also, in this partitioning, some records can be redundant in more than one organization. One realistic scenario of such partitioning is the case in which department of vehicles in Texas has all the records about people in Texas, however, it does not have any of such information about people in California and vice versa (see also Ceri & Pelagetti, 1984).

Figure 2. Horizontal partitioning

	SSN	Dob	Credit history	Annual income	Job	Insurance
1	123-...	1-8-90			Engineer	
2	321-...	2-1-02			teacher	
3						
4						
5	143-...	1-1-62			Artist	
6	325-...	1-1-82			Lawyer	
7						
8						
9	223-...	1-1-92			Professor	
10	521-...	1-1-72			driver	

Org 1 (rows 1–2), Org 2 (rows 5–8), Org 3 (rows 3–6), Org 4 (rows 7–10)

Figure 3. Vertical partitioning

	SSN	Dob	Credit history	Annual income	Job	Insurance
1	123-...	1-8-90			Engineer	
2	321-...	2-1-02			teacher	
3						
4						
5	143-...	1-1-62			Artist	
6	325-...	1-1-82			Lawyer	
7						
8						
9	223-...	1-1-92			Professor	
10	521-...	1-1-72			driver	

Org 1 (SSN), Org 2 (Dob), Org 3 (Credit history, Annual income, Job, Insurance), Org 4 (Job, Insurance)

2.1.2 Vertical Partitioning

In vertical partitioning each organization has part of the fields/attributes about some entity in the dataset. For example, in a dataset of patient records, an insurance organization knows specific attributes about the patients such as their ids, cost of treatment, drug used, duration of treatments. However, such insurance organization has no specific information about the illnesses, readings (blood pressure, sugar level, etc.). Figure 3 presents an example of vertical partitioning for the same dataset used in Figure 2. Notice that some organizations such as organization 1 has only information about SSN and date of birth. Organization 4 has information about the annual income, occupation, and the auto insurance company. In real time scenario, there might be different ID used for each person. For example, Department of Motor Vehicles might use driver license to identify a person, on the other hand FBI might have both driver license and SSN and use both to identify persons. In this study, we assume that there is a unique id that identifies each person, and all organizations are using this id.

2.1.3 Hybrid Partitioning

Hybrid partitioning is the combination of vertical and horizontal partitioning. This means that an organization might have a complete record about some entities, however, it lacks some of the attributes about others. Such lack of information presents optional information, such as race, age,

Figure 4. Hybrid partitioning

	SSN	Dob	Credit history	Annual income	Job	Insurance
1	123-...	1-8-90			?	
2	321-...	?			Teacher	
3			?	?		
4			?			?
5	?...	1-1-62			Artist	
6	325-...	1-1-82			?	
7			?			
8						
9	?...	1-1-92			Professor	
10	521-...	1-1-72			driver	

etc. So, it is up to the person to provide it or not; hence, it might be available or unavailable.

Figure 4 presents an example of hybrid partitioning of a dataset among four organizations. The question mark in Figure 4 denotes unknown field value. Notice that some records are complete in some organizations, for example, organization 4 has all the fields of record number 10. However, organization 4 lacks some attributes, such as occupation, of record number 6.

3. POLICY REPRESENTATION AND ENFORCEMENT

In this section, we present the representation of organization policy and the details of enforcing them. But before we present that, we introduce some terminology and definitions.

Policy

In this section, we refer to policy as an xml document that is mainly designed to inform which attributes can be released. Figure 5 presents a policy of an organization in which such organization can only release the attributes of type of employment, county of birth, and income type for each record it has about people. Such scheme can be extended to include encoded data or randomized data, i.e., what are the attributes that we should encode them (using randomization) before releasing them. For more details on policy enforcement in XML we refer to Bertino et al. (2004).

Release Factor

The release factor is the percentage of attributes which are released from the dataset by an organization. For example, assume we have a dataset that has 40 attributes and "Organization 1" re-

Figure 5. Example of xml policy

```
<?xml version="1.0"?>
  <DATASET>
   <RELEASE_ATTR>
     <REL_ATTRIB>full_or_part_time_employment</REL_ATTRIB>
     <REL_ATTRIB>country_of_birth_mother</REL_ATTRIB>
     <REL_ATTRIB>income_type</REL_ATTRIB>
   </RELEASE_ATTR>
  </DATASET>
```

Figure 6. an example of an xml file used for partitioning and sharing

```
<?xml version="1.0"?>
<ORGANIZATIONS>
        <ORGANIZATION>
    <ORG_ID>1</ORG_ID>
    <XML_POLICY_FN>org_1.xml</XML_POLICY_FN>
    </ORGANIZATION>
    <ORGANIZATION>
    <ORG_ID>2</ORG_ID>
    <XML_POLICY_FN>org_2.xml</XML_POLICY_FN>
    </ORGANIZATION>
    <ORGANIZATION>
    <ORG_ID>3</ORG_ID>
    <XML_POLICY_FN>org_3.xml</XML_POLICY_FN>
    </ORGANIZATION>
    <NUM_ORG>3</NUM_ORG>
    <DATASET_FN>census_income/census_income_50k.dat</DATASET_FN>
    <ARFF_PREFIX>census_income</ARFF_PREFIX>
    <TEST_CASE_ID>census_income_test_20_1</TEST_CASE_ID>
    <DATASET_PROCESSOR>
        <CLASS_NAME>processors.CensusIncomeProcessor</CLASS_NAME>
        <ATTRIB_FN>census_income/attributes.xml</ATTRIB_FN>
    </DATASET_PROCESSOR>
    <POLICY_DIR>census_income_20/testcases/test_case_1</POLICY_DIR>
    <DELIM>,</DELIM>
</ORGANIZATIONS>
```

Organization information

Data set & Processing data

leases 8 attributes. The release factor in this case is 8/40=20%. Here, we use the release factor to analyze the amount of information loss as a result of sharing and applying policies. The release factor is crucial in determining the information loss due to the enforcement of policies.

3.1 Policy Structure and Details

In this section, we present the structure of the xml files that we used to configure partitioning and policy enforcement.

Figure 6 presents an example of partitioning a dataset among three organizations. In the top part of the xml file, noted by organization information, we state the number of organizations, and each organization id and its releasing policy. Each releasing policy file is an xml file which is similar to Figure 5, in which we define the attributes/fields that we can release.

The second part of the xml in Figure 6 is details about the dataset file, dataset preprocessor, and meta data about that. Table 1 presents the name and definition of each xml tag in the configuration xml file.

Notice that we randomly assign a record to an organization. Once all records are assigned to organizations, we start applying the policy of that organization. In the GUI, the user can choose the type of data partitioning (see Figure 7). Notice that the user can use the browse xml button to find his policy file, then from the drop box, the user can choose either horizontal, vertical, or hybrid partitioning.

Notice that in the previous xml configuration file, we did not mention the releasing factor. That is because each test case is a single test case that is specific for a set of attributes provided by the user. Alternatively, the user can choose batch processing, in which she chooses the releasing factor step and the GUI generates a set of test cases. In other words, the system will generate a set of xml files similar to Figure 6. In this study, we adopt the batch processing because, first, we need large number of test cases. Next, each test case should represent different releasing factor. Finally, we need to see the effects of different releasing factor on the information loss.

Figure 8 presents an example of xml file used in batch processing. In addition to the xml tags Figure 6, we added few xml tags to indicate the

Table 1. XML tags names and their definitions

Xml tag	Definition
ORG_ID	Unique organization id.
XML_POLICY	The xml file that contains policy, see Figure 5.
NUM_ORG	The number organization involved in data sharing.
Dataset Information	
DATASET_FN	The dataset file name including its path.
ARFF_PREFIX	The arff prefix file name.
TEST_CASE_ID	A unique id for the test case generated.
Dataset Processor	
CLASS_NAME	Java class name of the processor dedicated for this dataset.
ATTRIB_FN	The file name that contains all the attributes in this dataset along with their types (for example, nominal, binary, etc.)
POLICY_DIR	The directory where the xml policies of the organizations reside in.
DELIM	The delimiter used to separate fields in the dataset.

Figure 7. Processing dataset and policy enforcement GUI

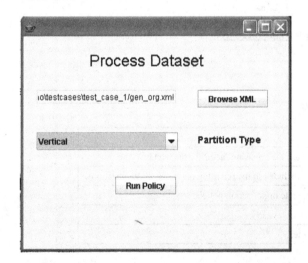

releasing factor step, template information for xml generation, and policy directory to build the directory structure of the test cases (see Table 2). Notice that the RELEASE_FACTOR indicates the step of increasing the number of attributes. For example, if the RELEASE_FACTOR is 10, that means we will generate 10 test cases from 1 to 10 and the number of attributes released for all organization in these test cases is 10, 20, 30, 40, 50, ..., 100%, respectively. The MANDATORY_ATTRIB is the list of attributes that all organizations have to release. This is very convenient because it allows the system to enforce a unique id to be released; hence, it can connect different attributes from different organizations and remove duplicates. Figure 9 presents the list of test cases generated from Figure 8.

4. DATA SHARING

4.1 Overview

The data sharing happens among N organizations with three different partitioning (horizontal, vertical and hybrid). The dataset is divided into N parts randomly so that each organization has its own dataset. We used 3 different organizations for each test case, so that each partition uses its own partitioned dataset, that is, if the dataset's file name is dataset.dat, the dataset will be randomly distributed into three data files and named horizontal_dataset_org1.dat, horizontal_dataset_org2.dat and horizontal_dataset_org3.dat for horizon-

Figure 8. XML file used in batch processing

```
<?xml version="1.0"?>
 <TEST_CASE>
  <BASE_POLICY_DIR>/data/policy/</BASE_POLICY_DIR>
  <!-- make sure to have different tc_id for the bundle -->
  <TC_ID>census_income_4</TC_ID>
  <TEST_CASE_DIR>testcases</TEST_CASE_DIR>
  <NUM_ORG>3</NUM_ORG>
  <RELEASE FACTOR>4</RELEASE FACTOR>
  <ATTRIB_XML>attributes.xml</ATTRIB_XML>
  <DATASET_BASE>/data/dataset/census_income/</DATASET_BASE>
  <MANDATORY ATTRIB>income type</MANDATORY ATTRIB>
  <POLICY_XML>gen_org.xml</POLICY_XML>
  <ORG_PREFIX>org_</ORG_PREFIX>

  <!-- information about the dataset -->
  <DATASET_FN>census_income/census_income_50k.dat</DATASET_FN>
  <ARFF_PREFIX>census_income</ARFF_PREFIX>

  <!-- for each testcase bundle, used different test_case_id -->
  <TEST_CASE_ID>census_income_test_4</TEST_CASE_ID>
  <DATASET_PROCESSOR>
   <CLASS_NAME>processors.CensusIncomeProcessor</CLASS_NAME>
   <ATTRIB_FN>census_income/attributes.xml</ATTRIB_FN>
  </DATASET_PROCESSOR>
  <POLICY_DIR>census_policy_</POLICY_DIR>
  <DELIM>,</DELIM>
  <TEMPLATE FN>gen template.xml</TEMPLATE FN>
 </TEST_CASE>
```

Table 2. Additional xml tags used in batch processing

Xml tag	Definition
RELEASE_FACTOR	The step in which we increase the releasing factor for the next test case.
MANDATORY_ATTRIB	Mandatory attributes to be included in the releasing policy of all organizations.
TEMPLATE_FN	A template file used to generate organization policies.
TC_ID	Unique batch test case id.
TEST_CASE_DIR	The test case directory name.

tal partitioning. The same dataset will again be partitioned for vertical and hybrid partitionings.

4.2 Using the Policies

Our gui uses several policies to get information. It starts with a policy named *<dataset_file_*

name>_<release_factor>.xml. i.e census_income_10.xml

There are two parts in the policy. The first part of the xml policy shows how to name the directories and prefixes to eliminate overwriting, and uses some policies about the information that is needed to process the dataset. The second part is related to batch processing and partitioning. So

Figure 9. Generated test cases for Figure 8

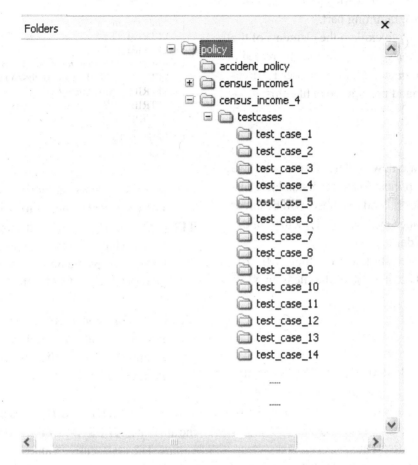

Figure 10. Batch processing GUI

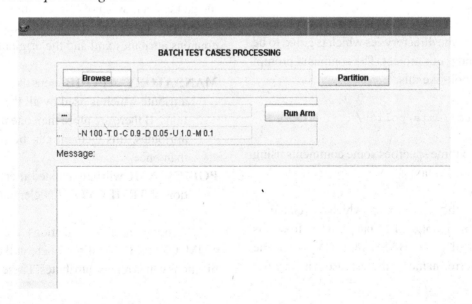

we are going to explain the first part which is not related to the programming part.

Before starting to explain the elements of the xml policy, let's assume that we have created a new project file named NewProj under H directory. The command prompt looks like this:

```
H:/NewProj
```

We will create new folders to save what we process and keep them in an understandable hierarchy. The files related to dataset will be under the "dataset" folder, and the policies will be under the "policy" folder.

Now, let's get started with the XML file shown above. The first line of the file is an XML declaration.

```
<?xml version="1.0"?>
```

Every XML file starts with an "XML declaration", which indicates several pieces of information that is used to parse the file. "1.0" is the XML version number which is the only official version of the XML specification.

The policy starts in the second line with "TEST_CASE" element. This element is the root of the tree which contains all the information in the file.

The **BASE_POLICY_DIR** element contains the name of the directory/ies which is going to be created under our project. The command prompt line will look like this.

```
H:/NewProj/data/policy/
```

The next line specifies some comments using <!—and --> syntax.

TC_ID is the test case id which is related to the xml policy file name. This folder is created under BASE_POLICY_DIR. The preferred name for the test case id is *"dataset*

Figure 11. Sample policy

```
<?xml version="1.0"?>
<ATTRIBUTES>
<ATTRIBUTE>
<ATTRIB_NAME>gender</ATTRIB_NAME>
<ATTRIB_TYPE>Female;Male</ATTRIB_TYPE>
<ATTRIB_NAME>age</ATTRIB_NAME>
<ATTRIB_TYPE>0:100</ATTRIB_TYPE>
</ATTRIBUTE>
</ATTRIBUTES>
```

name"_"release factor number" as shown in **Error! Reference source not found.**.

TEST_CASE_DIR contains the name of another folder which is created under TC_ID.

NUM_ORG keeps the number of organizations and **RELEASE_FACTOR** keeps the release factor number.

ATTRIB_XML contains each column name and its potential values in the dataset. The sample example for this policy is seen in Sample Policy 2 (Figure 11).

Here, **ATTRIB_NAME** gives us the name of the attribute, **ATTRIB_TYPE** gives the attribute values. The consecutive values are separated by ":", the other types are separated by ";"

Let's go back to our first XML policy. The element of the next line, **DATASET_BASE** has the name of a new set of folders which is created under the "NewProj" directory. This directory contains attributes.xml and the original dataset.

MANDATORY_ATTRIB keeps the name of the attribute which is used by all the organizations. If there are more than one mandatory attributes, this element can be used more than once.

POLICY_XML will be explained after the definition of **TEMPLATE_FN** element.

The number of organizations are given in NUM_ORG, let's say it's 3. There will be 3 organizations which release attributes. These organizations must have different names. The naming is generated by the program using a prefix which is given in **ORG_PREFIX** element. The new xml files will be named like this, org_1, org_2, .. org_N

DATASET_FN contains the original dataset file name.

ARFF_PREFIX is the prefix of a folder name which is generated for different test cases. The generated test case and its number is attached as a suffix to this name.

As we said before, part 2 is related to the programming part, however the element named

TEMPLATE_FN has the XML file name which helps the program generate the "gen_org. xml" defined in **POLICY_XML** element.

An example for TEMPLATE_FN file is seen in Figure 12.

gen_org.xml files in all of the test case folders will be a copy of this file except the values between "%". Those values will be generated by the program. The sample for POLICY_XML file is shown in Figure 13.

As it is seen in Figure 13, some of the elements are rewritten due to the number of organizations.

Figure 12. Example template

```
<?xml version="1.0"?>
<ORGANIZATIONS>
%ORGANIZATIONS%
<NUM_ORG>%NUM_ORG%</NUM_ORG>
<DATASET_FN>%DATASET_FN%</DATASET_FN>
<ARFF_PREFIX>%ARFF_PREFIX%</ARFF_PREFIX>
<TEST_CASE_ID>%TEST_CASE_ID%</TEST_CASE_ID>
<DATASET_PROCESSOR>
<CLASS_NAME>%CLASS_NAME%</CLASS_NAME>
<ATTRIB_FN>%ATTRIB_FN%</ATTRIB_FN>
</DATASET_PROCESSOR>
<POLICY_DIR>%POLICY_DIR%</POLICY_DIR>
<DELIM>%DELIM%</DELIM>
</ORGANIZATIONS>
```

Figure 13. Policy file

```
<?xml version="1.0"?>
<ORGANIZATIONS>
<ORGANIZATION>
<ORG_ID>1</ORG_ID>
<XML_POLICY_FN>org_1.xml</XML_POLICY_FN>
</ORGANIZATION>
<ORGANIZATION>
<ORG_ID>2</ORG_ID>
<XML_POLICY_FN>org_2.xml</XML_POLICY_FN>
</ORGANIZATION>
<ORGANIZATION>
<ORG_ID>3</ORG_ID>
<XML_POLICY_FN>org_3.xml</XML_POLICY_FN>
</ORGANIZATION>
<NUM_ORG>3</NUM_ORG>
<DATASET_FN>census_income/census_income_50k.dat</DATASET_FN>
<ARFF_PREFIX>census_income</ARFF_PREFIX>
<TEST_CASE_ID>census_income_test_10_1</TEST_CASE_ID>
<DATASET_PROCESSOR>
<CLASS_NAME>processors.CensusIncomeProcessor</CLASS_NAME>
<ATTRIB_FN>census_income/attributes.xml</ATTRIB_FN>
</DATASET_PROCESSOR>
<POLICY_DIR>census_income_10/testcases/test_case_1</POLICY_DIR>
<DELIM>,</DELIM>
</ORGANIZATIONS>
```

5. SUMMARY AND FUTURE CONSIDERATIONS

In this paper we discussed the tradeoffs between security and information sharing. Then discussed the system we have developed that not only shares data between organizations, but also computes the amount of information that is lost by enforcing policies. Specifically we defined the concept of "release factor" which is used to compute the information loss. We also used data mining tools to extract the useful nuggets from the information shared. Ultimately it is up to the analyst to use our tool as a guide to determine what policies to enforce. We believe that the work we have discussed in this paper is the first such effort on determining the information loss. As there is more and more push to migrate from a need to know to the need to share environment we believe that our work will be extremely useful.

There are several areas for future work. First we need to determine the release factor for a more robust set of policies such as those based on role based access control. Next we need to develop ways to compute the value of the information lost. For this we need to use semantic web technologies to add semantics to the information that will determine the value. Essentially we need algebra to compute the value of information from the value of the components of the information. Such robust tools can provide better support to the analyst and the policy makers to determine what policies to enforce under what conditions.

ACKNOWLEDGMENT

We thank the students Dilsud Cavus, Manjunath Reddy and Sirinivasan Iyer for their contributions to the project; in particular for the user interface implementation and Oracle expertise.

REFERENCES

Bertino, E., Carminati, B., Ferrari, E., Thuraisingham, B. M., & Gupta, A. (2004). Selective and Authentic Third-Party Distribution of XML Documents. *IEEE Transactions on Knowledge and Data Engineering, 16*(10), 1263–1278. doi:10.1109/TKDE.2004.63

Ceri, S., & Pelagetti, G. (1984). *Distributed database principles and systems*. New York: McGraw Hill.

Kumar, Y., Khan, L., & Thuraisingham, B. (2008). Trusted Computing Base for Assured Information Sharing. *Journal of Information Security and Privacy*.

Thuraisingham, B. (1998). *Data Mining: Technologies, techniques, Tools and Trends*. Boca Raton, FL: CRC Press.

Thuraisingham, B. M. (2008). Assured Information Sharing: Technologies, Challenges and Directions. *Intelligence and Security Informatics*, 1-15.

APPENDIX

System Manual

MainGUI: The Main GUI Chooser window is used to launch PD&M graphical environments. Main Window has three buttons:

1. **Load and Analysis**. Provides a simple GUI interface that allows loading the already generated rules and analyze rules by displaying the charts.
2. **Run ARM.** Provides an interface to choose the arff file and run Apriori algorithm, and displays the association rules, frequent item sets and their confidence.
3. **Process DataSet:** Provide the chooser window to select Single Processing dataset or Batch Processing.

RunArm: This GUI allows a user to select the preprocessed .arff file and select the options required for the association rules (for more about the options refer to Figure 20). By clicking **Run ARM** button the **Apriori** association rule algorithm is applied to the selected file with options selected.

Figure 14. Main GUI

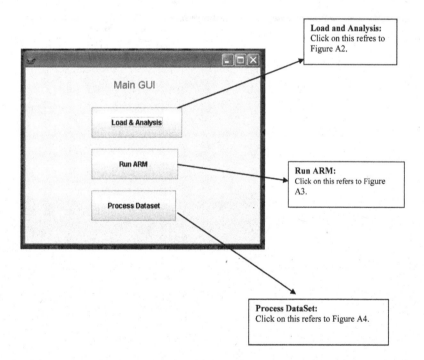

Figure 15. Load and Analyze GUI

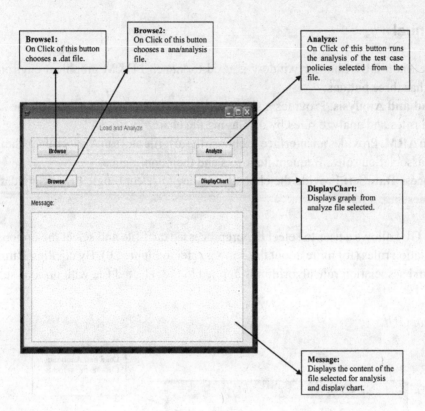

Figure 16. Run ARM GUI

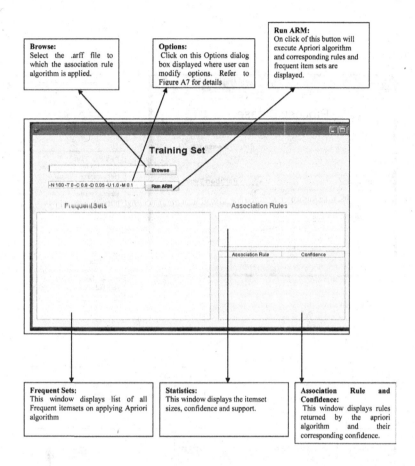

Figure 17. Main process data set GUI

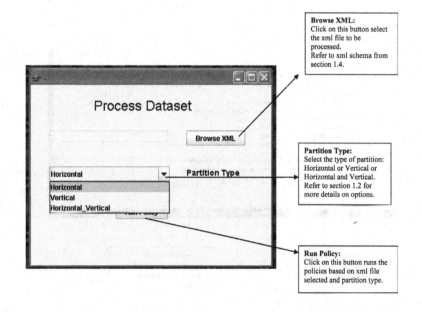

Figure 18. Process dataset GUI

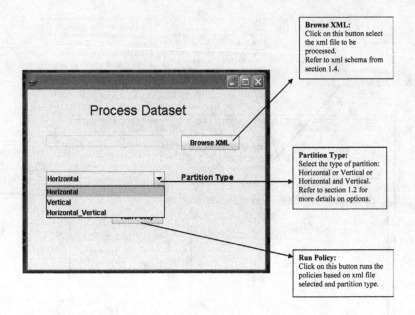

Figure 19. Batch processing GUI

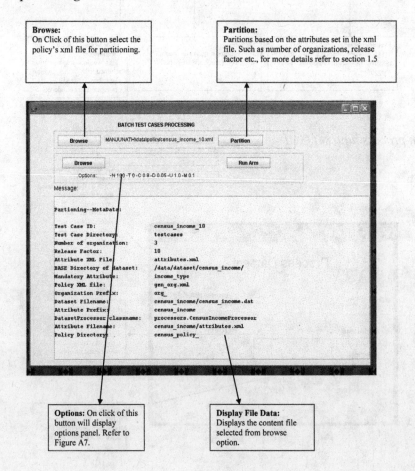

Figure 20. Options panel

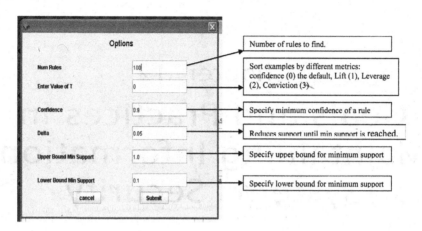

Chapter 12
Goals and Practices in Maintaining Information Systems Security

Zippy Erlich
The Open University of Israel, Israel

Moshe Zviran
Tel-Aviv University, Israel

ABSTRACT

With the rapid growth of information systems and networks, security is a major concern of organizations. The main goals of information systems security are confidentiality, integrity, and availability. The cornerstone of an organization's security lies in designing, developing and implementing proper information systems' security policy that balances security goals with the organization's needs. In this paper, the authors discuss the goals of information systems security and the techniques to achieve them. Specifically, the paper focuses on access control and the various authentication approaches, as well as intrusion detection and prevention systems. As attacks become more frequent and devastating, ongoing research is required to adapt and improve security technologies and policies to reflect new modes of attack to keep information systems secure.

INTRODUCTION

Computers are everywhere and affect almost every aspect of modern life. We store and process most of the information we use in computerized systems, both personal and organizational. One of the most prolific threats to computer systems are malicious code objects, such as viruses, worms, and Trojan horses. Antivirus software packages are specifically designed to detect and eradicate malicious code. These antivirus programs scan file systems, Web content, network traffic and electronic mail for signs of malicious code and either quarantine or block suspect programs from

DOI: 10.4018/978-1-4666-0026-3.ch012

entering the system. With the rapid growth of information and networked systems, security is a major concern for organizations, and the demand for effective computer security is increasing.

Information systems security involves blocking unauthorized malicious access to a system's resources and information. The main goals of information systems security are confidentiality, integrity, and availability (Solomon & Chapple, 2005). Confidentiality means the assurance that users obtain access only to information they have the right to access, integrity means the assurance that data be modified only by users who are authorized to modify it, and availability means the assurance that computer resources and information are available to authorized users whenever needed.

To achieve these security goals, various access control and intrusion detection and prevention systems are used. These security technologies rely on each other for their operation, thereby affecting each other's contribution (Cavusoglu, Raghunathan, & Cavusoglu, 2009). Hence, it is important to have a suitable configuration to benefit from the security techniques used.

Security requirements differ greatly from one system to another. Many security systems fail because their security policy designers protect the wrong things, or protect the right things but in the wrong way (Ross, 2008). The cornerstone of any organization's security lies in designing, developing and implementing proper information security policy that balances the security goals of confidentiality, integrity, and availability with the organization's needs.

Security policies are dynamic and should be comprehensive and flexible enough to accommodate changes in technology. Security policy should include technical and software controls like access controls, firewalls, intrusion detection systems (IDS), as well as intrusion prevention systems (IPS), together with sound physical and personnel security practices that supplement these technical controls.

Due to the continuous development of new types of malicious attacks, research is needed to improve and adapt security technologies and policies to keep information systems secure. Information systems can be made more secure with both technologies and management strategies and policies (Ross, 2008). Further research is needed to better understand human behavior and the applied psychology aspects of computer security.

In this paper, we discuss the main goals of information systems security and the security techniques used to achieve these goals. We focus on access control and the various authentication approaches as well as intrusion detection and prevention systems.

MAIN GOALS OF INFORMATION SYSTEMS SECURITY

There are various definitions of computer security; each views computer security from a different standpoint. Security professionals tend to define three interdependent information security goals: confidentiality, integrity, and availability (CIA) (Solomon & Chapple, 2005).

Confidentiality is the main goal of information security and refers to preventing confidential information from falling into the hands of unauthorized users. Access controls and encryption processes can prevent this.

Integrity refers to preventing unauthorized alteration and modification of data, either by unauthorized users such as hackers, or by authorized users making unauthorized modifications. Access controls prevent such modification of data by unauthorized users. In addition, to ensure integrity, a backup policy should be defined to protect against corruption or loss of data.

Availability aims at ensuring that computer resources and information are available for authorized users. It guarantees legitimate users the ability to access data for their intended use whenever they need. Access controls and intrusion detection systems are used to prevent unauthorized users from harming computer resources and information and to prevent denial-of-service (DoS) attacks.

Several methods and mechanisms are used to ensure CIA. Firewalls provide perimeter protection for a computer system through traffic filtering. They are used to screen incoming and outgoing traffic on a single computer or an entire network and determine whether the data received may be passed on to its destination. In addition, cryptography techniques that convert plaintext into ciphertext are used to facilitate the confidential exchange of information over insecure communication channels, such as the Internet. Encrypting data ensures that only the user in possession of the decryption key can decrypt the ciphertext and read the data.

Merely securing the perimeter with firewalls or routers is not sufficient. Authentication and authorization access controls are needed to prevent unauthorized users from entering a system and to prevent authorized users from accessing confidential information that they are not authorized to access. Access controls are also used to protect from unauthorized modification of data to achieve the integrity goal. There are various authentication approaches and methods; using more than one method can strengthen the authentication process.

When access control protection mechanisms fail, intrusion detection systems (IDS) and intrusion prevention systems (IPS) are used to achieve the security goals. Intrusion detection systems monitor data traffic to discover if an attacker is trying to break into a system. Intrusion prevention systems help to detect and protect against hackers attacks performing malicious harm actions using computer programs like viruses, worms and Trojan horses.

Threats to the security of information systems can also come from an authorized malicious insider. To mitigate this threat, which is the most difficult to prevent, a combination of access control mechanisms and intrusion detection and prevention systems is used.

USER AUTHENTICATION AND ACCESS CONTROL

Access control supports both the confidentiality and integrity goals of computer and information security. The three main, closely related components of access control – identification, authentication and authorization – should be operated separately (Auernheimer & Tsai, 2005). Each user is typically represented by a unique identifier, such as a user name. However, this is insufficient to ensure the user's actual identity. Therefore, a process of authentication is used to verify the user's claim. The authorization phase authenticates user access according to predefined criteria and user profiles. The two phases of identification and authentication provide reasonable protection from unauthorized users' accessing the computer system.

Authentication approaches can be classified into three types according to their distinguishing characteristics (Erlich & Zviran, 2009; Menkus, 1988).

- *Knowledge-based authentication*: Character-based, image-based, and question-and-answer-based
- *Possession-based authentication*: Token-based authentication (memory tokens and smart tokens)
- *Biometric-based authentication*: Physiological biometrics and behavioral biometrics

The classification of the authentication approaches is presented in Figure 1. The benefits and drawbacks of each approach are described below.

Knowledge-Based Authentication

The most widely used type of authentication is knowledge-based authentication – what the user knows. There are various types of knowledge-based authentication:

Figure 1. Classification of authentication approaches

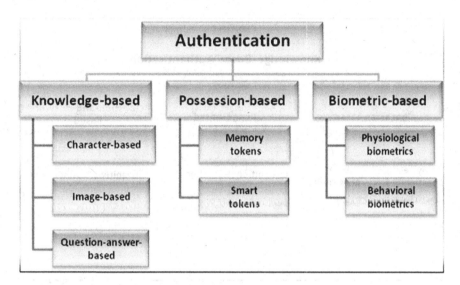

- Character-based authentication
- Image-based authentication (picture-based or graphical)
- Question-and-answer-based authentication

Character-based authentication consists of a series of characters, like passwords, pass-phrases or pass-sentences (Spector & Ginzberg, 1994) and PINs. The series of characters can be system-generated or user-generated with predefined rules. User-generated series of characters have been shown to be easier to remember but less secure than a system-generated series of characters, as they can be easily guessed (Lopez, Oppliger, & Pernul, 2004).

Image-based authentication (Picture-based or graphical) (Brostoff & Sasse, 2000; Thorpe & van Oorschot, 2004; Wiedenbeck, Waters, Birget, Brodskiy, & Memon, 2005) can be subdivided into recognition-based techniques and recall-based techniques (Qureshi, Younus, & Khan, 2009). In the recognition-based technique, users are presented with a set of images and have to recognize the images they selected when registering. In the recall-based technique, users are asked

to reproduce something they created or selected when registering.

Question-and-answer-based authentication (Bunnell, Podd, Henderson, Napier, & Kennedy-Moffat, 1997; Zviran & Haga, 1993) has been suggested to overcome the difficulty of remembering a series of characters. It is mainly used for secondary authentication. In a typical question-and-answer session, users are presented with several randomly selected brief questions from a set of questions stored in their profile in the operating system. Access to a system or to a particular application is granted only when the users' answers and those stored in their profile match. The two main types of question-and-answer authentication are *cognitive* and *associative* (Haga & Zviran, 1991). In the cognitive type, the user must provide the system with answers to personal fact-based or opinion-based questions. In the associative type, the user must provide the system with a set of word associations, consisting of cues and their unique associated responses.

The various types of knowledge-based authentication are presented in Figure 2. The tradi-tional, and by far the most widely used form of knowledge-based authentication is the password:

Figure 2. Knowledge-based authentication types

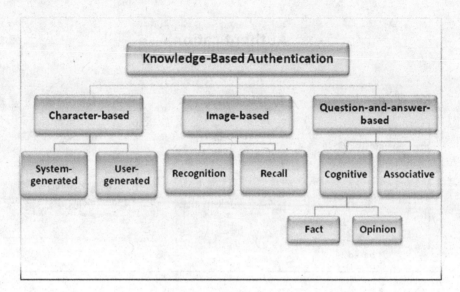

character-based authentication. Most computer systems are protected through user identification (like a user name) plus a password.

A password is conceptually simple for both system designers and end users. It consists of a secret series of characters, determined according to predefined rules. The user ID plus password combination acts as user identification and authentication, and serves to block unauthorized access to computing resources. In most systems, if used correctly, it can provide effective protection.

However, passwords are known to have a number of drawbacks due to human information processing limitations (Sasse, Brostoff, & Weirich, 2001; Yan, Blackwell, Anderson, & Grant, 2005). First, there is a tradeoff between memorability and security. Passwords should be difficult to guess and easy to remember. The generation of secure passwords poses a dilemma as difficult to guess and crack passwords are difficult to remember, and easy to remember passwords are easy to guess and crack. The most secure password is a random string of characters. Such passwords are difficult to guess by others, but at the same time are difficult to remember and thus compel the

users to write them down, which impairs their secrecy. Passwords that are easy to remember, such as names, nicknames, or initials, are also easy to crack.

In order to improve password security and protect from attack, such as dictionary and brute force attacks, password policy should apply rules for choosing and maintaining passwords (Carstens, McCauley-Bell, Malone, & DeMara, 2004; Erlich & Zviran, 2009; Smith, 2002; Tsai, Lee, & Hwang, 2006). The major rules are:

- Passwords should be encrypted or hashed
- Passwords should be limited in time and not reused
- Passwords should be non-dictionary and no-name
- Passwords should be of minimal length and have mixed types of characters
- Complex passwords should use acronyms, rhymes and mnemonic phrases, which are difficult to guess and easy to remember
- Passwords should not be shared and should not be written down
- The number of unsuccessful authentication attempts should be limited by the system

Passwords based on the rules above are more effective, more difficult to identify and to determine by cracking utilities. To overcome the problem of sniffing passwords when authentication is performed over the Internet, one-time dynamic passwords are used (Lamport, 1981; Shimizu, 2007). The one-time password can be implemented using smart cards – a kind of possession-based authentication discussed below.

Possession-Based Authentication

Possession-based or token-based authentication is based on what the user has. Possession-based authentication provides higher security than knowledge-based authentication. There are two main groups of tokens: memory tokens and smart tokens.

Memory tokens store information but do not process it. The most common memory token is the magnetic card, usually used together with a knowledge-based authentication mechanism such as a PIN number. Memory tokens are inexpensive to produce. Using them with PINs provides significantly more security than PINs or passwords alone.

Smart tokens, unlike memory tokens, incorporate one or more embedded integrated circuits that enable them to process information. Like memory tokens, most smart tokens are used for authentication together with a knowledge-based authentication mechanism such as a PIN. Of the various types of smart tokens, the most widely used are those that house an integrated chip containing a microprocessor. Their portability and cryptographic capacity have led to their wide use in many remote applications (Juang, 2004; Ku & Chen, 2004; Wu & Chieu, 2003). Due to their complexity, smart tokens are more expensive than memory tokens but provide greater flexibility and security and are more difficult to forge.

Most problems associated with tokens relate to their cost, administration, loss, and user dissatisfaction due to the inconvenience carrying them. In addition, presentation of a valid token does not prove ownership, as it may have been stolen or duplicated (Svigals, 1994).

Biometric-Based Authentication

Biometric-based authentication is based on what the user is, using certain physiological or behavioral features and characteristics associated with the user (Jain, Hong, & Pankanti, 2000; Kim, 1995; Wayman, Jain, Maltoni, & Maio, 2004). Biometric authentication is based on the fact that certain physiological or behavioral characteristics reliably distinguish one person from another. Biometric systems also enhance user convenience by alleviating the need to determine and remember passwords or to carry tokens. There are various kinds of biometrics (Matyas & Stapleton, 2000); biometric authentication is usually divided into two main categories: physiological and behavioral.

Physiological biometrics is based on the user's stable physical attributes. The best known are fingerprints, finger scans, hand geometry, iris scans, retina scans and facial scans. The most widely used physiological characteristic in systems that automatically recognize a user's identity are fingerprints (Ratha & Bolle, 2005; Wayman et al., 2004).

Behavioral biometrics is based on users' behavioral attributes. These are learned movements (Guven & Sogukpinar, 2003; O'Gorman, 2003; Yu & Cho, 2004). The best known are keystroke dynamics, signature dynamics, mouse dynamics and speech or voice verification.

Biometric authentications are technically complex and usually expensive, as they require special hardware. Biometrics involves both collection and comparison of characteristics. A biometric system can be viewed as a pattern recognition system consisting of three main modules: the sensor module, the feature-extraction module and the feature-matching module. The accuracy of the different biometric systems can be evaluated by the measurement of two types of errors

(Matyas & Stapleton, 2000): erroneous rejection, i.e., false non-match (type I error), and erroneous acceptance, i.e., false match (type II error). In a biometric system that provides a high level of authentication, the rate of these two errors is low.

Although all biometric technologies inherently suffer from some level of false match or false non-match, they provide a high level of security. Despite this, they do not have a high acceptance rate by users, as they are perceived as intrusive and an encroachment on privacy (Prabhakar, Pankanti, & Jain, 2003). Ethical issues of potential misuse of personal biometrics, such as tracking and monitoring productivity, also arise (Alterman, 2003). Thus, they are not popular and mainly used in systems with very high security needs. Biometric authentication is the most effective and accurate identification method as it cannot be easily stolen or shared. However, the digital scan or pattern is vulnerable to network analysis and, once stolen, can no longer be used (Ives, Walsh, & Schneider, 2004).

The *access control design* defines rules for users accessing computer resources and information. The design should consider the control techniques that best suit the organization and provide the highest degree of security. In choosing an authentication method, a number of factors need to be considered: effectiveness, ease of implementation, ease of use and user attitude and acceptance (Furnell, Dowland, Illingworth, & Reynolds, 2000; Zviran & Erlich, 2006). To strengthen the authentication process, the use of more than one type is recommended (Furnell, Papadopoulos, & Dowland, 2004; Yu & Cho, 2004).

Knowledge-based authentication is inexpensive and easy to implement and maintain. Passwords provide the most cost-effective solution; they are portable to other applications and easy to deploy. They are integrated into many operating systems and users are familiar with them. Improved security can be achieved through a secondary technique, like a cognitive or associative password.

Unfortunately, knowledge-based authentication is also the easiest to compromise and is less secure than tokens or biometric authentication methods, which are inherently more secure. On the other hand, tokens and biometric methods are more expensive to implement. User attitudes are very positive toward knowledge-based authentication, less so toward possession-based authentication and negative toward biometric-based authentication (Deane, Barrelle, Henderson, & Mahar, 1995; Prabhakar et al., 2003).

The relationship between human senses and authentication techniques should be exploited to ensure improvement in authentication, while preserving its practicality and ease of use. Creating a link between the human mind and the computer system for verification is a great challenge for researchers in the field of computer security (Qureshi et al., 2009).

INTRUSION DETECTION AND PREVENTION SYSTEMS

In general, it is assumed that users have already gone through an authentication phase using one or more of the authentication methods described. When the access control mechanisms fail, network-based and host-based *intrusion detection systems* (IDSs) are used to help to achieve security goals. IDSs continuously monitor and analyze activity and data traffic on a single computer or network, looking for suspicious actions to discover if an attacker is trying to break into a system. IDSs help to detect attacks in real time so that an appropriate response can be taken immediately. When the IDS detects suspicious activity, it takes a predefined action, according to its configuration. The response process can be a combination of automated and manual steps that validate detected intrusions and select an appropriate response. As far as possible, a good IDS should place minimal load on the system, thus not affecting the system's operation. An extension of the IDS is the *intrusion prevention system* (IPS), which not only detects an intrusion, but also responds and takes action to block it (Yue & Cakanyildirim, 2007). IPSs can be highly effective as a defensive tool but need to be configured with great care and attention. The intrusion detecting and prevention systems, even if properly configured, can miss some intrusions (false negative errors) or generate erroneous alerts (false positive errors). A false negative error, which occurs when an intrusion is missed, is more serious than a false positive error.

IDSs can be broadly classified into two categories based on their detection approaches: *signature-* or *misuse-based* and *knowledge-* or *anomaly-based* (Solomon & Chapple, 2005; Zanero, 2007).

A *signature-based* IDS compares the current system activity with a database of known attack signatures. To contain all known attack signatures, the database requires continuous updates when new attack signatures are available. Signature-based IDSs generally produce precise alerts and thus have a low false positive error rate.

A *knowledge-based* IDS examines activity while building a profile of normal activity over time. Thus, it can detect anomaly intrusions. Knowledge-based IDSs produce more false positive errors than signature-based IDSs, but can detect new and yet unknown types of attacks, which knowledge-based IDSs cannot detect, and they do not require continuous updates. However, knowledge-based IDSs are more difficult to design than signature-based IDSs.

IDSs can also be classified according to where they are placed and what data they inspect: *network-based* and *host-based*. A *network-based* IDS monitors all traffic on a particular network segment and can detect intrusions that cross it. It can be placed outside the main Internet firewall or inside the firewall. A *host-based* IDS monitors all network activity intended for a particular host computer and is useful for detecting intrusions involving a particular system; it can examine the system's entire input and output.

IDSs are traditionally based on characterization of an attack and tracking activity on the system to see if it matches that characterization. Some new intrusion detection systems are based on data mining (Barbará, Couto, Jajodia, & Wu, 2001) and recently, approaches that use artificial immune systems (AISs) for misbehavior detection have been developed (Schaust & Szczerbicka, 2008). Another new approach is AIP – active intrusion prevention (Green, Raz, & Zviran, 2007). AIP constantly examines all network activity to identify requests for data that may be used for hostile purposes. The AIP marks the data requested and when the attacker attempts to use it, the AIP recognizes it as a valid attack rather a false alert and blocks the attacker. The accurate identification of hostile events by AIPs yields a very low false positive error rate. Also, data obtained from an active intrusion prevention system can be analyzed and used to improve network security.

Security technologies rely on each other for their operations, thereby affecting each other's contributions. When used together, there is interaction between firewalls and IDS technologies. While the optimal configuration of an IDS does not change whether it is deployed alone or together with a firewall, the optimal configuration of a firewall has a lower detection rate when it is deployed with an IDS than when deployed alone (Cavusoglu et al., 2009). Hence, it is very important to ensure proper configuration to benefit from the security techniques of both the firewall and the IDS.

SUMMARY AND CONCLUSION

Information systems security involves blocking unauthorized malicious access to a system's resources and information while ensuring confidentiality, integrity, and availability. To achieve security goals, various access control techniques and intrusion detection and prevention systems are used. Solid security depends on intelligent layering, to put as many obstacles between the intruders and protect resources and information, while ensuring a clear path between the authorized users and the information they need.

Security requirements differ greatly from one system to another. The cornerstone of any organization's security effort lies in designing, developing and implementing a suitable information security policy that balances the security goals with the organization's needs.

Due to the rapid changes in technologies and as attacks become, not only more frequent but also more devastating, research is needed to adapt and improve security technologies and policies to respond to new modes of attack and to keep information systems secure.

REFERENCES

Alterman, A. (2003). A piece of yourself: Ethical issues in biometric identification. *Ethics and Information Technology*, 5(3), 139–150. doi:10.1023/B:ETIN.0000006918.22060.1f

Auernheimer, B., & Tsai, M. J. (2005). Biometric authentication for web-based course examinations. In *Proceedings of the 38th Annual Hawaii International Conference on System Science (HICSS'05)* (pp. 294-300).

Barbará, D., Couto, J., Jajodia, S., & Wu, N. (2001). ADAM: A testbed for exploring the use of data mining in intrusion detection. *SIGMOD Record*, 30(4), 15–24.

Brostoff, S., & Sasse, M. A. (2000). Are passfaces more usable than passwords? A field trial investigation. In McDonald, S., Waern, Y., & Cockton, G. (Eds.), *People and Computers XIV - Usability or Else! Proceedings of HCI2000* (pp. 405–424). Sunderland, UK: Springer.

Bunnell, J., Podd, J., Henderson, R., Napier, R., & Kennedy-Moffat, J. (1997). Cognitive, associative and conventional passwords: Recall and guessing rates. *Computers & Security*, 16(7), 629–641. doi:10.1016/S0167-4048(97)00008-4

Carstens, D. S., McCauley-Bell, P. R., Malone, L. C., & DeMara, R. F. (2004). Evaluation of the human impact of password authentication practices on information security. *Information Science Journal*, 7(1), 67–85.

Cavusoglu, H., Raghunathan, S., & Cavusoglu, H. (2009). Configuration of and interaction between information security technologies: The case of firewalls and intrusion detection systems. *Information Systems Research*, 20(2), 198–217. doi:10.1287/isre.1080.0180

Deane, F., Barrelle, K., Henderson, R., & Mahar, D. (1995). Perceived acceptability of biometric security systems. *Computers & Security*, 14(3), 225–231. doi:10.1016/0167-4048(95)00005-S

Erlich, Z., & Zviran, M. (2009). Authentication methods for computer systems security. In Khosrow-Pour, M. (Ed.), *Encyclopedia of information science and technology* (2nd ed., *Vol. 1*, pp. 288–293). Hershey, PA: Information Science Reference.

Furnell, S. M., Dowland, P. S., Illingworth, H. M., & Reynolds, P. L. (2000). Authentication and supervision: A survey of user attitudes. *Computers & Security*, 19(6), 529–539. doi:10.1016/S0167-4048(00)06027-2

Furnell, S. M., Papadopoulos, I., & Dowland, P. S. (2004). A long-term trial of alternative user authentication technologies. *Information Management & Computer Security*, 12(2), 178–190. doi:10.1108/09685220410530816

Green, I., Raz, T., & Zviran, M. (2007). Analysis of active intrusion prevention data for predicting hostile activity in computer networks. *Communications of the ACM, 50*(4), 63–68. doi:10.1145/1232743.1232749

Guven, A., & Sogukpinar, I. (2003). Understanding users' keystroke patterns for computer access security. *Computers & Security, 22*(8), 695–706. doi:10.1016/S0167-4048(03)00010-5

Haga, W. J., & Zviran, M. (1991). Question-and answer passwords. An empirical evaluation. *Information Systems, 16*(3), 335–343. doi:10.1016/0306-4379(91)90005-T

Ives, B., Walsh, K. R., & Schneider, H. (2004). The domino effect of password reuse. *Communications of the ACM, 47*(4), 75–78. doi:10.1145/975817.975820

Jain, A. K., Hong, L., & Pankanti, S. (2000). Biometric identification. *Communications of the ACM, 43*(2), 90–98. doi:10.1145/328236.328110

Juang, W. S. (2004). Efficient password authenticated key agreement using smart cards. *Computers & Security, 23*(2), 167–173. doi:10.1016/j.cose.2003.11.005

Kim, H. J. (1995). Biometrics, is it a viable proposition for identity authentication and access control? *Computers & Security, 14*(3), 205–214. doi:10.1016/0167-4048(95)97054-E

Ku, W.-C., & Chen, S.-M. (2004). Weaknesses and improvements of an efficient password based user authentication scheme using smart cards. *IEEE Transactions on Consumer Electronics, 50*(1), 204–207. doi:10.1109/TCE.2004.1277863

Lamport, L. (1981). Password authentication with insecure communication. *Communications of the ACM, 24*(11), 770–772. doi:10.1145/358790.358797

Lopez, J., Oppliger, R., & Pernul, G. (2004). Authentication and authorization infrastructures (AAIS): A comparative survey. *Computers & Security, 23*(7), 578–590. doi:10.1016/j.cose.2004.06.013

Matyas, S. M., & Stapleton, J. (2000). A biometric standard for information management and security. *Computers & Security, 19*(5), 428–441. doi:10.1016/S0167-4048(00)05029-X

Menkus, B. (1988). Understanding the use of passwords. *Computers & Security, 7*(2), 132–136. doi:10.1016/0167-4048(88)90325-2

O'Gorman, L. (2003). Comparing passwords, tokens, and biometrics for user authentication. *Proceedings of the IEEE, 91*(12), 2019–2040. doi:10.1109/JPROC.2003.819605

Prabhakar, S., Pankanti, S., & Jain, A. K. (2003). Biometric recognition: Security and privacy concerns. *IEEE Security and Privacy Magazine, 1*(2), 33–42. doi:10.1109/MSECP.2003.1193209

Qureshi, M., Younus, A., & Khan, A. A. (2009). Philosophical survey of passwords. *International Journal of Computer Science Issues, 1*, 8–12.

Ratha, N., & Bolle, R. (Eds.). (2005). *Automatic fingerprint recognition systems*. New York: Springer Verlag.

Ross, J. A. (2008). *Security engineering: A guide to building dependable distributed systems* (2nd ed.). New York: Wiley.

Sasse, M. A., Brostoff, S., & Weirich, D. (2001). Transforming the 'weakest link': A human/computer interaction approach to usable and effective security. *BT Technology Journal, 19*(3), 122–131. doi:10.1023/A:1011902718709

Schaust, S., & Szczerbicka, H. (2008). Artificial immune systems in the context of misbehavior detection. *Cybernetics and Systems, 39*(2), 136–154. doi:10.1080/01969720701853434

Shimizu, A. (2007). A dynamic password authentication method using a one-way function. *Systems and Computers in Japan, 22*(7), 32–40. doi:10.1002/scj.4690220704

Smith, R. E. (2002). *Authentication: From passwords to public keys*. Boston: Addison-Wesley.

Solomon, M. G., & Chapple, M. (2005). *Information security illuminated*. Boston: Jones and Bartlett Publishers.

Spector, Y., & Ginzberg, J. (1994). Pass-sentence: A new approach to computer code. *Computers & Security, 13*(2), 145–160. doi:10.1016/0167-4048(94)90064-7

Svigals, J. (1994). Smartcards: A security assessment. *Computers & Security, 13*(2), 107–114. doi:10.1016/0167-4048(94)90056-6

Thorpe, J., & van Oorschot, P. (2004). Graphical dictionaries and the memorable space of graphical passwords. In *Proceedings of the 13th USENIX Security Symposium*, San Diego, CA.

Tsai, C.-S., Lee, C.-C., & Hwang, M.-S. (2006). Password authentication schemes: Current status and key issues. *International Journal of Network Security, 3*(2), 101–115.

Wayman, J., Jain, A. K., Maltoni, D., & Maio, D. (Eds.). (2004). *Biometric systems: Technology, design and performance evaluation*. New York: Springer.

Wiedenbeck, S., Waters, J., Birget, J.-C., Brodskiy, A., & Memon, N. (2005). Passpoints: Design and longitudinal evaluation of a graphical password system. *International Journal of Human-Computer Studies, 63*(1-2), 102–127. doi:10.1016/j.ijhcs.2005.04.010

Wu, S.-T., & Chieu, B.-C. (2003). A user friendly remote authentication scheme with smart cards. *Computers & Security, 22*(6), 547–550. doi:10.1016/S0167-4048(03)00616-3

Yan, J., Blackwell, A., Anderson, R., & Grant, A. (2005). The memorability and security of passwords. In Cranor, L., & Garfinkel, S. (Eds.), *Security and usability: Designing secure systems that people can use* (pp. 121–134). Sebastopol, CA: O'Reilly & Associates.

Yu, E., & Cho, S. (2004). Keystroke dynamics identity verification: Its problems and practical solutions. *Computers & Security, 23*(5), 428–440. doi:10.1016/j.cose.2004.02.004

Yue, W. T., & Cakanyildirim, M. (2007). Intrusion prevention in information systems: Reactive and proactive responses. *Journal of Management Information Systems, 24*(1), 329–353. doi:10.2753/MIS0742-1222240110

Zanero, S. (2007). Flaws and frauds in the evaluation of IDS/IPS technologies. In *Proceedings of FIRST Conference - Forum of Incident Response and Security Teams,* Sevilla, Spain (pp. 167-177).

Zviran, M., & Erlich, Z. (2006). Identification and authentication: Technology and implementation issues. *Communications of the Association for Information Systems, 17*(4), 90–105.

Zviran, M., & Haga, W. J. (1993). A comparison of password techniques for multilevel authentication mechanisms. *The Computer Journal, 36*(3), 227–237. doi:10.1093/comjnl/36.3.227

This work was previously published in International Journal of Information Security and Privacy, Volume 4, Issue 3, edited by Hamid Nemati, pp. 40-50, copyright 2010 by IGI Publishing (an imprint of IGI Global).

Chapter 13
Factors Influencing College Students' Use of Computer Security

Norman Pendegraft
University of Idaho, USA

Mark Rounds
University of Idaho, USA

Robert W. Stone
University of Idaho, USA

ABSTRACT

Information systems administrators face a difficult balance between providing sufficient security to protect the organization's computing resources while not inhibiting the appropriate use of these resources. Striking this balance is particularly difficult in higher education due to the diversity of computer uses and users. This is accentuated by one large, diverse user group, namely students. To facilitate striking such a balance, a better understanding of students' motivations to use security measures is useful. A theoretically sound model linking student and system security characteristics to students' security behaviors is developed and presented in this paper. The model is operationalized using student responses to a web-based questionnaire. The empirical results show that training to use security measures has no impact on students' security behaviors while experience with security does. Furthermore, ease of security use positively impacts students' security behaviors through security self-efficacy. The influence of peers has similar impacts through security outcome expectancy.

DOI: 10.4018/978-1-4666-0026-3.ch013

INTRODUCTION

Information systems administrators in all organizations face a difficult balance between providing sufficient security to protect the organization's data and computing resources while not inhibiting the appropriate use of these resources and data. While this balance is difficult in any organization, for information systems administrators in higher education it is particularly difficult to accomplish. In higher education, the uses and users of information systems are very diverse, accentuated by a large, diverse user group, students. It is this challenging environment that is used to examine the factors influencing individuals' use of computer security.

Students not only use university computing resources for classroom-related activities, they also use these resources for a variety of personal activities. These personal activities make use of a wide range of computing resources. Such diversity of uses and activities makes providing a secure yet usable environment for computing resources very difficult. As a result, the information systems administrator in higher education faces a very difficult environment to provide appropriate security measures protecting data and computing resources while allowing reasonable ease of use of these resources and data.

In order to facilitate striking an appropriate balance between security and ease of information systems use, a better understanding of students' motivations to use these security measures would be useful. Such insights are of interest for at least two reasons. First, information systems of American universities have been subject to a significant number of security attacks since 2001 (Shroff & Vogel, 2009). These attacks most certainly lead to greater information system security measures being implemented on campuses. Increased information system security inherently affects students since students constitute a major user group of these information systems. Hence, a better understanding of students' security attitudes and behaviors are important to information system

administrators in higher education. Secondly, in a more general organizational context students may serve as a reasonable proxy for the attitudes of employees in general toward security.

These concepts motivate the research that follows. A theoretically sound model linking student and system security characteristics to students' security behaviors is developed and presented. The model is operationalized using student responses to a web-based questionnaire regarding their knowledge and use of security measures. Based on this data, the operationalized model is tested and the results presented. Using these results, discussion and policy implications for information system administrators in higher education as well as conclusions are offered.

THE THEORETICAL MODEL

The research extends the works of Rounds, Pendegraft, and Stone (2008) and Rounds Pendegraft, Pendegraft, and Stone (2008) by examining the attitudes and behaviors of students toward computer security. A formal model of student security attitudes and behaviors is presented and empirically examined. The theoretical model is grounded in social cognitive theory as pioneered by Bandura (1982, 1986). The application of social cognitive theory has been shown to be meaningful in explaining motivation, behavior, and affective reactions in a variety situations and applications. Among these applications are ones applied to computer and technology adoption and use characteristics. For example, social cognitive theory has been used to study the antecedents of knowledge management systems (Lin & Huang, 2008), computer system use (Stone & Henry, 2001), computer users' organizational commitment (Stone & Henry, 2003), and computer users' perceptions of job control and stress (Henry & Stone, 1999). Other studies have used key constructs from social cognitive theory (e.g., self-efficacy and outcome expectancy or perceived usefulness) in their theoretical model and empirical analysis. For example, Hasan (2007) examined the role of computer self-efficacy and system complexity as antecedents to the acceptance of technology. Similarly, Hsu and Chao (2004) used Internet self-efficacy to study electronic service acceptance by users. Finally, Zhao, Mattila, and Li-Shan (2008) used post-training self-efficacy to study customers' use of self service technologies.

The model used in this research has at its heart self-efficacy and outcome expectancy. Self-efficacy is the evaluation by the individual regarding their perceived ability to successfully complete the specific task at hand. Outcome expectancy (i.e., perceived usefulness) is the perceived result or outcome the individual anticipates receiving by successfully completing the specific task at hand. Henry and Stone (1999) have shown that self-efficacy generally has a meaning impact on outcome expectancy. Both self-efficacy and outcome expectancy have meaningful impacts on the individual's attitudes toward the task. These attitudes have meaningful impacts on the task or behavior through the individual's behavioral intentions to perform the task.

There are four classes of antecedents to self-efficacy and outcome expectancy (Bandura, 1986). The first antecedent class is personal mastery which is based on the individual's prior experiences with, and performance of, the specific task. A second category is physiological factors or arousal. Such antecedents include the individual's interest or concern with the task or their emotional response to the task. The third group of antecedents is vicarious experience by the individual with the task. Examples of this class of antecedent include watching others perform the task and listening to others explain how to perform the task. The final category of antecedents is social persuasion which focuses on the influences of social networks and norms of people important to the individual and the impacts of these on the individual with respect to the task.

The theoretical model applied to university students' security attitudes and behaviors is shown in Figure 1. The antecedents of security self-efficacy and outcome expectancy include experience with security (personal mastery), ease of use regarding the security measures (physiological factors), peer influence (social persuasion), and training to use security (vicarious experience). All four antecedents are predicted to have significant, positive impacts on both security self-efficacy and outcome expectancy. Security self-efficacy is proposed to have a meaningful, positive impact on security outcome expectancy. Both these expectancies are predicted to have significant, positive influences on university students' attitudes toward using security. These attitudes are predicted to have meaningful impacts on students' behavioral intentions to use security measures which, in turn, have positive impacts on students' security behaviors.

THE EMPIRICAL STUDY

The ultimate goal for the empirical study is to provide suitable conditions to test the model regarding student security attitudes and behaviors. To this end, a questionnaire was developed containing items measuring the various constructs in the theoretical model. The target population was students at a mid-sized university in the western United States. The questionnaire was Internet-based and developed and distributed using Web Surveyor. An email invitation to complete the questionnaire containing the URL of its web site was distributed via a university listserv to 1000 student email addresses selected randomly from a list of 11,174 undergraduate student email addresses. A total of 101 usable responses were received producing a 10% response rate.

The Sample

Data on two demographic variables were also collected from the respondents. The summary

Figure 1. The theoretical model

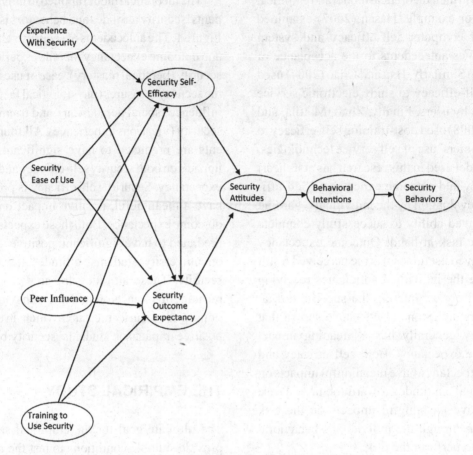

statistics for these demographic variables, gender and age, are shown in Table 1. The sample consisted of 53% males and 47% females. The average respondent age was 21.88 years with a minimum of 18 years and a maximum of 52 years of age. As with any survey research, the possible presence of non-response bias in the sample needs evaluation. The hope is to illustrate that the characteristics of the sample respondents are consistent with the potential respondents in the population from which the sample was drawn. Several tests were performed on the sample to evaluate the possible presence of non-response bias. These tests are described below.

The demographic variables collected on the questionnaire were also available for the student population. Comparing the portion of males and

females in the sample to those in the university undergraduate student population (46% female and 54% male) indicated no meaningful differences between the sample and the population. Similarly, when comparing the mean age of the respondents to the average age of undergraduate students at the university (22 years), no meaningful differences were found.

While these results do indicate a lack of non-response bias, additional tests were performed since only two demographic variables were in common between the sample and the population. These additional tests used the approach of Armstrong and Overton (1977) which orders the responses by response date. The lower quartile of the ordered distribution (i.e., the first responses received) simulates the sample respondents while

Table 1. The sample demographics

Gender*		
Gender	**Frequency**	**Percentage**
Female	46	47%
Male	51	53%
Age*				
Number	**Mean**	**Standard Deviation**	**Minimum**	**Maximum**
97	21.88	4.79	18	52

* Four missing values.

the upper quartile simulates the non-respondents. Demographic variables and variables key in the study are compared between the simulated respondents and non-respondents to evaluate the possible presence of non-response bias in the sample. The first tests performed using the simulated respondents and non-respondents examined age and gender for any differences between these groups. The results validated those found when the sample was compared to the population. The second set of tests performed compared the measures used in the empirical analysis (described in the next section) across the simulated respondents and non-respondents. The tests were performed using multiple analysis of variance. The results showed no meaningful differences between these groups for any of the measures individually or as a group. Based upon these and the previously discussed results, it is concluded that non-response bias appears not to be a meaningful problem for the analysis that follows.

The Measures

The constructs in the theoretical model were measured using items from the questionnaire. Due to a relatively small sample size, the responses to each set of items were summed to form the measures used in the analysis. For all the items except those used in the security behaviors measure, the response scale on the individual questionnaire items was a five point Likert-type scale. The

respondents were provided a statement and then asked to evaluate it as Strongly Disagree (1); Disagree (2); Neutral (3); Agree (4); or Strongly Agree (5). In the security behaviors measure, the first item was "Approximately how often do you update the definition files for your antivirus program(s)?" The respondents were given the response scale of Everyday; Every week; Every month; Every semester; and less often. The remaining three items in this measure requested a number from the respondent. These three items asked the respondent how many web sites/accounts they have, how many different passwords they use on these accounts, and how frequently they change the password on their university email account.

All of the measures and the questionnaire items forming them are shown in Table 2. Also shown in Table 2 is each measure, its mean, standard deviation, minimum value, and maximum value.

Estimation of the Model

The theoretical model was estimated using the summated items discussed above to measure the theoretical constructs. The estimation method was CALIS (i.e., Covariance Analysis of Linear Structural Equations) in PC SAS version 9.2. The estimation method was maximum likelihood. The fit of the model to the data was acceptable as summarized by several statistics. These statistics are shown is Table 3. The goodness of fit index was 0.89 while Bentler's comparative fit index

Table 2. The measures, summary statistics, and questionnaire items

Measures and Questionnaire Items	Mean	Standard Deviation	Minimum	Maximum
Experience with Security	6.33	2.23	2	10
I have a great deal of experience using computer security.				
Changing the security level on my computer is something I have a great deal of experience doing.				
Ease of Use	9.02	2.32	3	15
Changing security level on a computer is simple.				
Changing security levels on a computer is intuitively obvious.				
My interactions with security features are clear and understandable.				
Peer Influence	6.96	2.21	3	15
My peers encourage me to increase the security level on my computer.				
People who influence my behavior think that I should increase the security on my computer.				
People who are important to me think that I should increase the security on my computer.				
Training to Use Security	5.28	2.10	2	10
I have had a great deal of training to use computers.				
I have had a great deal of training to use security.				
Security Self-Efficacy	14.39	3.62	4	20
I am confident in my ability to use computer security.				
I have the skills to successfully use computer security.				
I have the ability to adjust computer security measures.				
I have the knowledge to successfully change the security level on my computer.				
Security Outcome Expectancy	8	1.65	4	10
Having high security on my computer saves me time in the long run.				
Having security on my computer saves me effort in the long run.				
Security Attitudes	11.73	1.99	7	15
Increasing security is a good idea.				
It is important to worry about computer security.				
I like having high security on my computer.				
Behavioral Intentions	7.14	1.66	2	10
I intend to continually adjust my computer security measures on my computer as needed throughout my career.				
I intend to review the security measures on my computer on a regular basis.				
Security Behaviors	14.32	5.65	5	34
Approximately how often do you update the definition files for your antivirus program(s)?				
How many web sites/accounts do you regularly use that require passwords?				
For the web sites in the previous question, about how many different passwords do you use?				
Approximately how often do you change your university email account password?				

Table 3. Summary statistics of the fit between the model and the data

Statistic	Value
Goodness of Fit Index	0.89
Adjusted Goodness of Fit Index	0.71
Root Mean Square Residual	0.12
ChiSquare	54.54*
degrees of freedom	17
Normed Chi-Square	3.21
Bentler's Comparative Fit Index	0.87
Bentler & Bonett's Non-normed Index	0.73
Bentler & Bonett's Normed Index	0.84
Bollen Normed Index	0.65
Bollen Non-Normed Index	0.88

* Statistically significant at a 1% level.

was 0.87. The normed chi-square statistic was slightly greater than 3. Bentler & Bonett's normed index was 0.84 and Bollen non-normed index was 0.88. These values indicate a good fit between the model and the data. The remaining values provide less clear results as to the quality of this fit. The adjusted goodness of fit index was 0.71 and the root mean square residual was 0.12. Furthermore, Bentler & Bonett's non-normed index was 0.73 and the Bollen normed index was 0.65.

The estimated path model is shown in Figure 2 using standardized path coefficients. The training to use security antecedent had no meaningful impacts on either security self-efficacy or security outcome expectancy. Similarly, ease of use had no meaningful impact on security outcome expectancy. All the other paths from antecedents to either security self-efficacy and security outcome expectancy had statistically significant impacts. The hypothesized path from security self-efficacy to security outcome expectancy was not found to be meaningful. The empirical results also indicated that security self-efficacy and security outcome expectancy both have meaningful impacts on students' security attitudes. These security attitudes were found to have meaningful impacts on students' behavior intentions to use

security and these behavioral intentions significantly impact their security behaviors.

DISCUSSION AND POLICY IMPLICATIONS

The results indicate that security self-efficacy and security outcome expectancy impact security attitudes which in turn influences behavioral intentions to use security measures and ultimately security behaviors by students. These results indicate that to improve students' security behaviors, policy makers should consider security self-efficacy and outcome expectancy. More specifically, policies should focus on appropriately changing the meaningful antecedents of security self-efficacy and outcome expectance. These antecedents include providing students meaningful experiences with security, selecting security measures considering their ease of use, and trying to find ways to exploit peer influences on students' security self-efficacy and outcome expectancy and ultimately security behaviors.

Traditionally, training to use security is a major emphasis of university security policies. Voss and Siegel (2009) confirm the importance of informa-

Figure 2. The empirical results using standardize path coefficients

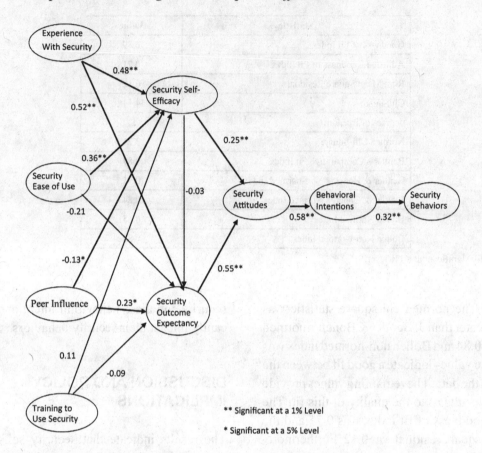

** Significant at a 1% Level

* Significant at a 5% Level

tion system security training at universities. They point out that providing training is a common response to the threat. Surprisingly, our results suggest that training is not an effective strategy since these empirical results indicate that training has no meaningful impact on security behaviors via security self-efficacy and outcome expectancy. This result calls into question the use of traditional training when attempting to encourage security behaviors among university students.

Another set of interesting results is based on the impact of the peer influence antecedent on security self-efficacy and outcome expectancy. Peer influence positively impacts security outcome expectancy but negatively impacts security self-efficacy, both at a 5% significance level. The results indicate that peers encouraging students to increase the security on their computer increases students' perceptions of the positive results to expect from this increase in security. However, peer encouragement to increase security on their computer reduces these students' confidence in their abilities to successfully increase this security. Peers encouraging students to increase their computer security may well overwhelm these students and undermine their confidence to successfully adjust their own computer security. Coupling these two results could lead to replacing traditional training with the use of peers demonstrating how to adjust the security level on their computer. The demonstration of how to adjust computer security could offset the negative impact of overwhelming students and thereby positively impact security self-efficacy.

As is theoretically expected, experience with security had meaningful, positive impacts on both security self-efficacy and security outcome expectancy. These results indicate that experienced security users understand the benefits from its use as well as have the confidence in their ability to successfully use security. Furthermore, these results may imply that, overtime, if meaningful experiences using security can be provided to students that these experiences will positively impact security behaviors. The security's ease of use also had significant and positive impacts on security self-efficacy but insignificant impacts on security outcome expectancy. Easy to use security measures improve students' confidence in their ability to successfully use the security. However, the ease of use does not influence students' perceptions of the benefits to be received from security measures. Considering ease of use for the typical student user when developing security measures may well lead to improved security behaviors.

The rest of the empirical results were as theoretically expected. Security self-efficacy and security outcome expectancy have meaningful and positive impacts on security attitudes. In turn, security attitudes of students' positively impact students' behavioral intentions to use security. Behavioral intentions then have significant and positive impacts on the security behaviors of students.

CONCLUSION

In summary, the general policy implications from these results are that formal security training has no value in impacting students' security behaviors. On the other hand, adopting security mechanisms that are easy to use appears desirable. Providing security experiences to students also leads to improved security behaviors. Finally, the positive affect of peer influence suggests that using security advocates chosen from the user community is an effective tactic. In a more general context,

the theoretical model, grounded in social cognitive theory, appears to be a valid foundation upon which to explain student attitudes, intentions and behaviors regarding computer security.

REFERENCES

Armstrong, J. S., & Overton, T. S. (1977). Estimating nonresponse bias in mail surveys. *Journal of Marketing Research, XIV*, 396–402. doi:10.2307/3150783

Bandura, A. (1982). Self-efficacy mechanism in human agency. *The American Psychologist, 37*, 122–147. doi:10.1037/0003-066X.37.2.122

Bandura, A. (1986). *Social foundation of thought and action: A social cognitive theory*. Upper Saddle River, NJ: Prentice-Hall.

Cline, J. (2009). What's behind the rash of university data breaches? *Computerworld Security*. Retrieved from http://www.computerworld.com/s/article/9129036/What's_behind_the_rash_of_university_data_breaches

Hasan, B. (2007). Examining the effects of computer self-efficacy and system complexity on technology acceptance. *Information Resources Management Journal, 20*(3), 76–88.

Henry, J. W., & Stone, R. W. (1999). The effects of computer self-efficacy and outcome expectancy on end-user job control and stress. *Journal of International Information Management, 8*(1), 23–34.

Hsu, M., & Chao, C. (2004). Internet self-efficacy and electronic service acceptance. *Decision Support Systems, 38*(3), 369–381. doi:10.1016/j.dss.2003.08.001

Lin, T., & Huang, C. (2008). Understanding knowledge management system usage antecedents: an integration of social cognitive theory and task technology fit. *Information & Management, 45*(6), 410–417. doi:10.1016/j.im.2008.06.004

Rounds, M., Pendegraft, N., & Stone, R. (2008). *Student computer security behavior and interest in training.* Paper presented at the Mountain Plains Management Conference, Idaho Falls, ID.

Rounds, M., Pendegraft, R., Pendegraft, N., & Stone, R. (2008, May 18-20). Student survey on computer security awareness and responsiveness. In *Proceedings of the Information Resource Management Conference,* Niagara Falls, ON, Canada (p. 48).

Shroff, R. H., & Vogel, D. R. (2009). Assessing the factors deemed to support individual student intrinsic motivation in technology supported online and face-to-face discussions. *Journal of Information Technology Education, 8,* 59–85.

Stone, R. W., & Henry, J. W. (2001). The roles of computer self-efficacy, outcome expectancy, and attribution theory in impacting computer system use. *Journal of International Information Management, 10*(1), 32–41.

Stone, R. W., & Henry, J. W. (2003). The roles of computer self-efficacy and outcome expectancy in influencing the computer end-user's organizational commitment. *Journal of End User Computing, 15*(1), 38–53.

Voss, B. D., & Siegel, P. M. (2009). Keeping up the guard in a down economy. *EDUCAUSE Review,* 10–22.

Zhao, X., Mattila, A. S., & Li-Shan, E. T. (2008). The role of post-training self-efficacy in customers' use of self service technologies. *International Journal of Service Industry Management, 19*(4), 492–505. doi:10.1108/09564230810891923

This work was previously published in International Journal of Information Security and Privacy, Volume 4, Issue 3, edited by Hamid Nemati, pp. 51-60, copyright 2010 by IGI Publishing (an imprint of IGI Global).

Chapter 14

A Game Theoretic Approach to Optimize Identity Exposure in Pervasive Computing Environments

Feng Zhu
The University of Alabama in Huntsville, USA

Sandra Carpenter
The University of Alabama in Huntsville, USA

Wei Zhu
Intergraph Co., USA

Matt W. Mutka
Michigan State University, USA

ABSTRACT

In pervasive computing environments, personal information is typically expressed in digital forms. Daily activities and personal preferences with regard to pervasive computing applications are easily associated with personal identities. Privacy protection is a serious challenge. The fundamental problem is the lack of a mechanism to help people expose appropriate amounts of their identity information when accessing pervasive computing applications. In this paper, the authors propose the Hierarchical Identity model, which enables the expression of one's identity information ranging from precise detail to vague identity information. The authors model privacy exposure as an extensive game. By finding subgame perfect equilibria in the game, the approach achieves optimal exposure. It finds the most general identity information that a user should expose and which the service provider would accept. The authors' experiments show that their models can reduce unnecessary identity exposure effectively.

DOI: 10.4018/978-1-4666-0026-3.ch014

INTRODUCTION

We expose personal information frequently in our daily tasks. Often, we unnecessarily expose too much information. For example, Bob proves that he is an adult by using his driver's license. At the same time, he unnecessarily exposes his driver's license number, birth date, name, home address, sex, eye color, hair color, and height. Different amounts of exposure may have dramatic differences in sensitivity. If Bob just proves that he is older than a certain age, the verifying party only knows that he is one of billions of adults. In contrast, his driver's license information uniquely identifies him in the world. In pervasive computing environments, we interact with intelligent ambient environments. Much more personal information is expressed in digital forms, is communicated over networks, and is permanently stored. Multiple types of ID cards such as employee IDs, driver's licenses, passports, and credit cards are already using embedded processors and can communicate over wireless networks. Proper identity exposure becomes more critical to protect our privacy because identities are associated with our daily activities, preferences, context, and other sensitive information. Without privacy protection, pervasive computing may become a distributed surveillance system (Campbell, Al-Muhtadi et al., 2002).

Exposing the appropriate amount of personal identity information to the appropriate parties is challenging. First, we may have many types of identities associated with our different life roles. To access pervasive services, with which we may or may not be familiar, a variety of identity elements need to be exposed. Second, users may not be able to make rational exposure choices. Many people's privacy awareness is very limited. For example, people carelessly provide their detailed personal information on the Internet (Dyson, 2006). Third, unnecessary exposure may be lured, requested, and forced. Stores give discounts to customers who provide their personal information. At the checkout register, customers are often asked for their home phone numbers, by which their home addresses and names can be found. According to the Georgetown Study of 361 randomly selected U.S. commercial websites with a minimum of 32,000 unique visitors in a month, the common practice is that almost all service providers (more than 90%) collected various identity information (Culnan, 2000). Data show that service providers extensively use identity information (NativeForest.org, 2009). Some may even aggressively sell their customers' identity information (Gellman, 2002).

The laws and regulations that protect privacy provide protection only on data usage (Langheinrich, 2001). Privacy exposure is often left up to an individual's decision. Once personal information is unnecessarily exposed, it is out of a user's control. Langheinrich suggests that privacy should be built into in pervasive computing systems because law makers and sociologists are still addressing yesterday's and today's information privacy issues (Langheinrich, 2001).

Anonymity is an approach to prevent identity exposure (Chaum, 1981, 1985; Campbell, Al-Muhtadi et al., 2002; Beresford & Stajano, 2003; Gruteser & Grunwald, 2003). It hides users' identities such that a user is not discernible from other users. Anonymity protects privacy by hiding the identity information, but sometimes exposure is necessary. A critical issue is the appropriate exposure: whether the requested identity information should be exposed and what identity information should be exposed. Several research works use policy-based approaches (Leonhardt & Magee, 1998; Snekkenes, 2001; Langheinrich, 2002; Hong & Landay, 2004), such that users' personal information is not exposed unless service providers' policies meet users' preferences and policies. The systems require users to have the special skills required to specify policies. But users might still sacrifice their privacy for convenient service access.

We propose a Hierarchical Identity model that defines a lattice structure to express a user's identity information from precise to general. More general identity information can represent a larger set of users. If a piece of general identity information can be used to access a service, a user's privacy is more likely to be protected because he is less likely to be uniquely identified.

The main contribution of this paper is that we propose a negotiation approach to identify proper identity information for exposure. We call our approach the RationalExposure model. To the best of our knowledge, this is the first paper that uses game theory for modeling optimal identity exposure. We model the service providers' decisions and users' privacy exposure as an extensive game (an economic model). Our approach provides optimal results regardless of a person's negotiation skills. Our model helps users to determine whether they should provide the requested identity information and what identity elements they should expose. The proposed identity information to expose will meet authentication or verification requirements, but is as general as possible. Unlike other approaches, our model provides a good balance between the benefit of service access and the risk of privacy exposure. In addition, we provide strategies to interact with unfamiliar service providers.

We built a prototype system and related software, and simulated a CD shopping scenario in our lab. Participants used PDAs to view additional information about CDs and went through a checkout process. During the checkout process, participants were asked for identity information, which they provided via the PDAs. Compared to the control group, the group that used the software with the RationalExposure model exposed much less identity information.

The remainder of the paper is structured as follows. First, we discuss related work and illustrate our Hierarchical Identity model. We then model privacy exposure as an extensive game and describe our prototype system. We also present our experimental design and results. Lastly, we outline our future work and describe our contribution.

RELATED WORK

The research on Internet privacy provides good experience and lessons for pervasive computing. In ten years of evolution, the Platform for Privacy Preferences Project (P3P) has provided a standard for websites and users' Internet browsers to communicate with each other about privacy preferences (Cranor, Dobbs et al., 2006). Using machine-readable languages, websites express the data collected and their privacy practices. Internet browsers employ user-defined policies to determine the release of identities and other personal information. Besides the machine readable version, an Internet browser may prompt a user for a human-readable version. If sensitive personal information will be collected, a user can make decisions. In pervasive computing environments, a standard for specifying a machine-readable version and a user-friendly version is important for heterogeneous devices to communicate with each other.

Several systems proposed for pervasive computing environments were based on P3P or other traditional mechanisms. Cranor and Reagle's "*buckets*" approach (Cranor & Reagle, 1998) and the Privacy AWareness System (*pawS*) (Langheinrich, 2002) are P3P-based privacy awareness systems. Privacy Server Protocol extended the P3P and enables clients and servers to exchange negotiation messages (Thibadeau, 2000). Leonhardt and Magee use high level policies for access control and privacy protection (Leonhardt & Magee, 1998). The approach is based on two classical security models: Lampson's access matrix and the Bell and LaPadula's (BLP) security labels (Bishop, 2003). These systems, however, are not an ideal solution for pervasive computing environments because the policies are too complex for average users to understand and define (Soppera & Burbridge, 2004).

Confab is a privacy sensitive framework for pervasive computing environments (Hong & Landay 2004). It enables application developers to enforce policies, send privacy notifications, and manipulate private data. In addition, it enables users to control their privacy information in three interaction patterns: optimistic (share information with others), pessimistic (detect privacy information abuse), and mixed-initiative (request users to make exposure decisions). Confab's data model is used to represent context information including locations, activities, and services. Confab and other frameworks (Campbell, Al-Muhtadi et al., 2002; Soppera & Burbridge, 2004) do not provide sophisticated methods to help users make decisions. Our approach complements the frameworks and improves their usability by helping users to make rational decisions.

When a user has many identity elements, identity management becomes a usability issue. Identity federation is an approach to address this issue by using third parties (Ragouzis, Hughes et al., 2006; Ferg, Fitzpatrick et al., 2007). For web applications, cross domain single sign-on systems have been developed and are evolving rapidly. Behind the scenes, service providers and identity providers link a user's accounts on different websites and share related attributes with each other. Therefore, a user needs to log in only once for accessing protected websites across administrative domains. Although identity federation improves usability, the usage of a single identity for various applications across different domains may sacrifice privacy. The identity providers are aware of all websites with which a user authenticates. Furthermore, the identities in federation systems are attractive targets for identity theft and need to be properly protected (Bhargav-Spantzel, Squicciarini et al., 2006).

Another method to address the usability issue of identity management is to aggregate and manage all identity information on the user's device.

Microsoft Windows CardSpace aggregates a user's identity information as identity cards and supports user authentication with various websites (Chappell, 2006). It supports several types of digital tokens such as user names, x.509 certificates, and Kerberos tickets. A user's web browser, a website, and CardSpace exchange messages to identify the identity information needed and available. CardSpace highlights the cards that meet the website's requirements and lets the user select a card. Our Master Key design also aggregates users' digital identity tokens on a single device and enables key initiated entity authentication for pervasive computing environments (Zhu, Mutka et al., 2006). Besides simple aggregation of the identity information, the proposed approach in this paper uses a game theoretic approach to expose more general or partial identity information.

Sometimes, a service provider needs to verify a user's identity. A desired feature is that users and service providers can expose and verify individual identity elements. Thus, a user needs to expose only the necessary elements. Bauer et al. proposed a Merkle authentication tree based approach (Bauer, Blough et al., 2008) which uses a binary tree structure to represent and verify signatures of individual elements (Merkle, 1989). A service provider verifies the identity element, which is a leaf node element in the Merkle tree, based on hash results of the tree nodes on the authentication path. The Merkel authentication tree may be integrated to our framework, if a service provider or a user wants to verify the other party's identity elements.

Automated trust negotiation systems enable unfamiliar parties on the Internet to establish trust and exchange identity information (Bonatti & Samarati, 2000; Winslett, Yu et al., 2002; Bertino, Ferrari et al., 2004). The main purpose of the systems is to establish mutual trust by exchanging verifiable identity information such as certificates. During trust negotiation, a user and a service provider in turn request the other party's identity information and provide their own identity information. For example, the user may require the service provider to provide a certificate from a Better Business Bureau, and then a service provider may require credit card information from a user. The systems protect sensitive attributes by exchanging one piece of information in a message. In a round, if both the user's and a service provider's requirements are met, the process proceeds. Automated trust negotiation systems may also be integrated with identity federation systems (Bhargav-Spantzel, Squicciarini et al., 2007). Combinations of identity federation and trust negotiation improve usability. Moreover, PP-Trust-X extended a trust negotiation system (Trust-X) to further protect credential privacy (Squicciarini, Bertino et al., 2007). In PP-Trust-X, types of identity information are exchanged and evaluated before the actual information is exposed. These automated trust negotiation systems rely on exposure policies. Nevertheless, if the policies are specified by automated trust negotiation system designers, they are abstract and less flexible. If users need to define policies, this process may be too challenging for average users. Instead of using policies, our game theoretic approach analyzes potential exposure strategies between a user and a service provider and finds optimal exposure by taking both users' and service providers' strategies into consideration.

In our previous work (Zhu, Zhu et al., 2007), we proposed a progressive and probabilistic exposure strategy to protect privacy among familiar users and service providers. In this study, a user and a service provider exchanged their identities and other sensitive data over multiple rounds. During each round, partial information (several encoded bits) was exchanged. If there was any mismatch in the identity verification in any round, the interaction stopped. Since only part of their identities and other sensitive information were exchanged, the other parties may not be able to properly guess the identity and service information.

Role-Based Access Control (RBAC) inspires our work (Sandhu, Coyne et al., 1996). RBAC has been widely used in computer systems, especially in database systems. Permissions are granted to roles and roles are assigned to users. With the role as a level of indirection between users and permissions, users can be easily reassigned from one role to another. Role Hierarchies in RBAC might seem similar to our Hierarchical Identity model, as both models use hierarchical structures. However, it is important to distinguish between the two concepts. Roles in RBAC have two basic characteristics: role membership and role permission. From a role, its users and granted permissions can be easily determined. Neither operation is essential in our Hierarchical Identity model. Instead, it is critical to express all identity elements of a single person as a hierarchy in our model. In RBAC, roles towards the root of a hierarchical structure have less permission, whereas in the Hierarchical Identity model nodes towards the root express more specific identity information.

Identity information may be protected via anonymous systems (Chaum, 1981, 1985). Recent systems focus on location privacy in pervasive computing. Snekkenes uses lattices to reduce the preciseness of location, identity, time, and speed information in location-based applications (Snekkenes, 2001). Mix Zone achieves location privacy via a short-term anonymous identity in a geographical area (Beresford & Stajano, 2003). Gruteser and Grunwald propose k-anonymous location information through spatial and temporal cloaking (Gruteser & Grunwald, 2003). A more general anonymous identity system, idemix, exposes and protects users' identity information via unlinkability (Camenisch & Herreweghen, 2002). Users create pseudonyms and acquire signing statements (credentials) for the pseudonyms and associated identity elements from identity providers. Instead of directly exposing the credentials, one uses a zero-knowledge proof to ensure a service provider that he has the identity elements. Service providers cannot link users' identity information in different transactions. Similarly, VeryIDX uses an aggregate zero-knowledge proof to ensure a service provider that a user is

Figure 1. (a). An identity and its elements. (b) The Hierarchical Identity model

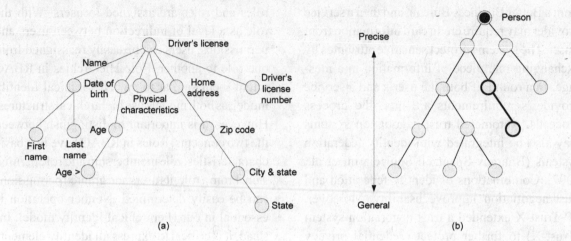

(a)

(b)

the owner of the requested identity elements and has the knowledge of the secrets for the credentials (Paci, Bertino et al., 2009). Unlike these anonymous and unlinkable systems, the focus of our approach is help users decide whether they should expose the requested identity information and what they should expose.

THE HIERARCHICAL IDENTITY MODEL

We propose to aggregate all digital identities of a person on a single device. Handheld devices such as smartphones are good candidates because people always carry them. Via the devices, users can manage digital identities and interact with service providers.

The major purpose for the Hierarchical Identity model is to facilitate proper identity exposure. The model enables exposure of identity information in different levels of details. For different activities and applications with different authentication and verification requirements, the proper identities or identity elements can be provided. For example, Bob proves that he is a resident of a city to access the city zoo at a discounted price. As a resident, he gains access to a community pool. Note that

precise exposure of Bob's home address meets both authentication requirements, but privacy is not well protected.

We express an identity and its elements in the hierarchical structure as shown in Figure 1(a). From bottom to top, identity elements become more and more specific and eventually become the person's identity. An identity element (or a set of identity elements) is more general, if more people have the same identity element (or a set of elements). Thus, a user is less likely to be identified by exposing more general identity information. A piece of identity information is precise, if the number of persons in the set is small or even unique. Therefore, the person is more likely to be identified.

All types of identity of a person are aggregated together in a hierarchical lattice structure as shown in Figure 1(b). The top-level node represents a person. The second-level nodes are different types of identity that one acquires, for example, a driver's license and a credit card. Other nodes (below the second-level) are subsets of the identity elements.

For each type of identity (driver's license, for example), the identity elements form a tree structure as shown in Figure 1(a). Identity elements (or a set of identity elements) may appear more than once in different types of identity, (one's name on the driver's license and on the student ID card, for example). The same identity element stores in the same node in the lattice structure as highlighted in Figure 1(b). In each of these nodes, a list of the identity elements of different types is maintained. Other information, such as the associated type, is also stored with the element. If one does not have the requested identity element, a different type of the identity element may be used as an alternative. The following definition formalizes the above description.

Definition 1. The Hierarchical Identity Model has the following properties:

A person has a set of different types of identity, $\{I_i\}_{i \in N}$.

I_i may have a set of children, $\{I_j\}_{j \in N}$. I_j may be a type of identity, an identity element, or a set of identity elements.

I_m and I_n satisfy the partial order, $\leq$, if I_m is a child of I_n. The set of people that I_m represents, $\{P_a\}_{a \in N}$, contains the set of people that I_n represents, $\{P_b\}_{b \in N}$. That is $\{P_b\} \subseteq \{P_a\}$. I_m is at least as general as I_n.

I_p may have a set of children, $\{I_k\}_{k \in N}$. I_q may have a set of children, $\{I_l\}_{l \in N}$. If $I_p = I_q$, for each element $I_a \in \{I_k\}_{k \in N}$ there exist an element $I_b \in \{I_l\}_{l \in N}$, such that $I_a = I_b$. Similarly, a child of I_q have an equivalent identity element as a child of I_p.

The main benefit of the Hierarchical Identity model is that along the hierarchical lattice structure from top to bottom, more and more general identity information can be found to represent a person.

FINDING THE PROPER IDENTITY TO EXPOSE

In pervasive computing environments, we interact with many service providers. In the meantime, the intelligent devices that we wear and carry may interact with service providers' intelligent devices. We may or may not be familiar with the service providers. When we request to access a service, a service provider may ask for our identity. Should we give the identity? Or should we provide only some elements of the identity? In traditional computing environments, this usually is not a problem. For example, users know that they need to provide user names and passwords to access computers; users and service providers agree on the exposure. In our current daily life, people often make their own identity exposure decisions. For example, Bob may be asked for his driver's license at a checkout register. Should he give it?

We start our discussion with this simple example and model it as an extensive game. Then, a service provider will not acquire a better payoff if he or she takes any other exposure action.) Next, we will define the payoff functions for users and service providers. Afterward, we will discuss the strategy to interact with unfamiliar service providers. Last, we will illustrate how extensive games are built from the Hierarchical Identity model. We assume that a user interacts with a service provider in the vicinity and the user wants to access the service and trusts the service provider.

Identity Exposure as an Extensive Game

We model the interaction between a user and a service provider as an extensive game, using a supermarket checkout process as our scenario. An extensive game means that a user and a service provider take turns making decisions and taking actions. In the game, Bob provides his credit card information via his smartphone. The store's computer asks for his digital driver's license. Then, Bob makes a decision on whether to expose his driver's license information. Afterward, the store makes a decision.

In the following discussion, we use "Bob" to refer to himself, as well as to the smartphone that aggregates his digital identity information. We use "the store" to refer to the store and the computer at a checkout kiosk. Figure 2 starts with Bob's turn to make a decision. Bob may quit the service; he may accept the request and give his driver's license information; or he may propose other identity information. Let's suppose that Bob proposes to provide only his name. Now, it is the store's turn to make decisions. The store may either abort the checkout service or finish the transaction. Therefore, there are five outcome cases. In case 1, Bob provides only his name, and the store finishes the transaction. In case 2, he provides only his name, and the store aborts the process. In case 3, he quits the checkout process. In case 4, he gives his driver's license information, and the store aborts the transaction. In case 5, he gives his driver's license information, and the transaction finishes.

In Figure 2, we also show the user's and the service provider's payoffs in the parentheses of each outcome. The first number indicates the user's payoff, whereas the second number shows the service provider's payoff. The numbers represent the preference of a user and a service provider in an ordinal order. In this example, Bob's preference is {case 1} > {case 5} > {case 3, case 2} > {case 4}. That is, Bob prefers to get the same service by giving only his name. He also prefers to access the service, rather than not access it, even at the price of giving his driver's license information. His least preferred outcome is that he gives his driver's license information without accessing the service. It is possible that two or more outcomes have the same payoff value. This means that the user or the service provider is

Figure 2. An extensive game between a user and a service provider

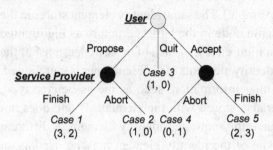

indifferent about the outcomes. For example, case 2 and case 3 have the same payoff value for Bob. Thus, he may choose either outcome. Moreover, we assume that users' preferences are known. The preferences may be acquired via surveys (Zhu, Carpenter et al., 2009) or from similar decisions that they have made. We formally define the identity exposure game as follows.

Definition 2. An identity exposure game has the following components:

Two players, u and s – a user and a service provider.

A set of outcomes, $\{o_i\}_{i \in N}$: in our example, there are the five outcomes: *(Propose, Finish)*, *(Propose, Abort)*, *(Quit, -)*, *(Accept, Abort)*, and *(Accept, Finish)*.

Each player chooses and takes one action $a_i^j \in \{a_i\}_{i \in N}$ at step j. Note that at different steps, the actions may be different.

The user and the service provider have their preferences, which are represented by payoff values. For example, the payoff values for the user and the service provider in case 1 are:

$$p_u(Propose, Finish) = 3,$$

and $p_s(Propose, Finish) = 2$,

respectively.

Identifying the Optimal Identity Exposure Strategy in an Extensive Game

To determine optimal identity exposure, the user has a device that runs the RationalExposure model, and we assume that the software that a service provider runs is rational. That, is they will choose outcomes according to their preferences. Any chosen action leads to an outcome that is at least as good as any other outcome. The payoff functions that we will define are used to determine the preferences.

In this subsection, we assume that the outcomes are known. This is likely because the user and the service provider may have learned the outcomes from their previous interactions. We also assume that the user's and the service provider's preferences are known. Even if a user and a service provider interact with each other for the first time, the outcomes, actions, and preferences may still be predicted with a high probability because a user may have interacted with many other similar service providers for the same type of service.

Given an extensive game, we start from the bottom of the tree and consider the subtrees of height 2. We walk through our example in Figure 2 to demonstrate the game. There are two subtrees for which the service provider makes choices. In the left subtree, the user has proposed to give only his name on the driver's license. The service provider may choose "*Abort*" or "*Finish.*" "*Abort*" gives the service provider a payoff of 0, whereas "*Finish*" gives him a payoff of 2. Thus, he will choose "*Finish.*" Similarly, in the right subtree, the service provider will choose "*Finish*" with a payoff of 3. He provides the service and also acquires the user's driver license.

After the selections of optimal actions for all subtrees, we move up one level of the tree and consider the subtrees with height of 1. In our example, there is one subtree for which the user makes choice. He may choose "*Propose,*" "*Quit,*" or "*Accept.*" From our discussion in the previ-

ous paragraph, if the user chooses "*Propose,*" the service provider will choose "*Finish.*" The user's payoff is 3. If the user chooses "*Accept,*" the service provider will choose "*Finish.*" The user's payoff is 2. If the user chooses "*Quit,*" his payoff is 0. Therefore, the user's best choice is "*Propose.*"

The process of finding the best choices in the subtrees continues, until the root of the tree is reached. This process is known as backward induction in Game Theory (Osborne 2004). In our example, we have reached the root of the tree. So, the user chooses "*Propose,*" and then the service provider chooses "*Finish.*" The subgame perfect equilibrium is obtained and the choices are optimal for the both user and service provider. Using backward induction, we can always find a subgame perfect equilibrium in an identity exposure game. We prove the following proposition.

Proposition 1. In an identity exposure game, an optimal exposure can always be found by using backward induction. (There is an assumption in the proof that an exposure game has finite levels and each subtree has finite branches. We will prove that assumption.)

Proof. We use mathematical induction to prove the proposition.

Base: For a tree (game) of height 1, either the user or the service provider makes a choice. Without loss of generality, we assume the user makes the choice. The user compares the payoffs of all the outcomes and can select one outcome that is at least as good as every other outcome, reaching the subgame perfect equilibrium.

Inductive step: Assume that we can find a subgame perfect equilibrium of a tree with height of n or less using the backward induction. Then for a tree with height of $n+1$, we consider each child of the root as a subtree with height of n or less. Hence for each subtree, we can find a subgame perfect equilibrium. Now, we move to the root. The best payoff

Figure 3(a). Two components of the user's payoff function. (b). User's payoff function. (c). Two components of the service provider's payoff function. (d). Service provider's payoff function. (e). The user's modified payoff function. (f). The service provider's modified payoff function.

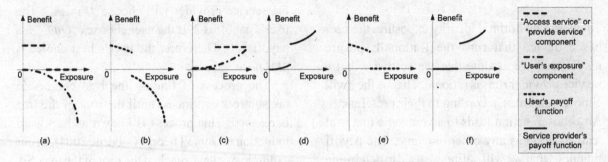

value of each child is known. This can be considered as a tree of height 1. Therefore, the user (or the service provider) can choose the optimal outcome.

Payoff Functions

We believe that users want to protect their privacy while they access services. Service providers want to acquire more personal information about users while they provide services. We define their payoff functions as follows.

Definition 3. A user's payoff function and a service provider's payoff function at each node are, respectively:

$$P_u = Access\ serice\ -\ User's\ exposure \tag{1}$$

$$P_s = Provide\ serice\ +\ User's\ exposure \tag{2}$$

"Access service" and *"Provide service"* in equation (1) and (2) are the benefits that a user and a service provider get, respectively. Note that they may not be the same value for the user and the service provider. For different services, users and service providers acquire different profit from *"Access service"* and *"Provide service."* For *"User's exposure,"* a user usually obtains

negative benefit by exposing his personal information. On the contrary, a service provider often obtains positive benefit. He might sell users' personal information and their preferences, or he might improve his services by using users' information data.

From a user's perspective, *"Access service"* may bring him constant amount of benefit for a service, which is independent of his personal information exposure. After a certain point (threshold), the user may not want to expose more personal information and therefore quits the negotiation. Then, the benefit becomes zero as shown in Figure 3(a). The *"User's exposure"* component in equation (1), however, keeps reducing the benefit as *"User's exposure"* increases. Thus, the payoff function that adds the two components together has two segments as shown in Figure 3(b).

Similarly, from a service provider's perspective as shown in Figure 3(c), *"Provide service $\times$ Weight_s"* brings him a constant benefit, unless the service provider does not get enough identity information from a user and aborts. Then, the benefit is zero. The *"User's exposure"* component in equation (2) is a non-decreasing function. The more the user exposes the more benefit a service provider receives. The service provider's payoff function is shown in Figure 3(d) by adding the two components.

Figure 4. User and service provider interaction cases. (a-b) Two boundary cases in which the user and the service provider find agreements. (c). The user and the service provider quit negotiation. (d). The user and the service provider find agreement.

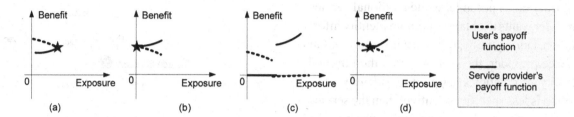

From the two payoff functions shown in Figure 3(b) and (d), the game does not seem to be fair to the user. The user may risk exposing his personal information without getting the service. On the contrary, the service provider's payoff function is always positive.

To address the problem, the user plays a modified game. Instead of giving his identity information during negotiation, the user proposes what identity information he will provide. Only after the user and the service provider agree on the identity information and service access does the user expose his identity elements. If the negotiation is unsuccessful, the user will not expose any identity information. Therefore, the user's and the service provider's payoff functions are changed as shown in Figure 3(e) and (f), respectively. Both the user and the service provider have non-negative payoff functions.

Our model does not require users to specify quantitative values for their payoff functions. Instead, we assume that the more general an identity element is, the better payoff a user will acquire. In addition, users may rate identity elements and inform the RationalExposure model whether they think the identity elements are important to keep private. Therefore, users' payoff values are expressed in the ordinal numbers. During the interactions with service providers, our model learns service providers' preferences. And thus, service providers' payoff values are also expressed in ordinal numbers at the users' side.

While we discuss the payoff functions in this and next subsections, the smooth curves in Figures 3 and 4 may be considered as approximation to the ordinal numbers without loss of generality.

Strategies to Interact with Unfamiliar Service Providers

When interacting with an unfamiliar service provider, an essential question is whether a user and a service provider will reach an agreement. Different services offer a user different amounts of benefit, such that a payoff function may be higher or lower. For different services, a user may be willing to expose different amount of identity information. Similarly, service providers may weigh their benefit differently and accept different types of identities.

The two boundary cases are shown in Figure 4(a), a user provides the identity information that the service provider originally requested. This is the maximum identity information that a service provider asks. In Figure 4(b), a user proposes minimal exposure that he is willing to give and the service provider accepts. Beyond the two boundary cases, a user and a service provider cannot reach any agreement. The user's and the service provider's payoff functions do not intersect with each other. Therefore, the user does not gain the access to the service and he does not expose his identity information as shown in Figure 4(c). Between the two boundary cases, shown in Figure 4(d), a user and a service provider can reach an agreement on the identity exposure for a service access.

A rational user wants to expose as little identity information as possible, while a rational service provider wants to obtain maximum identity information. During the negotiation with an unfamiliar service provider, the user proposes the minimal identity information. If the proposed identity information is less specific (sensitive) than the service provider requires, the user gradually increases his exposure. Likewise, the service provider gradually decreases his identity request. Figure 4(d) provides another way to interpret the strategy. As the user exposes more, his payoff value moves down along his payoff function curve from left to right. If the service provider requests less, his payoff value moves down along his payoff function curve from right to left. Eventually, the user and the service provider reach an agreement on the exposure of the identity information.

We use Figure 5 to illustrate a more detailed analysis. The game starts after a user receives a service provider's identity request. If a user "*Accepts*" the request, it is the case shown in Figure 4(a). Otherwise, the rational user will choose other actions. If the user chooses to "*Quit,*" the user does not want to negotiate and use the service. If the user chooses to "*Propose,*" he proposes the minimal identity information. If the service provider "*Accepts*" the proposal, it is the case shown in Figure 4(b). The proposal may be that the user does not expose any identity information. If the service provider "*Aborts*" the service, the service provider's last request is the minimum identity information that he needs. Or, the service provider does not want to negotiate. If the service provider "*Requests*" more identity information, he decreases his requirement as little as possible. The user and the service provider may keep negotiating, until they agree on the exposure or one party quits. If one party quits, the user's maximum exposure is still less than the service provider's minimum requirement. This is the case shown in Figure 4(c). If the two parties agree on

Figure 5. The user's strategy to interact with an unfamiliar service provider

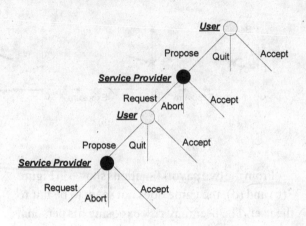

the exposure, we find an agreement, which is the case shown in Figure 4(d).

If a user does not have the requested identity element, he may search his Hierarchical Identity Model. If there is an equivalent identity in his Hierarchical Identity lattice structure, he may propose it. By exploring other potential identity elements, a user maximizes the probability of successful negotiation with a service provider. Similarly, a service provider may maximize his successful negotiation rates by allowing multiple equivalent identity elements.

Both a user and a service provider may quit a negotiation. If one party decides to stop, it may explicitly send a message to inform the other party. Alternatively, a user and a service provider may implicitly notify the other party by repeating the same request or proposal. Implicit notification enables a user or a service provider to make a final decision on whether they will accept the request or the proposal.

USING THE HIERARCHICAL IDENTITY MODEL TO BUILD AN EXPOSURE GAME

Each type of services has its own exposure game. If there is no available tree to represent the game, a user builds the tree when he interacts with a service provider for the first time. The service provider asks for identity information. The user builds the top level branches. For example, when a user is asked for his home address as shown in Figure 6, he has the choices of "*Propose,*" "*Quit,*" and "*Accept.*" If the requested identity information in his Hierarchical Identity is found, all the children in the subtree are traversed. The most general identity information will be used as the user's proposal.

The service provider may take action for each action that the user takes (except "*Quit*"). He may choose to "*Request*" more or other information, "*Abort*" the service, or "*Accept*" the proposal and provide the service. If the negotiation is along the path in the Hierarchical Identity from the original requested identity to the most general identity the user proposes, the tree that represents the exposure game looks like the tree in Figure 6.

If multiple leaf nodes are found in the Hierarchical Identity, those identity elements may be alternative identity elements to propose as shown in Figure 6 (dotted line). Rules or statistics may be used to determine which identity to propose. For example, eye color is rarely used and should be a lower priority identity element to propose. If several identities are good choices, a user may randomly select one identity element, whereby he tries different identities in different games.

During the negotiation, if the service provider requests an identity element that is not in the subtree of the originally requested identity, then the user searches the new requested identity element in the Hierarchical Identity and finds the most general identity element in its children. The user's proposal will be the top level branch (an alternative proposal) as shown in Figure 6 (dotted line). If the service provider's request is in the subtree, but it is not on the path of the most general identity information to the originally requested information, then the common parent of the two is found. In Figure 6, we show that an

Figure 6. Build an identity exposure extensive game from the Hierarchical Identity model

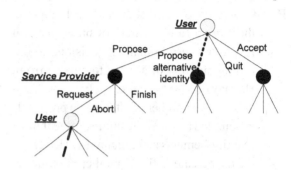

alternative proposal (dashed line) is added at the third level of the tree.

A user and a service provider make their proposals and requests. The orders of requests express their preferences. From the service provider's request order, the user finds the service provider's preferences in the games. Similarly, the service provider finds the user's preferences.

An exposure extensive game may be dynamic. The tree that represents the game might expand as the user interacts with a service provider multiple times or after the user interacts with different service providers. Moreover, a user's identity may expire, in which case the user needs to prune the trees of extensive games that use the expired identity. Similarly, after a new identity is acquired, a user may update his games with the new identity.

The above discussion about a tree representing an exposure game is general. A user may have many different choices of identity information to expose at any step during an interaction. He may propose different identity elements or different identities to a service provider. The service provider may not accept the user's proposal and request new information. The process may continue between a user and a service provider, and such a process includes any identity exposure interactions between a user and a service provider. Is an interaction guaranteed to finish? We prove the following proposition to show that a game always finishes.

Proposition 2. A tree representing an exposure game has finite levels and finite branches.

Proof. First, we prove that at any level of a tree, there are a finite number of branches. If it is a user's turn to make a decision, he has a finite number of actions to choose from. He may choose "*Accept,*" "*Quit,*" or "*Propose.*" The number of alternative proposals is bounded by the finite number of leaf node identity elements in the hierarchy. Therefore, the user creates a finite number of branches for each node in which he makes a decision. Similarly, if it is a service provider's turn to make a decision, he may "*Accept*" a user's proposal, "*Abort*" the service, or "*Request*" other identity information from a finite set of possibilities. Thus, the service provider creates finite numbers of branches for each node in which he makes a decision.

Second, we prove that a tree has a finite number of levels. A user has a finite number of identities. In the extreme case that the service provider requests all identity information (n pieces of identities and identity elements) that the user has and the user replies, the tree's height will be up to 2*n. If the service provider asks for some identity information that he has previously asked, the user quits. If the service provider asks for some identity information that the user does not have, the user may quit or propose alternative identity information (the user may propose only the identity information that has not yet been proposed). Therefore, the tree will not grow infinitely. Although a user may acquire new identities in the future, he has finite number of identities at any given time.

PROTOTYPE DESIGN AND IMPLEMENTATION

When an identity is requested, the application invokes the RationalExposure model. Figure 7 shows the architecture design of the RationalExposure model. In our prototype system, we explicitly specify an identity request. An application may use a parser to process an incoming identity request and invoke the RationalExposure model. In addition, speech to text software may be used to extract a vocal identity request.

The Extensive Game module handles two types of games. First, if a service provider is capable of negotiation, the RationalExposure model processes the negotiation using the Extensive Game module as we discussed previously. The module uses the connection that the application has established with the service provider. In each negotiation message, the module notifies the application whether it is in the negotiation mode or it has concluded the negotiation. In the former case, the application forwards the message, whereas in the latter case the RationalExposure model provides the application a suggestion and related information. Second, if the service provider is not capable of negotiation, the RationalExposure model considers the game as a one-round game. The user may accept a request, quit the transaction, or make a final proposal. Then, the service provider makes a decision.

The Game Management module constructs both types of games for a type of identity if a user interacts with service providers that may or may not be able to negotiate. The two types of games are also associated with each other. When a user changes preferences, the games are updated together.

The suggestion module helps users to determine whether an exposure is necessary and prompts users with related information. Figure 8(a) shows an exposure recommendation and related information in the prototype application. The appropriate levels of detail in the messages help users to make decisions. At the current stage, the messages are focused on the users' perspective. On the other hand, service providers may also provide further explanations about why an identity element is requested. Therefore, users will

Figure 7. The architecture of the RationalExposure model

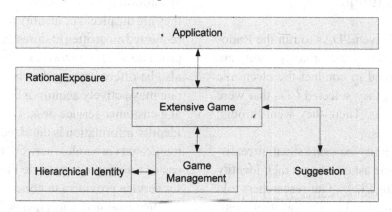

Figure 8. Screenshots of the prototype applications with and without the RationalExposure model. (a) The RationalExposure model makes an exposure suggestion and explains the reason. (b) Without Rational Exposure, a user makes the decision when a phone number is requested. (c) The prototype application enables users to view additional information about a music album.

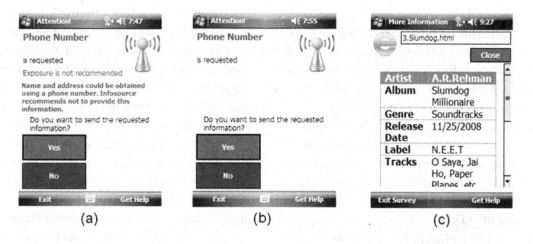

(a)   (b)   (c)

have more complete view of an identity exposure in the context.

We run the RationalExposure model on Windows Mobile 6.0. The RationalExposure model is implemented as a DLL and the prototype application calls the DLL when identity information is requested. Figure 8(a) and (b) show the versions with and without the RationalExposure model. One of our prototype applications provides users information about CD albums and singers and enables users to listen to sample songs via handheld devices as shown in Figure 8(c).

EVALUATION AND EXPERIMENTS

To evaluate the RationalExposure model, we recruited participants to come to our lab and use the software. They went through a CD shopping experiment and were asked for their identity information. Although the software was new to them, they have experienced the shopping and identity exposure situation during the checkout process in their daily life.

Experiment Settings

Participants were given PDAs to run the RationalExposure model and the prototype software that we implemented to conduct the electronic transactions. First, they selected CDs that were displayed on shelves. Then, they went through the checkout process.

To make the identity exposure situation realistic, participants were asked to input their identity information into the PDAs. Our researchers told participants to consider the PDAs as their smart phones or their cell phones, so that they could input their identity information once and then use it many times. Each time a user needed to disclose his or her identity for a transaction on the PDA, he or she needed to unlock the identity with a password.

To protect participants' personal information, we immediately deleted their credit card and driver's license information as they were inputted. Participants, however, did not know their information was not stored on the PDAs.

Participants used the PDAs to listen to sample songs and to read additional information about CD albums and singers. When they finished shopping, they completed their transactions using their credit cards and other identity information "stored" in the PDAs.

One hundred participants attended our experiments during the spring semester of 2009. All of them were college students and approximately 90% of them were 23 or younger. We acquired complete samples from 97 participants. Two of the participants did not want to input their credit card numbers into the PDAs, and another participant did not have a credit card.

During the checkout process, participants were asked for four pieces of information: credit card number, phone number, information on their driver's licenses, and whether he or she wanted to become a VIP member (which required them additionally to provide their monthly income and an email address). We chose to request phone numbers and information on their driver's licenses because they are the pieces of identity information that are requested most often in stores during the checkout processes. In some stores, VIP membership might also be offered during the checkout process. Or, one may actively acquire it by filling out a form at a customer service desk. Unfortunately, when identity information is digitized and can be communicated via wireless networks, it becomes much easier for people to provide the information and for service providers to collect it.

We separated participants into two groups: those who completed transactions with and without the RationalExposure model. In the control group that used the software without RationalExposure model, participants made their own exposure decisions. All participants had to provide their credit card numbers and driver's license information in order to checkout. The phone number and VIP membership were optional. For the group that used the RationalExposure model, the software suggested that users not provide their phone numbers. (We programmed the server software such that the service provider would finish the transaction with the phone numbers.) This group also observed a message on the PDA that the RationalExposure model was negotiating with the service provider (store) when a participant's driver's license was requested. After the negotiation, the RationalExposure model prompted users that only their names on the driver's licenses were required. (We programmed the server software, so that the service provider would accept the name in the negotiation.) Then, users made their exposure decisions (whether to provide their names). For the VIP membership, the RationalExposure condition group did not get suggestions from the model. Instead, they made their own decisions just as the control group did. We wanted to know whether their behavior would be different from the control group after they had been prompted by two rational exposure suggestions.

Table 1. Experimental results

Condition	Control Group 42 Participants	Rational Exposure Group 55 Participants
Phone Number	36 (86%) provided	21 (38%) provided
Driver's license	37 (88%) provided driver's license information	49 (89%) provided the name on the driver's license
VIP	19 (45%) applied	24 (44%) applied

Experimental Results and Key Findings

Forty-two participants were in the control group, and fifty-five participants used the software with the RationalExposure model. Table 1 shows the experimental results. In the control group, most participants (86%) provided their phone numbers if it was requested. Participants in the RationalExposure group saw a message that suggested they not provide their phone number. Furthermore, the message stated that one's name and address could be known, if he or she provided the phone number as shown in Figure 8(a). Twenty-one out of fifty-five participants (38%) gave their phone numbers in spite of this suggestion. We ran a one-tailed two proportions Z-test. The null hypothesis was that the two groups were equally likely to provide their phone numbers, while the alternative hypothesis was that the RationalExposure group was less likely to provide their phone numbers. The test showed that our RationalExposure model helped users to avoid unnecessary exposure ($Z = 5.6$ and *p-value* < 0.001).

In a second study that we conducted later, we asked participants ($n = 46$) from the same population who had provided their phone numbers why they did so. We did not tell them that their names and addresses could be found by their phone numbers, but some participants clearly understood that. In addition, they wrote in their surveys that they did not mind getting advertisements in the mail and they liked to receive coupons.

Driver's license information was mandatory for the control group to finish transactions. More than a dozen identity elements are on a driver's license. These identity elements are sensitive and important. Most people are aware that identity information on their driver's license is important to keep private as shown in our survey (Zhu, Carpenter et al., 2009). However, it seems that they are accustomed to providing their driver's licenses. Without the RationalExposure model, 88% of the participants chose to give the full digital version of the driver's license. For the RationalExposure group, only participants' names on their driver's licenses were required. Similarly, about 89% percent of them provided the requested information and finished the transactions. Thus, by using the RationalExposure model, we can effectively help users to reduce the extent of their identity exposure by providing only the necessary information.

We wanted to know whether participants would behave differently after using the RationalExposure model, so all participants (both the control and RationalExposure groups) made their own VIP membership decisions. It seems that there was no difference between the two groups. Forty-five percent and forty-four percent of the participants in the control and RationalExposure groups, respectively, applied for the VIP memberships. Thus, users of the RationalExposure model did not quickly learn to be protective of their identity information, indicating that software interventions may be necessary to help users make more rational decisions. We speculate that after a longer period of using the RationalExposure model, users might more carefully expose their identity information. This possibility can be tested in future research.

CONCLUSION AND FUTURE WORK

We have modeled identity exposure between a user and a service provider as an extensive game. The user and service provider negotiate the identity information that the user wants to provide and the service provider requests and accepts. We have expressed one's identity information in our Hierarchical Identity model. It facilitates the use of identity information in a more general manner, so that users are less likely to be identified. We have provided strategies to interact with unfamiliar service providers and learn their preferences. We have also presented formal definitions and proven the properties of our model.

To help us understand user reactions and their acceptance of the game theoretic models, we conducted a three-step process in usability studies. In the first step, participants input their identity information into PDAs and were trained to use the RationalExposure model on the PDAs. In the second step, we mimicked purchases in stores and participants' responses to identity requests via the PDAs. In the third step, participants completed a survey. Our experimental results showed that users avoided exposing identity information or exposed less sensitive information when using the RationalExposure model.

In this paper, we have not addressed special exposure situations. For example, in a medical emergency, Bob would want to expose as much patient identity information as possible in order for medical emergency personnel to find his medical history quickly. These special exceptions require a special implementation. Our model is capable of expressing the payoff functions in this case as well. The *"User's exposure"* component is expressed as non-decreasing functions. Thus, both Bob and medical personnel acquire better payoffs when Bob exposes more information. It can be proven that negotiations in these cases still converge.

The game theoretic model discussed in this paper may not work well when the information about identity exposure is incomplete. That is, users may not have the knowledge or they may be uncertain whether they should keep the requested identity elements private. In an extreme case, they may interact with unfamiliar services or service providers. The fundamental problem is the asymmetric information between users and service providers. Service providers know which identity elements are really needed and they may learn whether users are willing to provide the information. But, users do not have this same information and service providers may use the information to their advantages. We are building game theoretic systems to address issues such as reputation, purpose of identity collection, and exposure strategies that are related to incomplete information.

Another challenge for identity exposure lies in the various users' preferences. Some users may like to supply their identity information to acquire services; some users may be willing to trade their information for product discounts; and some users may want to protect their identity information by paying monthly fees (e.g., pay $5 a month to not be listed in phone books). We do not discuss the expression and storage of users' preferences in this paper. Part of users' preferences may be learned via surveys and analysis of their attitudes as we did in (Zhu, Carpenter et al., 2009), and part of their preferences may be acquired when our software prompts exposure messages to users and asks them to make decisions. We are designing additional mechanisms to better store and reflect users' preferences.

In the paper, we assume that a user interacts with a trusted service provider in the vicinity. If the assumption does not hold, trust establishment needs to be addressed before or during the negotiation of identity exposure. During the trust negotiation or during the identity exposure games, additional software may be needed to determine whether a service provider is malicious. These are important issues for identity exposure systems, yet they are beyond the scope of this paper.

ACKNOWLEDGMENT

The authors are grateful to Dr. Danny Soroker for helping them to greatly improve this paper. The preliminary version of this paper was published in the proceedings of the 2009 IEEE Annual Conference on Pervasive Computing and Communications (Percom 2009).

REFERENCES

Dauer, D., Blough, D. M., et al. (2008). Minimum Information disclosure with Efficiently Verifiable Credentials. In *Proceedings of the 4th Workshop on Digital Identity Management,* Alexandria, VA.

Beresford, A., & Stajano, F. (2003). Location Privacy in Pervasive Computing. *IEEE Pervasive Computing / IEEE Computer Society [and] IEEE Communications Society,* 47–55.

Bertino, E., & Ferrari, E. (2004). Trust-X: A Peer-to-Peer Framework for Trust Establishment. *IEEE Transactions on Knowledge and Data Engineering, 16*(7), 827–842. doi:10.1109/TKDE.2004.1318565

Bhargav-Spantzel, A., Squicciarini, A., et al. (2007). Trust Negotiation in Identity Management. *IEEE Security & Privacy,* 55-63.

Bhargav-Spantzel, A., & Squicciarini, A. C. (2006). Establishing and Protecting Digital Identity in Federation Systems. *Journal of Computer Security, 14*(3), 269–300.

Bishop, M. (2003). *Computer Security.* Reading, MA: Addison Wesley.

Bonatti, P., & Samarati, P. (2000). Regulating service access and information release on the Web. In *Proceedings of the 7th ACM Conference on Computer and Communications Security,* Athens, Greece.

Camenisch, J., & Herreweghen, E. V. (2002). Design and Implementation of idemix Anonymous Credential System. In *Proceedings of the 9th ACM Conference on Computer and Communications Security,* Washington, DC.

Campbell, R., Al-Muhtadi, J., et al. (2002). *Towards Security and Privacy for Pervasive Computing.* Paper presented at the International Symposium on Software Security, Tokyo.

Chappell, D. (2006). *Introducing Windows Card-Space.* Chappell & Associates.

Chaum, D. (1981). Untraceable electronic mail, return addresses, and digital pseudonyms. *Communications of the ACM, 24*(2), 84–90. doi:10.1145/358549.358563

Chaum, D. (1985). Security Without Identification: Transaction Systems to Make Big Brother Obsolete. *Communications of the ACM, 28*(10). doi:10.1145/4372.4373

Cranor, L., Dobbs, B., et al. (2006). *The Platform for Privacy Preferences 1.1 (P3P1.1) Specification.* W3C.

Culnan, M. (2000). Protecting Privacy Online: Is Self-Regulation Working? *Journal of Public Policy & Marketing, 19*(1), 20–26. doi:10.1509/jppm.19.1.20.16944

(1998). Designing a Social Protocol: Lessons Learned from the Platform for Privacy Preferences Project. In Cranor, L. F., & Reagle, J. (Eds.), *Telephony, the Internet, and the Media.* Mahwah, NJ: Lawrence Erlbaum Associates.

Dyson, E. (2006). Privacy Protection: Time to Think and Act Locally and Globally. *First Monday.*

Ferg, B., Fitzpatrick, B., et al. (2007). *OpenID Authentication 2.0.*

Gellman, R. (2002). Privacy, Consumers, and Costs: How The Lack of Privacy Costs Consumers and Why Business Studies of Privacy Costs are Biased and Incomplete.

Gruteser, M., & Grunwald, D. (2003). *Anonymous Usage of Location-Based Services Through Spatial and Temporal Cloaking*. Paper presented at the 1st International Conference on Mobile Systems, Applications and Services, New York.

Hong, J., & Landay, J. (2004). *An Architecture for Privacy-Sensitive Ubiquitous Computing*. Paper presented at the 2nd International Conference on Mobile Systems, Applications, and Services, Boston.

Langheinrich, M. (2001). Privacy by Design - Principles of Privacy-Aware Ubiquitous Systems. In *Ubicomp 2001 Proceedings* (LNCS 2201, pp. 273-291. Langheinrich, M. (2002). *A Privacy Awareness System for Ubiquitous Computing Environments*. Paper presentd at the 4th International Conference on Ubiquitous Computing, Göteborg, Sweden.

Leonhardt, U., & Magee, J. (1998). Security Considerations for a Distributed Location Service. *Journal of Network and Systems Management, 6*(1), 51–70. doi:10.1023/A:1018777802208

Merkle, R. C. (1989). A Certified Digital Signature. In *Proceedings of the 9th Annual International Cryptology Conference on Advances in Cryptology.*

NativeForest.org. (2009). *Native Forest Netwok's Guide to Stopping Junk Mail.*

Osborne, M. (2004). *An Introduction to Game Theory*. New York: Oxford University Press.

Paci, F., & Bertino, E. (2009). An Overview of VeryIDX - A Privacy-Preserving Digital Identity Management System for Mobile Devices. *Journal of Software, 4*(7), 696–706. doi:10.4304/jsw.4.7.696-706

Ragouzis, N., & Hughes, J. (2006). *Security Assertion Markup Language (SAML) V2.0 Technical Overview*. OASIS Open.

Sandhu, R., & Coyne, E. (1996). *Role-Based Access Control Models*. IEEE Computer.

Snekkenes, E. (2001). Concepts for Personal Location Privacy Policies. In *Proceedings of the 3rd ACM Conference on Electronic Commerce,* Tampa, FL.

Soppera, A., & Burbridge, T. (2004). Maintaining privacy in pervasive computing—enabling acceptance of sensor-based services. *BT Technology Journal, 22*(3), 106–118. doi:10.1023/B:BTTJ.0000047125.97546.4a

Squicciarini, A., & Bertino, E. (2007). PP-Trust-X: A system for Privacy Preserving Trust Negotiations. *ACM Transactions on Information and System Security, 10*(3).

Thibadeau, R. (2000). *Privacy Server Protocol: Short Summary*. Pittsburgh, PA: Carnegie Mellon University.

Winslett, M., & Yu, T. (2002). Negotiating Trust on the Web. *IEEE Internet Computing,* 30–37. doi:10.1109/MIC.2002.1067734

Zhu, F., Carpenter, S., et al. (2009). Understanding and Minimizing Identity Exposure in Ubiquitous Computing Environments. In *Proceedings of the 2009 International Conference on Mobile and Ubiquitous Systems: Computing, Networking and Services (Mobiquitous 2009),* Toronto, ON, Canada.

Zhu, F., Mutka, M., et al. (2006). The Master Key: A Private Authentication Approach for Pervasive Computing Environments. In *Proceedings of the 2006 IEEE Annual Conference on Pervasive Computing and Communications.*

Zhu, F., & Zhu, W. (2007). Private and Secure Service Discovery via Progressive and Probabilistic Exposure. *IEEE Transactions on Parallel and Distributed Systems, 18*(11), 1565–1577. doi:10.1109/TPDS.2007.1075

This work was previously published in International Journal of Information Security and Privacy, Volume 4, Issue 3, edited by Hamid Nemati, pp. 1-20, copyright 2010 by IGI Publishing (an imprint of IGI Global).

Chapter 15
Hiding Message in Map along Pre–Hamiltonian Path

Sunil Kumar Muttoo
University of Delhi, India

Vinay Kumar
National Informatics Centre, India

ABSTRACT

In this paper, an algorithm to embed information in a map along Hamiltonian path is presented. A file based data structure in which a graph is treated as a composition of three components, node, segment and intermediate points that constitute a segment, is used to store a graph. In a map with N nodes, each node can represent $\lceil log_2 N \rceil$ bits from message bit strings. Any bits (≥ 0) from message between bit strings represented by adjacent nodes are embedded in a segment. In the case of a multi graph, a segment is selected based on the last two bits in the nodes. A pre Hamiltonian path is determined in the map starting from node represented by the first $\lceil log_2 N \rceil$ bits from message string to the last bit string $\lceil log_2 N \rceil$. The method is tested on different maps and messages of different sizes and robust results have been observed. Retrieval is based on the key (S, |m|, $\sum$) and traversing along the pre Hamiltonian path starting from node S.

1. INTRODUCTION

The steganographic algorithm introduced in this paper uses a planar graph (Berge, 1962) as cover object. A planar graph is also called a map. Normal data structure used to represent a graph does not provide enough redundancy for hiding.

DOI: 10.4018/978-1-4666-0026-3.ch015

Before discussing the details, background of the approach, motivation behind the paper and the contribution that this paper can provide to the computing world need to be discussed.

1.1 Background

Steganography is the art of hiding a secret message inside a cover (*host*) object. The purpose is to allow two parties to communicate surreptitiously, without raising suspicion from an eavesdropper. Steganography (Katzenbeisser & Petitcolas, 2000) and cryptography (Stallings, 1999) are two techniques used for secret communication. Cryptography attempts to hide the *contents* of a message while steganography attempts to hide the *existence* of a message (Anderson & Petitcolas, 1998). A digital cover object may be an image, audio, video or a graph –a vector data. The cover object with embedded secret message is called stego object i.e.

```
cover + secret message = stego
```

Stego object is the medium that carries the secret message (hidden data). Main requirement for any steganographic technique is undetectability, robustness, tamper resistance and embedding capacity (Cole, 2003; Johnson & Jajodia, 1998a). These properties of any steganographic algorithm are mainly influenced by following four factors:

- The choice of the cover object,
- The selection rule used to identify individual elements of the cover that could be modified (or used without any modification) during embedding,
- The type of embedding operations that modifies the cover elements, and
- The number of embedding changes.

The embedding capacity and robustness in steganographic algorithm are so diagonally opposite placed that it is difficult to achieve both simultaneously at the maximum level (Saloman, 2003; Kumar & Muttoo, 2008, 2009b). Thus, a steganographic algorithm achieves robustness at low embedding capacity. The placement of embedding changes in the cover is called a selection channel. A channel is kept secret by the communicating partners in the similar way a secret key is maintained in cryptography. After embedding, stego medium should maintain similarity with cover to avoid any detection of the hidden data. It is achieved by minimizing the distortion in the cover medium while embedding the hidden data (Anderson & Petitcolas, 1998).

The way a cover is stored in digital form plays an important role in minimizing distortion introduced in cover while embedding secret message. A cover is collection of some basic elements. Basic element in image is pixel while that in a graph is node and segment. A segment consists of many intermediate points (Kumar & Muttoo, in press). More is the amount of bits available to store one element of a cover medium, less is the visible distortion after embedding and vice versa.

1.2 Motivation

Today map is used for various purposes e.g. routing, tourism, online tracking of vehicle movement etc. It is freely exchanged using electronic communication devices like PDA and GPS. Using more generic cover for hiding relevant but secret message raises less or no suspicion at all. Moreover, with emergence of Geographic Information System (GIS), many countries have either developed their national spatial database or are in process of developing it. Out of the two main approaches: vector and raster, vector form takes less number of bits to store the same amount of spatial features (Kumar & Muttoo, 2006; Hetzl & Mutzel, 2005). This makes a vector form of spatial data more suitable for transmission and therefore it can be used to hide information at store as well as to hide information while transmitting data using public network that includes both wired and wireless.

Further according to Kerckhoff's principle, the security of a hidden message must depend on keeping the stego key secret. It must not depend on keeping the steganographic algorithm secret (Cox et al., 2005, 2007). Further, if a particular type of cover is in use for longer period, it is easy for steganalyst to develop a tool to defeat the process. A GIS based vector covers i.e. map or planer graph can help in introducing confusion by using very relevant map for covert communication.

Although there exists a number of steganographic methods as mentioned in (Johnson & Jajodia, 1998a; Kumar & Muttoo, in press) many of them are image based. A number of image based graph theoretic approach using image as cover are also developed and reported (Hetzl & Mutzel, 2005). There are very few approaches that discuss about steganographic process using graph as a cover. A work presented in (Kumar & Muttoo, 2009a) describes a data structure for a planar graph (map) that is used in the steganographic algorithm presented in the paper.

1.3 Contribution

The algorithm presented in this paper makes the following contributions.

*   Firstly we present the complete implementation of a steganographic method that uses a graph as cover and the method is capable of embedding a considerably large payload in the basic components of a graph and yet maintains a fine balance between robustness and embedding capacity.
*   The algorithm opens door for using spatial data as cover for covert communication. Since cover used is relevant to a particular situation, it raises little or no suspicion that a spatial data is used for steganographic purpose. For example if security measure is to be tightened or some terrorist is to be nabbed in a particular region on a particular occasion then the message can be sent from Intelligence Bureau to security agency very well hidden in the map of that location or route of the program of an important person.
*   A map used as a cover can contain many hidden messages simultaneously without compromising with basic characteristics of a graph like degree spectrum, adjacency

matrix, length of segments and known isomorphism because there exists many pre Hamiltonian paths in a planar graph (or map).

1.4 Approach

A graph consists of three basic components: node, segments and intermediate points that constitutes segments (Kumar & Muttoo, 2009a). The given message is converted into bit strings. A pre Hamiltonian path (Bollobas, 1983; Bondy & Murty, 1976) is determined in the map as the embedding proceeds. For N nodes map, each node can represent $\lceil \log_2 N \rceil$ bits from message bit strings. First $\lceil \log_2 N \rceil$ bit from message string is taken as start node in the pre Hamiltonian path. Next node in the path represents another $\lceil \log_2 N \rceil$ bits from message string. It is possible that there are zero or more bits between two bit strings represented by adjacent nodes. These bits are embedded into a segment between the two nodes. Each intermediate point has coordinates in the form of (x, y) with respect to the map extent which is independent of the viewing area of the screen of the computer on which the map is displayed. A bit to be hidden in a segment is embedded in (x, y) based on hamming distance between x and y. Odd hamming distance (x, y) represents bit 0 and even hamming distance represents bit 1. If the corresponding bit of the message matches with hamming distance (x, y) nothing needs to be done, else LSB of either x or y is toggled to make the hamming distance represent the bit of the message.

In case of a multi graph, a segment is selected based on the last two bits in the 'from' node. 'from node' in a segment $e_{1,2} = (v_i, v_j)$ is the node v_i. The approach retains the graph characteristic of the cover graph in stego graph and makes the task difficult for steganalyst. A map is used as cover object in the steganographic approach presented in this paper. A map selected may or may not be Hamiltonian. While embedding, all nodes of the map may not be used, thus many times pre Hamiltonian path suffices the requirement.

The paper is organized in six sections. In Section 2 we describe basic concept of map, planar graph and data structure used to store a map in a conventional vector GIS. In Section 3 we introduce the embedding algorithm, in Section 4 the extraction method is explained. The method is illustrated using an example in Section 5. The algorithm is analyzed for its robustness, completeness and suitability from steganalyst point of view under the heading steganalysis in Section 6. The paper is concluded in Section 7.

2. DATA STRUCTURE FOR VECTOR MAP

The data structure presented here is used in an in-house developed software named GISNIC for providing low cost Geographic Information System (GIS) solution in India. The corresponding author of this paper has been project leader of the software development team. The concept related to the data structure is described in (Kumar & Sharma, 2006; Kumar & Muttoo, 2009a). A brief introduction is presented here to enable reader to understand the algorithm based on the data structure.

A map is graphical representation of some geographic area. The data structure presented in this paper is for vector GIS where information is written in form of two dimensional coordinates (x, y) in a plane. The three basic components: node segments and intermediate points, of map are stored in the following file:

1. Node
2. Segment
3. Data
4. Segment.dbf

Out of the four files, segment.dbf is a database file and others are binary files. Node contains

Box 1.

```
typedef struct
{
         long       node_num-
ber;
         float      x_coord;
         float      y_coord;
} node_info;
```

information about nodes in the record format node_info defined in Box 1.

Segments are stored in three files. A segment has attributes like: segment number, number of intermediate points, coordinates of these intermediate points, a rectangular extent within which the segment lies –the Maximum Bounding Rectangle extent (Kumar & Muttoo, 2009a), length of segment, the node pairs -start and end node defining the segment, name of the segment. Since number of intermediate points varies from segments to segment and all such intermediate points are stored in a file called data, information regarding from where the intermediate points in data file starts is stored in segment binary file under the field offset_in_datafile. All attributes are arranged in the record formats in respective files shown in Box 2.

The problem of identifying a segment with pair of nodes is resolved by using a triplet <segment_number, start_node, end_node>. This is also required to give shape to a graph while drawing it on the screen. The choice of database format is driven with a vision to extent this data structure to link with some additional attributes of segment that may help in hiding more information in a graph (Egenhofer & Franzosa, 1991).

Mathematically, a graph is represented as G = (V, E) where V is set of nodes and E is set of segments. In a map both V and E are nonempty. A segment has a start and an end node. All other points on the segments are called intermediate

Box 2.

```
segment binary file
typedef struct
{
          long      segment_number;
          float     x_min, y_min, x_max, y_max;  // MBR extent
          long      nunber_of_intermediate_points;
          long  offset_in_datafile;
     //offset in data file where intermediate points are
} segment_info;

data binary file
typedef struct // Structure of data binary file
{
          float     x_coord, y_coord;
} Intermediate_point_rec;

segment.dbf
   1. segment_number, 'N', 6, 0
   2. NAME, 'C', 20
   2. LENGTH, 'N', 12, 4
   3. FR_NODE, 'N', 6, 0
   4. TO_NODE, 'N', 6, 0
```

points. There is no provision for overlapping segments. The point where two segments cross is treated as intersection in a map and it is treated as node and overlapping segments are further divided into segments at the intersection. The process through which we achieve this is called cleaning. A node may be an end node of one segment and the start node of other segment. It is also possible for a node to be start node or end node of many segments. Each node is unique and will be used to identify a segment as pair of nodes (u, v). It is mandatory to assign a unique identification number to each node and each segment. It is also possible to have more than one segment between a pair of nodes (Kumar, 2002).

In order to facilitate display of a graph on a screen independent of its resolution and size, coordinates of leftmost top corner and rightmost bottom corner (or rightmost top corner and leftmost bottom corner) are also stored in a file in a database file extent.dbf. There may exist more than one graph within the same extent and all such graphs are stored with different names. Files related to a graph are kept in a directory and call the directory as graph. Information about number of graphs and its attribute is written in graph.dbf. Thus metadata about graphs (maps) are written in

1.   Extent.dbf
2.   Graph.dbf
3.   <Name of graph as directory>

3. EMBEDDING ALGORITHM

Let M be the message to be embedded in the cover map $G = (V, E)$. Suppose number of nodes in G is N and number of bits in message is $|m|$. The bit string in message M is denoted by m. Theoretically, there are n! Hamiltonian paths (Frank, 1974) in a Hamiltonian graph (Fenner & Frieze, 1983) and a path can start from any node in the graph. Out of so many paths available, we have to select the path in which maximum bits from m are represented by nodes of G. For example if bit string

```
m = 01010011 11100010 01110001
11010110 11110100
```

```
5, 3, 14, 2, 7, 1, 13, 6, 15, 4, ...
```

$$v_1, s_{1,2}, v_2, s_{2,3}, v_3, \ldots, s_{N-1,N}, v_N$$

We use a restricted backtracked algorithm (Kumar, 2002) to find pre Hamiltonian path. The gist of algorithm is to visit next node, prune the graph by dropping the visited intermediate node as and when its neighbor is visited. While selecting the neighbor to visit next, it is ensured that no backtracking to the current node will be needed in most of the cases. Wherever there is absolutely no way to break the tie, a node having smallest node number is taken.

The bits represented by nodes need no embedding because it is naturally embedded in the nodes. A bit (or bit string) is said to be naturally embedded in a part of cover if the functional output of that part is equal to the corresponding bit string of the message to be embedded (Kumar & Muttoo, 2009a). To embed $s_{i,j}$ bits we use intermediate points in the segment $e_{i,j}$ between nodes v_i and v_j. Each Intermediate Point (IP) is represented by its coordinate (x, y). Starting from first IP from node v_i we embed bits string $s_{i,j}$ in the same number of IPs in $e_{i,j}$. The embedding of kth bit in $s_{i,j}$ is done as follows:

- If $((s_{i,j})_K == 1)$ then
- if (HAM distance $IP_K(x, y) ==$ EVEN) skip and go to embed next bit from $s_{i,j}$ else
- make HAM Distance $IP_K(x, y) ==$ EVEN by changing least significant bit (LSB) of either x or y depending on whether (dy < dx) or (dy > dx) respectively.
- Similarly if $((s_{i,j})_K == 0)$ then
- if (HAM distance $IP_K(x, y) ==$ ODD) skip and go to embed next bit from $s_{i,j}$ else
- make HAM Distance $IP_K(x, y) ==$ ODD by changing LSB of either x or y depending on whether (dy < dx) or (dy > dx) respectively.

Now the problem is to resolve the issues of variable number of bits to be embedded in the different segments. Since there is no mechanism to include counting of the bits to indicate at the time of extraction, it is essential to include some marker in some way to indicate the end of embedded bits in a segment. We call this marker as checksum $(s_{i,j})$. In the segment.dbf file, "NAME" field is used to keep description of the segment. The segment may represent road, rail, lane, river, its tributaries etc. This field is used to store the number of bits embedded in the segment. Let $|(s_{i,j})|$ be number of bits in bit string $s_{i,j}$ and $0 \leq |s_{i,j}| \leq 25$. The 25 is the extreme value and it has never been found that 25 bits are to be embedded in a segment, the maximum value found is ≤ 21 and many times it is 0. Thus only least significant five bits of concatenated string of the bits represented by the respective node number are XORed with $|s_{i,j}|$ i.e.

$$\text{checksum}\left(s_{i,j}\right) = LSB_5(v_i \| v_j) \oplus |s_{i,j}|$$

Where LSB_5 represents the operation of taking least significant 5 bits from $(v_i \| v_j)$. Now the checksum value is incorporated in the field "NAME" by replacing last character of name of the segment with the *symbol* computed as follows.

symbol = ['Σ' + checksum $(s_{i,j})$]

Here Σ is a roman alphabet forming part of the key and 'Σ' is ASCII code of the alphabet. The reverse process is applied while extracting the message from stego graph. It is explained later in the Section 4. The above computation may produce some graphics character or control character and we use the same for the purpose. The key of embedding is the triplet $(v_1, |m|, Σ)$ i.e. (<Start node of the pre Hamiltonian path>, <length of message in bits (or bytes)>, Alphabet to compute number of bits in the segment). Having addressed the issues involved in embedding, the stepwise algorithm is presented in Algorithm 1.

Algorithm 1: Stepwise algorithm for embedding message in a map

- Convert message M into bit strings m.
- Compute value $\lceil \log_2 N \rceil$ and take first $\lceil \log_2 N \rceil$ bits from m and find node number v_1 of the embedding path.
- Find a path - pre Hamiltonian, $\pi = v_1, v_2, v_3, ..., v_N$, in the cover map using restricted backtracked algorithm described in (Kumar, 2002) in such a way that $| s_{1,2} | <$ Number of intermediate points in $e_{1,2}$.
- Find next bit string $\lceil \log_2 N \rceil$ that matches node number v_2.
- Let the number of bits between bits sequence represented by v_1 and v_2 be $s_{1,2}$. Embed bit string $s_{1,2}$ in segment $e_{1,2} = (v_1, v_2)$ using hamming distance of coordinate value of IPs. Embed value $|s_{1,2}|$ in name of segment.
- If v_i be the current node on the path π and v_j be the next node from v_i on the path then $s_{i,j}$ represents bit strings between $\lceil \log_2 N \rceil$ bits represented by node v_i and $\lceil \log_2 N \rceil$ bit string represented by node v_j. Repeat step 4 and 5 until entire message is embedded in G = (V, E).

4. EXTRACTION ALGORITHM

Let the stego map received be G = (V, E) with |V|= N and stego key is (x, |m|, Σ). We compute $\lceil \log_2 N \rceil$ to find the number of bits represented by a node in the stego map. Initialize the message string to string represented by x. Find a pre-Hamiltonian path using restricted backtracked algorithm (Kumar, 2002). Let the path obtained in G be $\pi = x, v_2, v_3, ..., v_N$. The algorithm always determines unique pre Hamiltonian path if the start node is given.

Once node v_2 is found, the bit string $s_{1,2}$ is retrieved from the segment $e_{1,2}$, if any. To determine whether any bits are embedded in segment, we use segment name from segment.dbf.

checksum $(s_{i,j})$ = symbol – 'Σ'

$|s_{i,j}| =$ [Least significant 5 bit in $(v_1 \| v_2)$] $\oplus$ checksum $(s_{i,j})$

Now retrieve bit string $s_{i,j}$ from $e_{i,j}$ starting with first IPs from v_1. Following the process along the path, repeat the process until the message length becomes equal to m. The message retrieved is then

m = $v_1, s_{1,2}, v_2, s_{2,3}, v_3, ..., s_{N-1,N}, v_N$

Message M is then formed by converting each byte into corresponding character. Last node v_N may not represent the complete $\lceil \log_2 N \rceil$ bits. If any bits are to be discarded then most significant bits from bit string representing last nodes in the path are discarded. Now let us see an example to illustrate the implementation process.

5. IMPLEMENTATION

Suppose the message to be embedded is, "AREA IS COMMUNALLY SENSITIVE. HIGH ALERT FROM 11 AM TO 5 PM". Now after removing all spaces, punctuation marks and treating all charac-

Box 3. Binary string representing the message

```
m = 01000001 01010010 01000101 01000001 01001001 01010011 01000011 01001111
    01001101 01001101 01010101 01001110 01000001 01001100 01001100 01011001
    01010011 01000101 01001110 01010011 01001001 01010100 01001001 01010110
    01000101 01001000 01001001 01000111 01001000 01000001 01001100 01000101
    01010010 01010100 01000110 01010010 01001111 01001101 00110001 00110001
    01000001 01001101 01010100 01001111 00110101 01010000 01001101
```

ters in upper case, the ASCII code in hexadecimal corresponding to the message M is

```
41 52 45 41 49 53 43 4F 4D 4D 55 4E
41 4C 4C 59 53 45 4E 53 49 54 49 56
45 48 49 47 48 41 4C 45 52 54 46 52
4F 4D 31 31 41 4D 54 4F 35 50 4D
```

The binary equivalent of the above hexadecimal string m is given in Box 3.

Total number of characters in M is 47 and therefore

$$|m| = 47 * 8 = 376$$

Let the cover map be G= (V, E) in which |V| = 65 i.e. N = 65. And number of segments is equal to 93. The map is shown in Figure 1 $\lceil \log_2 65 \rceil = 7$, thus each node is represented by 7 bits. The first 7 bits in m is 0100000 and it corresponds to node number 32. The second seven bits corresponds to node number 18 which is adjacent to 32 and segment $e_{32, 18}$ has sufficient number of intermediate points, 10, to hide 5 bits from message between bits string represented by node 32 and node 18. The rearranged (mapped) message string m with nodes and segments in map is given in Box 4. Bold bit strings represent nodes.

Figure 1. Map of 65 nodes and 93 segments

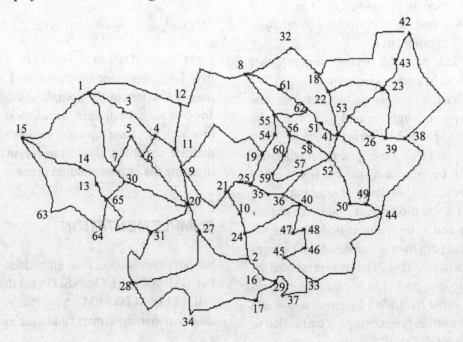

Box 4. Rearranged binary string showing bits covered by nodes and to be hidden in segment

```
m = 0100000 10101 0010010 0 0101010 000010100100101 0100110 1000011 0100111
    101 0011010 10 0110101 0101 0101001 11001000001010 0110001 00110001 0110010
    1010 0110100 0101010 0111001 010011 0100100 101 0101000 100100101 0101100
    1000101010 0100001 0 0100101 0 0011101 0010000 1 0000010 1 0011000 1 0001010
    101001 0010101 00010 0011001 01001 0010011 11010011010011 0001001 10 0010100
    00010100110101010101000 0011110 0110101010 1000001 001101
```

The sequence of nodes traveled to embed the message is:

```
32, 18, 42, 38, 39, 26, 53, 41, 49,
50, 52, 57, 36, 40, 44, 33, 37, 29,
16, 2, 24, 10, 21, 25, 19, 9, 20, 30,
65 and 13.
```

Node 13 represents only 6 bits to complete the message of size |m|. Therefore while retrieving message from the map, if any bits are to be discarded then most significant bits from bit string representing last nodes in the path are discarded. Path traveled according to algorithm is described briefly in Section 3. And details about the same can be found in (Kumar, 2002). The path can be traced from the map depicted in Figure 1. We compute checksum for number of bits embedded in a segment. For example $|s_{1,2}| = 5$. These 5 bits are embedded in segment $e_{32,18}$.

checksum $(s_{1,2}) = LSB_5 (32 \| 18) \oplus 5 = 10010 \oplus 00101 = 10111 = 23$

The checksum value is incorporated in the name of the segment $e_{32,18}$ i.e. in "SSROAD". Let us take $\Sigma = C$. The last character D is now replaced with

'Σ' + 23 = 'Z'

Similarly last char in name of respective segment is modified. For illustration, few embeddings are shown in Table 1.

There are 10 intermediate points in segment $e_{32,18}$. The coordinates of first five intermediate points in the segment $e_{32,18}$ are (1213468, 1376293), (1213630, 1376495), (1213751, 1376657), (1213953, 1376819) and (1214074, 1376859). Bit string 10101 is to be embedded in it. Now even, odd sequence of hamming distance of these five intermediate points is (9, 8, 9, 8, 7).

Table 1. Embedding checksum value for segment containing bits from message

Segment Number	Name	Figures within () is $|s_{i,j}|$ and figure out side is number of Intermediate points in that segment.	From Node	To Node
$e_{32,18}$	SSROAZ	10 (5)	32	18
$e_{18,42}$	HIGHWAD	17 (1)	18	42
.....		.....	...	...
$e_{29,16}$	LANE1	8 (0)	29	16
			....	...
$e_{20,30}$	LINKROAY	31 (22)	20	30
$e_{30,65}$	SUBWA\	17 (10)	30	65
$e_{65,13}$	FOOTPATH	6 (0)	65	13

Figure 2. Map after embedding of the message M

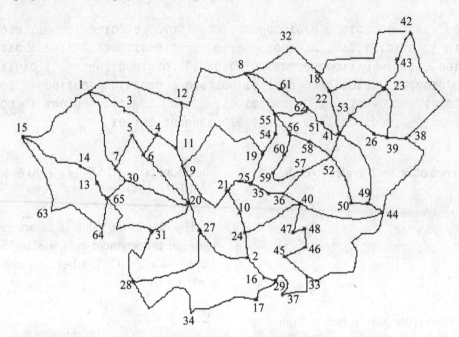

Now all five points need to be nagged. The difference in y coordinate of first point and second point is 198. And that in respective x coordinate is 162. Therefore LSB of y coordinate of first point is flipped. Similarly LSB of y coordinate in second point, of x coordinate of third, fourth and fifth point is flipped. Thus nagged points are now represented as (1213468, 1376292), (1213630, 1376494), (1213750, 1376657), (1213952, 1376819) and (1214073, 1376859). Proceeding the same way the embedding is completed. The map of Figure 1 after embedding of message is shown in Figure 2.

Clearly both the maps are visually same. The redundancy in the Name field is used to hide checksum that contains count of the number of bits hidden in the segment. The key to be sent is either (32, 47, C) or (32, 376, C). Retrieval is done according to the algorithm described in Section 4. It is to be noted that column 3 in Table 1 is not a part of the seg.dbf. It is mentioned here to explain the embedding process.

6. STEGANALYSIS

The necessary evil of a steganographic algorithm is the distortion that it adds to the cover object while embedding the message. A good steganographic algorithm maximizes the information embedded into the cover object and minimizes the distortion induced (Halevi & Krawczyk, 2005; Stegoarchive, 2010). In the case of an algorithm using image as cover object, the distortion induced in the cover to produce stego can be measured using various statistical values like: average absolute difference (AD), mean squared error (MSE), L^p-norm, Laplacian mean squared error (LMSE), peak signal to noise ratio (PSNR) and histogram similarity (HS), on the pixels of cover and stego object.

However in case of graph (vector map) various graph characteristics like: Adjacency, Degree spectrum, Known isomorphism, Number of nodes and segments, Spatial position of nodes and segments, Curvature of segments, Regions adjacency and area within each region and Spatial position of each intermediate point of the cover map are to be

Figure 3.

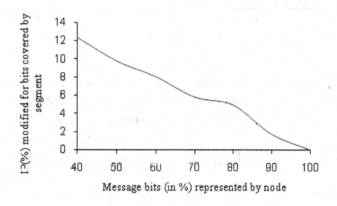

preserved in the stego map to avoid any suspicion and to make the algorithm robust.

Therefore to ensure that the algorithm presented is robust, statistically imperceptible and induces minimum ($\cong 0$) distortion (Aspert et al., 2002), the algorithm is put to test under the three criteria and results obtained are presented herein.

6.1 Statistical Imperceptibility

Imperceptibility implies that a change is impossible or difficult to perceive by the mind or senses. The change are so subtle, slight, or gradual as to be barely perceptible or an imperceptible. The same concept is applicable in case of a steganographic algorithm. The graph in Figure 3 shows the overall impact on cover. The graph is based on the result obtained while embedding various messages in different maps.

Let S be the number of segments and ip_k ($1 \leq k \leq S$) be number of intermediate points in k^{th} segment. The total intermediate points IP_G in map G is

$$IP_G = \sum_{k=1}^{S} ip_k.$$

Out of the total m bits of message let N_C and S_C be bits covered by nodes and segment respectively of the map, then

$$m = N_C + S_C$$

N_C needs no change in cover for embedding. However S_C causes changes in some intermediate points. S_C is spread over to ($N_C - 1$) segments. Number of bits in each segment is determined randomly by sequence of node coverage (Box 2, Section 5). Further S_C is at the most 10% of IP_G and most of the time $S_C <<< IP_G$. Table 2 shows the statistics observed about amount of intermediate points as % of S_C displaced with respect to node coverage of message. Obviously larger is the node coverage lesser is the number of intermediate points affected.

From the table the expected number of change is only one sixth of

[(60 * 0.123 + 50 * 0.0975 + 40 * 0.08 + 30 * 0.58 + 20 * 0.049 + 10 * 0.017 + 0] = 18.345

i.e. (18.345 /6) = 3. 0575% of S_C.

Table 2. % of S_C displaced with respect to node coverage

Message bits Covered by Node	40	50	60	70	80	90	100
(% of S_C) intermediate points affected	12.3	9.75	8	5.8	4.9	1.7	0

In the worst case S_C is 10% of IP_G. Let δ be the number of intermediate points nagged (miniscule displacement). Then

$$\delta < .1 * 3.0575\% \text{ of } IP_G = 0.30575\% \text{ of } IP_G$$

The range is within imperceptible (excellent) range of embedding.

6.2 Distortion

While embedding message into cover map, no additional features like node, segment or points are added to map. The characteristics of the algorithm ensures that the adjacency of nodes, degree spectrum, isomorphism with known maps, feature counts and region adjacency of cover map are preserved in stego map. The nagging (miniscule displacement) is introduced in one of the coordinates (either x or y) of a few intermediate points. On an average only δ of the total internal points are affected. The value of δ is calculated in the previous subsection.

Let (x, y) be the coordinate of on intermediate point to be nagged to hide corresponding bit from message. Nagging is done by either flipping the LSB of x coordinate or of y coordinate so that the Hamming distance between x and y becomes odd from even or vice versa for message bit 0 or 1 respectively. If the map scale is 1:50000 or even of further low scale, the flipping of LSB is going to displace the intermediate point in actual by an order of $< 10^{-5}$. Thus on an average the sum of absolute displacements in a map of scale 1:50000 will be

$$= \delta * 2 * 10^{-5} < 10^{-5}.$$

It is obvious that all displacements are not in one direction. Some displacement may be towards left, some towards right, even some towards upward and some towards downwards. Taking the sign into account, the mean of the total displacement is $\cong 0$. Thus it retains the curvature of the segment as well as area bounded by group of segments (Kumar & Muttoo, 2009a).

6.3 Robustness

Robustness is a measure of strength of a steganographic algorithm such that the outcome of the embedding (hidden message) remains relatively unaffected by the presence of a small number of unusual or incorrect data values. While embedding a message in a map using the algorithm only less than .3% of total intermediate points are displaced. Thus probability of getting an intermediate point nagged is very low. Also nagging, if any, is confined to very few intermediate points, therefore, stego map obtained using the algorithm withstand editing of some intermediate points carrying the payloads. The information may be retrieved using contextual meaning. However the stego can withstand editing of all intermediate points carrying no payloads.

The stego map withstands editing of point features, cleaning of the map and building of polygons. Because these simplification processes neither alter nodes (number) nor coordinate of any of the intermediate points. A vector map is exported and imported from one format to another like ASCII, DXF, E00, etc. while using the same map in different GIS software. The steganographic algorithm presented retains all the features of the stego after export (and then import) or other way.

However as any steganographic algorithm suffers from the tempering related to editing of the stego object, this approach is also prone to editing of the graph to the drastic extent.

7. CONCLUSION

In this paper, an original method is presented to embed some information into a map. A map is a planar graph. The data structure used to represent a graph i.e. planar graph is file based that stores the three components: node, segment and intermediate points of a segment in graph. The method uses small displacements in a few intermediate points by the way of toggling LSB of coordinates of x or y when the hamming distance between x and y does not match the corresponding bits of the message to be embedded in the segment. The displacement is restricted to conform to geometric invariance (Weiss, 1993) when viewed using a graphics tool or analyzing using any GIS tools for measuring aerial distances between any two points represented by the map. The stego map remains robust even after undergoing transformations (Saloman, 2003). The embedding and extraction is based on symmetric key steganography (Katzenbeisser & Petitcolas, 2000). The key depends on the triplet of values < Start node of the Hamiltonian path, length of message in bits (or bytes), an alphabet>. It is also proved that number of bits that can be accommodated in a segment without changing the basic characteristics like adjacency, degree spectrum, planarity, etc. of a graph is proportional to the length and smoothness of the curve of segment.

The file based data structure provides embedding capacity in a map (planar graph) and the key of the algorithm secures the embedded message against known steganalysis method that includes brute force for guessing key. The algorithm tested on a number of covers and different messages yielded interesting results. The relationship shown in Figure 3 clearly explains that when all bits are associated with nodes then no bit is embedded in segment and hence no displacement in any of the intermediate points. Even if some bits are embedded in the segment, number of displacements required has been below 50%.

The concept of planar graph is used in Geospatial field as map. With the advent of Geographical Information System (GIS) technology, many nations are investing in building the National spatial databases. The resources can be used in steganography for maintaining the privacy and secrecy of message during communication by embedding them in very relevant map of one's own town or colony or related events.

ACKNOWLEDGMENT

We are thankful to our colleagues and seniors for their continuous support and encouragements. Though finding sufficient redundancy in a conventional data structure of a graph is a challenge in itself, even then our determination continued to be bold and positive. The successful implementation of (Kumar & Sharma, 2006) has shown the way to achieve this. We are grateful to all those who provided suggestions for improvement of this work. It is our pleasure to acknowledge the cooperation extended by seniors at NIC and all faculty members at Department of Computer Science, University of Delhi. At last but not the least, we are sincerely grateful to anonymous referees who provided judicious and constructive suggestions to improve this paper.

REFERENCES

Anderson, R., & Petitcolas, F. (1998). On the Limits of Steganography. *IEEE Journal on Selected Areas in Communications, 16*(4), 474–481. doi:10.1109/49.668971

Aspert, N., Drelie, E., Maret, Y., & Ebrahimi, T. (2002). Steganography for Three-Dimensional Polygonal Meshes. In *Proceedings of SPIE, 47th Annual Meeting 2002* (pp. 705-708).

Berge, C. (1962). *Theory of Graphs and its Application*. London: Methuen Press.

Bollobas, B. (1983). Almost all regular graphs are Hamiltonian. *European Journal of Combinatorics, 4*, 97–106.

Bondy, J. A., & Murty, U. S. R. (1976). *Graph Theory with Applications*. Amsterdam, The Netherlands: Elsevier.

Cole, E. (2003). *Hiding in Plain Sight: Steganography and the Art of Covert Communication*. New York: Wiley Publishing.

Cox, I. J., Kalkar, T., Pakura, G., & Scheel, M. (2005). Information Transmission and Steganography. In *Digital Watermarking* (LNCS 3710, pp. 15-29).

Cox, I. J., & Matthew, L. Miller, M. L., Bloom, J. A., Fridrich, J., & Kalkar, T. (2007). Digital Watermarking and Steganography. San Francisco: Morgan Kaufmann Publishers.

Egenhofer, M., & Franzosa, R. (1991). Point-set topological spatial relations. *International Journal of Geographical Information Systems, 5*(2), 161–174. doi:10.1080/02693799108927841

Fenner, T. I., & Frieze, A. M. (1983). On the Existence of Hamiltonian Cycles in a Class of Random Graphs. *Discrete Mathematics, 45*, 301–305. doi:10.1016/0012-365X(83)90046-8

Frank, R. (1974). A Search Procedure for Hamilton Paths and Circuits. *Journal of the ACM, 21*(4).

Halevi, S., & Krawczyk, H. (2005, May). *Strengthening Digital Signatures via Randomized Hashing*. IETF.

Hetzl, S., & Mutzel, P. (2005). A Graph-Theoretic Approach to Steganography. In *CMS* (LNCS 3677, pp. 119-128).

Johnson, N.F., & Jajodia, S. (1998a). Exploring Steganography: Seeing the Unseen. *IEEE Computer*, 26-34.

Johnson, N. F., & Jajodia, S. (1998b, April). Steganalysis of Images Created Using Current Steganography Software. In *Proceedings of the Second Information Hiding Workshop*, Portland, OR.

Katzenbeisser, S., & Petitcolas, F. A. P. (2000). *Information Hiding Techniques for Steganography and Digital Watermarking*. Norwood, MA: Artech House.

Kumar, V. (2002). *Discrete Mathematics*. New Delhi, India: BPB Publication.

Kumar, V., & Muttoo, S. K. (2008). Relevance of Steganography, in General, and Graph Theoretic Approach in particular, in Indian Security Concern and Measure. In *Proceedings of the 2nd National Conference, INDIACom-2008* (pp. 183-188).

Kumar, V., & Muttoo, S. K. (2009a). A data structure for graph to facilitate hiding information in a graph's segments - A Graph Theoretic Approach to Steganography. *International Journal of Communication Networks and Distributed Systems, 3*(3), 268–282. doi:10.1504/IJCNDS.2009.026879

Kumar, V., & Muttoo, S. K. (2009b). Principle of Graph Theoretic Approach to Digital Steganography. In *Proceedings of the 3rd National Conference, INDIACom-2009* (pp. 161-165).

Kumar, V., & Muttoo, S. K. (in press). A Graph Theoretic Approach to Sustainable Steganography. *International Journal of Information and Computer Security*.

Kumar, V., & Sharma, V. (2006). Overcoming 64kb data size limit in handling large spatial data in GISNIC while cleaning and building topology. *International Journal of Information Technology and Management*, 5(1), 77–86. doi:10.1504/IJITM.2006.008715

Saloman, D. (2003). *Data Privacy and Security*. New York: Springer.

Stallings, W. (1999). *Cryptography & Network Security: Principles and Practice*. New York: Prentice Hall.

StegoArchive. (2001). *Steganography Information, Software and News to enhance your Privacy*. Retrieved from http://www.StegoArchive.com

Weiss, I. (1993). Review – Geometric Invariants and Object Recognition. *International Journal of Computer Vision*, *10*, 207–231. doi:10.1007/BF01539536

This work was previously published in International Journal of Information Security and Privacy, Volume 4, Issue 3, edited by Hamid Nemati, pp. 21-34, copyright 2010 by IGI Publishing (an imprint of IGI Global).

Chapter 16
Probabilistic Inference Channel Detection and Restriction Applied to Patients' Privacy Assurance

Bandar Alhaqbani
Queensland University of Technology, Australia

Colin Fidge
Queensland University of Technology, Australia

ABSTRACT

Traditional access control models protect sensitive data from unauthorised direct accesses; however, they fail to prevent indirect inferences. Information disclosure via inference channels occurs when secret information is derived from unclassified (non-secure) information and other sources like metadata and public observations. Previously, techniques using precise and fuzzy functional dependencies were proposed to detect inference channels. However, such methods are inappropriate when probabilistic relationships exist among data items that may be used to infer information with a predictable likelihood of accuracy. In this paper, the authors present definitions and algorithms for detecting inference channels in a probabilistic knowledge base and maximising an attacker's uncertainty by restricting selected inference channels to comply with data confidentiality and privacy requirements. As an illustration, a healthcare scenario is used to show how inference control can be performed on probabilistic relations to address patients' privacy concerns over Electronic Medical Records. To limit an attacker's ability to know secret data selected inference channels are restricted by using a Bayesian network that incorporates the information stored within a medical knowledge base to decide which facts must be hidden to limit undesired inferences.

DOI: 10.4018/978-1-4666-0026-3.ch016

INTRODUCTION

Information systems are essential in many organisations to improve upon and automate business processes. In addition, they extend information accessibility to users outside the organisation's physical boundary (e.g., through the Internet). Data that is stored and managed by these systems is captured from day-to-day operations and is a crucial input for decision making processes. Damage to, and misuse of, mission-critical data may affect not only a single user or application, but may have disastrous consequences for the entire organisation; therefore securing this data becomes a mandatory requirement.

Information security breaches are typically categorised as *unauthorised data observation*, *incorrect data modification*, and *data unavailability* (Bertino & Sandhu, 2005). Unauthorised data observation is defined as the direct or indirect disclosure of information to users not entitled to gain access to such information. The consequences of such an illegal access may be heavy losses to the organisation from both financial and human points of view as such breaches affect data confidentiality and privacy. Though the term 'data privacy' is often used as a synonym for 'data confidentiality', the two are quite different. Traditional data confidentiality mechanisms aim to give the *owner* of data control over its accessibility, whereas privacy means giving the *subject* of data control over who accesses it. A particular concern with data that has confidentiality or privacy implications is that once information has been released into the public domain it can never be effectively recalled.

Data confidentiality and privacy are breached once an attacker gets access to protected information, either by having illegal direct access to a protected data object or by *inferring* its value via legal accesses to related data objects. The problem of illegal direct access has gained lots of attention in database research in the last two decades. Applying Mandatory Access Control (MAC) is one of the proposed solutions to con-

trol direct accesses to confidential and private data (Brodsky, Farkas, & Jajodia, 2000). This is done by assigning security labels to data objects and security clearances to users, and employing a security-dominating access relation.

However, an attacker who can access unclassified (non-secure) data may still be able to infer secure information by employing metadata. For example, the observation that "Alice is taking the medication didanosine" and the general medical knowledge that "didanosine is prescribed only to treat HIV infections" can be combined easily to produce the information that Alice is an HIV patient. This problem is known in the literature as an *inference channel* whereby an attacker can combine several pieces of publicly-accessible information in order to infer confidential or private information.

In many situations, however, the relationships between facts are probabilistic or statistical in nature, rather than absolute. For instance, if a particular medication is used to treat several diseases then knowing that a patient takes this medication can be used to infer that the patient has a specific disease only with a certain likelihood. In this paper we present an inference channel detection and restriction technique that uses a Bayesian network and analyses causal probability between data elements. In particular, quantifying the probabilistic size of the channel allows us to restrict it to below a desired threshold, rather than just eliminating it entirely. We illustrate the approach using a healthcare scenario in which patients have privacy concerns over what can be learnt from their Electronic Medical Records (EMRs). We give abstract definitions for what information can be inferred from such records and how such inferences can be limited by hiding specific data items. We then present practical algorithms for restricting inference channels that breach a patient's privacy desires. Also we show our implemented application that uses the developed algorithms.

BACKGROUND

Inference channels are a well known problem that may affect data confidentiality and privacy policies in many organisations, including those involved in healthcare. As an extreme example of a privacy violation, Sweeney (Sweeney, 2002) was able to infer the privileged medical data of William Weld, former governor of the state of Massachusetts, by linking the state's Group Insurance Commission's published "anonymized" medical data, including only each patient's zip code, birth-date, and sex, but omitting their name, to a voter registration list for governor Weld's home city which included each voter's name, zip code, birth-date, and sex. Only one person matched governor Weld's zip code, birth-date, and sex, allowing Sweeney to retrieve his medical data.

Inference control mechanisms are introduced to overcome the security problem caused by inference channels. Static and dynamic approaches to detect and eliminate inference channels have been proposed. These approaches rely on using some information such as database constraints and functional dependencies among database relations to detect inference channels, but they employ different mechanisms to eliminate the detected channels. However, these approaches are incapable of detecting inference channels in a context where the relationship between data objects varies according to the captured data. Nor

do they allow us to leave a channel "open" but restrict its potential impact to an acceptable level.

For example, in the medical domain there is a well established probabilistic relationship between diseases and symptoms, and between symptoms and medications. A disease causes several symptoms; however, these symptoms might be caused by more than one disease. Also, each disease has a causal probability towards each symptom; this information is usually available in medical decision support systems (Goggin, Eikelbom, & Atlas, 2007). Similarly, a particular medication may be used to treat a variety of symptoms and, when there is a choice of medications, there is a statistical likelihood of a doctor prescribing a particular one which can be determined, for instance, from drug companies' sales data. Thus, the inference relation between the disease, the captured symptoms, and the medications prescribed in a patient's medical record will depend on their causal probabilities (which themselves may vary over time).

In this paper, we are interested in a healthcare scenario where a patient has a privacy concern over a certain disease in his medical record. The patient's medical record is represented by columns and rows (Figure 1). The columns represent the date and time of the consultation, the diagnosed disease identified by the medical practitioner, the patient's exhibited symptoms, and the medications prescribed. Each row represents a particular medical event (consultation). We assume that diseases act independently of one another and all captured

Figure 1. Patient's medical record

Date and time of consultation	Diagnosed disease	Exhibited symptoms	Prescribed medications
T_1	D_1	S_1, S_2	M_7, M_8
T_2	D_2	S_2, S_3	M_4, M_5, M_8
T_3	D_3	$S_1, S_2, S_3, S_4, S_5, S_6$	$M_1, M_2, M_3, M_4, M_5, M_6$

Figure 2. Patient's privacy - case scenario

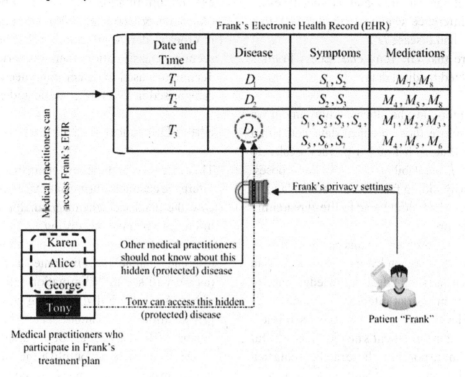

information that is related to a particular disease is recorded in one time event. We use the following scenario to demonstrate a patient's privacy problem (Figure 2).

"Frank" is a patient who has an Electronic Medical Record (EMR) within a hospital. Frank had suffered from mental illness (D_3) which is recorded in his EMR. Frank is concerned about the disclosure of this medical data to his health insurance company. He does not want anyone to know that he had D_3 because he is worried that this information might be communicated to his health insurance company. However, Frank still wants to allow his General Practitioner (GP) "Tony" to have access to it — as a trusted GP. The hospital's EMR system applies Mandatory Access Control (MAC) principles — security clearance for users and security labelling for data items. As per the EMR settings, there are four types of security levels: Top-Secret (TS), Secret (S), Classified (C), and Unclassified (UC). As per

the hospital policy, all patients' medical histories have a C security label, and medical practitioners have C security clearance. Accesses by medical practitioners to a patient's EMR are allowed if the medical practitioner participates in the patient's treatment plan. According to Frank's treatment plan, Tony is not the only person who can access Frank's EMR.

In order to fulfil Frank's privacy desire, hiding the protected disease (D_3) from his medical record is insufficient on its own, because this information can be inferred from recorded medical data, so we need to detect and hide those medical data (symptoms and medications) that may create an inference channel which could be used for undesired access. Therefore, in order to conform to Frank's privacy desire, we need to satisfy the following requirements:

- Protect against direct and indirect accesses (via inference channels) to the fact that Frank had disease D_3.
- Ensure that GP Tony *can* access Frank's protected medical data.

Furthermore, in a healthcare environment we need to disclose those medical data items that do *not* conflict with Frank's privacy desire to maximise their availability for legitimate purposes. Unnecessarily hiding facts about patients' medications or diseases could lead to life-threatening treatment errors.

To solve this problem, in this paper we follow a probabilistic approach by applying a Bayesian network that uses a medical knowledge base to detect and then restrict inference channels to an acceptable level. This process is executed on each medical event in the patient's medical record. Our approach aims to both hide those medical data that have high inference probability to a 'protected' disease, and to disclose the maximum amount of non-inferential medical data.

RELATED WORK

Inference control mechanisms are introduced to detect and eliminate the occurrence of harmful inference channels. Successful inference attacks affect users' and organisations' data confidentiality and privacy. Many research projects in database security have addressed this problem and several detection and elimination techniques have been proposed for inference channels (Farkas & Jajodia, 2002). In this section, we introduce these techniques and highlight their limitations with respect to the problem introduced above.

Detection Techniques

Inference attacks usually occur by combining metadata (e.g., database constraints) (Bertino & Sandhu, 2005; Farkas & Jajodia, 2002) and/or external information (e.g., public observations) (An, Jutla, & Cercone, 2006) with retrieved data in order to derive information that has a higher security classification than the original data. Techniques used to detect inference channel are categorised in two forms: static and dynamic.

Static Detection Techniques

This category includes mechanisms that detect inference channels during database design. In this case the database schema is analysed to detect inference channels according to specific confidential and privacy policies, and those detected inference channels are eliminated in a certain way (as we will see in "Elimination (Hiding) Techniques") to ensure that inferring confidential or private information cannot occur while using the database (Brodsky et al., 2000; Farkas & Jajodia, 2002). In order to accomplish the analysis task, the database architect needs to consider all the available information that will help an attacker to accomplish his task.

For example, Su and Ozsoyoglu noted that database constraints such as functional and multivalued dependencies are helpful information for detecting inference channels (Su & Ozsoyoglu, 1991). They introduced inference detection algorithms which use functional dependency information, however their approach is based on absolute functional dependencies, and does not consider inference channels that result from imprecise (e.g., probabilistic) functional dependencies. Hale and Shenoi (Hale & Shenoi, 1997) then extended the functional dependency scope and introduced imprecise (fuzzy) functional dependencies that are extracted from public knowledge, e.g., published salary scales for executives. They proved that it is possible to detect inference channels by combining fuzzy functional dependencies with non-inferential precise functional dependencies; 'fuzzy inference' was the name given to this inference type. However, the fuzzy approach tends to build fuzzy functional dependencies using imprecise common knowledge but does not consider precisely quantifiable causal relations among data elements. By contrast, our approach can capture these causally probabilistic relations from well-researched and published medical knowledge. Furthermore, the two aforementioned approaches rely on functional dependencies whereas our approach employs causally probabilistic relations.

Buczkowski (Buczkowski, 1990) was the first researcher to use a probabilistic approach to quantify the capability of inference channels. He demonstrated his solution on a satellite network system. Like us, Buczkowski used a Bayesian network to determine the probabilistic relations among data, however his approach differs from ours in the process of calculating the probability of dependent data. Also our approach is unique in that we allow for the fact that the prior probability of contracting a disease varies over to time. Chang and Moskowitz (Chang & Moskowitz, 2000) have used Bayesian networks to limit the inference capability of certain data. Their approach aims to retain the functionality of the disclosed data to within a certain ratio by calculating the information loss that will occur once the inference channel is eliminated. In their solution, they used the data that are recorded in the relation (table) to compute the probabilistic inference among data in order to determine the inference capability; however, this approach would not allow them to have an accurate probabilistic result because they have not considered all possible values that a particular data field may have. Also, they did not consider the causal dependencies between data.

By contrast, our approach analyses all the possible data through the use of the medical knowledge base and applies a Bayesian network to compute the inference probability by taking into account the dependencies among data and their prior probabilities. As an additional feature, our approach allows patients to set their desired privacy levels (e.g., low, medium, high, or extreme) that are then used as an evaluation threshold for each inference channel.

Dynamic Detection Techniques

This category includes mechanisms that detect inference channels at run (query) time (Biskup & Bonatti, 2002; Farkas & Jajodia, 2002; Sicherman, Jonge, & de Riet, 1983). Each user's query is evaluated according to a certain confidential policy, where previously-answered queries are considered in the process. Controlled Query Evaluation (CQE) was developed by Biskup and Bonatti as a dynamic approach to the inference problem in logical databases (Biskup & Bonatti, 2001, 2002, 2004, 2007). After each query, the system checks whether the answer to that query — combined with the previous answers and possibly a priori assumptions — would enable the user to infer any secret information. This approach is computationally expensive (Farkas & Jajodia, 2002) but it increases data availability because inference channel detection is conducted on a case-by-case, data-specific basis, rather than on generic database schemata.

In our approach, we assume that the user, typically a medical practitioner, has a predefined query which returns a patient's *whole* medical record (or, at least, as much as this user is allowed to see). In this paper, we are interested in the online EHR systems where only the current medical data is of interest and people would not normally keep old snapshots, therefore the problem of incremental queries is not relevant in our situation. Nevertheless, our approach also aims to maximise data availability by examining potential inferences on the data, rather than schema, level.

Elimination (Hiding) Techniques

Once undesirable inference channels have been detected, we need to restrict their capabilities until we have satisfied relevant confidentiality and privacy policies. This process is achieved by applying inference channel elimination techniques.

The security labelling technique introduced by Mandatory Access Control (MAC) assigns 'high' security labels to those data that are secrets and 'low' security labels to those data that are non-secrets at the database design stage. Users are each assigned a security clearance, so that only users whose security clearance dominates the data security labels are allowed access. However, to protect against the occurrence of inference channels a relabeling mechanism is required to hide any non-secure data via which inferences can be made about secret data, which then means assigning high security labels to these data. However, this operation may result in overly-restrictive classifications which affect data availability (Biskup & Bonatti, 2001; Brodsky et al., 2000; Farkas & Jajodia, 2002). By contrast, our goal is to maximise data availability so, where possible, we aim to restrict the probabilistic size of inference channels, rather than eliminate them entirely.

Lying and refusal techniques (Biskup & Bonatti, 2001, 2004) have been introduced as a mechanism to follow within Controlled Query Evaluation, in which false data or no data, respectively, is returned in situations where answering a query accurately and completely may create an inference channel. However, in a healthcare context, neither of these approaches is acceptable. Providing false information to medical practitioners, or withholding vital information, may result in a life-threatening situation for the patient. Therefore, we do not consider these techniques in our solution. (In particular, if our inference channel technique hides some data then it will be obvious to the user via inspection of the metadata, e.g., a blank field in the medical record, that this has occurred. This in itself may be considered an inference channel, because it reveals that the patient has something to hide, but we consider this relatively unimportant in our application).

Similarly, techniques such as data anonymization and generalization (Sweeney, 2002) may be acceptable for medical research applications, but are not suitable for medical diagnostic scenarios, so are considered to be outside the scope of our research as well.

MEDICAL DATA RESOURCES

The healthcare sector has enjoyed substantial benefits by employing information systems. For instance, Electronic Medical Records (EMRs) are transforming cumbersome paper-based medical histories into easily stored and retrieved digital formats. However, these advances have raised significant security concerns, especially patient privacy. Preserving patients' privacy is an important requirement that, if not satisfied, may cause patients to withhold data or even falsify data, with potentially life-threatening consequences (Chhanabhai & Holt, 2007). In this section, we introduce the two main medical data resources that are used in our probabilistic analysis: the Medical Knowledge Base and Electronic Medical Records.

Medical Knowledge Base

The Medical Knowledge Base (MKB) is a crucial input to medical diagnosis systems. In our scenario it is used to derive the causal probability relationship between two medical data items (e.g., a disease and its symptoms). Usually, this information is used in clinical decision support systems which offer diagnostic support to physicians to enhance their diagnostic accuracy and reduce the overall rate of misdiagnosis. MKB information is entered and reviewed on a continuous basis by medical experts. Information such as the causal probability (Pearl, 2006) between a certain disease and its symptoms, and the statistical prior probability of the occurrence of a certain disease in a given population are captured within the MKB (Goggin et al., 2007). The statistical prior probability of getting a particular disease varies over time, e.g., the probability of contracting malaria in India in 1976 was 94%, but in 2006 the probability had decreased to 0.092%. Similarly, the probability that a particular medication will be prescribed to treat a certain symptom can be determined from drug companies' sales data. Figure 3 gives an example of the kind of data that may be contained

Figure 3. Medical knowledge base

Disease – Symptom Causal Probability					Symptom – Medication Treatment Probability					Disease Statistical Prior Probability		
	S_1	S_2	S_3	S_4		M_1	M_2	M_3	M_4	P_0-P_1	P_1-P_2	P_2-P_3
D_1	35%	15%	40%	0%	S_1	15%	0%	0%	0%	D_1	80%	60%	60%
					S_2	30%	0%	0%	0%				
D_2	0%	0%	40%	30%	S_3	0%	50%	0%	0%	D_2	60%	70%	50%
					S_4	0%	0%	40%	55%				

within the medical knowledge base at a particular time and is used in our solution in "Probabilistic Inference Channel Detection and Restriction".

Electronic Medical Records

An Electronic Medical record is a patient-centric medical record maintained by a particular health-care provider (e.g., a hospital) (Garets & Davis, 2006). It has information that is recorded about each patient admitted for each visit, e.g., admission and referral data, diagnostic image data, and medical history. The patient's medical history captures information such as the diseases and symptoms that the patient has suffered, and the medications they have been prescribed. Figure 3 is a simple example that shows the visualisation of a patient's medical history within the EMR.

MEDICAL DATA RELATIONS

Diseases, symptoms and medications are data items that are related to one another. A disease presents itself through one or more symptoms, and a particular symptom may be treated by one or more medications. This causality helps to establish relations among these three components. We use the Medical Knowledge Base to retrieve causal probability (C_Pr) values, i.e. the probability that an effect will occur by knowing the occurrence

of the cause, to determine these relations. There are three different relations that we can identify among these components: two direct relations (disease–symptom, and symptom–medication) and an indirect relation (disease–medication). We use the following definitions for each of these three relations:

Definition 1 (Disease-Symptom Relation ($\overline{DS}$)). Let D (Disease List)=$\{D_1,D_2,...,D_n\}$ be the list of all known diseases and S(Symptom List)$\{S_1,S_2,...,S_m\}$ be the list of all recognised symptoms. A disease x is in relation with a symptom y if and only if the causal probability of exhibiting symptom y by having disease x is greater than zero.

$$\overline{DS} = \{x : D; y : S \mid C\_Pr(y \mid x) > 0\}$$

Definition 2 (Symptom-Medication Relation ($\overline{SM}$)). Let M(Medication List)=$\{M_1,M_2,...,M_k\}$ be the list of all prescribed medications. A symptom y is in relation with a medication z if and only if the causal probability of having symptom y by being observed to take medication z is greater than zero.

$$\overline{SM} = \{y : S; z : M \mid C\_Pr(z \mid y) > 0\}$$

Figure 4. Disease, symptoms, and medications relations

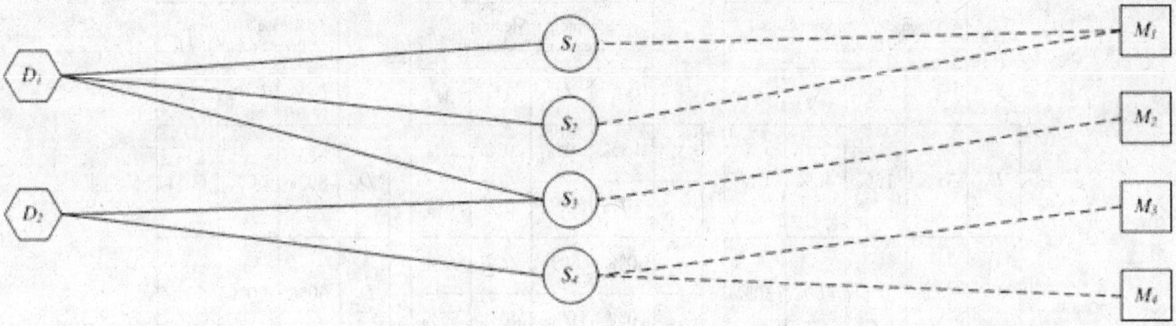

Definition 3 (Disease-Medication Relation ($\overline{DM}$)). A disease x is in relation with a medication z if and only if z treats one of the symptoms that are caused by x. Let R_i be a relation (set of pairs) with domain X_i and range Y_i. Then the relational composition $R_i \circ R_j$ is the relation

$$\{x{:}X_i;y{:}Y_j|\exists\ z{:}(x,z) \in R_i \wedge (z,y) \in R_j\}.$$

$$\overline{DM} = \overline{DS} \circ \overline{SM}$$

As an example, Figure 4 shows causally probabilistic relations among some diseases, symptoms, and medications, as determined by the Medical Knowledge Base in Figure 3. Each line (solid or dashed) represents a non-zero causal probability between two data items. Now, we apply our aforementioned definitions to extract the $\overline{DS}$, $\overline{SM}$ and $\overline{DM}$ relations (represented textually as sets of pairs).

$$\overline{DS} =$$
$$\{(D_1,S_1),(D_1,S_2),(D_1,S_3),(D_2,S_3),(D_2,S_4)\}$$
$$\overline{SM} =$$
$$\{(S_1,M_1),(S_2,M_1),(S_3,M_2),(S_4,M_3),(S_4,M_4)\}$$
$$\overline{DM} =$$
$$\{(D_1,M_1),(D_1,M_2),(D_2,M_2),(D_2,M_3),(D_2,M_4)\}$$

PROBABILISTIC INFERENCE CHANNEL DETECTION AND RESTRICTION

Inference channel detection has proven to be a complex challenge (Brodsky et al., 2000) which requires accurate analysis of implicit information flow that might occur due to the disclosure of particular sets of data elements. In our case the goal is to disclose as much information about the patient's medical history as is consistent with their privacy desires and the medical practitioner's needs. In this section, we start by introducing various properties for the 'disclosed' symptom list and medications list, and demonstrate via four examples why inference channel detection is difficult and varies according to the medical data knowledge. We then present our probabilistic solution, capable of detecting inference channels in complicated contexts.

Properties

Privacy requirements vary among people, so for each potentially sensitive fact in a patient's medical history the desired 'privacy protection level' might vary as well (e.g., low, medium, high, and extreme). We assume that patients can choose such levels for their own healthcare data, and we use them to quantify the permitted leaked knowledge that someone can gain by inferring information about the patient. Let Infer($Y|X$)

denote the 'inference probability' (Buczkowski, 1990) that knowing fact X will lead one to conclude that Y is true. In other words, it represents the likelihood that we will conclude Y given X. The higher the value, the greater the danger of someone making a correct inference about confidential data. Informally, it can be thought of as the 'size' or 'width' of the inference channel. In order to reduce the privacy impact of a detected inference channel, we keep reducing its size until we reach a satisfactory privacy level. We define two criteria, namely privacy protection threshold and maximum entropy probability distribution, that can be employed individually or collaboratively to define the foreseen satisfactory privacy level.

Definition 4 (Privacy Protection Threshold (PPT)). Privacy protection threshold determines the severity of inference channels, and is determined by means of privacy protection levels. A privacy protection level (PPL) is a discrete value that is set by the user to express his privacy protection level. Each PPL is associated with an assigned inference threshold (t). Let $PPL = \{Low, Medium, High, Extreme\}$, d be a protected medical disease and X be a medical data item. In order to say that disclosure of X creates an illegal inference channel, the following condition must be satisfied:

$$Infer(d|X) \begin{cases} \geq 75, & \text{when } PPL = Low \\ \geq 50, & \text{when } PPL = Medium \\ \geq 25, & \text{when } PPL = High \\ > 0, & \text{when } PPL = Extreme \end{cases}$$

Definition 5 (Maximum Entropy Probability Distribution (MEPD)). Maximum entropy probability distribution is a disease inferential probability distribution of a given medical data whose entropy is the highest inferential probability among other diseases. Let $d \in D$, where $D = \{D_1, D_2, ..., D_n\}$, be a protected disease and X be a medical data item. In order to say that

disclosure of X creates an illegal inference channel, the following condition must be satisfied:

$$\forall\ y \in D \quad \bullet \quad Infer(d\ |\ X) > Infer(y\ |\ X)$$

By using Definitions 4 and/or 5, we can define the characteristics of an acceptable Disclosed Symptom List (DSL) and Disclosed Medication List (DML), i.e., the information we will allow to be displayed in the patient's Electronic Health Record.

Property 1 (Disclosed Symptoms List (DSL)). Let $d \in D$, where $D = \{D_1, D_2, ..., D_n\}$, be a protected disease, and $SL \subset S$, where $S = \{S_1, S_2, ..., S_m\}$, be a symptoms list. SL is considered acceptably safe from the risk of inferring an illegal indirect disclosure of d, with regard to a certain criterion and privacy threshold t, and can be used as a disclosed symptoms list, if it satisfies the relevant criterion's condition:

PPT condition: $Infer(d\ |\ SL) < t$

MEPD condition:
$$\exists\ y \in D \quad \bullet \quad Infer(d\ |\ SL) \leq Infer(y\ |\ SL)$$

Property 2 (Disclosed Medications List (DML)). Let $d \in D$, where $D = \{D_1, D_2, ..., D_n\}$, be a protected disease, and $ML \subset M$, where $M = \{M_1, M_2, ..., M_k\}$, be a medications list. iML is considered acceptably safe from the risk of inferring an illegal indirect disclosure of d, with regard to a certain criterion and privacy threshold t, and can be used as a disclosed medications list, if it satisfies the relevant criterion's condition:

PPT condition: $Infer(d|ML) < t$

MEPD condition:
$$\exists\ y \in D \quad \bullet \quad Infer(d\ |\ ML) \leq Infer(y\ |\ ML)$$

Figure 5. Unique disease-symptom-medication relations

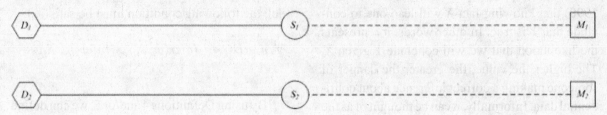

Exactly how Infer($d|ML$) is calculated for a particular disease d and symptom or medication list ML is explained below. For sake of simplicity, we use the privacy protection threshold as our evaluation criterion; however the same approach can be applied when using the maximum entropy distribution measure (MEDB).

PRIVACY-PRESERVING DATA DISCLOSURE

In this section we present our probabilistic approach for detecting the data that causes inference channels within a patient's Electronic Medical Record. Also we show how to determine an appropriate disclosed data list that satisfies both patient's privacy desires and medical practitioners' requirement for maximum disclosure of medical data.

Inference Channel Detection and Restriction

Our inference channel detection process is highly dependent on the medical knowledge base, and this process gets complicated as the number of relations within the knowledge base increases. In the following examples we present our probabilistic approach to detecting and restricting inference channels within an electronic medical record in successively more challenging situations.

Example 1. *Assume a patient has a medical record containing a timestamp/disease/symptoms/ medications event* (T_1, D_1, S_1, M_1). *The patient classifies disease* D_1 *as private data and chooses a 'medium' privacy protection level. Further assume that the medical knowledge base contains the relations shown in Figure 5, where each solid or dashed line represents a causal probability that is greater than zero. In order to achieve the patient's stated privacy desire, we need to hide* D_1 *to protect against direct accesses. Also, we need to evaluate the inference capability of symptom* S_1 *and medication* M_1 *with respect to disease* D_1.

As per Definitions 1 and 3, symptom S_1 and medication M_1 are in relation with disease D_1. As S_1 is the *only* symptom that is in relation ($\overline{DS}$) with D_1, this makes its inference probability immediate; the same concept applies to M_1.

$$Infer(D_1 \mid S_1) = Infer(D_1 \mid M_1) = 100\%$$

Therefore, hiding symptom S_1 and medication M_1 is mandatory because their inference probabilities are greater than the patient's privacy threshold. However, detecting inference channels in Example 1 is an easy process as symptoms and medications that are in relation with disease D_1 do not have any relation with other diseases.

Example 2. *Let us extend the relations in Figure 5 and add a link between disease D2 and symptom* S_1 *(Figure 6).*

In this scenario, we find that symptom S_1 and medication M_1 are in relation with diseases D_1

and D_2. Therefore, it can not be said that S_1 and M_1 have an immediate inference channel with regard to disease D_1; however they might have a probabilistic inference capability. Therefore, in order to detect whether or not there is an inference channel we use a Bayesian inference probabilistic approach (Griffiths & Yuille, 2006; Pearl, 2003; Pearl & Russell, 2003; Stephenson, 2000). Bayesian networks allow statistical inference in which evidence or observations are used to update or to newly infer the probability that a hypothesis may be true. The name "Bayesian" comes from the frequent use of Bayes' theorem in the inference process.

Definition 6 (Bayesian Inference Theorem). Let ε be a finite set of events and $(\varepsilon, \Pr)$ be a probability space. Let $E, H_1, H_2, ..., H_k \in \varepsilon$ be compound events, none of which has zero probability. Then the posterior probability of hypothesis H_i given evidence E is:

$$\Pr(H_i \mid E) = \frac{\Pr(H_i)C\_\Pr(E \mid H_i)}{\sum_{j=1}^{k} \Pr(H_j)C\_\Pr(E \mid H_j)}$$

where,

- $\Pr(H_i)$ and $\Pr(H_j)$ represent null hypotheses, that were inferred before new evidence E, and are called prior probabilities.
- $C\_\Pr(E \mid H_x)$ is the causal probability of seeing the effect E given that the hypothesis (cause) H_x is true.

Definition 6 is a generic definition for Bayesian inference, however we adapt it to derive our definition for symptom inference probabilities. Let R be a relation (set of pairs) with domain X and range Y. Then the *image* of relation R through a set $S \subseteq X$ is the set $\{y : Y \mid \exists\, s : s \in S \land (s,y) \in R\}$, denoted as $R\langle S \rangle$. We allow the image of a singleton set

$R\langle \{s\} \rangle$ to be abbreviated $R\langle s \rangle$. Let R be a relation (set of pairs) with domain R and range Y. Then the *inverse relation* R^{-1} is defined as $R^{-1} = \{y : Y; x : X \mid (x,y) \in R\}$.

Definition 7 (Symptom Inference Probability). Let $d \in D$, where $D = \{D_1, D_2, ..., D_n\}$, be a protected disease, and $s \in S$, where $S = \{S_1, S_2, ..., S_m\}$, be a symptom. Then the inference probability of a patient having disease d by knowing a patient has symptom s is calculated as follows:

$$Infer(d \mid s) = \frac{\Pr(d)C\_\Pr(s \mid d)}{\sum_{e \in \overline{DS}^{-1}\langle s \rangle} \Pr(e)C\_\Pr(s \mid e)}$$

In this definition inverse relation $\overline{DS}^{-1}$ maps symptoms to diseases, so applying it to symptom s returns the set of all disease e which cause this symptom.

For example 2, we can use Definition 7 with the provided causal probabilities in Figure 6 to determine the inference probability of disease D_1 with respect to symptom S_1.

$$\begin{aligned} Infer(D_1 \mid S_1) &= \frac{\Pr(D_1)C\_\Pr(S_1 \mid D_1)}{\sum_{e \in \{D_1, D_2\}} \Pr(e)C\_\Pr(S_1 \mid e)} \\ &= \frac{0.4(0.3)}{0.4(0.3) + 0.3(0.6)} = 40\% \end{aligned}$$

As a result, knowing that a patient has symptom S_1 increases our suspicion that the patient has been infected by disease D_1, but does not guarantee this conclusion. However, the disclosure of symptom S_1 is not considered to create a harmful inference channel according to the patient's 'medium' privacy protection level.

Next, we want to evaluate whether or not knowing that the patient has been prescribed medication M_1 could infer any information about the presence of disease D_1. In order to calculate D_1's inference probability with respect to M_1, we need

Figure 6. Symptom related to two diseases

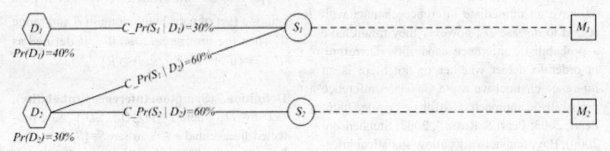

to calculate the transitive inference probability between medications, symptoms and diseases in the Medical Knowledge Base. Firstly, we need to find those symptoms that are in relation with both disease D_1 and medication M_1 to define the inference path from M_1 to D_1. Definition 8 shows how these symptoms can be identified.

Definition 8 (Shared Symptoms List). Let $d \in D$, where $D = \{D_1, D_2, ..., D_n\}$, be a disease, $m \in M$, where $M = \{M_1, M_2, ..., M_k\}$, be a medication, and $S = \{S_1, S_2, ..., S_m\}$ be a set of symptoms. The shared symptoms list between disease d and medication m in the Medical Knowledge Base is defined as follows:

$$Sh(d, m) = \{s : S \mid s \in (\overline{DS}\langle d \rangle \cap \overline{SM}^{-1}\langle m \rangle)\}$$

Secondly, we use a Bayesian theorem to calculate the inference probability of each symptom in list $Sh(D_1, M_1)$ with respect to medication M_1. In order to accomplish this calculation we derive Definition 9 from Definition 6.

Definition 9 (Symptom-Medications Inference Probability). Let $s \in S$, where $S = \{S_1, S_2, ..., S_m\}$, be a symptom, and $m \in M$, where $M = \{M_1, M_2, ..., M_k\}$, be a medication. Then the inference probability of symptom s by knowing the patient takes medication m is defined as follows:

$$Infer(s \mid m) = \frac{\Pr(s) C\_\Pr(m \mid s)}{\displaystyle\sum_{e \in \overline{SM}^{-1}\langle m \rangle} \Pr(e) C\_\Pr(m \mid e)}$$

Thirdly, we use Definition 7 to derive the inference probability of disease D_1 by knowing that the patient has a symptom $s \in Sh(D_1, M_1)$. This process is repeated for each shared symptom. Finally, we use Definition 10 to calculate the transitive inference (medication inference probability). This definition uses the previous inference values by multiplying each inference arc (symptom–medication and disease–symptom) to get the inference ratio for the medication.

Definition 10 (Medication Inference Probability). Let $d \in D$, where $D = \{D_1, D_2, ..., D_n\}$, be a disease, $s \in S$, where $S = \{S_1, S_2, ..., S_m\}$, be a symptom, and $m \in M$, where $M = \{M_1, M_2, ..., M_k\}$, be a medication. Then the inference probability of disease d by knowing a patient takes medication m is defined as follows:

$$Infer(d \mid m) = \frac{\displaystyle\sum_{s \in Sh(d,m)} Infer(d \mid s) Infer(s \mid m)}{\displaystyle\sum_{e \in \overline{DM}^{-1}\langle m \rangle} \sum_{s \in Sh(e,m)} Infer(e \mid s) Infer(s \mid m)}$$

Now, we use Definition 10 to calculate the inference probability created by knowing that the patient in our example takes medication M_1.

Figure 7. Medication used to treat two symptoms related to two diseases

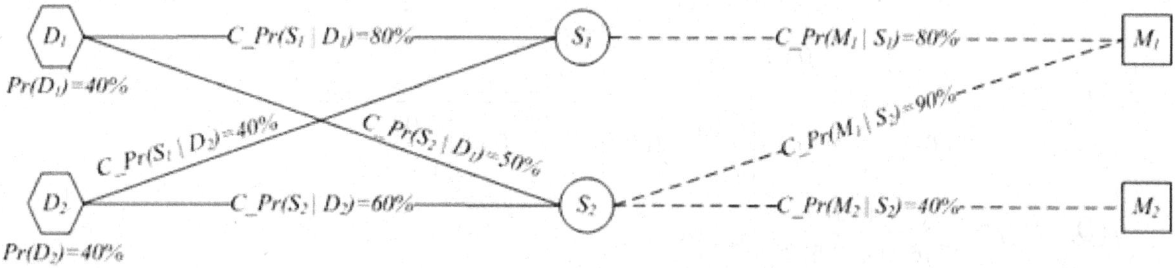

$$Infer(D_1 \mid M_1) = \frac{Infer(D_1 \mid S_1)Infer(S_1 \mid M_1)}{\displaystyle\sum_{e \in \{D_1, D_2\}} \sum_{s \in Sh(e, M_1)} Infer(e \mid s)Infer(s \mid M_1)}$$

$$= \frac{0.4(1)}{0.4(1) + 0.6(0.1)} = 40\%$$

The inference probability of disease D_1 by using medication M_1 is smaller than 50%, which means that disclosing M_1 will not breach the patient's stated privacy desire. As a result, the disclosure of both symptom S_1 and medication M_1 is acceptable in this extended example.

Example 3. *Assume a patient has a medical record containing a timestamp/ disease/ symptoms/ medications event* $(T_2, D_1, \{S_1, S_2\}, \{M_1, M_2\})$. The patient classifies disease D_1 as private data and chooses a 'medium' privacy protection level. The available medical knowledge is represented in Figure 7. In order to achieve the patient's stated privacy desire, we need to hide disease D_1 to protect against direct accesses. Also, we need to evaluate the inference capability of the exhibited symptoms and the prescribed medications.

From the medical knowledge (Figure 7), we notice that symptoms S_1 and S_2, and medications M_1 and M_2, are all in relation with diseases D_1 and D_2 which makes our inference detection task more difficult because we need to consider all these connections in the inference probability process.

We start our inference probability evaluation by considering individual data items at first. We use Definition 7 to evaluate the inference prob-

ability for disease D_1 caused by the individual symptoms S_1 and S_2:

$$Infer(D_1 \mid S_1) = \frac{0.4(0.8)}{0.4(0.8) + 0.4(0.4)} = 67\%$$

$$Infer(D_1 \mid S_2) = \frac{0.4(0.5)}{0.4(0.5) + 0.4(0.6)} = 46\%$$

As a result, symptom S_1 must not be disclosed because it fails to satisfy the patient's privacy setting on its own, but we can reveal that the patient has symptom S_2 because knowing this does not allowing someone to conclude that the patient has disease D_1 with enough certainty to violate the privacy requirement. Next, we evaluate the inference probability caused by medications M_1 and M_2 with respect to disease D_1 using Definition 10: (see Exhibit 1)

Thus the disclosure that the patient takes medication M_2 does not breach the patient's privacy desire; whereas revealing that the patient takes medication M_1 fails to meet this privacy constraint. Overall, therefore, symptom S_2 and medication M_2 satisfy the privacy protection threshold (PPT) disclosure condition as per Properties 1 and 2, and so revealing that the patient has symptom S_2 and takes medication M_2 does not create an illegal inference channel.

Example 4. let us extend this example by adding two additional relations in the medical knowledge base (Figure 8).

Exhibit 1.

$$Infer(D_1 \mid M_1) = \frac{0.67\left(\frac{0.8}{1.7}\right) + 0.46\left(\frac{0.9}{1.7}\right)}{0.67\left(\frac{0.8}{1.7}\right) + 0.46\left(\frac{0.9}{1.7}\right) + 0.33\left(\frac{0.8}{1.7}\right) + 0.55\left(\frac{0.9}{1.7}\right)} = 56\%$$

$$Infer(D_1 \mid M_2) = \frac{0.46(1)}{0.46(1) + 0.55(1)} = 46\%$$

Figure 8. Joint probability

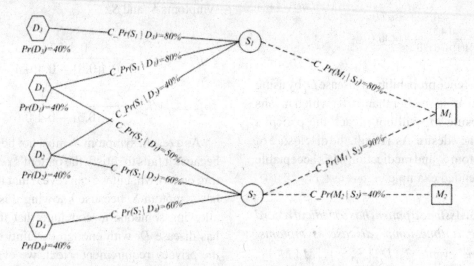

We start by calculating the inference probability of the patient's exhibited symptoms, with respect to disease D_1:

$$Infer(D_1 \mid S_1) = \frac{0.4(0.8)}{0.4(0.8) + 0.4(0.8) + 0.4(0.4)} = 40\%$$

$$Infer(D_1 \mid S_2) = \frac{0.4(0.5)}{0.4(0.5) + 0.4(0.6) + 0.4(0.6)} = 29\%$$

Therefore, neither symptom S_1 nor S_2, on their own, could breach the patient's 'medium' privacy policy and create an illegal inference channel since their inference probabilities are lower than 50%. However, the joint knowledge that the patient has both symptoms S_1 and S_2 might create a harmful inference channel; therefore, we need to analyze their joint inference probability. In order to avoid the need to have conditional probabilities for all combinations of symptoms we use the Noisy-OR approach (Bender, 1996), another type of Bayesian network used to calculate the joint probability of several effects. This approach is used in diagnosis decision support system (Heckerman, 1990) where the inference of a symptom using multiple diseases is calculated. However, in our approach we are interested in the opposite direction where we aim to compute the inference of a disease by knowing some symptoms.

Definition 11 (Noisy-OR). Let X be a set of random variables, $Z \subset X$ and $y \in X$. Variables of X are either *in-relation* or *not in-relation* with each other. The random variable y is called the

Exhibit 2.

$$Infer(D_1 \mid \{S_1, S_2\}) = \frac{1 - \prod_{s \in \{S_1, S_2\}} (1 - Infer(D_1 \mid s))}{\sum_{e \in \{D_1, D_2\}} 1 - \prod_{s \in \{S_1, S_2\}} (1 - Infer(e \mid s))}$$

$$= \frac{1 - (1 - 0.4)(1 - 0.29)}{[1 - (1 - 0.4)(1 - 0.29)] + [1 - (1 - 0.2)(1 - 0.35)]} = 54\%$$

noisy-OR of X if it is *in-relation* with some variables of X and *not in-relation* with others.

$$\Pr(y \mid Z) = 1 - \prod_{x \in Z} (1 - \Pr(y \mid x))$$

In order to calculate the inference probability that is caused by combinations of symptoms or medications, we need to find the diseases that are in relation with these symptoms and medications. We use Definitions 12 and 13 to extract the diseases list that shares the same symptoms or medications list.

Definition 12 (Diseases with Joint Symptoms (DJS)). Let $Z \subset S$, where $S = \{S_1, S_2, \ldots, S_m\}$, be a set of symptoms, and $DJS(Z)$ be the list of diseases that cause the occurrence of all symptoms in Z, such that $DJS(Z) \subset D$, where $D = \{D_1, D_2, \ldots, D_n\}$.

$$DJS(Z) = \bigcap_{s \in Z} \overline{DS}^{-1} \langle s \rangle$$

Definition 13 (Diseases Shring Medications (DSM)). Let $Y \subset M$, where $M = \{M_1, M_2, \ldots, M_k\}$, be a set of medications, and $DSM(Y)$ be the list of diseases that is treated by all medications in Y joint medications, such that $DSM(Y) \subset D$, where $D = \{D_1, D_2, \ldots, D_n\}$.

$$DSM(Y) = \bigcap_{m \in Y} \overline{DM}^{-1} \langle m \rangle$$

Now, we substitute Definitions 7 and 10 into Definition 11 to create Definitions 14 and 15. These definitions calculate the inference probability by using the Noisy-OR approach and then divide the result by the inference probability of each disease by knowing the joint symptoms and medications lists, respectively.

Definition 14 (Joint Symptoms Inference Probability). Let $d \in D$, where $D = \{D_1, D_2, \ldots, D_n\}$, be a disease, and $Z \subset S$, where $S = \{S_1, S_2, \ldots, S_m\}$, be a set of symptoms. Then the inference probability of disease d from knowing that a patient has symptoms Z is defined as follows:

$$Infer(d \mid Z) = \frac{1 - \prod_{e \in Z} (1 - Infer(d \mid s))}{\sum_{e \in DJS(Z)} 1 - \prod_{s \in Z} (1 - Infer(e \mid s))}$$

Definition 15 (Joint Medications Inference Probability). Let $d \in D$, where $D = \{D_1, D_2, \ldots, D_n\}$, be a disease, and $Y \subset M$, where $M = \{M_1, M_2, \ldots, M_k\}$, be a set of medications. Then the inference probability of disease d by knowing that a patient takes medications Y is defined as follows:

$$Infer(d \mid Y) = \frac{1 - \prod_{m \in Y} (1 - Infer(d \mid m))}{\sum_{e \in DSM(Y)} 1 - \prod_{m \in Y} (1 - Infer(e \mid m))}$$

Exhibit 3.

$$\text{Infer}(D_1 \mid \{M_1, M_2\}) =$$

$$\frac{1 - \displaystyle\prod_{m \in \{M_1, M_2\}} (1 - Infer(D_1 \mid m))}{\displaystyle\sum_{e \in \{D_1, D_2, D_4\}} 1 - \prod_{m \in \{M_1, M_2\}} (1 - Infer(e \mid m))} =$$

$$\frac{1 - (1 - 0.35)(1 - 0.29)}{[1 - (1 - 0.35)(1 - 0.29)] + [1 - (1 - 0.28)(1 - 0.35)] + [1 - (1 - 0.17)(1 - 0.35)]} =$$

$$35\%$$

Now, let us apply Definition 14 to calculate the joint inference probability of symptoms S_1 and S_2, with respect to disease D_1. (see Exhibit 2)

Thus the combination of both symptoms S_1 and S_2 creates an illegal inference channel as their joint inference probability is greater than 50%. Therefore, we need to hide either S_1 or S_2 to block this illegal inference channel. Now, we evaluate the inference probability caused by medications M_1 and M_2 by using Definition 10:

Infer($D_1 \mid M_1$) = 35%

Infer($D_1 \mid M_2$) = 29%

Here the inference probability caused by the individual medications does not breach the patient's privacy policy. Our next task is to evaluate their joint inference probability using Definition 15: (see Exhibit 3)

(In general, the ability to infer that a patient has a disease from their prescribed medications will be less than or equal to the ability to do so from their exhibited symptoms because symptoms are directly related to diseases whereas medications are related indirectly. This will not be the case, however, if all of the symptoms associated with a disease are not exhibited by the patient, or recorded by the doctor, even though the appropriate medication has been prescribed).

Therefore, the disclosure that the patient takes both medications M_1 and M_2 still satisfies the patient's privacy requirement.

Disclosable Data

Notice in Example 4 that to eliminate the undesired inference channel caused by revealing a combination of symptoms or medications we have a choice of hiding the fact that the patient has either symptom S_1 or S_2, but we do not need to hide both. In general, we usually have a number of alternative choices of 'disclosable' symptoms and medications lists all of which preserve the patient's privacy requirement. In Definitions 16 and 17, we define all of the disclosable symptoms lists and disclosable medications lists that preserve the patient's privacy.

Definition 16 (Privacy-preserving disclosed symptoms lists). Let $d \in D$, where $D = \{D_1, D_2, ..., D_n\}$, be the patient's diagnosed disease, $Z \subset S$, where $S = \{S_1, S_2, ..., S_m\}$, be the patient's exhibited symptoms. The privacy-preserving disclosed symptoms lists (*PDSLs*) that satisfy the patient's privacy desire to protect against inferring disease d with respect to privacy threshold t is defined as follows. PZ denotes the powerset (set of all subsets) of set Z.

$$PDSLs = \{Y : PZ \mid \text{Infer}(d \mid Y) < t\}$$

Definition 17 (Privacy-reserving disclosed medications lists). Let $d \in D$, where $D = \{D_1, D_2, ..., D_n\}$, be the patient's diagnosed disease, and $G \subset M$, where $M = \{M_1, M_2, ..., M_k\}$, be the patient's prescribed medications. The privacy-preserving disclosed medications lists (*PDMLs*) that satisfy the patient's privacy desire to protect against inferring disease d with respect to privacy threshold t is defined as follows:

$$PDMLs = \{Y : PG \mid \text{Infer}(d \mid Y) < t\}$$

As per Definitions 16 and 17 we can determine the disclosed lists for Example 4:

$$PDSLs = \{\{S_1\}, \{S_2\}\}$$

$$PDMLs = \{\{M_1, M_2\}\}$$

Optimum Disclosed Data List

Definitions 16 and 17 comply with the privacy constraint, which was our first stated aim, and allow several acceptable solutions. However, we still need to narrow down our selection criterion in order to satisfy our second motivational goal which was maximising the availability of data for use by medical practitioners. Revealing nothing at all would satisfy the patient's privacy needs, but is obviously not an acceptable solution. Therefore, we also wish to maximise the size of the disclosed lists. In Definitions 18 and 19, we define the desired disclosed symptoms lists and medications lists that satisfy both privacy and availability requirements. This is done by choosing the longest acceptable lists. (Other criteria could also be introduced based on medication relevant to the current diagnosis scenario).

Definition 18 (Disclosed symptoms list). Let *PDSLs* be the set of privacy-preserving disclosed symptom lists. A valid disclosed symptom list

(*DSL*) is then a member of the set $\{X : PDSLs \mid \forall Y : PDSLs \bullet |Y| \le |X|\}$.

Definition 19 (Disclosed medication list). Let *PDMLs* be the set of privacy-preserving disclosed medications lists. A valid disclosed medication list (*DML*) is then a member of the set $\{X : PDMLs \mid \forall Y : PDMLs \bullet |Y| \le |X|\}$.

By using Definitions 18 and 19 we conclude our final disclosed lists for our running example, telling us which symptom and medications we can reveal without creating an unacceptable risk of inference about the patient's private data:

$$DSL = \{S_1\}$$

$$DML = \{M_1, M_2\}$$

We can thus reveal that this patient exhibited symptom S_1 and take medications M_1 and M_2 with creating an unacceptable ability to infer to that he has disease D_1.

ALGORITHM

In the previous section we introduced our inference probabilistic detection and restriction approach through a series of definitions. In this section, we present two practical algorithms for inference channel elimination that use different inference evaluation criteria.

Privacy Protection Threshold

Figure 9 shows our algorithm that uses the privacy protection threshold to produce a disclosed symptom list consistent with the definitions above. The overall strategy is to perform a series of 'blocking rounds' in which we try blocking increasingly large subsets of symptoms from the patient's symptoms list until the inference level

Figure 9. Algorithm using PPT for calculating a disclosed symptoms list

Algorithm:	Disclosure process using PPT for non-inferential symptoms
INPUT	1. Protected disease d 2. Patient's exhibited symptom list SL 1. Patient's privacy protection level PPL 3. Medical Knowledge Base
OUTPUT	Disclosed symptom list DSL

METHOD	1. <u>Determine patient's privacy threshold t</u>
	
	$$t = \begin{cases} 75\%, \text{ when } PPL = Low \\ 50\%, \text{ when } PPL = Medium \\ 25\%, \text{ when } PPL = High \\ 0\%, \text{ when } PPL = Extreme \end{cases}$$
	
	2. <u>Initialise process:</u>
	  • $Subset\_Size \leftarrow 1$
	  • $Blocked\_Symptom\_List \leftarrow \Phi$
	3. <u>Start filtering process:</u>
	
	While $Infer(d \mid SL - Blocked\_Symptom\_List) \geq t$ **do**
	
	a) **For** each set $X \subseteq SL$ such that $\mid X \mid = Subset\_Size$ **do**
	
	If $Infer(d \mid X) \geq t$ **then**
	
	$Blocked\_Symptom\_List \leftarrow Blocked\_Symptom\_List \cup \{x\}$,
	where $x \in \{s : X \mid \forall u : X \bullet Infer(d \mid s) \geq Infer(d \mid u)\}$
	
	b) $Subset\_Size \leftarrow Subset\_Size + 1$
	4. $DSL \leftarrow SL - Blocked\_Symptom\_List$

for the disease of interest falls below the given threshold. The algorithm, like the definitions above, is nondeterministic when more than one acceptable solution is possible.

This algorithm starts by quantifying the privacy threshold, and then initialises two variables: Subset_Size is used to determine the size of the sets that we will consider hiding in each blocking round, and Blocked_Symptom_List is used to store those symptoms that will be blocked. Next, we iteratively apply Definition 14 to detect whether the patient's diagnosed symptoms, less the blocked symptoms list, can infer the protected disease. As long as this is the case, we increase the size of the blocked symptoms list and fill it with symptoms exhibited by the patient that allow the illegal inference channel, starting with

the symptom that has the highest inference capability and working downwards. Thus we begin by blocking as few symptoms as possible, but keep increasing the number of symptoms blocked until the inference channel's size does not exceed the given threshold t. (The algorithm is guaranteed to terminate; in the worst case, all the patient's symptoms will be blocked).

The worst-case time complexity of the algorithm is $O(2^n)$ where n is the number of the patient's exhibited symptoms (the length of list SL). Although the time complexity is exponential in n, the algorithm is nevertheless useful in practice because the number of the patient's exhibited symptoms is usually small.

The same algorithm can be used to filter the patient's prescribed medications and to produce

Figure 10. Algorithm using MEPD for calculating a disclosed symptoms list

Algorithm:	Disclosure process using MEPD for non-inferential symptoms
INPUT	1. Protected disease d 2. Patient's exhibited symptom list SL 3. Medical Knowledge Base
OUTPUT	Disclosed symptom list DSL

METHOD	1. Initialise process:
	   • $Found \leftarrow False$
	2. Start filtering process:
	   Repeat
	   i. $Z = DJS(SL) - \{d\}$
	   ii. **While** $|Z| \neq 0$ and $Found$ **do**
	      Let $z \in Z$
	      If $Infer(z \mid SL) < infer(d \mid SL)$ then
	       $Z \leftarrow Z - \{z\}$
	      Else
	       $Found \leftarrow True$
	   iii. **If not** $Found$ **then**
	      $SL \leftarrow SL - \{x\}, where$
	      $x \in \{s : SL \mid \forall u : SL \bullet infer(d \mid s) \geq infer(d \mid u)\}$
	   ix. if $|SL| = 0$ then
	      $Found \leftarrow True$
	   Until $Found$
	3. $DSL \leftarrow SL$

the disclosed medication list. The only difference is that we have to consider medications in our analytical steps instead of symptoms and to apply the appropriate definitions that are related to medication inference analysis.

Maximum Entropy Probability Distribution

Figure 10 outlines our algorithm that uses the MEPD criterion to produce a disclosed symptom list consistent with the aforementioned definitions. The approach we follow in this algorithm is to compare the inference probability of the protected disease against the inference probability of those diseases that are in relation with the investigated symptoms. If the inference probability of the protected disease is the highest among other diseases, we reduce the size of the inference channel

by removing a symptom from the investigated symptoms. We keep doing this process until the inference probability of the protected disease does not exceed that of all other diseases. The algorithm, as the former one, is nondeterministic in sense there are more than one acceptable solution.

The algorithm starts by noting no disease that has higher inference probability than the protected disease d is found. Next, an iterative process starts, and will end once we find a disease that has higher inference probability than d. Inside the iterative process, we use Definition 12 to produce the disease list Z where each disease is in relation with the investigated symptoms SL. A second comparison iterative process is initiated to compare the inference probability of d against other diseases in Z and continues while there is a disease in Z and we have not found a disease with a probability higher than d's. Inside the comparison iterative process, we process the inference probability comparison with the help of Definition 7. If we find a disease that has higher inference probability than the protected disease d, we quit the two iterative processes. Otherwise, we remove the disease that fails to dominate d's inference probability from the list Z and continue our comparison iterative process. If it appears that d's inference probability is the highest, we reduce its inference channel by removing the symptom that has the highest inference capability from the investigated symptom list SL, and we continue our iterative process by computing the new disease list Z. However, once we reach a state where a disease with a higher probability than d's is found, the symptoms in set SL are the disclosed symptom list that will not create a harmful inference channel.

The worst-case time complexity of the algorithm is $O(n * m)$ where n is the number of the patient's exhibited symptoms (the length of list SL) and m is the number of diseases in the longest disease list $DJS(SL)$ that is associated with any single symptom in SL.

In order to produce the disclosed medication list, we can employ the same algorithm by considering medications in our analytical steps instead of symptoms and to apply the medication related definitions in our inference analysis.

IMPLEMENTATION

To demonstrate the practicality of our approach we have implemented the algorithm's steps in Figure 9 as a Java application (Figure 11) for calculating both non-inferential disclosed symptoms and medications lists. Also, we have configured a MySQL database server that stores medical knowledge data. Our Java application uses the MySQL database server to retrieve the causal probability between medical data. We built a user interface panel for entering the patient's privacy settings, including his sensitive disease and his desired privacy protection level. Also, we use this interface panel to enter medical data, i.e.

Figure 11. Inference detection and restriction application

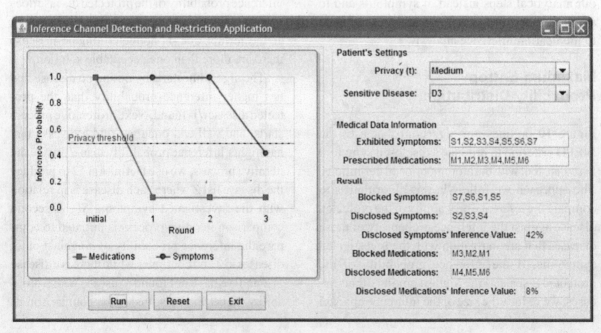

symptoms and medications, that belong to the sensitive disease.

Whereas the definitions in "Probabilistic inference channel detection and restriction" and the algorithm's steps in Figure 9 are nondeterministic and may produce more than one equally-valid result, the program instead follows a strictly sequential process in each 'blocking round' and is thus deterministic. It considers the data elements in the symptoms and medications lists in order of appearance.

The resulting disclosed and blocked medical data (symptoms and medications) are shown in the interface panel. Also, we have included a graph that shows the symptoms' and medications' inference capability for disclosing the sensitive disease at the initial state and after executing each round. This graph thus clearly shows the impact of each data filtering round on the ability to infer the sensitive disease. In the case illustrated we can see that the

inference channel is made acceptably small after 3 rounds because the ability to infer that the patient has the selected disease from *either* the exhibited symptoms or prescribed medications is below the privacy threshold.

CASE SCENARIO

As a larger example, let us revisit the healthcare scenario from the background section and use our implemented application to detect and restrict those inference channels created by the patient's exhibited symptoms and prescribed medications. Let us assume that Frank selected the 'medium' privacy protection level with regard to his protected disease D_3. Figure 12 represents the medical knowledge base that we use in our inference channel detection process. For simplicity's sake

Figure 12. Case scenario - medical knowledge base

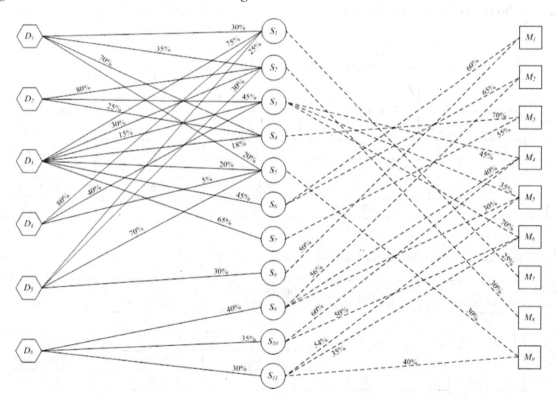

we assume that the prior probabilities for diseases $D_1,...,D_6$ are equal.

Table 1 and Table 2 show the results of our inference detection process by using our Java application that is applied to Frank's exhibited symptoms and prescribed medications. In each round the number of, blocked symptoms or medications is increased until the inference channel's size is below the threshold. As a result, the disclosed lists are:

$$DSL=\{S_2,S_3,S_4\}$$

$$DML=\{M_4,M_5,M_6\}$$

In order to hide the (blocked) symptoms and medications that allow an inference channel via Frank's Electronic Medical Record (EMR), we need to change the security classification of these medical data to make them inaccessible by medical practitioners. Changing their security classification from C (Classified) to S (Secret) will prevent their accessibility by medical practitioners who have C (Classified) security clear-

ance as per MAC's rule. To allow Tony to gain access to these protected medical data we need to change his security clearance, in Frank's profile, to S (Secret). As a consequence, the medical practitioners' – excluding Tony's – inference capability of disease D_3 is limited and cannot exceed 50%, whereas Tony is the only one who can know about this protected disease. As a result, Frank's privacy requirement is satisfied.

CONCLUSION AND FUTURE WORK

In this paper, we have presented an extended probabilistic inference channel detection approach for detecting indirect leakage of private information, and presented a mechanism to improve privacy by maximising an attacker's uncertainty by disclosing only those data items that do not create harmful inference channels. To maximize data availability we reduced the probabilistic size of an inference channel to an accepted level, rather than eliminating it entirely. We applied this approach in the healthcare domain in order to satisfy patients'

Table 1. Inference channel detection using symptoms

Round No.	Symptom list (SL)	Infer(D3|SL)	Inference channel caused by (X)	Infer(D3|X)	Blocked list
1	$\{S_1,S_2,S_3,S_4,S_5,S_6,S_7\}$	100%	$\{S_6\}$	100%	$\{S_6\}$
	$\{S_1,S_2,S_3,S_4,S_5,S_7\}$	100%	$\{S_7\}$	100%	$\{S_6,S_7\}$
2	$\{S_1,S_2,S_3,S_4,S_5\}$	100%	$\{S_1,S_2\}$	53%	$\{S_6,S_7,S_1\}$
3	$\{S_2,S_3,S_4,S_5\}$	100%	$\{S_3,S_4,S_5\}$	100%	$\{S_6,S_7,S_1,S_5\}$
4	$\{S_2,S_3,S_4\}$	42%	Nil	Nil	$\{S_6,S_7,S_1,S_5\}$

Table 2. Inference channel detection using medications

Round No.	Medication list (ML)	Infer(D3|ML)	Inference channel caused by (X)	Infer(D3|X)	Blocked list
1	$\{M_1,M_2,M_3,M_4,M_5,M_6\}$	100%	$\{M_1\}$	55%	$\{M_1\}$
			$\{M_2\}$	54%	$\{M_1,M_2\}$
			$\{M_3\}$	54%	$\{M_1,M_2,M_3\}$
3	$\{M_4,M_5,M_6\}$	8%	Nil	Nil	$\{M_1,M_2,M_3\}$

growing demand for privacy of electronic data which still giving medical practitioners maximum access to other data. We assumed an Electronic Medical Record (EMR) was the data source for our inference control solution, and that a patient selects a 'protected' disease. Our probabilistic approach then used a medical knowledge base to identify inference channels by using two individual or collaborative criteria, and filter out data items in order to satisfy the patient's privacy protection requirement, while maintaining data availability by hiding the minimum number of data items.

However, the solution is limited to detecting inference channels existing within an individual medical event only, under the assumption that diseases act independently of each other. Therefore, we intend to do a further extension to accommodate dependency relationships between diseases, and between medical events (EMR records).

REFERENCES

An, X., Jutla, D., & Cercone, N. (2006). Auditing and Inference Control for Privacy Preservation in Uncertain Environments. In *Smart Sensing and Context* (LNCS 4272, pp. 159-173).

Bender, E. A. (1996). Bayesian Networks. In *Mathematical Methods in Artificial Intelligence* (pp. 299–327). Washington, DC: IEEE Computer Society Press.

Bertino, E., & Sandhu, R. (2005). Database Security - Concepts, Approaches, and Challenges. *IEEE Transactions on Dependable and Secure Computing, 2*(1), 2–19. doi:10.1109/TDSC.2005.9

Biskup, J., & Bonatti, P. (2001). Lying Versus Refusal for Known Potential Secrets. *Data & Knowledge Engineering, 38*(2), 199–222. doi:10.1016/S0169-023X(01)00024-6

Biskup, J., & Bonatti, P. (2004). Controlled Query Evaluation for Known Policies by Combining Lying and Refusal. *Annals of Mathematics and Artificial Intelligence, 40*(1-2), 37–62. doi:10.1023/A:1026106029043

Biskup, J., & Bonatti, P. A. (2002). Confidentiality Policies and Their Enforcement for Controlled Query Evaluation, In *Proceedings of the 7th European Symposium on Research in Computer Security* (LNCS 2502, pp. 39-54).

Biskup, J., & Bonatti, P. A. (2007). Controlled Query Evaluation with Open Queries for a Decidable Relational Submodel. *Annals of Mathematics and Artificial Intelligence, 50*(1-2), 39–77. doi:10.1007/s10472-007-9070-5

Brodsky, A., Farkas, C., & Jajodia, S. (2000). Secure Databases: Constraints, Inference Channels, and Monitoring Disclosures. *IEEE Transactions on Knowledge and Data Engineering, 12*(6), 900–919. doi:10.1109/69.895801

Buczkowski, L. J. (1990). Database Inference Controller. In Spooner, D. L., & Landwehr, C. E. (Eds.), *Database Security, III: Status and Prospects* (pp. 311–322). Amsterdam, The Netherlands: Elsevier Science.

Chaing, L. W., & Ira, S. M. (2001). An Integrated Framework for Database Privacy Protection. In *Proceedings of the IFIP TC11/ WG11.3 Fourteenth Annual Working Conference on Database Security: Data and Application Security, Development and Directions* (pp. 161-172). Deventer, The Netherlands: Kluwer, B.V.

Chhanabhai, P., & Holt, A. (2007). Consumers are ready to accept the transition to online and electronic records if the they can be assured of the security measures. *Medscape General Medicine, 9*(1).

Farkas, C., & Jajodia, S. (2002). The Inference Problem: A Survey. *SIGKDD Explorations Newsletter, 4*(2), 6–11. doi:10.1145/772862.772864

Garets, D., & Davis, M. (2006). *Electronic Medical Record vs. Electronic Health Record: Yes, There is a Difference*. Gartner.

Goggin, L. S., Eikelbom, R. H., & Atlas, M. D. (2007). Clinical decision support systems and computer aided diagnosis in otology. *Otolaryngology - Head and Neck Surgery, 136*(4S), S21–S26. doi:10.1016/j.otohns.2007.01.028

Griffiths, T. L., & Yuille, A. L. (2006). *Technical Introduction: A Primer on Probabilistic Inference*. Los Angeles: Department of Statistics, UCLA.

Hale, J., & Shenoi, S. (1997). Catalytic Inference Analysis: Detecting Inference Threats due to Knowledge Discovery. In *Proceedings of the IEEE Symposium on Security and Privacy* (pp. 188-199).

Heckerman, D. (1990). A Tractable Inference Algorithm for Diagnosing Multiple Diseases. In *Proceedings of the Fifth annual Conference on Uncertainty in Artificial Intelligence* (pp. 163-172).

Pearl, J. (2003). Statistics and Causal Inference: A Review. *Test, 12*(2), 281–345. doi:10.1007/BF02595718

Pearl, J. (2006). *Two journeys into human reasoning*. Los Angeles: UCLA Cognitive systems Laboratory.

Pearl, J., & Russell, S. (2003). Bayesian Networks. In Arbib, M. A. (Ed.), *Handbook of Brain Theory and Neural Networks* (pp. 157–160). Cambridge, MA: MIT Press.

Sicherman, G. L., Jonge, W. D., & de Riet, R. P. V. (1983). Answering queries without revealing secrets. *ACM Transactions on Database Systems, 8*(1), 41–59. doi:10.1145/319830.319833

Stephenson, T. A. (2000). *An Introduction to Bayesian Networks Theory and Usage*. IDIAP.

Su, T., & Ozsoyoglu, G. (1991). Controlling FD and MVD Inferences in Multilevel Relational Database Systems. *IEEE Transactions on Knowledge and Data Engineering, 3*(4), 474–485. doi:10.1109/69.109108

Sweeney, L. (2002). Achieving k-Anonymity Privacy Protection Using Generalization and Suppression. *International Journal of Uncertainty. Fuzziness and Knowledge-Based Systems, 10*(5), 571–588. doi:10.1142/S021848850200165X

This work was previously published in International Journal of Information Security and Privacy, Volume 4, Issue 3, edited by Hamid Nemati, pp. 35-59, copyright 2010 by IGI Publishing (an imprint of IGI Global).

Compilation of References

(1998). Designing a Social Protocol: Lessons Learned from the Platform for Privacy Preferences Project. In Cranor, L. F., & Reagle, J. (Eds.), *Telephony, the Internet, and the Media*. Mahwah, NJ: Lawrence Erlbaum Associates.

Ackoff, R. L. (1974). *Redesigning the Future*. New York: Wiley-Interscience.

AdmitOne Security Inc. (2008). *Home*. Retrieved from http://www.admitonesecurity.com/

Agre, P., & Rotenberg, M. (1998). *Technology and Privacy: The New Landscape*. Boston: MIT Press.

ALEXA. (2008). *Top 100 most visited websites*. Retrieved from http://www.alexa.com/ site/ds/top_sites?ts_mode=lang&lang=en

Alterman, A. (2003). A piece of yourself: Ethical issues in biometric identification. *Ethics and Information Technology*, 5(3), 139–150. doi:10.1023/B:ETIN.0000006918.22060.1f

Altiris. (2005). *System Security: A Comprehensive Approach*. Retrieved from http://wp.bitpipe.com/resource/org_950672243_424/SystemSecurityACompApproach_edp.pdf

An, X., Jutla, D., & Cercone, N. (2006). Auditing and Inference Control for Privacy Preservation in Uncertain Environments. In *Smart Sensing and Context* (LNCS 4272, pp. 159-173).

Anderson, J., & Rachamadugu, V. (2008). *Managing Security and Privacy Integration across Enterprise Business Process and Infrastructure*. Paper presented at the IEEE International Conference on Services Computing.

Anderson, R., & Petitcolas, F. (1998). On the Limits of Steganography. *IEEE Journal on Selected Areas in Communications*, 16(4), 474–481. doi:10.1109/49.668971

Anonymous. (2008, July 7). ICO: UK privacy watchdog spearheads debate on the future of European Privacy Law. *M2 Presswire*.

Anonymous,. (2009a). Axis Technology, LLC; Axis Technology Unveils Breakthrough Data Masking Platform to Help Companies Ensure Compliance with New Federal and State Privacy Standards. *Managed Care Weekly Digest*,32.

Anonymous,. (2009b). EMC Corporation; Healthcare Organizations Deploy RSA Solutions to Improve Privacy and Efficiency of Patient Care. *Managed Care Weekly Digest*, 50.

Anonymous. (2009c). *Indian Information Technology Act, 2000 in Doldrums*. Retrieved from http://www.webnewswire.com/node/450791

Anonymous. (2009d, July 10). Understanding Ops Key To Effective Data Privacy. *Operations Management*.

Anton, A. I., Earp, J. B., Qingfeng, H., Stufflebeam, W., Bolchini, D., & Jensen, C. (2004). Financial privacy policies and the need for standardization. *IEEE Security & Privacy*, 2(2), 36–45. doi:10.1109/MSECP.2004.1281243

Armstrong, J. S., & Overton, T. S. (1977). Estimating nonresponse bias in mail surveys. *Journal of Marketing Research*, XIV, 396–402. doi:10.2307/3150783

Ashworth, L., & Free, C. (2006). Marketing Dataveillance and Digital Privacy: Using Theories of Justice to Understand Consumers' Online Privacy Concerns. *Journal of Business Ethics*, 67(2), 107–123. doi:10.1007/s10551-006-9007-7

ASIS. (2003). *General Security Risk Assessment Guideline.*

Aspert, N., Drelie, E., Maret, Y., & Ebrahimi, T. (2002). Steganography for Three-Dimensional Polygonal Meshes. In *Proceedings of SPIE, 47ᵗʰ Annual Meeting 2002* (pp. 705-708).

Aston University. (2001). *Data Protection Policy.* Retrieved November 7, 2010, from http://www1.aston.ac.uk/EasySiteWeb/GatewayLink.aspx?alId=6607

Auernheimer, B., & Tsai, M. J. (2005). Biometric authentication for web-based course examinations. In *Proceedings of the 38th Annual Hawaii International Conference on System Science (HICSS'05)* (pp. 294-300).

Australia. (2004). *AS/NZS 4360: 2004 Risk Management.*

Azin-Khan, R., Nicholson, J., Liotta, A., & Hodgkinson, D. (2008, May). New Spanish Regulations Tighten Up Data Protection Requirements. *Privacy & Data Security Law Journal.*

Bamba, B., Liu, L., Pesti, P., & Wang, T. (2008). Supporting anonymous location queries in mobile environments with privacygrid. In *Proceeedings of WWW 2008* (pp. 237-246).

Bandura, A. (1982). Self-efficacy mechanism in human agency. *The American Psychologist, 37,* 122–147. doi:10.1037/0003-066X.37.2.122

Bandura, A. (1986). *Social foundation of thought and action: A social cognitive theory.* Upper Saddle River, NJ: Prentice-Hall.

Barbará, D., Couto, J., Jajodia, S., & Wu, N. (2001). ADAM: A testbed for exploring the use of data mining in intrusion detection. *SIGMOD Record, 30*(4), 15–24.

Barnes, M. E. (2006). Falling Short of the Mark: The United States Response to the European Union's Data Privacy Directive. *Northwestern Journal of International Law & Business, 27*(1), 171.

Baskerville, R. (1988). *Designing Information Systems Security.* New York: John Wiley & Sons.

Baskerville, R. (1993). Information Systems Security Design Methods: Implications for Information System Development. *ACM Computing Surveys, 25*(4), 375–414. doi:10.1145/162124.162127

Bauer, D., Blough, D. M., et al. (2008). Minimum Information disclosure with Efficiently Verifiable Credentials. In *Proceedings of the 4th Workshop on Digital Identity Management,* Alexandria, VA.

BBB. (2003). *A Review of Federal and State Privacy Laws.* Retrieved from http://www.bbbonline.org/UnderstandingPrivacy/library/fed_statePrivLaws.pdf

Bender, S. S., & Postley, H. J. (2007). *Key sequence rhythm recognition system and method* (U.S. Patent No. 7,206,938).

Bender, E. A. (1996). Bayesian Networks. In *Mathematical Methods in Artificial Intelligence* (pp. 299–327). Washington, DC: IEEE Computer Society Press.

Bennett, S., & Paez, M. (2009). *Protecting Social Security Numbers: Federal Legislation in Sight.* Retrieved from http://www.jonesday.com/pubs/pubs_detail.aspx?pubID=S5920

Beresford, A., & Stajano, F. (2003). Location Privacy in Pervasive Computing. *IEEE Pervasive Computing / IEEE Computer Society [and] IEEE Communications Society,* 47–55.

Bergadano, F., Gunetti, D., & Picardi, C. (2002). User authentication through keystroke dynamics. *ACM Transactions on Information and System Security, 5*(4), 367–397. doi:10.1145/581271.581272

Berge, C. (1962). *Theory of Graphs and its Application.* London: Methuen Press.

Bertino, E. (2002). Access Control for XML Documents. *Data & Knowledge Engineering, 43*(3).

Bertino, E. (2004). Selective and Authentic Third Party Distribution of XML Documents. *IEEE Transactions on Knowledge and Data Engineering, 16*(10). doi:10.1109/TKDE.2004.63

Bertino, E., Carminati, B., Ferrari, E., Thuraisingham, B. M., & Gupta, A. (2004). Selective and Authentic Third-Party Distribution of XML Documents. *IEEE Transactions on Knowledge and Data Engineering, 16*(10), 1263–1278. doi:10.1109/TKDE.2004.63

Bertino, E., & Ferrari, E. (2004). Trust-X: A Peer-to-Peer Framework for Trust Establishment. *IEEE Transactions on Knowledge and Data Engineering, 16*(7), 827–842. doi:10.1109/TKDE.2004.1318565

Bertino, E., & Sandhu, R. (2005). Database Security - Concepts, Approaches, and Challenges. *IEEE Transactions on Dependable and Secure Computing, 2*(1), 2–19. doi:10.1109/TDSC.2005.9

Bhargav-Spantzel, A., Squicciarini, A., et al. (2007). Trust Negotiation in Identity Management. *IEEE Security & Privacy,* 55-63.

Bhargav-Spantzel, A., & Squicciarini, A. C. (2006). Establishing and Protecting Digital Identity in Federation Systems. *Journal of Computer Security, 14*(3), 269–300.

BioChec. (2008). *Home.* Retrieved from http://www.biochec.com/

Bishop, M. (2003). *Computer Security.* Reading, MA: Addison Wesley.

Biskup, J., & Bonatti, P. A. (2002). Confidentiality Policies and Their Enforcement for Controlled Query Evaluation, In *Proceedings of the 7th European Symposium on Research in Computer Security* (LNCS 2502, pp. 39-54).

Biskup, J., & Bonatti, P. (2001). Lying Versus Refusal for Known Potential Secrets. *Data & Knowledge Engineering, 38*(2), 199–222. doi:10.1016/S0169-023X(01)00024-6

Biskup, J., & Bonatti, P. (2004). Controlled Query Evaluation for Known Policies by Combining Lying and Refusal. *Annals of Mathematics and Artificial Intelligence, 40*(1-2), 37–62. doi:10.1023/A:1026106029043

Biskup, J., & Bonatti, P. A. (2007). Controlled Query Evaluation with Open Queries for a Decidable Relational Submodel. *Annals of Mathematics and Artificial Intelligence, 50*(1-2), 39–77. doi:10.1007/s10472-007-9070-5

Bolle, R., Connell, J., Pankanti, S., Ratha, N., & Senior, A. (2004). *Guide to biometrics.* New York: Springer.

Bollobas, B. (1983). Almost all regular graphs are Hamiltonian. *European Journal of Combinatorics, 4,* 97–106.

Bonatti, P., & Samarati, P. (2000). Regulating service access and information release on the Web. In *Proceedings of the 7th ACM Conference on Computer and Communications Security,* Athens, Greece.

Bondy, J. A., & Murty, U. S. R. (1976). *Graph Theory with Applications.* Amsterdam, The Netherlands: Elsevier.

Boneh, D., Crescenzo, G., Ostrovsky, G., & Persiano, G. (2004). Public-key Encryption with Keyword Search. In *Proceedings of the European Conference on Cryptology (EUROCRYPT).*

Boneh, D., Kushilevitz, E., Ostrovsky, R , & Skeith, W. (2007). *Public Key Encryption that Allows PIR Queries* (Cryptology ePrint Archive, Rep. No. 2007/073). Retrieved from http://eprint.iacr.org/

Bormuth, J. R. (1966). Readability: A new approach. *Reading Research Quarterly, 1,* 79–132. doi:10.2307/747021

Boyens, C., & Fischmann, M. (2003). Profiting from Untrusted Parties in Web-Based Applications. In *Proceedings of the 4th International Conference on Electronic Commerce and Web Technologies (EC-Web).*

Boyens, C., & Günther, O. (2002). Trust Is not Enough: Privacy and Security in ASP and Web Service Environments. In *Proceedings of the Sixth East-European Conference on Advances in Databases and Information Systems.*

Braithwaite, W. R. (2005). *HIPPA Administrative Simplification: Practical Privacy and Security.* Retrieved from http://ehr.medigent.com/assets/collaborate/2005/04/02/eHI Privacy&Security Tutorial a.ppt

Brinkhoff, T. (2002). A framework for generating network-based moving objects. *GeoInformatica, 6*(2), 153–180. doi:10.1023/A:1015231126594

Brodie, C., Karat, C., & Karat, J. (2005). Usable Security and Privacy: A Case Study of Developing Privacy Management Tools. In *Proceedings of the Symposium on Usable Privacy and Security (SOUPS '05).* New York: ACM Digital Library.

Brodsky, A., Farkas, C., & Jajodia, S. (2000). Secure Databases: Constraints, Inference Channels, and Monitoring Disclosures. *IEEE Transactions on Knowledge and Data Engineering, 12*(6), 900–919. doi:10.1109/69.895801

Brostoff, S., & Sasse, M. A. (2000). Are passfaces more usable than passwords? A field trial investigation. In McDonald, S., Waern, Y., & Cockton, G. (Eds.), *People and Computers XIV - Usability or Else! Proceedings of HCI2000* (pp. 405–424). Sunderland, UK: Springer.

Brown, M., & Rogers, S. J. (1993). User identification via keystroke characteristics of typed names using neural networks. *International Journal of Man-Machine Studies, 39*(6), 999–1014. doi:10.1006/imms.1993.1092

BSI. (2002). *Information Security Management—Part 2: Specification for Information Security Management Systems*. Retrieved from http://www.isaca-london.org/presentations/bs7799part2.pdf

Buczkowski, L. J. (1990). Database Inference Controller. In Spooner, D. L., & Landwehr, C. E. (Eds.), *Database Security, III: Status and Prospects* (pp. 311–322). Amsterdam, The Netherlands: Elsevier Science.

Bump, C. (2005). *Data Security: Translating Legal Requirements into Internal Policies*. Retrieved from http://www.privacyassociation.org/docs/sum05/10-3D-Bump.pdf

Bunnell, J., Podd, J., Henderson, R., Napier, R., & Kennedy-Moffat, J. (1997). Cognitive, associative and conventional passwords: Recall and guessing rates. *Computers & Security, 16*(7), 629–641. doi:10.1016/S0167-4048(97)00008-4

Camenisch, J., & Herreweghen, E. V. (2002). Design and Implementation of idemix Anonymous Credential System. In *Proceedings of the 9th ACM Conference on Computer and Communications Security*, Washington, DC.

Campbell, R., Al-Muhtadi, J., et al. (2002). *Towards Security and Privacy for Pervasive Computing*. Paper presented at the International Symposium on Software Security, Tokyo.

Caralli, R., & Wilson, W. (2003). *The Challenges of Security Management*. Retrieved from http://www.cert.org/archive/pdf/ESMchallenges.pdf

Carnaghan, C. (2006). Business Process Modeling Approaches in the Context of Process Level Audit Risk Assessment: an Analysis and Comparison. *International Journal of Accounting Information Systems*, 170–204. doi:10.1016/j.accinf.2005.10.005

Carstens, D. S., McCauley-Bell, P. R., Malone, L. C., & DeMara, R. F. (2004). Evaluation of the human impact of password authentication practices on information security. *Information Science Journal, 7*(1), 67–85.

Cavusoglu, H., Raghunathan, S., & Cavusoglu, H. (2009). Configuration of and interaction between information security technologies: The case of firewalls and intrusion detection systems. *Information Systems Research, 20*(2), 198–217. doi:10.1287/isre.1080.0180

Cegielski, C. G. (2008). Toward the Development of an Interdisciplinary Information Assurance Curriculum: Knowledge Domains and Skill Sets Required of Information Assurance Professionals. *Decision Sciences Journal of Innovative Education, 6*(1), 29–49. doi:10.1111/j.1540-4609.2007.00156.x

Centers for Medicare & Medicaid Services (CMS). (2002). *CMS Information Security Risk Assessment (RA) Methodology-Version #1.1*. Baltimore, MD: Department of Health & Human Services.

Ceri, S., & Pelagetti, G. (1984). *Distributed database principles and systems*. New York: McGraw Hill.

Cha, S., & Srihari, S. N. (2000). Writer Identification: Statistical Analysis and Dichotomizer. In *Advances in Pattern Recognition - Proceedings of SPR and SSPR 2000* (LNCS 1876, pp. 123-132).

Chaing, L. W., & Ira, S. M. (2001). An Integrated Framework for Database Privacy Protection. In *Proceedings of the IFIP TC11/ WG11.3 Fourteenth Annual Working Conference on Database Security: Data and Application Security, Development and Directions* (pp. 161-172). Deventer, The Netherlands: Kluwer, B.V.

Chall, J. S. (1988). The beginning years. In Zakaluk, B. L., & Samuels, S. J. (Eds.), *Readability: Its past, present, and future*. Newark, DE: International Reading Association.

Chang, Y., & Mitzenmacher, M. (2005). Privacy Preserving Keyword Searches on Remote Encrypted Data. In *Proceedings of the Applied Cryptography and Network Security, Third International Conference*, New York (pp. 442-455).

Chappell, D. (2006). *Introducing Windows CardSpace*. Chappell & Associates.

Chari, S. N., & Cheng, P. C. (2003). BlueBoX: A Policy-Driven, Host-Based Intrusion Detection System. *ACM Transactions on Information and System Security, 6*(2), 173–200. doi:10.1145/762476.762477

Chaturvedi, A., Bhatkar, E., & Sekar, R. (2006). Improving Attack Detection in Host-Based IDS by Learning Properties of System Call Arguments. In *Proceedings of the IEEE Symposium on Security and Privacy.*

Chaum, D. (1981). Untraceable electronic mail, return addresses, and digital pseudonyms. *Communications of the ACM, 24*(2), 84–90. doi:10.1145/358549.358563

Chaum, D. (1985). Security Without Identification: Transaction Systems to Make Big Brother Obsolete. *Communications of the ACM, 28*(10). doi:10.1145/4372.4373

Chen, Y., Hwang, K., & Kwok, Y.-K. (2005). *Collaborative Defense against Periodic. Shrew DDoS Attacks in Frequency Domain.* ACM Transactions on Information and System Security.

Chhanabhai, P., & Holt, A. (2007). Consumers are ready to accept the transition to online and electronic records if the they can be assured of the security measures. *Medscape General Medicine, 9*(1).

Choi, S.-S., Yoon, S., Cha, S.-H., & Tappert, C. C. (2004). Use of histogram distances in iris authentication. In *Image Analysis and Recognition – Proceedings of MSCE-MLMTA*, Las Vegas, NV (pp. 1118-1124). New York: Springer.

Chor, B., & Gilboa, N. (1997). Computationally private information retrieval (extended abstract). In *STOC '97: Proceedings of the Twenty-Ninth Annual ACM Symposium on Theory of Computing* (pp. 304-313). New York: ACM Press.

Chor, B., Goldreich, O., Kushilevitz, E., & Sudan, M. (1995). Private Information Retrieval. In *Proceedings of the IEEE Symposium on Foundations of Computer Science.*

Chow, C.-Y., & Mokbel, M. F. (2007). Enabling private continuous queries for revealed user locations. In. *Proceedings of SSTD, 2007,* 258–275.

Clarke, R. (2000). *Beyond the OECD Guidelines: Privacy Protection for the 21st Century.* Retrieved November 8, 2010, from http://www.rogerclarke.com/DV/PP21C.html

Clarkson, K., Miller, R., Gaylord, J., & Cross, F. (2009). *Business Law Text and Cases, Legal, Ethical, Global, and E-commerce Environment* (11th ed.). Mason, OH: South-Western, Cengage Learning.

Clement, A., Ley, D., Costantino, T., Kurtz, D., & Tissenbaum, M. (2008). The PIPWatch Toolbar: Combining PIPEDA, PETs and market forces through social navigation to enhance privacy protection and compliance. In *Proceedings of the 2008 IEEE International Symposium on Technology and Society.*

Clifford Chance. (2007). *Theft of Laptop Results in 980, 000 Fine.* Retrieved from http.//www.clifford chance.com/expertise/Publications/details.aspx?FilterName=@URL&contentitemid=11704

Clifton, C., Kantarcioglu, M., & Vaidya, J. (2002). *Defining Privacy for Data Mining.* Retrieved from http://cimic.rutgers.edu/~jsvaidya/pub-papers/ngdm-privacy.pdf

Cline, J. (2009). What's behind the rash of university data breaches? *Computerworld Security.* Retrieved from http://www.computerworld.com/s/article/9129036/What's_behind_the_rash_of_university_data_breaches

Cole, E. (2003). *Hiding in Plain Sight: Steganography and the Art of Covert Communication.* New York: Wiley Publishing.

Coleman, E. B., & Blumenfeld, P. J. (1963). Cloze scores of nominalization and their grammatical transformations using active verbs. *Psychological Reports, 13,* 651–654.

Cox, I. J., & Matthew, L. Miller, M. L., Bloom, J. A., Fridrich, J., & Kalkar, T. (2007). Digital Watermarking and Steganography. San Francisco: Morgan Kaufmann Publishers.

Cox, I. J., Kalkar, T., Pakura, G., & Scheel, M. (2005). Information Transmission and Steganography. In *Digital Watermarking* (LNCS 3710, pp. 15-29).

Cranor, L., Dobbs, B., et al. (2006). *The Platform for Privacy Preferences 1.1 (P3P1.1) Specification.* W3C.

Cresson-Wood, C. (2004). Why Information Security is Now Multi-Disciplinary, Multi-Departmental, and Multi-Organizational in Nature. *Computer Fraud & Security, 1,* 16–17. doi:10.1016/S1361-3723(04)00019-3

Culnan, M. (2000). Protecting Privacy Online: Is Self-Regulation Working? *Journal of Public Policy & Marketing, 19*(1), 20–26. doi:10.1509/jppm.19.1.20.16944

Curtin, M., Tappert, C., Villani, M., Ngo, G., Simone, J., St. Fort, H., et al. (2006). Keystroke biometric recognition on long-text input: A feasibility study. In *Proceedings of the International MultiConference of Engineers & Computer Scientists (IMECS)*, Hong Kong.

Cybertrust. (2005). *Adopting BS 7799-2:2002—practical, Achievable Security.* Retrieved from http://www.Cybertrust.com.

Dalal, P. (2009). *Data Protection Regulations in India.* Retrieved from http://www.legalnewsandviews.blogspot.com/2009/04/data-protection-regulations-in-india-html

Dale, E., & Chall, J. S. (1949). The concept of readability. *Elementary English*, 26-23.

Damiani, E., De Capitani Vimercati, S., Jajodia, S., Paraboschi, S., & Samarati, P. (2003). Balancing Confidentiality and Efficiency in Untrusted Relational DBMSs. In *CCS '03: Proceedings of the 10th ACM Conference on Computer and Communications Security*. New York: ACM Press.

Dash, J. (2001). Schools Push Soft Skills for Info Security Majors. *Computerworld, 35*(6), 24.

Davies, J. (2008). Does Europe need a single law on what staff can do in cyberspace? *People Management, 14*(8).

Davis, F. D. (1989). Perceived Usefulness, Perceived Ease of Use, and User Acceptance of Information Technology. *Management Information Systems Quarterly, 13*(3), 20. doi:10.2307/249008

Davison, A. (1984). Readability formulas and comprehension. In *Comprehension instruction: Perspectives and suggestions*. New York: Longman.

Deane, F., Barrelle, K., Henderson, R., & Mahar, D. (1995). Perceived acceptability of biometric security systems. *Computers & Security, 14*(3), 225–231. doi:10.1016/0167-4048(95)00005-S

Deflem, M., & Shutt, J. E. (2008). Law enforcement and computer security threats and measures. In Bidgoli, H. (Ed.), *Global perspectives in information security: legal, social, and international issues*. New York: Wiley.

DeMarco, T. (1979). *Structured Analysis and System Specification*. New York: Yourdon Press.

DeVries, B. W., Gupta, G., Hamlen, K. W., Moore, S., & Sridhar, M. (2009). ActionScript Bytecode Verification with Co-Logic Programming. In *Proceedings of the ACM SIGPLAN Workshop on Programming Languages and Analysis for Security (PLAS)*.

Dhillon, G., & Backhouse, J. (2001). Current Directions in IS Security Research: towards socio-organizational perspectives. *Information Systems Journal, 11*(2), 127–153. doi:10.1046/j.1365-2575.2001.00099.x

Domingo-Ferrer, J. (2002). A Provably Secure Additive and Multiplicative Privacy Homomorphism. In *Proceedings of the Information Security, 5th International Conference*.

Dowling, D. (2007). *European Union Data Protection Law and US-Based Multinational Banks: A Compliance Primer*. New York: White & Case LLP. Retrieved from http://www.whitecase.com/publications_09012007_1/

Du, Y., & Chang, C.-I. (2007). The problems of using ROC curve as the sole criterion in positive biometrics identification. In *Proceedings of SPIE 6579*.

DuBois, F. (2004). Globalization Risks and Information Management. *Journal of Global Information Management, 10*(1), 1–5.

Duda, R. O., Hart, P. E., & Stork, D. G. (2001). *Pattern Classification*. New York: Wiley.

Dunn, G., & Everitt, B. S. (2004). *An introduction to mathematical taxonomy*. Mineola, NY: Dover.

Dyson, E. (2006). Privacy Protection: Time to Think and Act Locally and Globally. *First Monday*.

Earp, J., Anton, A., & Jarvinen, O. (2002). *A Social, Technical, and Legal Framework for Privacy Management and Policies*. Paper presented at the Americas Conference on Information Systems.

Egenhofer, M., & Franzosa, R. (1991). Point-set topological spatial relations. *International Journal of Geographical Information Systems, 5*(2), 161–174. doi:10.1080/02693799108927841

Eloff, J., & Eloff, M. (2003). Information Security Management—A New Paradigm. In. *Proceedings of SAICSIT, 2003*, 130–136.

EPIC. (n.d.). *EPIC Online Guide to Practical Privacy Tools.* Retrieved November 7, 2010, from http://epic.org/privacy/tools.html

Erlich, Z., & Zviran, M. (2009). Authentication methods for computer systems security. In Khosrow-Pour, M. (Ed.), *Encyclopedia of information science and technology* (2nd ed., *Vol. 1*, pp. 288–293). Hershey, PA: Information Science Reference.

European Union. (1995). *Directive 95/46/EC of the European Parliament.* Retrieved from http:europa.eu.int/comm/internal_market/privacy/index_en.htm

Eysenbach, G., Powell, J., Kuss, O., & Sa, E. R. (2002). Empirical studies assessing the quality of health information for consumers on the World Wide Web: a systematic review. *Journal of Americican Medcial Association, 287*(20), 2691–2700. doi:10.1001/jama.287.20.2691

Farkas, C., & Jajodia, S. (2002). The Inference Problem: A Survey. *SIGKDD Explorations Newsletter, 4*(2), 6–11. doi:10.1145/772862.772864

Federal Trade Commission. (1998). *Privacy online: A report to congress, June 98.* Retrieved from http://www.ftc.gov/reports/privacy3/

Federal Trade Commission. (2008a). *Children Online Privacy Act (COPA).* Retrieved from http://www.ftc.gov/ogc/coppa1.htm

Federal Trade Commission. (2008b). *The Gramm-Leach Bliley Act.* Retrieved from http://www.ftc.gov/privacy/privacyinitiatives/glbact.html

Fenner, T. I., & Frieze, A. M. (1983). On the Existence of Hamiltonian Cycles in a Class of Random Graphs. *Discrete Mathematics, 45*, 301–305. doi:10.1016/0012-365X(83)90046-8

Ferg, B., Fitzpatrick, B., et al. (2007). *OpenID Authentication 2.0.*

Ferrell, K. (2004, September 22). Cybercrime Spins Out Of Control. *TechWeb.com.*

Finkel, R. A., & Bentley, J. L. (1974). Quad trees: A data structure for retrieval on composite keys. *Acta Informatica, 4*, 1–9. doi:10.1007/BF00288933

Fischmann, M., & Günther, O. (2003). Privacy Tradeoffs in Database Service Architectures. In *Proceedings of the First ACM Workshop on Business Driven Security Engineering (BIZSEC).*

Fisher, R. P. (1984). *Information Systems Security.* Englewood Cliffs, NJ: Prentice-Hall.

FISMA. (2006). *FY2006 Report to Congress on Implementation of the Federal Information Security Management Act of 2002.* Retrieved November 7, 2010, from http://www.whitehouse.gov/omb/inforeg/reports/2006_fisma_report.pdf

Flesch, R. (1974). *The art of readable writing.* New York: Harper.

Frank, R. (1974). A Search Procedure for Hamilton Paths and Circuits. *Journal of the ACM, 21*(4).

Freshfields Bruckhaus Deringer. (2008). *Data privacy protection across Asia.* Retrieved from http://www.freshfields.com/practices/intellectual/publications/?year=2008

Friedman, J. H. (2001). Greedy function approximation: a gradient boosting machine. *Annals of Statistics, 29*(5), 1189–1232. doi:10.1214/aos/1013203451

Funk, J. A., & Toher, J. P. (2004). Big Brother Is Watching: A Survey of the Regulatory Landscape Impacting Outsourcing Transactions. *Law Journal Newsletters, 2*(3).

Furnell, S. M., Dowland, P. S., Illingworth, H. M., & Reynolds, P. L. (2000). Authentication and supervision: A survey of user attitudes. *Computers & Security, 19*(6), 529–539. doi:10.1016/S0167-4048(00)06027-2

Furnell, S. M., Papadopoulos, I., & Dowland, P. S. (2004). A long-term trial of alternative user authentication technologies. *Information Management & Computer Security, 12*(2), 178–190. doi:10.1108/09685220410530816

Gaines, H. F. (1956). *Cryptanalysis: A study of ciphers and their solution.* Mineola, NY: Dover.

Gamma. (2006). *History of 27000.* Retrieved from http://www.gammassl.co.uk/bs7799/history.html

Gamma. (2006). *IS 17799*. Retrieved from http://www.gammassl.co.uk/bs7799/

GAO. (1999). *Information Security Risk Assessment—Practices of Leading s. Accounting and Information Management Division*. Washington, DC: United States General Accounting Office.

Garets, D., & Davis, M. (2006). *Electronic Medical Record vs. Electronic Health Record: Yes, There is a Difference*. Gartner.

Gartner. (2008). *2008 Data Breaches and Financial Crimes Scare Consumers Away*. Retrieved November 7, 2010, from http://www.internetretailing.net/news/data-theft-concerns-beginning-to-hit-internet-shopping-volumes

Gates, F., Natkovich, O., Chopra, S., Kamath, S. M., Kamath, P., Narayanamuthry, S. M., et al. (2009). Building a High-Level Dataflow System on top of Map-Reduce: The Pig Experience. In *Proceedings of the Thirty-Fifth International Conference on Very Large Data Bases (VLDB) (Industrial, Applications and Experience Track)*, Lyon, France.

Gazaleh, M.(2008). Online Trust and Perceived Utility for Consumers of Web Privacy Statements: UK Overview – WBS.

Gedik, B., & Liu, L. (2005). Location privacy in mobile systems: A personalized anonymization model. In. *Proceedings of ICDCS, 2005*, 620–629.

Gellman, R.(2002). Privacy, Consumers, and Costs: How The Lack of Privacy Costs Consumers and Why Business Studies of Privacy Costs are Biased and Incomplete.

Gerber, M., & von Solms, R. (2001). From Risk Analysis to Security Requirements. *Computers & Security, 20*(7), 577–584. doi:10.1016/S0167-4048(01)00706-4

Gerber, M., & von Solms, R. (2008). Information security requirements – Interpreting the legal aspects. *Computers & Security, 27*(5-6), 124–135. doi:10.1016/j.cose.2008.07.009

Ghemawat, P. (2001). *Distance still matters: The hard reality of global expansion*. Harvard Business Review.

Ghinita, G., Karras, P., Kalnis, P., & Mamoulis, N. (2007). Fast data anonymization with low information loss. In. *Proceedings of VLDB, 2007*, 758–769.

Ghinita, G., Tao, Y., & Kalnis, P. (2008). On the anonymization of sparse high-dimensional data. In. *Proceedings of ICDE, 2008*, 715–724.

Gilbert, F. (2008, February). Hot Issues in Cyberspace: Critical Information Privacy and Security Issues. *The Practical Lawyer*.

Gilinas, U., Sutton, S., & Fedorowics, J. (2004). *Business Process and Information Technology*. Mason, OH: Thomson South-Western.

Gindin, S. (1997). *Lost and Found in Cyberspace-Informational Privacy in the Age of the Internet*. Retrieved from http://www.info-law.com/lost.html

Giot, R., El-Abed, M., & Rosenberger, C. (2009a). Keystroke dynamics with low constraints svm based passphrase enrollment. In *Proceedings of the IEEE International Conference on Biometrics: Theory, Applications, and Systems (BTAS 2009)*.

Giot, R., El-Abed, M., & Rosenberger, C. (2009b). GREYC keystroke: a benchmark for keystroke dynamics biometric systems. In *Proceedings of the IEEE International Conference on Biometrics: Theory, Applications, and Systems (BTAS 2009)*.

Goggin, L. S., Eikelbom, R. H., & Atlas, M. D. (2007). Clinical decision support systems and computer aided diagnosis in otology. *Otolaryngology - Head and Neck Surgery, 136*(4S), S21–S26. doi:10.1016/j.otohns.2007.01.028

Goh, E.-J. (2003). *Secure Indexes* (Cryptology ePrint Archive: Rep. No. 2003/216). Retrieved from http://eprint.iacr.org/2003/216/

Goldreich, O. (2001). Foundations of Cryptography: *Vol. I. Basic Tools*. Cambridge, UK: Cambridge University Press.

Goldreich, O. (2004). Foundations of Cryptography: *Vol. II. Basic Applications*. Cambridge, UK: Cambridge University Press.

Green, I., Raz, T., & Zviran, M. (2007). Analysis of active intrusion prevention data for predicting hostile activity in computer networks. *Communications of the ACM, 50*(4), 63–68. doi:10.1145/1232743.1232749

Griffiths, T. L., & Yuille, A. L. (2006). *Technical Introduction: A Primer on Probabilistic Inference.* Los Angeles: Department of Statistics, UCLA.

Gritzalis, D., Theoharidou, M., & Kalimeri, E. (2005). Towards an Interdisciplinary InfoSec Education Model. In *Proceedings of the 4th IFIP World Conference on Information Security Education*, Moscow Russia (pp. 22-35).

Gruteser, M., & Grunwald, D. (2003). *Anonymous Usage of Location-Based Services Through Spatial and Temporal Cloaking.* Paper presented at the 1st International Conference on Mobile Systems, Applications and Services, New York.

Gunetti, D., & Picardi, C. (2005). Keystroke analysis of free text. *ACM Transactions on Information and System Security*, *8*(3), 312–347. doi:10.1145/1085126.1085129

Guven, A., & Sogukpinar, I. (2003). Understanding users' keystroke patterns for computer access security. *Computers & Security*, *22*(8), 695–706. doi:10.1016/S0167-4048(03)00010-5

Hacıgümüs, H., Iyer, B., Li, C., & Mehrotra, S. (2002). Executing SQL over Encrypted Data in the Database-Service-Provider Model. In *Proceedings of the 28th SIGMOD Conference on the Management of Data*. New York: ACM.

Hadoop. (n.d.). Retrieved from http://hadoop.apache.org

Haga, W. J., & Zviran, M. (1991). Question-and-answer passwords: An empirical evaluation. *Information Systems*, *16*(3), 335–343. doi:10.1016/0306-4379(91)90005-T

Hale, J., & Shenoi, S. (1997). Catalytic Inference Analysis: Detecting Inference Threats due to Knowledge Discovery. In *Proceedings of the IEEE Symposium on Security and Privacy* (pp. 188-199).

Halevi, S., & Krawczyk, H. (2005, May). *Strengthening Digital Signatures via Randomized Hashing.* IETF.

Hama. (n.d.). Retrieved from http://cwiki.apache.org/labs/cloudsglossary.html

Hamlen, K. W., & Jones, M. (2008). Aspect-Oriented In-lined Reference Monitors. In *Proceedings of the ACM SIGPLAN Workshop on Programming Languages and Analysis for Security (PLAS)*.

Hamlen, K. W., Morrisett, G., & Schneider, F. B. (2006). Certified In-lined Reference Monitoring on. NET. In *Proceedings of the ACM SIGPLAN Workshop on Programming Languages and Analysis for Security (PLAS)*.

Handley, M., Kreibich, C., & Paxson, V. (2001). Network Intrusion Detection: Evasion, Traffic Normalization, and End-to-End Protocol Semantics. In *Proceedings of the USENIX Security Symposium* (pp. 115-131).

Hargis, G., Hernandez, A. K., Hughes, P., Ramaker, J., Rouiller, S., & Wilde, E. (1998). *Developing quality technical information: A handbook for writers and editors.* Upper Saddle River, NJ: Prentice Hall.

Hasan, B. (2007). Examining the effects of computer self-efficacy and system complexity on technology acceptance. *Information Resources Management Journal*, *20*(3), 76–88.

Heckerman, D. (1990). A Tractable Inference Algorithm for Diagnosing Multiple Diseases. In *Proceedings of the Fifth annual Conference on Uncertainty in Artificial Intelligence* (pp. 163-172).

Henry, J. W., & Stone, R. W. (1999). The effects of computer self-efficacy and outcome expectancy on end-user job control and stress. *Journal of International Information Management*, *8*(1), 23–34.

Hentea, M., Dhillon, H., & Dhillon, M. (2006). Towards Changes in Information Security Education. *Journal of Information Technology Education*, *5*, 221–233.

Hetzl, S., & Mutzel, P. (2005). A Graph-Theoretic Approach to Steganography. In *CMS* (LNCS 3677, pp. 119-128).

Hevner, A. (2007). A Three Cycle View of Design Science Research. *Scandinavian Journal of Information Systems*, *19*(2), 87–92.

Hevner, A., & March, S., J. P., & Ram, S. (2004). Design Science Research in Information Systems. *Management Information Systems Quarterly*, *28*(1), 75–105.

Himma, K. E. (2008). Legal, social, and ethical issues of the internet. In Bidgoli, H. (Ed.), *Global perspectives in information security: legal, social, and international issues.* New York: Wiley.

HIPAA. (2008). *Health insurance portability and accountability act of 1996*. Retrieved from http://www.cms.hhs.gov/HIPAAGenInfo/Downloads/HIPAALaw.pdf

Hochhauser, M. (2002). The effects of HIPAA on research consent forms. *Patient Care Management, 17*(5), 6–7.

Hofstede, G., & Hofstede, G. J. (2005). *Cultures and Organizations: Software of the Mind*. New York: McGraw-Hill.

Holder, J. T., & Grimes, D. E. (2007). Government Regulated Data Privacy: The Challenge for Global Outsourcer. *Georgetown Journal of International Law, 38*(3), 16.

Hong, J., & Landay, J. (2004). *An Architecture for Privacy-Sensitive Ubiquitous Computing*. Paper presented at the 2nd International Conference on Mobile Systems, Applications, and Services, Boston.

Hsu, M., & Chao, C. (2004). Internet self-efficacy and electronic service acceptance. *Decision Support Systems, 38*(3), 369–381. doi:10.1016/j.dss.2003.08.001

Hussain, A., Heidemann, J., & Papadopoulos, C. (2003). A Framework for Classifying Denial of Service Attack. In *Proceedings of ACM SIGCOMM* (pp. 99-110).

IBM. (2004). *IBM PCI cryptographic coprocessor*. Retrieved from http://www.ibm.com/security/cryptocards.

IBM. (2005). *IBM Security Assessment Services*. Retrieved from http://www-935.ibm.com/services/au/igs/pdf/ibm-security-assessment-services.pdf

Irvine, C. E., Chin, S-K., & Frincke, D. (1998). Integrating Security Into the Curriculum. *IEEE Computer*, 25 -30.

ISO/IEC 17799. (2005). *Information technology - Security techniques - Code of practice for information security management*. Retrieved from http://www.iso.org/iso/en/prods-services/popstds/informationsecurity.html

Ives, B., Walsh, K. R., & Schneider, H. (2004). The domino effect of password reuse. *Communications of the ACM, 47*(4), 75–78. doi:10.1145/975817.975820

IWS. (2008). *Highest Internet Penetration Rate*. Retrieved from http://www.internetworldstats.com/top25.htm

Jahangir, N., & Begum, N. (2007). Effect of Perceived Usefulness, Ease of Use, Security and Privacy on Consumer Attitude and Adaptation in the Context of E-Banking. *Journal of Management Research, 7*(3).

Jain, A. K., Hong, L., & Pankanti, S. (2000). Biometric identification. *Communications of the ACM, 43*(2), 90–98. doi:10.1145/328236.328110

Jamal, K. (2005). Enforced Standards Versus Evolution by General Acceptance: A Comparative Study of E-Commerce Privacy Disclosure and Practice in the United States and the United Kingdom. *Journal of Accounting Research, 43*, 73–96. doi:10.1111/j.1475-679x.2004.00163.x

Jayaratna, N. (1993). Research Notes: Information Systems as Social Systems: Research at the LSE. *International Journal of Information Management, 13*(4), 299–301.

Jena. (n.d.). Retrieved from http://jena.sourceforge.net

Jensen, C., & Potts, C. (2004a). Privacy Policies as Decision-Making Tools: A Usability Evaluation of Online Privacy Notices. In *Proceedings of ACM Conference on Human Factors in Computing Systems: CHI 2004* (pp. 471-478).

Jensen, C., & Potts, C. (2005). Privacy Practices of Internet Users: Self-report versus Observed Behavior. *International Journal of Human Computer Studies*.

Jensen, C., & Potts, C. (2004b). *Privacy Policies Examined: Fair Warning or Fair Game*. Georgia Tech.

Jin, C., Wang, H., & Shin, K. G. (2003). Hop-Count Filtering: An Effective Defense against Spoofed Traffic. In *Proceedings of the 10th ACM conference on Computer and Communications Security* (pp. 30-41).

Jin, L., Ke, X., Manuel, R., & Wilkerson, M. (2004). Keystroke dynamics: A software based biometric solution. In *Proceedings of the 13th USENIX Security Symposium*.

Johnson, N. F., & Jajodia, S. (1998b, April). Steganalysis of Images Created Using Current Steganography Software. In *Proceedings of the Second Information Hiding Workshop*, Portland, OR.

Johnson, N.F., & Jajodia, S. (1998a). Exploring Steganography: Seeing the Unseen. *IEEE Computer*, 26-34.

Johnson, A. (2009). Business and Security Executives Views of Information Security Investment Drivers: Results from a Delphi Study. *Journal of Information Privacy & Security, 5*(1), 3.

Jones, M., & Hamlen, K. W. (2009). Enforcing IRM Security Policies: Two Case Studies. In *Proceedings of the IEEE Intelligence and Security Informatics Conference (ISI)*.

Juang, W. S. (2004). Efficient password authenticated key agreement using smart cards. *Computers & Security, 23*(2), 167–173. doi:10.1016/j.cose.2003.11.005

Jung, B., Han, I., & Lee, S. (2001). Security Threats to Internet: A Korean Multi-industry Investigation. *Information & Management, 38*(8), 487–498. doi:10.1016/S0378-7206(01)00071-4

Jurafsky, D., & Martin, J. H. (2000). *Speech and language processing*. Upper Saddle River, NJ: Prentice.

Kalnis, P., Ghinita, G., Mouratidis, K., & Papadias, D. (2007). Preventing location-based identity inference in anonymous spatial queries. *IEEE Transactions on Knowledge and Data Engineering, 19*(12), 1719–1733. doi:10.1109/TKDE.2007.190662

Kantarcioglu, M., & Clifton, C. (2004). *Security Issues in Querying Encrypted Data* (Tech. Rep. TR-04-013). West Lafayette, IN: Purdue University.

Karimi, J., & Knsynski, B. (1991). Globalization and information management strategies. *Journal of Management Information Systems, 7*(4), 7–26.

Katzenbeisser, S., & Petitcolas, F. A. P. (2000). *Information Hiding Techniques for Steganography and Digital Watermarking*. Norwood, MA: Artech House.

Kido, H., Yanagisawa, Y., & Satoh, T. (2005). Protection of location privacy using dummies for location-based services. In *Proceedings of the ICDE Workshops* (p. 1248).

Kim, H. J. (1995). Biometrics, is it a viable proposition for identity authentication and access control? *Computers & Security, 14*(3), 205–214. doi:10.1016/0167-4048(95)97054-E

King, S. T., & Chen, P. M. (2003). Backtracking intrusions. *SIGOPS Oper. Syst. Rev., 37*(5), 223–236. doi:10.1145/1165389.945467

Kirkland & Ellis. (2008). *New Laws Significantly Regulate Business Practices Relating to Personal Information*. Retrieved from http://www.kirkland.com/siteFiles/Publications/044FFB8745AE1B2ED379DF50D8897FD2.pdf

Klare, G. R. (1963). *The Measurement of Readability*. Ames, IA: Iowa State University Press.

Kobsa, A. (2007). Privacy-enhanced personalization: Multi-pronged strategies are needed to reconcile the tension between personalization and privacy. *Communications of the ACM, 50*(8), 24–33. doi:10.1145/1278201.1278202

Kokolakis, S. A., Demopoulos, A. J., & Kiountouzis, E. A. (2000). The Use of Business Process Modeling in Information Systems Security Analysis and Design. *Information Management & Computer Security, 8*(3), 107–116. doi:10.1108/09685220010339192

Kumar, V., & Muttoo, S. K. (2008). Relevance of Steganography, in General, and Graph Theoretic Approach in particular, in Indian Security Concern and Measure. In *Proceedings of the 2nd National Conference, INDIACom-2008* (pp. 183-188).

Kumar, V., & Muttoo, S. K. (2009b). Principle of Graph Theoretic Approach to Digital Steganography. In *Proceedings of the 3rd National Conference, INDIACom-2009* (pp. 161-165).

Kumar, Y., Khan, L., & Thuraisingham, B. (2008). Trusted Computing Base for Assured Information Sharing. *Journal of Information Security and Privacy.*

Kumaraguru, P., & Cranor, L. (2006). Privacy in India: Attitudes and Awareness. In *Privacy Enhancing Technologies* (LNCS 3856, pp. 243-258).

Kumar, V. (2002). *Discrete Mathematics*. New Delhi, India: BPB Publication.

Kumar, V., & Muttoo, S. K. (2009a). A data structure for graph to facilitate hiding information in a graph's segments -A Graph Theoretic Approach to Steganography. *International Journal of Communication Networks and Distributed Systems, 3*(3), 268–282. doi:10.1504/IJCNDS.2009.026879

Kumar, V., & Muttoo, S. K. (in press). A Graph Theoretic Approach to Sustainable Steganography. *International Journal of Information and Computer Security.*

Kumar, V., & Sharma, V. (2006). Overcoming 64kb data size limit in handling large spatial data in GISNIC while cleaning and building topology. *International Journal of Information Technology and Management, 5*(1), 77–86. doi:10.1504/IJITM.2006.008715

Ku, W.-C., & Chen, S.-M. (2004). Weaknesses and improvements of an efficient password based user authentication scheme using smart cards. *IEEE Transactions on Consumer Electronics*, *50*(1), 204–207. doi:10.1109/TCE.2004.1277863

Kuzmanovic, A., & Knightly, E. W. (2003). Low-Rate TCP-Targeted Denial of Service Attacks. In *Proceedings of ACM SIGCOMM* (pp. 75-86).

Lamport, L. (1981). Password authentication with insecure communication. *Communications of the ACM*, *24*(11), 770–772. doi:10.1145/358790.358797

Langheinrich, M. (2001). Privacy by Design - Principles of Privacy-Aware Ubiquitous Systems. In *Ubicomp 2001 Proceedings* (LNCS 2201, pp. 273-291. Langheinrich, M. (2002). *A Privacy Awareness System for Ubiquitous Computing Environments*. Paper presentd at the 4th International Conference on Ubiquitous Computing, Göteborg, Sweden.

Laudon, K. C., & Traver, C. G. (2008). *E-Commerce, Business, Technology, Society* (4th ed.). Upper Saddle River, NJ: Pearson International.

Lazarevic, A., & Kumar, V. (2005). Feature bagging for outlier detection. In *Proceedings of the Eleventh ACM SIGKDD international Conference on Knowledge Discovery in Data Mining* (pp. 157-166).

Lee, W., & Stolfo, S. (1998). Data mining approaches for intrusion detection. In *Proceedings of the 7th USENIX Security Symposium*, San Antonio, TX (pp. 79-94).

LeFevre, K., DeWitt, D. J., & Ramakrishnan, R. (2005). Incognito: Efficient full-domain k-anonymity. In. *Proceedings of SIGMOD*, *2005*, 49–60.

Leggett, J., & Williams, G. (1988). Verifying identity via keystroke characteristics. *International Journal of Man-Machine Studies*, *28*(1), 67–76. doi:10.1016/S0020-7373(88)80053-1

Leggett, J., Williams, G., Usnick, M., & Longnecker, M. (1991). Dynamic identity verification via keystroke characteristics. *International Journal of Man-Machine Studies*, *35*(6), 859–870. doi:10.1016/S0020-7373(05)80165-8

Lehigh University Benchmark (LUBM). (n.d.). Retrieved from http://swat.cse.lehigh.edu/projects/lubm

Leonhardt, U., & Magee, J. (1998). Security Considerations for a Distributed Location Service. *Journal of Network and Systems Management*, *6*(1), 51–70. doi:10.1023/A:1018777802208

Levine, D. S. (2001). One on One with Charles Cresson Wood of InfoSecurity Infrastructure. *Techbiz Online*. Retrieved from http://sanfrancisco.bizjournals.com/sanfrancisco/stories/2001/10/15/newscolumn7.html

Li, Y., & Guo, L. (2008). TCM-KNN scheme for network anomaly detection using feature-based optimizations. In *Proceedings of the ACM Symposium on Applied Computing* (pp. 2103-2109).

Liberty Alliance Project. (2003). *Privacy and Security Best Practices*. Retrieved from http://ehr.medigent.com/assets/collaborate/2005/04/03/final_privacy_security_best_practices.pdf

Linklaters. (2009a). *Data Protection 2009- Current Issues in Privacy and Data Protection*. Retrieved from http://www.linklaters.com/pdfs/seminars/dpconference2009.pdf

Linklaters. (2009b). *Technology Media and Communications*. Retrieved from http://www.linklaters.com/TMTnews/index.asp?issuestoryid=4014&languageid=1&opendivs=,16

Lin, T., & Huang, C. (2008). Understanding knowledge management system usage antecedents: an integration of social cognitive theory and task technology fit. *Information & Management*, *45*(6), 410–417. doi:10.1016/j.im.2008.06.004

Liu, F., Hua, K. A., & Cai, Y. (2009). *Query l-diversity in location based services*. Paper presented at the International Workshop on Privacy-Aware Location-based Mobile Services (PALMS).

Liu, H., & Yu, L. (2005). Towards integrating feature selection algorithms for classification and clustering. *IEEE Transactions on Knowledge and Data Engineering*, *17*(3), 1–12.

Loch, K. D., Carr, H., & Warkentin, M. E. (1992). Threats to Information Systems: Today's Reality, Yesterday's Understanding. *Management Information Systems Quarterly*, 173–186. doi:10.2307/249574

Long, J., & White, G. (2010). *On the Global Knowledge Components in an Information Security Curriculum – A Multidisciplinary Approach*. Education & Information Technologies.

Lopez, J., Oppliger, R., & Pernul, G. (2004). Authentication and authorization infrastructures (AAIS): A comparative survey. *Computers & Security*, *23*(7), 578–590. doi:10.1016/j.cose.2004.06.013

Luo, X., & Chang, R. K. C. (2005). On a New Class of Pulsing Denial-of-Service Attacks and the Defense. In *Proceedings of Network and Distributed System Security Symposium*.

Lwin, M.O., Wirtz, J., & Williams, J.D. (2007). Consumer online privacy concerns and responses: a power-responsibility equilibrium perspective. *Journal of the Academy of Marketing Science*.

Machanavajjhala, A., Gehrke, J., Kifer, D., & Venkitasubramaniam, M. (2006). l-diversity: Privacy beyond k-anonymity. In *Proceedings of ICDE 2006* (p. 24).

Mahout. (n.d.). Retrieved from http://lucene.apache.org/mahout/

Matyas, S. M., & Stapleton, J. (2000). A biometric standard for information management and security. *Computers & Security*, *19*(5), 428–441. doi:10.1016/S0167-4048(00)05029-X

McLaughlin, G. H. (1969). SMOG grading - a new readability formula. *Journal of Reading*, *22*, 639–646.

McNabb, A., Monson, C., & Seppi, K. (2007). MRPSO: MapReduce particle swarm optimization. In *Proceedings of the 9th annual conference on genetic and evolutionary computation (GECCO 2007)* (p. 177). New York: ACM Press.

Menkus, B. (1988). Understanding the use of passwords. *Computers & Security*, *7*(2), 132–136. doi:10.1016/0167-4048(88)90325-2

Merkle, R. C. (1989). A Certified Digital Signature. In *Proceedings of the 9th Annual International Cryptology Conference on Advances in Cryptology*.

Meyerson, A., & Williams, R. (2004). *On the complexity of optimal k-anonymity* (pp. 223–228). PODS.

Microsoft. (2005). *Service Management Functions—Security Management*. Retrieved from http://www.microsoft.com/technet/itsolutions/cits/mo/smf/mofsmsmf.mspx

Microsoft-TechNet. (2000). *Security Threats*. Retrieved from http://www.microsoft.com/technet/security/bestprac/bpent/sec1/secthret.mspx#EGAA

Milberg, S., Smith, J., & Burke, S. (2000). Information privacy: Corporate management and national regulation. *Organization Science*, *11*(1), 35–57. doi:10.1287/orsc.11.1.35.12567

Millar, J. (2001). *Quality in Teaching & Learning Framework and Current Risks to Quality and Action Plan*. Retrieved from http://www.ecu.edu.au/GPPS/acad_secret/assets/ctlc/011204agn.pdf

Millar, S. A. (2006). Privacy and security: Best practices for global security. *Journal of International Trade Law and Policy*, *5*(1), 36–49. doi:10.1108/14770020680000539

Milne, G. R. (2000). Privacy and ethical issues in database/interactive marketing and public policy: a research framework and overview of the special issue. *Journal of Public Policy & Marketing*, *19*, 1–6. doi:10.1509/jppm.19.1.1.16934

Milne, G. R., & Culnan, M. J. (2002). Using the Content of Online Privacy Notices to Inform Public Policy: A Longitudinal Analysis of the 1998–2001 U.S. Web Surveys. *The Information Society*, *18*(5), 345–360. doi:10.1080/01972240290108168

Milne, G. R., & Culnan, M. J. (2004). Strategies for Reducing Online Privacy Risks: Why Consumers Read (or Don't Read) Online Privacy Notices. *Journal of Interactive Marketing*, *18*(3), 15–29. doi:10.1002/dir.20009

Mokbel, M. F., Chow, C.-Y., & Aref, W. G. (2006). *The new casper: Query processing for location services without compromising privacy* (pp. 763–774). VLDB.

Monrose, F., Reiter, M. K., & Wetzel, S. (2002). Password hardening based on keystroke dynamics. *International Journal of Information Security*, *1*(2), 69–83. doi:10.1007/s102070100006

Monrose, F., & Rubin, A. D. (2000). Keystroke dynamics as a biometric for authentication. *Future Generation Computer Systems*, *16*(4), 351–359. doi:10.1016/S0167-739X(99)00059-X

Moore, D., Voelker, G. M., & Savage, S. (2001). Inferring Internet Denial-of-Service Activity. In *Proceedings of the 10th USENIX Security Symposium.*

Morelli, J. (2007). Hybrid filing schemes: the use of metadata signposts in functional file plans. *Records Management Journal, 17*(1), 17. doi:10.1108/09565690710730679

Moretti, C., Steinhaeuser, K., Thainer, D., & Chawla, N. (2008). Scaling Up Classifiers to Cloud Computers. In *Proceedings of the IEEE ICDM.*

Morrison-Foerster. (2008). *European Law & Regulations: A survival guide for technology companies.*

Moses, T. (Ed.). (2005, February). eXtensible Access Control Markup Language (XACML) Version 2.0. *OASIS Standard.* Retrieved from http://docs.oasis-open.org/xacml/2.0/access_control-xacml-2.0-core-spec-os.pdf

Musthaler, L. (2008, November 10). New approach to a network-based data privacy application. *Network World.*

Muys, A. (2006). *Building an Enterprise-Scale Database for RDF Data.*

NativeForest.org. (2009). *Native Forest Netwok's Guide to Stopping Junk Mail.*

NCES. (1992). *The National Adult Literacy Survey.* Retrieved from http://www.informatics-review.com/FAQ/reading.html

Net, I. Q. (2002). *Enterprise Security: Moving from Chaos to Control with Integrated Security Management.* Retrieved from http://download.netiq.com/CMS/WHITE-PAPER/NetIQ_WP_EnterpriseSecurity.pdf

Newman, A., Hunter, J., Li, Y. F., Bouton, C., & Davis, M. (2008). In *Proceedings of a Scale-Out RDF Molecule Store for Distributed Processing of Biomedical Data Semantic Web for Health Care and Life Sciences Workshop (WWW 2008).*

Nicolett, M., & Easley, M. (2002). *The Emerging IT Security Management Market.* Retrieved from http://www.dataquest.com/resources/110800/110845/110845.pdf

Ning, P., & Xu, D. (2004). Hypothesizing and reasoning about attacks missed by intrusion detection systems. *ACM Transactions on Information and System Security, 7*(4), 591–627. doi:10.1145/1042031.1042036

NSW. (2003a). *Information Security Guideline for NSW Government – Part 1 Information Security Risk Management.* Retrieved from http://www.albany.edu/acc/courses/ia/inf766/nswinfosecriskmanagementpt11997.pdf

NSW. (2003b). *Information Security Guideline for New South Wales (NSW) Government - Part 2 Examples of Threats and Vulnerabilities.* Retrieved from http://www.oict.nsw.gov.au/content/2.3.17-Security-Pt2.asp

NTIA. (2002). *National Telecommunications and Information Administration. A Nation Online: How Americans Are Expanding Their Use of the Internet.* Retrieved from http://www.ntia.doc.gov/ntiahome/dn/

O'Gorman, L. (2003). Comparing passwords, tokens, and biometrics for user authentication. *Proceedings of the IEEE, 91*(12), 2019–2040. doi:10.1109/JPROC.2003.819605

Obaidat, M. S., & Sadoun, B. (1999). Keystroke dynamics based authentication. In Jain, A. K., Bolle, R., & Pankanti, S. (Eds.), *Biometrics: Personal Identification in Networked Society* (pp. 213–230). New York: Springer.

Office of Management and Budget (OMB). (2003). *OMB Guidance for Implementing the Privacy Provisions of the E-Government Act of 2002.* Retrieved November 7, 2010, from http://www.whitehouse.gov/omb/memoranda_m03-22/

Office of Management and Budget (OMB). (2007). *Statement of the Honorable Karen Evans Administrator for Electronic Government and Information Technology Office of Management and Budget Before the Committee on Government Reform U.S. House of Representatives.* Washington, DC: Executive Office of the President.

Open, C. A. *Implementation.* (n.d.). Retrieved from http://www.openca.org/projects/openca/

O'Reilly, J. (2008). Don't Stick Your Head in the Sand. *Vital Speeches of the Day, 74*(6), 9.

Organization for Economic Cooperation and Development (OECD). (1980). *Guidelines Governing the Protection of Privacy and Transborder Flows of Personal Data.* Retrieved November 7, 2010, from http://www.oecd.org/document/18/0,3343,en_2649_34255_1815186_1_1_1_1,00.html

Osborne, M. (2004). *An Introduction to Game Theory*. New York: Oxford University Press.

Oz, E. (1994). Barriers to international data transfer. *Journal of Global Information Management, 2*(2), 22–29.

Paci, F., & Bertino, E. (2009). An Overview of VeryIDX - A Privacy-Preserving Digital Identity Management System for Mobile Devices. *Journal of Software, 4*(7), 696–706. doi:10.4304/jsw.4.7.696-706

Paez, M., & Galil, Y. (2005). *New York Enacts Data Security and Notification Law*. Retrieved from https://extranet.jonesday.com/pubs/pubs_detail.aspx?pubID=S2813

Peacock, A., Ke, X., & Wilkerson, M. (2004). Typing patterns: A key to user identification. *IEEE Security & Privacy, 2*(5), 40–47. doi:10.1109/MSP.2004.89

Pearl, J. (2006). *Two journeys into human reasoning*. Los Angeles: UCLA Cognitive systems Laboratory.

Pearl, J. (2003). Statistics and Causal Inference: A Review. *Test, 12*(2), 281–345. doi:10.1007/BF02595718

Pearl, J., & Russell, S. (2003). Bayesian Networks. In Arbib, M. A. (Ed.), *Handbook of Brain Theory and Neural Networks* (pp. 157–160). Cambridge, MA: MIT Press.

Pellet. (n.d.). Retrieved from http://clarkparsia.com/pellet

Pereira, J. (2009). Corporate News: CVS to Pay $2.25 Million In Privacy Case. *Wall Street Journal*, p. B.4. Retrieved from http://proquest.umi.com/pqdweb?did=1647569251&Fmt=7&clientId=2138&RQT=309&VName=PQD

Perkins, E., & Markel, M. (2004). Multinational data-privacy laws: an introduction for IT managers. *IEEE Transactions on Professional Communication, 47*(2), 85–94. doi:10.1109/TPC.2004.828207

Peslak, A. R. (2005b, April). Privacy Policies of the Largest Privately Held Companies – A Review and Analysis of the Forbes Private 50. In *Proceedings of ACM SIGMIS Conference 2005*, Atlanta, GA.

Peslak, A. (2005). Internet Privacy Policies: A Review and Survey of the Fortune 50. *Information Resources Management Journal, 18*, 29–41.

Peslak, A. R. (2005a). Privacy Policies: A Framework and Survey of the Fortune 50. *Information Resources Management Journal, 18*(1), 29–41.

Peslak, A. R. (2006). Current Privacy Issues and Factors: Development and Analysis. *Journal of Information Technology Impact, 6*(3), 171–186.

Peslak, A. R. (2007). Progress in Internet Privacy Policies: a Review and Survey of US Companies from 1998 through 2006. In Khosrow-Pour, M. (Ed.), *Emerging Information Resources Management and Technologies* (*Vol. 6*). Hershey, PA: Idea Group Inc.

Pirim, T., James, T., Boswell, K., Reithel, B., & Barkhi, R. (2008). An empirical Investigation of an Individual's Perceived need for Privacy and Security. *International Journal of Information Security and Privacy, 2*(1), 42–53.

Pollach, I. (2005). A Typology of Communicative Strategies in Online Privacy Policies: Ethics, Power and Informed Consent. *Journal of Business Ethics, 62*(3), 221–235. doi:10.1007/s10551-005-7898-3

Powers, D. M. (2008). Cyberlaw: the major areas, development, and information security aspects. In Bidgoli, H. (Ed.), *Global perspectives in information security: legal, social, and international issues*. New York: Wiley.

Prabhakar, S., Pankanti, S., & Jain, A. K. (2003). Biometric recognition: Security and privacy concerns. *IEEE Security and Privacy Magazine, 1*(2), 33–42. doi:10.1109/MSECP.2003.1193209

Privacy International. (2003). *Privacy and Human Rights 2003: Overview*. Retrieved November 7, 2010, from http://www.privacyinternational.org/survey/phr2003/overview.htm

Qureshi, M., Younus, A., & Khan, A. A. (2009). Philosophical survey of passwords. *International Journal of Computer Science Issues, 1*, 8–12.

Ragouzis, N., & Hughes, J. (2006). *Security Assertion Markup Language (SAML) V2.0 Technical Overview*. OASIS Open.

Ramanujam, S., Gupta, A., Khan, L., & Seida, S. (2009). R2D: Extracting relational structure from RDF stores. In *Proceedings of the ACM/IEEE International Conference on Web Intelligence*, Milan, Italy.

Rasmussen, M. (2003). *Analyst Report: IT Trends 2003 – Information Security Standards, Regulations and Legislation.* Retrieved from http://www.csoonline.com/analyst/report721.html

Ratha, N., & Bolle, R. (Eds.). (2005). *Automatic fingerprint recognition systems.* New York: Springer Verlag.

Reay, I. K., Beatty, P., Dick, S., & Miller, J. (2007). A survey and analysis of the P3P protocol's agents, adoptions, maintenance, and future. *IEEE Transactions on Dependable and Secure Computing, 4*(2), 151–164. doi:10.1109/TDSC.2007.1004

Reay, I., Dick, S., & Miller, J. A. (2009). *Large-scale empirical study of online privacy policies: stated actions vs. legal obligations.* ACM Transactions on the Web.

Reidenberg, J. R. (2000). Resolving conflicting international data privacy rules in cyberspace. *Stanford Law Review, 52*(5), 1315–1367. doi:10.2307/1229516

Revett, K. (2008). Keystroke dynamics. In *Behavioral biometrics: A remote access approach* (pp. 73–136). New York: Wiley. doi:10,1002/9780470997949.ch4

Ritzmann, M. (2009). *Strategies for managing missing or incomplete data in biometric and business applications.* Unpublished doctoral dissertation, Pace University, New York.

Rivest, R., Adleman, L., & Dertouzos, M. (1978). On Data Banks and Privacy Homomorphisms. In DeMillo, R., Dobkin, D., Jones, A., & Lipton, R. (Eds.), *Foundations of Secure Computation.* New York: Academic Press.

Rodrigues, R. N., Yared, G. F. G., Costa, C. R., Yabu-Uti, J. B. T., Violaro, F., & Ling, L. L. (2006). *Biometric access control through numerical keyboards based on keystroke dynamics* (. *LNCS, 3832,* 640–646.

Ross, J. A. (2008). *Security engineering: A guide to building dependable distributed systems* (2nd ed.). New York: Wiley.

Rounds, M., Pendegraft, N., & Stone, R. (2008). *Student computer security behavior and interest in training.* Paper presented at the Mountain Plains Management Conference, Idaho Falls, ID.

Rounds, M., Pendegraft, R., Pendegraft, N., & Stone, R. (2008, May 18-20). Student survey on computer security awareness and responsiveness. In *Proceedings of the Information Resource Management Conference,* Niagara Falls, ON, Canada (p. 48).

Rudraswamy, V., & Vance, D. A. (2001). Transborder data flows: Adoption and diffusion of protective legislation in the global electronic commerce environment. *Logistics Information Management, 14*(1/2), 127–136. doi:10.1108/09576050110362717

Ryder, R. (2004, February). *Connecticut Part C Stakeholders' Meeting.* Paper presented at the CASE Seminar, Clearwater, FL.

Saloman, D. (2003). *Data Privacy and Security.* New York: Springer.

Samarati, P. (2001). Protecting respondents' identities in microdata release. *IEEE Transactions on Knowledge and Data Engineering, 13*(6), 1010–1027. doi:10.1109/69.971193

Sandhu, R., & Coyne, E. (1996). *Role-Based Access Control Models.* IEEE Computer.

Sasse, M. A., Brostoff, S., & Weirich, D. (2001). Transforming the 'weakest link': A human/computer interaction approach to usable and effective security. *BT Technology Journal, 19*(3), 122–131. doi:10.1023/A:1011902718709

Saunders, C. (2002). *EU Oks spam ban, online privacy rules, Internet News.* Retrieved from http://www.internetnews.com/IAR/article .php/l154391

Savage, M. (2006). Protect what's Precious. *Information Security Magazine,* 23-28.

Savage, S., Wetherall, D., Karlin, A., & Anderson, T. (2000). Practical network support for IP traceback. In *Proceedings of ACM SIGCOMM,* Stockholm, Sweden (pp. 295-306).

Schaust, S., & Szczerbicka, H. (2008). Artificial immune systems in the context of misbehavior detection. *Cybernetics and Systems, 39*(2), 136–154. doi:10.1080/01969720701853434

Shimizu, A. (2007). A dynamic password authentication method using a one-way function. *Systems and Computers in Japan, 22*(7), 32–40. doi:10.1002/scj.4690220704

Shittu, H. (2001). *Resource Protection Mechanisms: Implementations in Operating Systems.* Retrieved from http://www.genixcorp.com/papers.html

Shrestha, A. (2004). *Information Security Management System (7799) for an Internet Gateway.* Retrieved from http://www.sans.org/reading_room/whitepapers/iso17799/1454.php

Shroff, R. H., & Vogel, D. R. (2009). Assessing the factors deemed to support individual student intrinsic motivation in technology supported online and face-to-face discussions. *Journal of Information Technology Education, 8,* 59–85.

Sicherman, G. L., Jonge, W. D., & de Riet, R. P. V. (1983). Answering queries without revealing secrets. *ACM Transactions on Database Systems, 8*(1), 41–59. doi:10.1145/319830.319833

Singh, R. I., Sumeeth, M., & Miller, J. (2010). Evaluating the Readability of Privacy Policies in Mobile Environments. *International Journal of Mobile Human Computer Interaction.*

Siponen, M. (2002). *Designing Secure Information Systems and Software.* Unpublished doctoral dissertation, University of Oulu, Finland.

Smith, R. E. (2000). *Ben Franklin's Web Site: Privacy and Curiosity from Plymouth Rock to the Internet.* Privacy Journal.

Smith, R. E. (2002). *Authentication: From passwords to public keys.* Boston: Addison-Wesley.

Smith, S., & Weingart, S. (1999). Building a high-performance, programmable secure coprocessor. [Special Issue on Computer Network Security]. *Computer Networks, 31,* 831–860. doi:10.1016/S1389-1286(98)00019-X

Snekkenes, E. (2001). Concepts for Personal Location Privacy Policies. In *Proceedings of the 3rd ACM Conference on Electronic Commerce,* Tampa, FL.

Snoren, A. C., Partridge, C., Sanchez, L. A., Jones, C. E., Tchakountio, F., Kent, S. T., et al. (2001). Hash-based IP Traceback. In *Proceedings of ACM SIGCOMM '2001,* San Diego, CA (pp. 3-14).

Sofaer, A. D., & Goodman, S. E. (2006). *Cyber Crime and Security. The Transnational Dimension.* Palo Alto, CA: Hoover Institution.

Solomon, M. G., & Chapple, M. (2005). *Information security illuminated.* Boston: Jones and Bartlett Publishers.

Song, D., Venable, P., & Perrig, A. (1997). *User recognition by keystroke latency pattern analysis.* Retrieved from http://citeseer.ist.psu.edu/song97user.html

Song, D., Wagner, D., & Perrig, A. (2000). Practical Techniques for Searches on Encrypted Data. In *Proceedings of the IEEE Symposium on Security and Privacy.*

Soppera, A., & Burbridge, T. (2004). Maintaining privacy in pervasive computing—enabling acceptance of sensor-based services. *BT Technology Journal, 22*(3), 106–118. doi:10.1023/B:BTTJ.0000047125.97546.4a

Spector, Y., & Ginzberg, J. (1994). Pass-sentence: A new approach to computer code. *Computers & Security, 13*(2), 145–160. doi:10.1016/0167-4048(94)90064-7

Squicciarini, A., & Bertino, E. (2007). PP-Trust-X: A system for Privacy Preserving Trust Negotiations. *ACM Transactions on Information and System Security, 10*(3).

SRC. (2008). *SMOG Readability Calculator.* Retrieved from http://www.harrymclaughlin.com/SMOG.htm

Srihari, S. N., Cha, S., Arora, H., & Lee, S. (2002). Individuality of Handwriting. *Journal of Forensic Sciences, 47*(4), 1–17.

Stallings, W. (1999). *Cryptography & Network Security: Principles and Practice.* New York: Prentice Hall.

Standler, R. (1997). *Privacy Law in the USA.* Retrieved from https:/www.rbs2.com/privacy.htm

StegoArchive. (2001). *Steganography Information, Software and News to enhance your Privacy.* Retrieved from http://www.StegoArchive.com

Stephens, D. O. (2007). Protecting Personal Privacy in the Global Business Environment. *Information Management Journal, 41*(3).

Stephens, D. (1999). The globalization of information technology in multinational corporations. *Information Management Journal, 33*(3), 66–71.

Stephenson, T. A. (2000). *An Introduction to Bayesian Networks Theory and Usage*. IDIAP.

Stevens, K. T., & Stevens, K. C. (1992). Measuring the Readability of Business Writing: The Cloze Procedure vs. Readability Formulas. *Journal of Business Communication, 29*, 367–382. doi:10.1177/002194369202900404

Stone, R. W., & Henry, J. W. (2003). The roles of computer self-efficacy and outcome expectancy in influencing the computer end-user's organizational commitment. *Journal of End User Computing, 15*(1), 38–53.

Straub, D. W., & Welke, R. J. (1998). Coping with Systems Risk: Security Planning Models for Management Decision Making. *Management Information Systems Quarterly, 22*, 441–469. doi:10.2307/249551

Su, T., & Ozsoyoglu, G. (1991). Controlling FD and MVD Inferences in Multilevel Relational Database Systems. *IEEE Transactions on Knowledge and Data Engineering, 3*(4), 474–485. doi:10.1109/69.109108

Svigals, J. (1994). Smartcards: A security assessment. *Computers & Security, 13*(2), 107–114. doi:10.1016/0167-4048(94)90056-6

Swartz, N. (2008). EU Panel: Delete Search Info Sooner. *Information Management Journal, 42*(4).

Sweeney, L. (2002). Achieving k-Anonymity Privacy Protection Using Generalization and Suppression. *International Journal of Uncertainty. Fuzziness and Knowledge-Based Systems, 10*(5), 571–588. doi:10.1142/S021848850200165X

Sweeney, L. (2002). k-anonymity: A model for protecting privacy. *International Journal of Uncertainty. Fuzziness and Knowledge-Based Systems, 10*(5), 557–570. doi:10.1142/S0218488502001648

Symantec. (2006). *Trends for July 05–December 05, Volume IX*. Retrieved from https://enterprise.symantec.com/enterprise/whitepaper.cfm

Symantec. (2008). *Trends for July 07–December 07, Volume XIII*. Retrieved from http://eval.symantec.com/mktginfo/enterprise/white_papers/b-whitepaper_internet_security_threat_report_xiii_04-2008.en-us.pdf

Tanenbaum, W. A., & Echegoyen, R. (2007, September). Getting a Grip on European Data Transfers. *New York Law Journal*.

Tao, R., Yang, L., Peng, L., Li, B., & Cemerlic, A. (2009). A Case Study: Using Architectural Features to Improve Sophisticated Denial-of-Service Attack Detections. In *Proceedings of 2009 IEEE Symposium on Computational Intelligence in Cyber Security*, Nashville, TN (pp. 13-18).

Tappert, C. C., Villani, M., & Cha, S. (2009). Keystroke Biometric Identification and Authentication on Long-Text Input. In Wang, L., & Geng, X. (Eds.), *Behavioral Biometrics for Human Identification: Intelligent Applications* (pp. 342–367). Hershey, PA: IGI Global.

Taylor, W. (1953). Cloze procedure: A new tool for measuring readability. *The Journalism Quarterly, 30*, 415–433.

Teer, F. E., Kruck, S. E., & Kruck, G. (2007). Empirical Study of Students' Computer Security - Practices/Perceptions. *Journal of Computer Information Systems, 3*(105).

Teifke, L. (2003). *The Importance of Privacy*. Retrieved November 7, 2010, from http://www.bankersonline.com/vendor_guru/alltel/alltel_privacy.html

Teswanich, W., & Chittayasothorn, S. (2007). A Transformation of RDF Documents and Schemas to Relational Databases. *IEEE Pacific Rim Conferences on Communications, Computers, and Signal Processing*, 38-41.

The Open Group. (2000). *Open Group Technical Standard—Authorization (AZN) API*. Retrieved from http://www.opengroup.org/onlinepubs/9690999199/toc.htm

Theoharidou, M., & Gritzalis, D. (2007). Common Body of Knowledge for Information Security. *IEEE Security & Privacy, 5*(2), 64–67. doi:10.1109/MSP.2007.32

Thibadeau, R. (2000). *Privacy Server Protocol: Short Summary*. Pittsburgh, PA: Carnegie Mellon University.

Thomas, R. E., & Maurer, V. G. (1997). Database marketing practice: protecting consumer privacy. *Journal of Public Policy & Marketing, 16*, 147–155.

Thorpe, J., & van Oorschot, P. (2004). Graphical dictionaries and the memorable space of graphical passwords. In *Proceedings of the 13th USENIX Security Symposium*, San Diego, CA.

Thuraisingham, B. M. (2008). Assured Information Sharing: Technologies, Challenges and Directions. *Intelligence and Security Informatics*, 1-15.

Thuraisingham, B. (1998). *Data Mining: Technologies, techniques, Tools and Trends*. Boca Raton, FL: CRC Press.

TNS & TRUSTe. (2008). *Internet users' knowledge, attitudes and concerns about behavioral targeting and its implications on their online privacy*. Retrieved November 7, 2010, from http://www.truste.org/about/press_release/03_26_08.php

Todd, J., & Vickers, K. (2003). Developing High-Tech Entrepreneurs: A Multidisciplinary Strategy. *Decision Sciences Journal of Innovative Education, 1*(2), 317–320. doi:10.1111/j.1540-4609.2003.00027.x

Totterdale, R. L. (2008). Enterprise content management-A usability study. *Issues in Information Systems*, IX.

Totterdale, R. L. (2009). *Exploring Barriers to the Categorization of Electronic Content in a Global Professional Services Firm*. Pittsburgh: Robert Morris University.

Tsai, C.-S., Lee, C.-C., & Hwang, M.-S. (2006). Password authentication schemes: Current status and key issues. *International Journal of Network Security, 3*(2), 101–115.

U.S. Coast Guard. (2003). *Marine Operations Risk Guide*. Retrieved from http://www.uscg.mil/hq/g-m/nmc/ptp/morg.pdf

U.S. Department of Defense. (1996). *Goal Security Architecture, Vol. 6, Version 3.0*. Retrieved from http://www2.umassd.edu/swarchresearch/tafim/v6.pdf

U.S. Department of Health and Human Services. (2003a). Health Insurance Reforms: Security Standards. *Federal Register, 68*(38).

U.S. Department of Health and Human Services. (2003b). *Summary of the HIPPA Privacy Rule*. Retrieved from http://www.hhs.gov/ocr/privacysummary.pdf

UB. (2003). *Understanding the .NET Code Access Security*. Retrieved from http://www.codeproject.com/dotnet/UB_CAS_NET.asp

Vaidyanathan, G., & Devaraj, S. (2003). A Five Framework for analyzing Online Risks in E-Businesses. *Communications of the ACM, 46*(12), 354–361. doi:10.1145/953460.953522

Van Eecke, P., & Truyens, M. (2008, June). Recent Events in EU Internet Law. *Journal of Internet Law*.

Verdon, D., & McGraw, G. (2004). Risk Analysis in Software Design. *IEEE Security & Privacy, 2*(4), 79–84. doi:10.1109/MSP.2004.55

Villani, M. (2006). *Keystroke biometric identification studies on long text input*. Unpublished doctoral dissertation, Pace University, New York.

Villani, M., Tappert, C., Ngo, G., Simone, J., St. Fort, H., & Cha, H.-S. (2006). Keystroke biometric recognition studies on long-text input under ideal and application-oriented conditions. In *Proceedings of the Computer Vision & Pattern Recognition Workshop on Biometrics*, New York.

Voss, B. D., & Siegel, P. M. (2009). Keeping up the guard in a down economy. *EDUCAUSE Review*, 10–22.

W3C. (n.d.). *SPARQL*. Retrieved from http://www.w3.org/TR/rdf-sparql-query

W3C. (n.d.). *The Platform for Privacy Preferences Project (P3P): Enabling smarter Privacy Tools for the Web*. Retrieved November 7, 2010, from http://www.w3.org/P3P/

Wagner, D., & Soto, P. (2002). Mimicry Attacks on Host-Based Intrusion Detection Systems, *Proceedings of the 9th ACM conference on Computer and communications security*, November 18–22, pp. 255 - 264

Walters, L. M. (2007). A Draft of an Information Systems Security and Control Course. *Journal of Information Systems, 21*(1), 123–148. doi:10.2308/jis.2007.21.1.123

Wang, H., Zhang, D., & Shin, K. (2004). Change-Point Monitoring for Detection for DoS Attacks. *IEEE Transactions on Dependable and Secure Computing*, 193–208. doi:10.1109/TDSC.2004.34

Warren, A., & Oppenheim, C. (2004). Integration of Roles? Implementing New Information Laws in UK Public Organizations. *Journal of Information Science, 30*(48), 48–59. doi:10.1177/0165551504041678

Wayman, J., Jain, A. K., Maltoni, D., & Maio, D. (Eds.). (2004). *Biometric systems: Technology, design and performance evaluation*. New York: Springer.

Web Design Directory. (2005). *Consumers Fret About Online ID Theft But Still Don't Protect Themselves*. Retrieved November 7, 2010, from http://www.designdir.net/newsst_1440.html

Weiss, I. (1993). Review – Geometric Invariants and Object Recognition. *International Journal of Computer Vision*, *10*, 207–231. doi:10.1007/BF01539536

White & Case. (2007). *Data Privacy*. Retrieved from http://www.whitecase.com/presentations/dataprivacy/

White, G., & Long, J. (2007). *Thinking Globally: Incorporating an International Component in Information Security Curricula*. Information Systems Education Journal.

Whitman, M. E., & Mattoro, H. J. (2005). *Principles of Information Security* (2nd ed.). Thomson Course Technology.

Whitmore, J. J. (2001). A Method for Designing Secure Solutions. *IBM Systems Journal*, *40*(3), 747–768.

Wiedenbeck, S., Waters, J., Birget, J.-C., Brodskiy, A., & Memon, N. (2005). Passpoints: Design and longitudinal evaluation of a graphical password system. *International Journal of Human-Computer Studies*, *63*(1-2), 102–127. doi:10.1016/j.ijhcs.2005.04.010

Wiederrich, S. (2003). *Enterprise Security—Workshop and Assessment*. Paper presented at the Microsoft Business Technology Symposium.

Wikipedia. (2005). *Security Management*. Retrieved from http://en.wikipedia.org/wiki/Security_management

Williams, A. (2003). *Privacy Matters – Why You Need to Pay Attention Now*. Retrieved November 7, 2010, from http://www.dww.com/?page_id=1060

Williams, P. (2001). Organized Crime and Cybercrime: Synergies, Trends, and Responses. *Global Issues (Washington, D.C.)*, *6*(2).

Winslett, M., & Yu, T. (2002). Negotiating Trust on the Web. *IEEE Internet Computing*, 30–37. doi:10.1109/MIC.2002.1067734

Wipro. (2008). *Improving Order-To-Cash Cycle*. Retrieved November 7, 2010, from http://www.wipro.com/pace/pdf/order2cash_in_telecom_mmi_a_nov08_073.pdf

Woo, D. H., & Lee, H.-H. S. (2007). Analyzing Performance Vulnerability due to Resource Denial-of-Service Attack on Chip Multiprocessors. In *Proceedings of the 1st workshop on Chip-Multiprocessor Memory Systems and Interconnects* (pp. 33-40).

Woodward, J. D. Jr, Orlans, N. M., & Higgins, P. T. (2002). *Biometrics*. New York: McGraw-Hill.

Wu, S.-T., & Chieu, B.-C. (2003). A user friendly remote authentication scheme with smart cards. *Computers & Security*, *22*(6), 547–550. doi:10.1016/S0167-4048(03)00616-3

Xiao, Z., Xu, J., & Meng, X. (2008). *p-sensitivity: A semantic privacy-protection model for location-based services*. Paper presented at the International Workshop on Privacy-Aware Location-Based Mobile Services (PALMS 2008).

Xiao, X., & Tao, Y. (2006). Simple and effective privacy preservation. In *VLDB 2006* (pp. 139–150). Anatomy.

Xu, T., & Cai, Y. (2008). *Exploring historical location data for anonymity preservation in location-based services*. Paper presented at INFOCOM.

Xu, T., & Cai, Y. (2007). *Location anonymity in continuous location-based services* (p. 39). GIS.

Yadav, S. B. (2008). SEACON: An Integrated Approach to the Analysis and Design of Secure Enterprise Architecture-Based Computer Networks. *International Journal of Information Security and Privacy*, *2*(1), 1–25.

Yan, J., Blackwell, A., Anderson, R., & Grant, A. (2005). The memorability and security of passwords. In Cranor, L., & Garfinkel, S. (Eds.), *Security and usability: Designing secure systems that people can use* (pp. 121–134). Sebastopol, CA: O'Reilly & Associates.

Yoon, S., Choi, S.-S., Cha, S.-H., Lee, Y., & Tappert, C. C. (2005). On the individuality of the iris biometric. *Proc. Int. J. Graphics. Vision & Image Processing*, *5*(5), 63–70.

Yu, E., & Cho, S. (2004). Keystroke dynamics identity verification: Its problems and practical solutions. *Computers & Security, 23*(5), 428–440. doi:10.1016/j.cose.2004.02.004

Yue, W. T., & Cakanyildirim, M. (2007). Intrusion prevention in information systems: Reactive and proactive responses. *Journal of Management Information Systems, 24*(1), 329–353. doi:10.2753/MIS0742-1222240110

Yu, L., & Liu, H. (2004). Efficient Feature Selection via Analysis of Relevance and Redundancy. *Journal of Machine Learning Research, 5*, 1205–1224.

Yu, Z., & Tsai, J. (2007). An efficient intrusion detection system using a boosting-based learning algorithm. *International Journal of Computer Applications in Technology, 27*(4), 223–231. doi:10.1504/IJCAT.2006.011994

Zanero, S. (2007). Flaws and frauds in the evaluation of IDS/IPS technologies. In *Proceedings of FIRST Conference - Forum of Incident Response and Security Teams,* Sevilla, Spain (pp. 167-177).

Zhang, K. (2009). *Adding user and service-to-service authentication to Hadoop.* Retrieved from https://issues.apache.org/jira/browse/HADOOP-4343

Zhao, X., Mattila, A. S., & Li-Shan, E. T. (2008). The role of post-training self-efficacy in customers' use of self service technologies. *International Journal of Service Industry Management, 19*(4), 492–505. doi:10.1108/09564230810891923

Zhu, F., Carpenter, S., et al. (2009). Understanding and Minimizing Identity Exposure in Ubiquitous Computing Environments. In *Proceedings of the 2009 International Conference on Mobile and Ubiquitous Systems: Computing, Networking and Services (Mobiquitous 2009),* Toronto, ON, Canada.

Zhu, F., Mutka, M., et al. (2006). The Master Key: A Private Authentication Approach for Pervasive Computing Environments. In *Proceedings of the 2006 IEEE Annual Conference on Pervasive Computing and Communications.*

Zhu, F., & Zhu, W. (2007). Private and Secure Service Discovery via Progressive and Probabilistic Exposure. *IEEE Transactions on Parallel and Distributed Systems, 18*(11), 1565–1577. doi:10.1109/TPDS.2007.1075

Zuckerman, A. (2001). Order in the courts? *World Trade, 14*(9), 26–29.

Zviran, M., & Erlich, Z. (2006). Identification and authentication: Technology and implementation issues. *Communications of the Association for Information Systems, 17*(4), 90–105.

Zviran, M., & Haga, W. J. (1993). A comparison of password techniques for multilevel authentication mechanisms. *The Computer Journal, 36*(3), 227–237. doi:10.1093/comjnl/36.3.227

About the Contributors

Hamid Nemati is an associate professor of information systems in the Department of Information Systems and Operations Management at the University of North Carolina at Greensboro. He holds a doctorate from the University of Georgia and a Master of Business Administration from the University of Massachusetts. Before coming to UNCG, he was on the faculty of J. Mack Robinson College of Business Administration at Georgia State University. He has extensive professional experience in various consulting, business intelligence and analyst positions and has consulted for a number of major organizations. His research specialization is in the areas of decision support systems, data warehousing, data mining, knowledge management and information privacy and security. He has presented numerous research and scholarly papers nationally and internationally. His articles have appeared in a number of premier professional and scholarly journals.

* * *

Bandar Alhaqbani is an Assistant Professor in the College of Public Health and Health Informatics, King Saud bin Abdulaziz University for Health Sciences, Saudi Arabia. His research interests span different topics in the area of information security, including, but not limited to, privacy, access control models, identity management, reputation systems, network security, and security of workflow management systems (WfMS). Also, he has over 8 years of experience in the Information Technology field within the healthcare domain.

Sandra Carpenter is Professor of Psychology at The University of Alabama in Huntsville. She received her Ph.D. in Social Psychology from the University of California in Santa Barbara. She leverages her training in social psychology to study applied issues. One line of research involves attempting to reduce the frequency with which people inappropriately disclose private information. A second line explores the development of workgroups and teams, primarily with respect to emergent cognitive processes related to taskwork and teamwork. Finally, she also studies culture change in the Caribbean. She is a member of the Society for Personality and Social Psychology and the International Network of Group Researchers.

Sung-Hyuk Cha is an Associate Professor of Computer Science with over 100 publications in pattern recognition and related fields. During his PhD years, he was affiliated with the Center of Excellence for Document Analysis and Recognition (CEDAR) at SUNY Buffalo where he made major contributions that include a dichotomy model to establish the individuality of handwriting, distance measures on histograms and strings, a nearest neighbor search algorithm, apriori algorithm, etc. He joined the School of CSIS at Pace University in 2001. His main interests include computer vision, data mining, and pattern matching and recognition. He is a member of AAAI, IEEE and its Computer Society and IS&T.

Zippy Erlich is on the faculty of the Computer Science department at the Open University of Israel and served as the head of the department for four years. She has developed curricula for undergraduate and graduate programs of study in Computer Science and headed development teams for a variety of B.Sc. and M.Sc. courses. She received her B.Sc. degree in mathematics and statistics, M.Sc. in applied mathematics – both from Tel-Aviv University, and Ph.D. in computer science from University of California, Los-Angeles. Before joining the Open University, she headed the Data Processing department of the Israeli Navy Computer Center. Her research interests include: Queuing theory and applications; Measurement of information systems success and user satisfaction; Open source code; Computer systems security; Data mining; Computer literacy and applications; Social networks and learning networks analysis; and e-Learning.

Sergei Evdokimov is a postdoctoral scholar at Humboldt University Berlin (Germany). In 2002 he graduated from the Belarusian State University in 2002, specializing in Applied Mathematics and Computer Sciense. In 2008 he obtained his doctorate degree at Humboldt University's Institute of Information Systems in Berlin. His research interests include database security, and privacy and security issues of ubiquitous computing.

Colin Fidge is Professor of Computer Science in the Faculty of Science and Technology, Queensland University of Technology, where he teaches software development and computing fundamentals. He received his PhD in 1990 from the Australian National University. His research interests are in the field of critical systems, including security-critical software engineering and networking, risk-aware business process modelling, and large-scale industrial asset management.

Matthias Fischmann obtained his master's degree in computer science and philosophy from Saarland University in Germany. Between 2000 and 2002, he held a position as a research and software engineer at SSH Communication Security Oy in Helsinki, Finland. Between 2002 and 2007, he worked at Humboldt University's Institute of Information Systems in Berlin. His work was focused on the security of distributed information systems, touching topics such as privacy- and integrity-preservation in the presence of untrusted services, anonymity, and reputation-based incentives. He obtained his doctorate degree in 2008. He is currently working as a consultant for Business & Decision.

Oliver Günther is Dean of the School of Business and Economics at Humboldt-Universität zu Berlin. There he also directs the Institute of Information Systems and Humboldt's Interdisciplinary Center on Ubiquitous Information. He also serves as Vice President of the German Informatics Society (GI) and as a member of the Advisory Board of SAP Research. Previously, he has held positions with the International Computer Science Institute in Berkeley and the University of California at Santa Barbara. He holds a Master degree from Karlsruhe Institute of Technology and M.S. and Ph.D. degrees from UC Berkeley.

Vinay Kumar is a postgraduate in Mathematics and did his MCA from School of Computer and System Science, Jawaharlal Nehru University, New Delhi. He is working as a Scientist in National Informatics Center, MoCIT, Government of India. He has authored a book on discrete mathematics. His area of interest is graph algorithm, steganography, discrete mathematics, data security and privacy.

Munir Majdalawieh is an academic researcher and a practicing Information Systems (IS) professional. He is an Assistant Professor of MIS at the American University of Sharjah (AUS). He obtained his Ph.D. in IS from George Mason University in Fairfax, Virginia, USA. He has written about internal auditing and control, IT security and privacy, risk management, corporate and IT governance, and strategic changes in IT/IS technologies and management in academic and practitioners' refereed journals and conference proceedings. He previously worked for Digital Equipment Corporation, Compaq Computer Corporation, Hewlett Packard, and Booz Allen Hamilton for more than 22 years. He is an active member of the IIA, ISACA, and RIMS.

Matt W. Mutka received the B.S. degree in electrical engineering from the University of Missouri-Rolla, the M.S. degree in electrical engineering from Stanford University, and the Ph.D. degree in Computer Science from the University of Wisconsin-Madison. He is on the faculty of the Department of Computer Science and Engineering, Michigan State University, East Lansing, Michigan, where he is currently professor and department chairperson. He has been a visiting scholar at the University of Helsinki, Helsinki Finland and a member of technical staff at Bell Laboratories in Denver, Colorado. His current research interests include mobile computing, wireless networking, and multimedia networking.

Sunil Kumar Muttoo is Associate Professor in Department of Computer Science, University of Delhi, India. He completed his M. Tech from IIT Kharagpur and Ph.D. from University of Delhi, India. His specialization is coding theory, information hiding.

Norman Pendegraft (Ph.D. UCLA) is Professor of Information Systems in the College of Business and Economics at the University of Idaho. He teaches database design and telecommunications management. His major research interest is information systems security.

Mark Rounds is an instructor in College of Business and Economics at the University of Idaho. He holds a BS in Computer Science for Montana State University, an MBA from the University of North Dakota, a MS in Computer Science from Washington State University and is currently a PhD candidate in Computer Science at the University of Idaho. His research focus is on Computer Security. Prior to beginning at the University of Idaho, Mark was the Director of Engineering for Tri Geo Network Security, providing security products for small to medium size businesses. Previous to that, he was a market analyst and later a sales manager for Advanced Hardware Architectures, a fabless semi-conductor firm.

Robert W. Stone (Ph.D. Purdue University) is currently a Professor of Accounting & Information Systems in the College of Business and Economics at the University of Idaho. His teaching interests are in Systems Analysis and Design and Accounting Information Systems. His research interests include organizational impacts from information system use and user acceptance of information systems. Professor Stone has published numerous research works, some of which have appeared in the Review of

Accounting Information Systems, Behavior, Research Methods, Instruments, & Computers, Journal of Business Research, Behaviour & Information Technology, Journal of Informatics Education Research, and Information Resources Management Journal.

Charles C. Tappert has a Ph.D. in Electrical Engineering from Cornell University. He worked on speech and handwriting recognition at IBM for over two decades, secured government contracts in speech recognition, and holds nine patents. After IBM, he taught at the U.S. Military Academy at West Point for seven years and has been a Professor of Computer Science at Pace University since 2000. He has over 100 publications and his research interests include pattern recognition, biometrics, pen computing and voice applications, human-computer interaction, and artificial intelligence.

Mary Villani is an Associate Professor in the Computer Systems Department at State University of New York (SUNY) Farmingdale. She holds a Doctor of Professional Studies degree from Pace University, and her dissertation topic was Keystroke Biometric Identification Studies on Long-Text Input. Publications in this area include several peer-reviewed external and internal conference papers. Prior to joining SUNY Farmingdale, she had a fifteen year computer consulting career in the Risk Management and Insurance industry. She has also written articles in the area of Risk Management and given invited presentations at conferences as a recognized expert.

Surya B. Yadav is the James & Elizabeth Sowell Professor of Telecom Technology in Rawls College of Business, Texas Tech University, Lubbock, Texas. He received his Bachelors of Science degree in electrical engineering from Banaras University in 1972, the M.Tech. degree from IIT Kanpur, India in 1974 and the Ph.D. degree in business information systems from Georgia State University, Atlanta in 1981. He has published in several journals including Communications of the ACM, IEEE Transactions on Software Engineering, IEEE Transactions on Systems, Man, and Cybernetics, Journal of Management Information Systems, and Decision Support Systems. His research areas include information quality, intelligent information retrieval systems, and system security.

Robert S. Zack is a computer professional with 27 years of experience with project management, systems analysis, and systems integration for financial services and pharmaceutical industries. He is currently a student in the Doctor of Professional Studies in Computing program at Pace University.

Feng Zhu received the B.S. degree in computer science from East China Normal University, the M.S. degree in computer science and engineering from Michigan State University, the M.S. degree in statistics from Michigan State University, and the Ph.D. degree from Michigan State University. He is an assistant professor at The University of Alabama in Huntsville. He was a program manager at Microsoft and a software engineer at Intel. His current research interests include pervasive computing, security for pervasive computing, computer networks, and distributed systems.

Wei Zhu received the Ph.D. degree in computer science and engineering from Michigan State University in 2006, the M.S. degree in statistics from Michigan State University in 2004, the M.S. degree in computer science and engineering from Michigan State University in 2001, and the B.S. degree in computer science from East China Normal University in 1994. Her research interests include human-computer interaction, computer graphics, augmented reality, and multimedia systems. She was a software design engineer at Microsoft Corporation. She is currently a software consultant at Intergraph Corporation.

Moshe Zviran is Associate Professor of Information Systems in the Faculty of Management, The Leon Racanati Graduate School of Business Administration, Tel Aviv University. He received his B.Sc. degree in mathematics and computer science and the M.Sc and Ph.D degrees in information systems from Tel Aviv University, Israel, in 1979, 1982 and 1988, respectively. He held academic positions at the Claremont Graduate University, California, the Naval Postgraduate School, California, and Ben-Gurion University, Israel. His research interests include information systems planning, measurement of IS success and user satisfaction, information systems security e-Business. He is also a consultant in these areas for a number of leading organizations. Prof. Zviran's research has been published in: MIS Quarterly, Communications of the ACM, Journal of Management Information Systems, IEEE Transactions on Engineering Management, Information and Management, Omega, The Computer Journal, Journal of Medical Systems and other journals. He is also co-author (with N. Ahituv and S. Neumann) of Information Systems for Management (Tel-Aviv, Dyonon, 1996) and Information Systems – from Theory to Practice (Tel-Aviv, Dyonon, 2001).

Index

A

access control 216, 220
access control framework 153
active intrusion prevention (AIP) 221
advanced business-centric personal data management system (ABC-PDMS) 177, 184
  data protection in 184
  five processes 186
alert correlation 20
alert fusion 20
anonymity 236
anonymization set 117
Anton et al. Study 101
artificial immune systems (AISs) 221
assessment view of system security 71
authentication approaches 216
authentication classification 39
availability 215

B

behavioral biometrics 219
binary-rewriter 160
Binding Corporate Rules (BCRs) 137
biometric-based authentication 219
boolean expressions 15

C

character-based authentication 217
cloaked query 120
cloud computing 153
  encrypted data storage 155
  security issues 151
  virtualization paradigm 151
computational private information retrieval 8
Confab 238
confidentiality 215

D

Dale-Chall index (DCI) 98
data at rest (DAR) 177, 185
database PH indistinguishability 7
  up to frequency 9
database privacy homomorphism 5
data confidentiality 271
data in processing (DIP) 177, 185
data in transmission (DIT) 177, 185
data partitioning 199
data protection
  controls domain 185
  legislation domain 185
  policies and procedures domain 185
Data Protection Directive (95/46 134
data sharing 198, 203
Data Sharing Miner and Analyzer (DASMA) system 197
Denials of Service (DoS) attacks 19
detection techniques 274
DigNet age 176
distributed DoS 20
dynamic detection techniques 275

E

Electronic Medical Records (EMRs) 271, 276-277
elimination (hiding) techniques 274-275
embedding algorithm 260, 267
empirical study 227
encrypted data storage
  for cloud computing 155
existing secure information system (SIS) design 60
Expand Cloak algorithm 121-122
exploit-based DoS attacks 19
extensive game 241
extraction algorithm 261

F

Fair Information Practices (FIP) 94
False Accept Rate (FAR) 40
False Reject Rate (FRR) 40
feature analysis 20
feature extraction 35
Federal Information Security Management Act
    (FISMA) 182
Flesch Grade Level (FGL) 97-98, 100
Flesch Readability Score (FRES) 97, 100
flooding-based DoS attack 19
Fog Index (FI) 98
free text 34
Fry graph 99

G

Geographic Information System (GIS) 256, 258
global information security 165
globalization 163
Gradient Boosting Trees (GBT) Model 21-22
Graham Leach Bliley Act (GLBA) 91
graph components 257

H

Hadoop distributed file system (HDFS) 151
    inadequacies 156
    overview 156
    secure query processing 156
    SUN XACML implementation into 159
hierarchical fallback model 49
hierarchical identitiy model 240
Hilbert Cloak 124
Hochhauser Study 102
homomorphism 11
horizontal partitioning 199
Host-based Intrusion Detection Systems (HIDSs)
    18-19
hybrid partitioning 200

I

IBM 4758 Cryptographic Coprocessor 155
identification classification 39
identity federation 238
I Love You virus 165
image-based authentication 217
imperceptibility 265
indistinguishability 5

inference channels 272
    detection 270, 277-278, 280, 291
    restriction 270, 277-278, 280, 291
information security 164
    global nature of 164
information security breaches 271
information systems security 215, 221
    main goals 214-215
In-lined Reference Monitors (IRM's) 159
integrity 215
intrusion detection systems (IDS) 214-216, 220
intrusion prevention systems (IPS) 215-216
IP spoofing 20

J

Jensen and Potts Study 99
jurisdictional laws 92

K

k-anonymity
    in Location-Based Services (LBS) 117
Kantarcioglu-Clifton model 7
keystroke biometric systems 33-34
    four components 35
keystroke-duration 37
k-nearest-neighbor (kNN) classifier 39
knowledge-based authentication 216, 220
knowledge-based IDS 221

L

l-diversity
    in Location-Based Services (LBS) 117
legal view of system security 74
Location-Based Services (LBS) 115
low-rate pulsing method 20

M

machine learning techniques 20
management view of system security 73
Mandatory Access Control (MAC) 271, 273, 275
mapping 11
maximum entropy probability distribution 289
Medical Knowledge Base (MKB) 276
memory tokens 219
mining shared data 198

N

Network-based Intrusion Detection Systems
  (NIDSs) 18-19

O

optimal identity exposure 242

P

password security 218
personal information exposure 236
Personal Information Protection and Electronic
  Documents Act (PIPEDA) 180
personalized query 120
physiological biometrics 219
Plan-Do-Check-Act (PDCA) 60, 76
Platform for Privacy Preferences Project (P3P) 181
Policy Decision Point (PDP) 159
Policy Enforcement Point (PEP) 159
possession-based authentication 219
principal component analysis (PCA) 106
privacy 134, 177-178
privacy framework 134
    business perspective 137
    legal perspective 134
    technical perspective 138
privacy homomorphism 2, 4
Privacy Impact Assessments (PIAs) 182
privacy policies 92
privacy policy statement 180
privacy protection laws 179
privacy protection solutions 181
privacy protection threshold 287
Private Information Retrieval problem (PIR) 8
process view of system security 70

Q

quansi-identifiers 117
Query Anonymization Time (QAT) 124
query homogeneity attack 116
Query Success Rate (QSR) 125
Question-and-answer-based authentication 217

R

RationalExposure model 237
raw keystroke data capture 35
readability evaluation methods 97
readability formulas 97

Receiver Operating Characteristic (ROC) 34, 40
Relative Anonymity Level (RAL) 125
Relative Anonymization Area (RAA) 125
releasing factor 198
Requirements of Human Readable Policies 94
resource view of system security 68
robustness 266
Role-Based Access Control (RBAC) 239

S

safe queries 10
sectoral laws 92
secure cloud data management 152
secure multipart computation (SMC) 155
secure query processing
    with Hadoop 156
Secure Virtual Machine (VM) Monitor 151
security design methods 60
security policies 215
security requirements analysis 60
security systems development 60
    five methods 60
Security Systems Development Life Cycle (SecS-
  DLC) 60
signature-based IDS 221
six-view perspective of system security (SVPSS)
    applicability of the 76
    assessment view 71
    legal view 74
    limitations 78
    management view 73
    process view 70
    resource view 68
    security risk determination 76
    threat view 66
smart tokens 219
SMOG Index (SMOG) 99
SMOG readability formula 92
social cognitive theory 226
static detection techniques 274
steganalysis 264
steganographic algorithm 256
steganography 255
Systems of Records Notices (SORNs) 182

T

theoretical model 226
threat view of system security 66

token-based authentication 219
tuple-wise encryption 15

U

unauthorised data observation 271
unsafe queries 10
unweighted m-match, k-Nearest-Neighbor (m-kNN)
    procedure 40-41

V

vertical partitioning 200

W

Weighted m-match, k-Nearest-Neighbor (Wm-kNN)
    procedure 40-41
Whitmore, James J. 62-63